MINDFUL MILITANTS

MINDFUL MILITANTS

The Amalgamated Engineering Union in Australia 1920–1972

T. SHERIDAN

Senior Lecturer in Economics, University of Adelaide

CAMBRIDGE UNIVERSITY PRESS

CAMBRIDGE

LONDON · NEW YORK · MELBOURNE

Published by the Syndics of the Cambridge University Press
The Pitt Building, Trumpington Street, Cambridge CB2 1RP
Bentley House, 200 Euston Road, London NW1 2DB
32 East 57th Street, New York, NY10022, USA
296 Beaconsfield Parade, Middle Park, Melbourne 3206, Australia

© Cambridge University Press 1975

Library of Congress Catalogue Card Number: 74—17503

ISBN: 0 521 20680

First published 1975

Photoset and printed in Malta by St Paul's Press Ltd

DEDICATED TO THE MEMORY OF MY FATHER
AND ALL OTHER ENGINEERS

Contents

Introduction

As its title suggests, the Amalgamated Engineering Union (Australian Section) was part of a much larger international organisation. The latter was the successor to the Amalgamated Society of Engineers, the first 'New Model' craft union, formed in Britain in 1851. The first overseas branch was established in Sydney in 1852 by 27 Society members who had emigrated after a lock out essentially aimed at destroying the infant organisation. In the nineteenth century the mobile British engineers also formed branches of the union in Canada, France, Constantinople, Bombay, South Africa, New Zealand, Malta, and the United States of America. As a result of an amalgamation with several smaller sectional societies in Britain, the name of the Society was changed in all parts of the world to that of the Amalgamated Engineering Union (A.E.U.) on 1 July 1920. In 1968 the Australian A.E.U. severed its links with the parent British union as a prelude to its amalgamation in 1972 with two other Australian unions to form the Amalgamated Metal Workers' Union.

Several factors go to make A.E.U. records particularly full and extensive compared with those of most other Australian unions. These include the A.E.U.'s centralised administrative structure, the education and aspirations of its members, and the need for accounting accuracy arising out of its friendly society activities. I began my own study of the A.E.U. in mid-1965 when a postgraduate scholar at the Australian National University. At that time K. D. Buckley of Sydney University had already been exploring the union's nineteenth century experience for several years. A mutually acceptable division of research was decided upon, with 1920 being taken as the obviously convenient watershed. Since, however, my doctoral thesis on the industrial history of the A.E.U. to 1954 was submitted over two years before Mr Buckley's book was published[1] it proved necessary for me to investigate independently

---

[1] *The Amalgamated Engineers in Australia, 1852–1920* (Canberra, 1970).

the history of the union in the late nineteenth and early twentieth centuries. In the following pages I have endeavoured to avoid traversing the ground covered so thoroughly by Mr Buckley — although certain brief backward references are inevitable in the opening chapters. The history of the parent British union to the end of World War II has been written by James B. Jefferys.[2]

The A.E.U. is of particular interest to students of Australian industrial relations and labour history for a number of reasons. Not the least of these is its unique British connections and constitution. The A.E.U. was also Australia's largest manufacturing union, and its craftsmen members, while congregated mainly in the strategic metal trades, were also employed in literally every other sector of the economy. Because of their strong bargaining position A.E.U. craftsmen invariably relied more on industrial pressure than political action to further their interests. In the process, the A.E.U.'s assertive independence occasionally brought confrontations with the rest of the labour movement, including federal and state Labor governments.

To most outsiders and laymen, however, the A.E.U. had two main claims to fame; the fitter's margin, and the controversies surrounding alleged 'communist control' of the union. Over the years the arbitration tribunals allotted an increasingly key role in the national wages pyramid to the wage rate of the typical A.E.U. tradesman, the fitter. A movement in the fitter's rate came to imply a parallel proportionate shift in virtually all other wage rates. Consequently, the tribunals ceased to determine its level by reference to current market value and relied rather on wider — and varying — national economic criteria. This trend stimulated the A.E.U.'s industrial aggression as its members sought to ensure that their actual earnings were not similarly artificially depressed.

In the 1940s A.E.U. policy began to be silhouetted in a new incendiary glare emitting from the explosive battle between Right and Left factions within the labour movement. Many outsiders became convinced that the union's industrial aggression stemmed in fact from a minority of communists elected to its policy-making bodies. Insiders knew better but the communists' political ideology was resented and suspected by some A.E.U. members who also sought to use the union's large affiliation to the Australian Labor Party (A.L.P.) to influence that party's policy along anti-communist lines. As a result the A.E.U. was wracked for 20 years by increasingly bitter internal dissensions. After the A.L.P. 'Split' of the mid-1950s the polemics and vituperation reached a peak of intensity as the opposing sides publicly battled for

[2] *The Story of the Engineers, 1800–1945* (London, 1945).

supremacy through the ballot box and the law courts. Not until the mid-1960s did the smoke finally clear and the right wing forces admit defeat and withdraw from the field. The length and passion of the A.E.U.'s internal struggles make this key union's experiences clearly distinguishable from that of its fellows in the trade union movement.

The ramifications of the fitter's margin and the notoriety of the Left—Right A.E.U. battles help explain certain changes in emphasis in the following pages. After essential scene setting in Chapters 1 and 2, the subsequent five chapters take the union's overall history up to 1945 and its general industrial experience to 1954. In these middle chapters, while endeavouring to consider all significant facets of A.E.U. history, I have attempted to trace in some detail the changing criteria by which the fitter's marginal rate was determined. When the wages story is taken up again in Chapter 10, the reasons behind each of the federal tribunal's margins decisions after 1954 are not examined so closely. This is for two main reasons: the tendency for margins and Basic Wage cases to be argued along increasingly similar lines in the years between the abolition of cost of living adjustments in 1953, and the final abandonment of the national margins and Basic Wage concepts in 1965; and the contemporary appearance of a snowballing body of literature critically analysing every aspect of both the actual and ideal behaviour of the federal tribunal.

In Chapters 8 and 9 the wages story is set aside while attention is focussed on the two decades of political struggle inside the A.E.U. Detailed examination is felt to be warranted not simply because of the obvious intrinsic interest and importance but also because of subsequent effects of the subjectivity of those involved. Nearly 20 years after the A.L.P. 'Split' considerable rancour still lingers within the labour movement. In assessing the roles played by the various pieces in that complicated and dynamic political jigsaw, the combatants themselves, to say nothing of the general public, remain confused by a variety of myths — often retrospective — concerning 'Groupers', communists, Catholics and radical A.L.P. men alike. The A.E.U. occupied an important position on labour's political board and the hectic events occurring within its ranks have been similarly obscured by the dust stirred up — if not manufactured — by contemporary passions. Objectivity was made all the more unlikely by the continuation of the A.E.U.'s internecine warfare long after the Split, and the exacerbating effects of certain aspects of the union's constitution. Some of the myths which consequently emerged about the A.E.U. seem to be in danger of hardening into folk-lore-and thus further hampering clear sighted examination of an already complex industrial relations scene.

Acknowledgements

A great number of people have earned my gratitude while I was preparing this book. In the first place it could never have been written without the co-operation of the officers and members of the A.E.U. who gave me complete and unrestricted access to all its records. My main debt is to Mr J. D. Garland, currently Joint Commonwealth Secretary of the Amalgamated Metal Workers Union, for his unfailing interest and prompt and efficient attention to all my requests. Other A.E.U. officers were generous with their time and assistance, and all agreed to submit to lengthy interviews at often inconvenient times in order to fit in with my schedules. Former A.E.U. officials were similarly gracious, some inviting me to their homes, others undertaking lengthy trips across Sydney and Melbourne in order to meet me. To all the following A.E.U. men I extend my heartfelt thanks; J. J. Arter, A. J. Bailey, L. Bird, R. Bruggy, W. Buckley, J. E. Burke, W. T. Butler, L. Carmichael, J. P. Devereux, L. E. Fitzpatrick, H. Fountain, H. J. Gillman, J. Goss, J. F. Halfpenny, N. Hill, A. E. Horsburgh, J. Hutson, W. C. Long, M. J. Malcolm, J. McDowell, M. O'Brien, J. L. Scott, A. E. Searle, F. N. Self, C. M. Southwell, G. J. Stead, H. E. Walklate, W. H. White, L. N. Wickham, A. C. Williams, and A. Wilson.

I would also like to thank T. L. Addison, K. G. Goodwin, J. B. Holmes of the Australasian Society of Engineers, J. Restarick of the Boilermakers' Society of Australia, J. W. Mead of the Department of Labour, Adelaide, and G. M. Nettelbeck of the Australian Metal Industries Association, Adelaide.

Useful comments on earlier manuscript drafts were offered by Dr R. A. Gollan, Dr J. A. Merritt and Dr D. W. Rawson all of the Research School of Social Sciences, Australian National University, Canberra. Ms K. Cheshire and Ms H. M. Wickens provided valuable research assistance. For typing services I have been indebted at one time or another to G. Duncan, J. Dutkiewicz, R. Erickson, G. Morgan, N. Richards, L. Tuckwell and J. Wood.

I should also like to thank the editors of *The Journal of Industrial Relations* and of *Labour History* for permission to reproduce in the book parts of papers originally written for those journals.

Above all I must thank my wife, Dr Kyoko Sheridan for her sympathy, support and understanding.

T. Sheridan

University of Adelaide
April 1974

Abbreviations

A.C.T.U.	Australian Council of Trade Unions.
A.E.U.	Amalgamated Engineering Union.
A.L.P.	Australian Labor Party.
A.R.U.	Australian Railways Union.
A.S.E.	Australasian Society of Engineers.
A.W.U.	Australian Workers Union.
B.S.A.	Blacksmiths' Society of Australasia.
C.A.R.	Commonwealth Arbitration Reports.
C.C.M.	A.E.U. Commonwealth Council Minutes.
C.L.R.	Commonwealth Law Reports.
C.P.D.	Commonwealth Parliamentary Debates.
C.P.A.	Communist Party of Australia.
D.L.P.	Democratic Labor Party.
E.T.U.	Electrical Trades Union of Australia.
F.E.D.F.A.	Federated Engine Drivers and Firemen's Association of Australasia.
F.I.A.	Federated Ironworkers' Association.
F.L.R.	Federal Law Reports.
I.A.R.	New South Wales Industrial Arbitration Reports.
I.C.M.	A.E.U. Investment Committee Minutes.
M.D.C.M.	A.E.U. Melbourne District Committee Minutes.
M.J.	A.E.U. Monthly Journal.
M.J.R.	A.E.U. Monthly Journal and Report.
M.P.C.M.	A.E.U. Melbourne District Political Committee Minutes.
M.R.	A.E.U. Monthly Report.
M.T.E.A.	Metal Trades Employers' Association.
N.C.C.	National Civic Council.
O.B.U.	One Big Union.
S.M.W.I.U.	Sheet Metal Working Industrial Union of Australia.

Note on Australian monetary values: Until 1931 £1 Australian = £1 sterling. Between 1931 and 1966 £1 Australian = £0.80 sterling. In 1966 when Australia adopted decimal currency £1 Australian became $2 Australian. The fixed links between the two currencies were severed, after the devaluation of sterling in 1967.

1

Engineers, engineering, and the A.E.U.

Craftsmen have played a vital role in the development of the varied group of industries producing metal and metal products. Despite changes in techniques and the scale of operations, and despite the growing diversity and complexity of the products themselves, the skilled worker has retained his key position in the metal workforce. The union organising the largest numbers of metal craftsmen between 1920 and 1972 was the Amalgamated Engineering Union. In this opening chapter the aim will be to outline the work performed by these men, its changing nature and the associated changes taking place in the composition of A.E.U. membership. Some statistics are inevitable but hopefully they have been kept to a minimum.[1]

I

The metal-using sectors of an industrial economy may broadly be divided into three: refining and smelting of metal ores, casting the refined metals into preliminary shapes and the machining and fitting processes whereby component metal parts are converted into their final form and assembled as finished products. Two small groups of highly skilled A.E.U. members, roll turners and patternmakers, were key employees in the refining and foundry processes respectively but the great majority of A.E.U. men possessed skills solely relevant to the third stage. The union's skilled members were employed in many enterprises other than those manufacturing metal goods but whether engaged in sugar mills, gold mines or newspaper offices their work was basically the same as that performed at the bench, in the machine-shop, or in the smithing section of an engineering establishment.

There are, however, several engineering occupations which the A.E.U.

---

[1] Any readers interested in more detailed statistics, and an explanation of compilation problems are referred to, T. Sheridan 'A History of the Amalgamated Engineering Union (Australian Section), 1920–1954', Ph.D. thesis, Australian National University, 1967, Ch. 1 and passim.

never attempted to organise. The most important of these is boilermaking and the reasons for the union's relative lack of interest in this trade are to be found in the particular sectional development of engineering societies in nineteenth century Britain. The existing boilermakers' union refused to join with the other craft bodies in forming the Amalgamated Society of Engineers in 1851. For the remainder of the century the latter made no attempt to extend its membership coverage to boilermaking occupations and when branches were established in Australia this section of the engineering trade was also ignored by the colonial Society. Similarly, the existence of a separate moulders' union in Britain precluded the Society from organising foundry workers. When, in the twentieth century, the Australian branches became interested in the formation of one union covering all metal workers, boilermakers and moulders had formed their own organisations and the obstacles to absorption or amalgamation proved insurmountable until the 1960s.

Within the occupations covered by the A.E.U. and its predecessor, there has been a continuous subdivision of tasks and a concomitant growth of job classifications. Ever since the introduction of Maudslay's slide rest lathe in 1800[2] the work of the original highly skilled millwrights who 'executed every kind of engineering operation, from making the wooden patterns to erecting in the mill the machines which had been constructed by their own hands'[3] has been broken up and distributed among more and more highly specialised operatives. Yet, while repetition processes and machines have multiplied and the number of semi-skilled engineering workers has increased, craftsmen have remained the key employees within the industry, even in the most advanced economies. Job specialisation has occurred at a slower rate in Australia because of the relatively small scale of operations. In 1920—1 the proportion of metal workers engaged in establishments employing less than 100 hands was 40 per cent. In 1967—8 the proportion was still 40 per cent. Even if the many small motor-repair shops are removed from the calculation the figure in 1967—8 remains as high as 32 per cent.[4] Compared

---

[2] For details of the basic technological developments in the engineering industry and associated changes in engineering occupations, see Nathan Rosenberg, 'Technological Change in the Machine Tool Industry 1840—1910' *Journal of Economic History*, xxiii, 4 December 1963, pp. 414—43; M. Daumas, 'Precision Mechanics' in C. Singer, E. J. Holmyard, A. R. Hall and T. Williams (Eds.) *A History of Technology* (Oxford, 1958), volume iv pp. 379—416; K. R. Gilbert, 'Machine Tools', ibid., pp. 417—41; D. F. Galloway, 'Machine Tools', ibid., Vol. v, pp. 636—57; Jefferys, op. cit., pp. 12—15 and *passim*; M. L. Yates, *Wages and Labour Conditions in British Engineering* (London, 1937), pp. 16—24.

[3] Sydney and Beatrice Webb, *Industrial Democracy* (London, 1913), p. 107.

[4] Calculated from Commonwealth Bureau of Census and Statistics, *Production Bulletin*, No. 15, *Manufacturing Industry*, No. 5.

with advanced overseas countries there existed in Australia, particularly prior to World War II, a greater time lag before new techniques percolated throughout the industry. Hence the role of the all-round skilled tradesmen has been of particular importance in the Commonwealth. During the period we are considering in this study craftsmen members of the Australian Section of the A.E.U. were generally called upon to perform a wider range of operations during their working lives than their confrères in Britain. The habit of many Australian engineers of describing themselves as 'fitters *and* turners', rather than separately as 'fitters' or 'turners' is indicative of the all-round capabilities expected of Commonwealth tradesmen.

The basic engineering crafts are those of smithing, fitting and machining. The work of a smith is essentially that of beating metals into shape after heating. Advances in electric and oxy-welding and cutting techniques have limited the importance of forging in certain areas and improvements in power hammers and other machine aids have made for greater precision and ease of handling. But while the exertion associated with smithing has been greatly reduced, the increased speed of operations has called for closer application to the work and the degree of skill required has not altered a great deal since the nineteenth century.

The fitter's fundamental task is to adjust or assemble parts of a machine. He was originally equipped with little more than a file, a chisel, a few taps and dies, and his own touch and experience, but since the mid-nineteenth century he has been supplied with various hand machines to aid his work. More importantly the fitter's job has been modified by the improvements in the machining processes. Greater accuracy and better finish of machined components have lessened the amount of real 'fitting' performed. The increasing emphasis on interchangeability of parts led to close attention being paid to tolerance. 'Go and Not-Go' gauges were developed to set machining limits which reduced the need for 'dead' accuracy in the fitter's work. The growing complexity and intricacy of metal products meant, however, that a skilled man was often still required to fit and erect the finished article. In the larger and more specialised establishments there was a subdivision of the fitter's job into bench fitter, tool and gauge maker, erector, and assembler. But in the many small jobbing and repair shops and in maintenance work in non-metal producing firms all-round versatility was still required.

Machinists have experienced a much greater subdivision of their trade during the twentieth century. The key machine tool is the centre lathe which is capable of performing a wide variety of metal-turning functions and which calls for the highest degree of skill from its operator. In large specialised engineering plants this general purpose lathe which once dominated all machine shops has now been transferred to the toolroom where only the most intricate and varied work is undertaken. For repetitive jobs other machines can be employed. These range from capstan and turret lathes, which might still require some degree of skill on the part of the turner, to fully automatic lathes several of which can be fed and tended by one semi-skilled employee.

The other basic machining processes are those of planing, shaping, slotting and drilling all of which were originally performed by craftsmen. In these fields also the development of improved specialist machines has largely reduced the amount of skill required by their operatives. Yet many of these innovations appeared only in the 1940s and the small scale of the Australian engineering industry greatly lessened their impact. Many machinists in the advanced European and American economies tended to operate only one single-purpose machine during their working lives but in Australia an employee would often be expected to use the whole range of tools in the machine shop. The lack of repetition work meant that there were relatively few employees who merely 'minded' machines set up for them by skilled tool setters. 'Process workers' who performed the simplest repetitive tasks only began to assume numerical importance in a few of the larger engineering establishments in the late 1930s. Even after the great war-induced expansion of the industry between 1940 and 1943 and its post-war consolidation these employees still represented only a relatively small proportion of the engineering workforce. In the jobbing shops each machinist performed constantly varying work on a number of machines and he often had to be as versatile as a fitter.

However, in addition to the specialised jobs provided by the limited sub-division of basic engineering crafts, completely new occupations arose in the train of changes in techniques and products. Some of the new work was closely akin to the traditional engineering tasks. Motor mechanics, for instance, were the direct descendants of engine fitters. On the other hand many of the new jobs came to demand skills completely different from those required by the main body of engineering work. One example is electric and oxy-welding and cutting which performed tasks hitherto undertaken by boilermakers, smiths, and other engineering craftsmen. More importantly the replacement of steam by electricity as a source of power, and the expansion in the production of electrical goods and appliances gave rise to many new occupations. They ranged from switchboard attendants to electricians and electrical fitters, and usually required training and knowledge markedly different from those possessed by metal tradesmen.

Unfortunately it is impossible to trace the change in the numbers of workers engaged in the various engineering occupations before the 1930s.

Statistics are available for six separate years between 1933 and 1966, but even these are of limited value. Occupation tables are set out in the 1933, 1947, 1961 and 1966 Census Reports, in the Civilian Register drawn up in 1943, and in the Occupation Survey undertaken by the Commonwealth Bureau of Census and Statistics in 1945. In each case the tables were compiled from information provided by members of the workforce. The period after the economic depression of the 1930s was that in which the greatest changes in technique and scale of operations took place within the engineering industry. A comparison between the numbers and proportions of employees following the different engineering occupations in 1933 and the mid-1960s might therefore be expected to illustrate both the extent of the subdivision of the traditional craftsmen's work and the rise of the new job classifications. Unfortunately, as with all other occupation surveys, analysis of the data is bedevilled by problems of definition, including the tendency of some employees to boost their occupational status.[5] It is therefore extremely difficult to make anything like confident comparisons.

Since, however, beggars can't be choosers, information concerning those occupations that appear to have been grouped relatively consistently in each Census have been set out in Tables 1.1–1.3. Because of the exceptional nature of developments in World War II, which are discussed in Chapter 7, the two wartime surveys have not been included. The broad and completely ambiguous categories of 'Engineers (Mechanical) not Professional', 'Mechanics (so described)', 'Engineers (so described)', and 'Metal Workers, n.e.c'. have been included as some reminder of the possible margin of error which may have been incorporated in any or all of the other classifications. The distinction made between 'traditional' and 'other' skills rests on the difference between the work performed by nineteenth century craftsmen and the newer skilled jobs appearing in the twentieth century.

Table 1.1 indicates the overall growth of the total metal trade workforce and all selected occupations save blacksmithing. In absolute terms the greatest expansion between 1933 and 1966 occurs among electrical mechanics, mainly in the 1950s in synchronisation with the boom in communications and the manufacture of television sets and other electrical consumer durables. Next comes the combined grouping of fitting and turning within which it is likely that turning would be relatively more significant than the 1933 breakdown suggests, for wartime demands caused turners to increase

---

[5] For comments on the lack of accuracy of occupation statistics see e.g. *Census of the Commonwealth of Australia, 30th June 1947, Statistician's Report*, p. 194; *Conference of British Commonwealth Statisticians, Canberra November 1951, Summary of Proceedings*, pp. 12–16.

Table 1.1: Workers Engaged in Various Engineering Occupations
1933—1966

	Year			
	1933	1947	1961	1966
Total metal workforce[a]	150,013	314,628	472,629	570,784
Traditional skills				
Blacksmiths	8,714	6,283	4,163	3,361
Fitters	14,430	48,526[d]	69,728[df]	81,137[dh]
Turners	3,252			
Patternmakers	1,186	1,647	n.a.	1,911
Toolmakers	1,097	6,429	10,847	13,256
SUB-TOTAL	28,679	62,885	84,738	99,665
Other Skills				
Welders	602	8,732	18.200[e]	22,691
Motor engineers, mechanics	15,326	35,371	59,357	67,141
Electrical mechanics[b]	17,182	33,517	70,345[g]	83,817[i]
SUB-TOTAL	33,110	77,620	147,902	173,649
Machinists (so described)	2,780	13,385	24,994	26,726
Process workers	—	11,151	40,968[e]	62,829
Indeterminate				
Engineers (mechanical) not professional	5,761	—		
Engineers (so described)	8,605	32,487	24,407	23,580
Mechanics (so described)	9,587	10,063		13,400
Metal workers n.e.c.[c]	—	—	14,272[e]	15,489
SUB-TOTAL	23,953	42,550	38,679	52,469
GRAND TOTAL	88,522	207,591	337,281	415,338

Sources: *Census of the Commonwealth of Australia*, 1933, 1947, 1961 and 1966.

[a]The 1933 total workforce figure was calculated by adding together the numbers employed in the following industrial groups: Founding, Engineering and Metal-working (including Motor Engineering); Manufacture of vehicles; Shipbuilding and Equipment; and Motor Garages which were included in the Land Transport classification in the Census. The 1947 workforce figure consists of the sum of employees engaged in: Founding, Engineering and Metal-working (including Shipbuilding); Manufacture, Assembly and Repair of Vehicles, Parts and Accessories; and Motor Engineering and Motor Garages (so described) which are constituents of the Road Transport and Storage industrial group in the Census. The 1961 and 1966 workforce figures consist of the sum of employees engaged in: Founding, Engineering and Metal Working; and Manufacture, Assembly and Repair of Ships, Vehicles, Parts and Accessories.

from 18 per cent of the total in 1933 to 35 per cent at the time of the 1945 Occupation Survey.[6] This change in the relative importance of the two largest traditional trades is indicative of the structural change of the industry, which began to place greater emphasis on machining interchangeable components rather than on fitting varied jobbing and repair work. Close behind these traditional skills come the repetitive process workers who were not significant enough to warrant separate citation in 1933, although literary evidence already indicates their existence in the 1920s. Table 1.2 confirms the natural expectation that the 1933–47 period encompassing the war-induced expansion contains the fastest growth rates for both the total work-force and all occupations except electrical mechanics, who increased slightly more quickly in the 1947–61 period. Over the whole 33 years, the outstanding relative growth performances are among the newer or repetitive jobs of process working, welding and machining, and in highly skilled toolmaking – always a key trade in an industrialising economy. The large groupings of electrical mechanics, fitters and turners, and motor mechanics all grew faster

[6] *Occupation Survey of the Commonwealth of Australia, 1st June 1945*, Table 27.

Table 1.1: (footnotes cont.)

[b]This category includes electrical fitters, electrical engineers, electricians, electrical mechanics (so described), wireless mechanics and radio mechanics. It does not include linesmen and telephone mechanics.

[c]This category is apparently a catch-all for indeterminate occupations in the sub-groups 'Toolmakers, machinists, plumbers, welders, platers and related workers'. It does not include trades such as moulders, boilermakers, or tradesmen's assistants.

[d]Separate figures for fitters and turners not available.

[e]In the 1961 Census the 23,203 female 'Metal and Electrical Factory Workers' are not subdivided into separate occupations. These three occupations were the only ones in the table in which women worked in the 1966 Census. A similar percentage (95.6%) of the 1961 total has been arbitrarily allocated among them in the same proportion as in 1966.

[f]Including 3,764 aircraft mechanics.

[g]Including 9,139 'Servicemen, mechanics' and an unknown number of 'radar mechanics and national and commercial radio and T.V. technicians'.

[h]Including 5,002 aircraft mechanics.

[i]Including 13,400 'Mechanics, servicemen (so described) and n.e.c.' and an unknown number of 'radar mechanics and national and commercial radio and T.V. technicians'

Table 1.2: The Growth of Various Engineering Occupations

	1933–47		1947–61		1961–6		1933–66	
	Over-all %	Simple yearly aver-age %	Over-all %	Simple yearly aver-age %	Over-all %	Simple yearly aver-age %	Over-all %	Simple yearly aver-age %
Total metal workforce	110	7.9	50	3.6	21	4.2	281	8.5
Traditional skills								
Blacksmiths	−18	−1.3	−34	−2.4	−19	−3.8	−61	−1.8
Fitters	174⎱	12.4⎱	44⎱	3.1⎱	16⎱	3.2⎱	359⎱	10.9⎱
Turners								
Patternmakers	39	2.9	n.a.	—	n.a.	—	61	1.8
Toolmakers	486	34.7	69	4.9	22	4.4	1,108	33.6
SUB-TOTAL	119	8.5	35	2.5	18	3.6	248	7.5
Other skills								
Welders	1,351	96.5	108	7.7	25	5.0	3,669	111.2
Motor engineers, mechanics	131	9.4	68	4.9	13	2.6	330	10.2
Electrical mechanics	95	6.9	110	7.9	19	3.8	389	11.8
SUB-TOTAL	134	9.6	91	6.5	17	3.4	425	12.9
Machinists (so described)	382	27.3	87	6.2	7	1.4	761	23.3
Process workers	∞	∞	267	19.1	53	10.6	∞	∞
Indeterminate	77	5.5	−9	−0.6	36	7.2	119	3.6
GRAND TOTAL	135	9.6	63	4.5	23	4.6	369	11.2

than the total metal workforce. Thus, as Table 1.3 indicates in another way, the small decline in the relative importance of the traditional engineering skills is more than accounted for by the fall in blacksmithing and pattern-making. Fitting, turning and toolmaking all increase in importance over the 33 year period, although falling slightly from their combined 1947 position in later years. Consideration of the selected occupations as proportions of the total metals workforce cannot be pursued very far because many of the workers concerned were engaged in other industries. Information on this point was provided only in the 1933 and 1947 Census Reports —and even then major problems of industry definition compounded the flaws in oc-cupation details. As a cautionary indicator we may note that, of those workers

Table 1.3: Various Engineering Occupations as a Proportion of the Total Metal Workforce

	Year			
	1933 %	1947 %	1961 %	1966 %
Total metal workforce	100	100	100	100
Traditional skills				
Blacksmiths	5.8	2.0	0.9	0.6
Fitters	9.6	15.4	14.7	14.2
Turners	2.2			
Patternmakers	0.8	0.5	n.a.	0.4
Toolmakers	0.7	2.1	2.3	2.3
SUB-TOTAL	19.1	20.0	17.9	17.5
Other skills				
Welders	0.4	2.8	3.9	4.0
Motor engineers, mechanics	10.2	11.2	12.5	11.7
Electrical mechanics	11.5	10.7	14.9	14.7
SUB-TOTAL	22.1	24.7	31.3	30.4
Machinists (so described)	1.9	4.3	5.3	4.7
Process workers	—	3.5	8.7	11.0
Indeterminate	15.9	13.5	8.2	9.2
GRAND TOTAL	59.0	66.0	71.4	72.8

considered to have satisfactorily defined their industry, the percentage engaged in the metal trades in 1933 and 1947 respectively were: Traditional Skills, 94 and 77 per cent; Other Skills, 67 and 68; Machinists 100 and 100; Process Workers, n.a. and 100 per cent.[7]

II

With the growth of the industry metal unionists increased as a proportion of all Australian trade union members. In 1912 they represented less than seven per cent of the total; by 1939 the figure had risen to 11 per cent, and by 1970 to 17 per cent.[8] During this period there were eight major unions enrolling workers in all sectors of the metal trades. Two of them, the A.E.U.

[7] For further details see Sheridan, op. cit., pp. 12–16.
[8] Commonwealth Bureau of Census and Statistics, *Labour Reports.*

and the Australasian Society of Engineers (A.S.E.) were direct rivals in their attempts to organise engineering workers. A third, the Blacksmiths' Society of Australasia (B.S.A.), also competed with the two larger bodies for recruits in the smithing section of the engineering trade. The titles of four of the remaining metal unions indicate their main spheres of interest. They were, the Boilermakers' Society of Australia, the Federated Moulders (Metals) Union of Australia, the Electrical Trades Union of Australia (E.T.U), and the Sheet Metal Working Industrial Union of Australia (S.M.W.I.U.). Generally speaking these bodies did not constitute direct rivals to A.E.U. Occasional jurisdictional disputes arose but competition was never as intense as with the A.S.E. The A.E.U. experienced remarkably little friction with the E.T.U. and seemed content to allow that body to organise a growing proportion of electrical workers while it concentrated its organisational efforts among the traditional engineering trades. The eighth significant metal union was the Federated Ironworkers' Association (F.I.A.). The A.E.U. seldom clashed with this body which largely enrolled tradesmens' assistants, labourers, and production workers in the iron and steel refining industry.

Several other unions attempted to organise workers engaged in specific sectors of the metal industries. Most important of these was the vehicle builders' union[9] which catered for workers employed in the assembly and manufacture of automobiles and whose aggressive recruiting policies often brought it into collision with the other metal unions. Smaller sectional unions were those in the agricultural implement and stovemaking industries. The first of these operated mainly in Victoria and South Australia while the latter was important only in New South Wales. Neither of them caused much friction with other unions largely because most of their potential rivals refused to enrol piece-workers common in these two sectors of the metal industry. In 1946 both organisations amalgamated with the S.M.W.I.U.

Another body of some importance in the history of the unionisation of metal trades workers was the Federated Engine Drivers and Firemen's Association of Australasia (F.E.D.F.A.). This organisation initially enrolled only stationary-engine drivers working in all sectors of the economy but came also to cater for crane drivers employed within the metal industries. Several other relatively unimportant unions organised small numbers of metal workers in various localities. More significant at times were the

---

[9] This union's full title was originally The Australian Coach, Motor Car, Tram, Waggon Builders, Wheelwrights and Rolling Stock Makers Employees Federation. During World War II it changed its name to that of the Vehicle Builders Employees Federation of Australia. Hereafter it will be referred to where relevant simply as the Coachmakers or the Vehicle Builders union.

'industrial' unions such as those of the coalminers, railwaymen, and gas-workers, which often competed with the eight principal metal unions for the recruitment of metal workers engaged in their particular industry. However, except in the railway workshops, the numbers of workers over whom such jurisdictional disputes arose were relatively insignificant.

The Commonwealth Bureau of Census and Statistics provides figures for the total membership of metal unions — 'industrial' unions not included — at the end of each year. By comparing these with Bureau estimates of average annual employment in the metal trades it is possible to obtain a very crude index of the degree to which the industry's workforce was unionised in any particular year. Table 1.4 sets out the details for various years which witnessed temporary peaks in the size of the workforce. The low 1937—8 figure is probably due to the lag in previously unemployed workers rejoining their unions after the depression. An annual series would reveal a decline on trend in the 1950s and 1960s in common with Australian unionisation as a whole.[10] However, the degree of unionisation in the metal trades is still relatively high throughout the period. By comparison three British estimates for the years 1939, 1947 and 1960 indicate that 37, 52 and 54 per cent respectively of the British engineering workforce were members of trade unions.[11]

An incomplete membership series for the A.S.E. from 1941 to 1971[12] indicates that in the 1950s and 1960s A.S.E. membership rose from around one third to over three quarters of the A.E.U. total. The reasons for this will be discussed in Chapter 10. No continuous series of membership figures are available for other organisations but it is certain that, except for a brief period during World War II when the F.I.A. absorbed the temporarily inflated membership of the Munition Workers' Union, the A.E.U. was always the largest metal union. In Table 1.4 A.E.U. estimates of its membership in December of each year have been aligned with the Census Bureau's figures for all metal unions and it will be seen that the A.E.U. usually accounted for between one quarter and one third of the total. However, this overstates the numerical importance of A.E.U. members within the metal trades because an unknown number were employed outside the metal industries. Of the other major metal unions only the A.S.E., B.S.A., and perhaps the E.T.U. would have been

[10] See e.g. G. W. Ford, 'Unions and the Future', in P. W. D. Matthews and G. W. Ford, *Australian Trade Unions* (Melbourne, 1968), Table 1.

[11] N. Barou, *British Trade Unions* (London, 1947) Appendix VIII; Allan Flanders, 'Great Britain' in W. Galenson (Ed.), *Comparative Labour Movements* (New York, 1952), pp. 1—103, Table 2; Royal Commission on Trade Unions and Employers' Associations, *Research Papers*, 6, by G. S. Bain (H.M.S.O., 1967) Table 10.

[12] Kindly provided to the author by the A.S.E. federal office.

likely to have a similar proportion of their membership engaged in other industries.

As in most manufacturing industries the majority of metal producing firms are located in New South Wales and Victoria. Within these states there is a further heavy concentration of employment in the capital cities of Sydney and Melbourne. A.E.U. membership was consequently greatest in the two major industrial states, which together accounted for two thirds of the total in most peacetime years, rising to three quarters during World War II. In 1920 the breakdown between New South Wales and Victoria was 40 and 23 per cent respectively, but over the years the gap narrowed until, by 1966, the figures were 35 and 32 per cent respectively. Next came Queensland, accounting for a proportion fluctuating between 12 and 18 per cent of the peacetime total, followed jointly by South and Western Australia, each with usually a little more than half the Queensland total. Tasmania's share of A.E.U. membership rose from 2 to 4 per cent over the whole period.

III

For many years after its formation the Australian Section of the union remained the strict preserve of craftsmen. In 1890, for example, the typical member of the 1,700-strong Amalgamated Society of Engineers was a highly skilled journeyman capable of turning his hand to practically any engineering task. In every essential the colonial society was closely comparable to its parent union at the date of its formation 40 years earlier. In Australia craftsmen had not been affected by the emergence of less skilled specialised machinists who were beginning to threaten the ascendancy of the society's members in Britain.[13] The society comprised almost entirely of fitters, turners, smiths, patternmakers, and the highly skilled planers, shapers and other 'first-class' machinemen. Within these occupations entry was limited to men aged between 21 and 40 years who had undergone at least five years' training at their trade. Most members, after the manner of an eighteenth-century millwright, had served a formal apprenticeship during which they had been indentured to their employers to serve for low wages in return for being taught the trade.

A central feature of the nineteenth-century 'New Model' unionism initiated by the Amalgamated Society of Engineers was the extensive system of benefits provided for members. In return for high weekly subscriptions

---

[13] For details of the contemporary British situation see Jefferys, op. cit., pp. 122–7, 156–7.

Table 1.4:   Trade Union Membership in the Metal Industries in
Selected Years

(i) Year	(ii) Metal workforce (000)	(iii) Metal unionists (000)	(iv) Col. (iii) as proportion of col. (ii) %	(v) A.E.U. member- ship (000)	(vi) Col. (v) as proportion of col. (iii) %
1914	84.9	42.1	50	13.0	31
1920–1	103.6	53.9	52	17.5	32
1928–9	127.3	82.7	65	23.5	28
1937–8	178.0	84.0	47	24.8	30
1943–4	341.0	206.8	61	71.2	34
1951–2	389.3	242.8	62	72.9	30
1960–1	512.7	292.4	57	79.6	27
1967–8	629.0	343.1	55	83.5	24

Sources: Commonwealth Bureau of Census and Statistics, *Production Bulletins*; *Secondary Industries Bulletin*; *Manufacturing Industry*; *Labour Reports*; Amalgamated Society of Engineers and A.E.U., *Monthly Reports*, *Monthly Journal and Reports*, *Monthly Trade Reports*, *Quarterly Reports*.

of between 1s. and 1/6d. (exclusive of special levies) members were entitled to 'Friendly' Benefits, covering them against loss of tools, accidents, sickness, old age and death, and 'Out of Work' Benefits covering them against unemployment caused by lack of work and industrial disputes. Unemployment Benefit and Sickness Benefit, for example, both commenced at 10s. per week and at a time when the average craftsman's wage was approximately 10s. per day such sums represented a valuable safeguard against economic fluctuations and personal misfortune. Lest unhealthy or incompetent members became a drain on the union's funds, applicants had to be without physical disabilities[14] and capable of earning the 'ordinary' rate of wages in the district. 'To the tendency to create an "aristocracy of labour" was added, therefore, the fastidiousness of an insurance company.'[15] The nicknames of 'Gentlemen Jims' and 'Tin Gods' acquired by Society members within the labour movement were not untainted with bitterness, for they formed a consciously elite group among

[14] Some applicants were rejected because they wore spectacles. See K. Buckley, 'A New Index of Engineering Unemployment 1852–94', in *The Economic Record*, 43, 101, 1967, p. 113. In Britain on one occasion a branch consulted head office about the advisability of admitting a 'worker who is a little round shouldered'. Jefferys, op. cit., p. 59.

[15] Sydney and Beatrice Webb, *The History of Trade Unionism, 1666–1920* (London, 1920), p. 323.

Australian engineering workers and their ranks included minor employers, senior management personnel and many foremen.

The exclusive nature of the union could not, however, be maintained in the face of the increasing specialisation and subdivision of the engineering trades which were taking place in Britain. In order to protect the interests of its craftsmen members the British section was forced to begin organising operatives of the new machines and processes. Such defensive reasons were to some small degree fortified by more altruistic motives derived from the contemporary British trend away from New Model craft unionism toward 'industrial' unionism. Consequently, beginning in 1892, the Amalgamated Society's entry rules were progressively widened until, in 1912, even engineering labourers were allowed to join the union. In the 1890s the union also relaxed its rules sufficiently to permit the entry to special membership sections of those workers who were ineligible to join the main Benefit sections because of 'age, infirmity or a lower [than the ordinary] rate of wages'.[16] Despite these important reforms, no allowance was made in Britain until 1926 for the increasing number of engineers who, although eligible, were uninterested in the Benefits side of the union's activities and hence were deterred from joining the A.E.U.

Fortunately for the union's position in the competitive Australian trade union environment a 1901 amendment to the rules gave members in the Commonwealth the power to meet the requirements of Australian labour legislation. Registration under the various Federal and State Arbitration Acts introduced in the 1900s broadly required that no restrictions should be placed on the admission of new members.[17] In the Amalgamated Society's case this meant that provision had to be made for the entry of those engineers uninterested in benefits. The New South Wales branches were the first to suitably amend the rules in order to register under the State Act in 1902. By 1905 'Arbitration' members, paying contributions of 4d. per week and entitled to dispute benefits only, were being enrolled in all States. In 1913 these new entrants became known as 'Industrial' members and their membership section came to cover all categories of engineering workers including labourers after the closure of their separate member-

[16] Jefferys, op. cit., p. 137.
[17] For example, the first *Commonwealth Conciliation and Arbitration Act* of 1904 did not allow for the registration of a union if, *inter alia*, 'the rules of the trade union or their administration do not provide reasonable facilities for the admission of new members or impose unreasonable conditions on the continuance of their membership . . .': J. H. Portus, *The Development of Australian Trade Union Law* (Melbourne, 1958), p. 183.

ship section in 1919. As the twentieth century progressed the attraction to members of Friendly Society-type benefits declined with the result that Industrial members came to represent an increasing proportion of A.E.U. total membership. By the start of World War II, Benefit members were in a minority and the trend was accelerated by the enormous inflow of workers entering the engineering trades through special wartime training schemes. Table 1.5 depicts the overall growth of non-Benefit members.

Table 1.5: Non-Benefit Members as a Percentage of Total A.E.U. Membership in each State in Selected Periods

	N.S.W. %	Vic. %	S.A. %	Qld. %	W.A. %	Tas. %	C'wealth %
1914–21	16.8	24.5	18.3	34.7	32.6	25.2	23.3
1922–7	16.1	31.5	21.1	51.1	43.7	45.9	29.5
1928–33	18.0	37.6	23.8	61.7	53.6	58.2	34.8
1934–9	25.8	51.7	37.9	69.8	62.4	74.5	46.4
1940–5	55.8	67.2	65.0	77.1	73.3	81.4	64.6
1946–54[a]	62.3	74.1	66.9	80.2	74.2	81.6	69.0
1955–61	65.0	80.6	70.7	85.1	75.9	82.1	74.5
1962–7	74.4	83.8	76.3	90.4	79.6	84.9	80.5

Sources: *A.E.U. Monthly Reports, Monthly Journal and Reports, Monthly Trade Reports, Quarterly Reports.*

[a]From 1948 onwards the A.E.U. records listed separately all female members and those tradesmen members trained under wartime training schemes. These membership categories have been added to Industrial members in the table.

It also indicates that the growth rate of the Industrial Section varied markedly between the states and that, particularly before World War II, Industrial members remained a much smaller percentage of the total in New South Wales and South Australia than elsewhere. In pre-war years Queensland, Tasmanian and West Australian members proved the least interested in benefits while the proportion of Victorian Industrial members approximated to the average for the whole Commonwealth. No fully satisfactory reason can be offered for these geographical differences. Important factors in the overall decline in the importance of the Benefit sections were the gradual improvement in Australian social security and the establishment of permanent full employment after 1939. Yet before World War II there was no significant disparity between either the welfare systems or unemployment rates in the six states which could explain the regional variations in the union's membership structure. Social security in Queensland certainly improved more rapidly than elsewhere under the Labor governments which were in power almost uninterruptedly from 1915. However, New South Wales was by no means backward in this sphere and, particularly in the 1920s under Labor governments, several important Bills were passed by the state legislature including the first Australian child endowment scheme and a very generous Workers' Compensation Act. One factor of probable relevance to the problem is the organising activity of other unions. Because of the varying regional strength of the F.I.A. a higher proportion of labourers, who were ineligible to join the Benefit sections, entered the A.E.U. in Queensland, West Australia and Tasmania. In addition the A.S.E., which offered its members only funeral and dispute benefits did not succeed in establishing effective branches in Queensland and Tasmania and it was of relatively minor significance in Victoria before World War II. Hence a larger proportion of those engineering workers who were willing to join a union but who were not interested in an extensive benefits system joined the A.E.U. in these states than elsewhere.

IV

During the transition period from 1892 onwards when the exclusive Amalgamated Society progressively opened its ranks to less skilled workers the Australian Section appears to have accepted the change far more readily than was the case in Britain. Although the ominous growth in the numbers of unorganised semi-skilled workers had largely prompted the successive lowering of membership qualifications, the animosity of the British rank and file craftsmen towards these potential job usurpers, combined with the long tradition of exclusiveness, prevented full advantage being taken of the new rules. In the pre-World War I period the recruitment of machinists was greatly hampered while the admission of labourers met with even greater rank and file hostility. Thus, 'After a few years of argument but little recruiting, the [unskilled] Section was abolished in 1917.'[18]

The Australian reaction to the rule changes was different largely because of the technological backwardness of the domestic engineering industry. In Britain Society members were already suffering from the competition of semi-skilled workers and their attitude, although short-sighted, was understandably coloured by their bitter experience. In Australia, where repetitive work and specialist machines were practically non-existent, the union's members were able to take a more objective view.[19] The skilled members of

[18] Jefferys, op. cit., p. 166.
[19] This is one area in which the conclusions I reached from an independent examination of the union's pre-1920 history differ from those of K. D. Buckley. When discussing the pre-World War I period, I feel Buckley at times confuses

the A.E.U. and the Amalgamated Society always remained utterly opposed to the 'handyman', the worker who had not been indentured and who had picked up his knowledge of the craftsman's trade — often only a single aspect — by observation and experimentation. But as far as semi-skilled machinists were concerned the Australian Section's aim was always to control the new processes and to safeguard the craftsman's position by securing the best possible rates of pay for the machinists. Fortunately specialisation occurred at a very slow pace in Australia. Although some of the older craftsmen may have scorned the less skilled newcomers, the union's approach was never hampered by the blind enmity characteristic of the British members when first confronted with the problem. Thus the federal executive could soberly appraise the 1901 rule changes,

So far as the engineering trade in Australasia is concerned, the question of automatic machines is not yet of any importance, competition has not reached that stage in this country, nor production so extensive to cause the introduction of these specialised machines, but that time is fast coming, and it is fortunate for us that the rules have been so far liberalised, that District committees will now be in a better position to meet and control such competition when it comes.[20]

Leading Australian officials urged that membership should be open to labourers some time before the British union took the reluctant and short-lived step.[21] When, however, the Australian branches were permitted to enrol unskilled workers the existence of the F.I.A. proved a restricting factor since the Society was unwilling to enter into a 'body-snatching' contest. Hence it was decided that labourers would be eligible for membership only if '. . .amalgamation with the Iron Workers' Assistants Union [sic] can be arranged, except in any State where no branch of that Union exists'.[22] This meant that recruitment was largely confined to West Australia, where the local branches of the F.I.A. amalgamated with the Society in 1915, Queensland where the unskilled union was seldom active outside Brisbane, and Tasmania where

the engineering craftsman's ageless opposition to the 'handyman' with separate attitudes towards accepting semi-skilled and unskilled workers into the union, and places too much emphasis on the minority 'conservative' view within the union. (*The Amalgamated Engineers*, pp. 133–4, 206–18).

[20] Amalgamated Society of Engineers, *Monthly Report*, January 1902, p. 4. (Hereafter the union's *Monthly Report* will be abbreviated to '*M.R.*' in the footnotes. The title of the Journal remained the same after the union altered its name in 1920. From 1935, however, it was published in a new format under the title *Monthly Journal and Report* ('*M.J.R.*'). In 1948 its title changed finally to *Monthly Journal*, ('*M.J.*').)

[21] See, e.g. *M.R.*, January 1911, pp. 12–13, February 1911, pp. 11–14.

[22] *Amalgamated Society of Engineers, 1913 Rules (Australian Section)*, Rule 23, Clause 10.

the F.I.A. was unimportant before the Second World War. Nevertheless the proportion of members in the unskilled Section F reached five per cent during its short five year life and this compares favourably with the British experience. After 1918 labourers could join the Industrial Section.

The acceptance of less skilled workers by a union hitherto confined to the craftsmen-aristocrats of the engineering world drew comment from outsiders. Employers ostensibly regretted the trend. The representative of the Broken Hill Proprietary Co. Ltd. at the engineers' first federal arbitration case in 1920 remarked that the union, 'must be getting down very much to have general labourers',[23] while a South Australian employer alleged that because of the 'deterioration' in membership standards many Society men arriving at his works were incapable of performing the work required of them.[24] The President of the Commonwealth Arbitration Court, Mr Justice Higgins, proved a more sympathetic observer. He recalled that Society members used to 'hold their noses aloft and scorned at the inferior men' but was pleased to hear that they had now 'seen the error of their ways'.[25]

Although less skilled members continued to rise in relative importance, the term 'Gentlemen Jims' was still being applied in the late 1940s and there is no doubt that the A.E.U. remained predominantly a craft union right up to the end of its separate existence in 1972. The literary evidence for this is overwhelming but unfortunately it is impossible to quantify the breakdown of A.E.U. members' skills. While we can be sure that the overwhelming majority of Benefit members were craftsmen, the increasingly important Industrial Section conceals the whole gamut of skills from toolmaker down to general labourer. Considerable detailed information is, however, available concerning entrants to A.E.U. in the years after 1905. This is contained in the several hundred thousand completed application forms which the union has retained. Obviously information about *entrants* to the union tells us nothing about the current membership of the A.E.U. at any one time, for we have no way of estimating membership turnover. A further drawback is that, because of the original need for the central supervision of benefits, entry forms for other than the Industrial Section and the shortlived labourers' section were sent to the Head Office in London prior to 1939.[26] Bearing these twin facts in mind, a consideration of Table 1.6 still proves illuminating. The Table sum-

---

[23] Commonwealth Arbitration Court, *Amalgamated Society of Engineers and The Adelaide Steamship Company and Others* (1920—21), Transcripts of Evidence, H. A. Mitchell, p. 91. (Hereafter referred to as *1920—1 Arbitration Case*).
[24] Ibid., S. Perry, pp. 3589—90.
[25] Ibid., p. 2789.
[26] The British Executive Council of the A.E.U. has since destroyed these forms.

marises the results of a sample survey of 9,706 A.E.U. application forms between the years 1914 and 1952.[27] It strongly suggests that A.E.U. members remained predominantly craftsmen in the period surveyed. The pre-1939 time periods are based on turning points in the rate of growth of A.E.U. membership but the 1939—52 period is simply divided into war and post-war years. In brief, the table indicates the great preponderance of skilled entrants, the importance of the apprenticeship system and the fact that a large proportion of recruits worked outside the metal trades. Much greater reliance can be placed on occupation details provided by A.E.U. recruits under the scrutiny of shop steward, organiser or Branch Secretary than those offered by Census respondents. In all, the entrants were engaged in 66 clearly defined occupations. The arbitrary classification of certain machining jobs by the author probably overstates the true proportion of semi-skilled entrants, particularly in the earlier years. A separate consideration of the characteristics of entrants to the Benefit Sections after 1939[28] suggests that the proportions of apprenticed recruits, skilled recruits — particularly in the traditional crafts, and recruits working in the metal trades, would all be higher in the pre-1939 period if Benefit application forms were available.

The sharp rise in the proportion of apprenticed entrants between 1928 and 1933 mainly reflects the relative fall of semi-skilled entrants during the Depression. In the years between 1940 and 1945 the number of entrants to the A.E.U. soared as a result of the emergency expansion of the metal industries and the inflow of male and female engineers into the various trades via special adult training schemes. Total A.E.U. membership rose from 28,000 in 1939 to 72,000 in mid-1944. As a consequence apprenticed entrants declined to approximately one third of the total despite the inclusion in the calculation for the first time of Benefit and Apprentice Sections representing 17 per cent of all war-time recruits. In the immediate post-war period the proportion apprenticed began to rise again. Among skilled entrants, of course, apprenticeship was well above average. Practically 90 per cent of recruits engaged in traditional skilled jobs had been apprenticed in the pre-1939 period.[29] Even during World War II a majority of recruits in this group had been apprenticed and after 1945 the proportion rose to 73 per cent. Although the percentage fell to 39 per cent during the war period, the majority of pre- and post-World War II entrants following other skilled

[27] T. Sheridan, 'Partial Anatomy of a Union: A Sample of A.E.U. Recruiting, 1914—1952', *The Journal of Industrial Relations*, 14, 3, 1972, pp. 238—63.
[28] Ibid., Table 3.
[29] Ibid., Table 4.

Table 1.6:   Characteristics of Entrants to A.E.U.

	Excluding benefit sections				All sections	
	1914–21	1922–27	1928–33	1934–39	1940–45	1946–52
Total sampled[a]	1,190	1,121	677	2,079	3,013	1,619
Characteristics	%	%	%	%	%	%
Occupation:						
Traditional skilled	57	50	58	53	52	50
Other skilled	20	25	24	25	14	20
Total skilled[b]	79	76	84	79	68	71
Semi skilled	15	16	10	16	29	24
Unskilled	6	8	6	5	3	5
Apprenticed	65	63	76	65	35	49
Employed in metal trades	70	68	60	69	75	67

Source: Sheridan, 'Partial Anatomy . . .', op. cit.

[a]7 sample application forms provided no date. Thus the total on this line adds to 9,699 only.

[b]Included in this total is the tiny proportion of entrants who were engaged in the skilled occupations of plumbing, moulding and boilermaking not usually organised by the A.E.U.

engineering occupations had also been apprenticed, and during the Depression the proportion rose to 72 per cent.

It is difficult to overstress the significance of apprenticeship in the history of the A.E.U. Generally speaking boys were indentured at low wages for a fixed period, usually five years, during which practical instruction and observation on the job was combined with theoretical instruction at technical schools. Right into the 1970s unions and metal employers alike regarded this as the best means of producing engineering craftsmen.[30] In addition the ancient trappings and jargon usually connected with entering indentures, and the ceremonies — dignified or bawdy — traditionally associated with a lad 'coming out of his time' at the end of the apprenticeship, greatly fortified the pride and sense of separateness or superiority in tradesmen's minds. That this was not simply an anachronistic hangover perpetuated by the A.E.U. and other craft unions is indicated by the evidence of employers before the

[30] See e.g. Industrial Commission of New South Wales, *Report of the Inquiry into The Apprenticeship System in New South Wales* (Sydney, 1968) (Hereafter referred to as the *Beattie Report*).

most recent inquiry into the apprenticeship system. In the view of a senior official of Australia's largest firm,

It is important that an apprentice should feel that he belongs to a system with a long history of pride in craftsmanship and that this sense of belonging is engendered and strengthened by the formalities connected with the signing and presentation of indentures. The [steel making] companies endeavour to foster this pride in craftsmanship by the presentation of completed indentures at formal ceremonies.[31]

A notable feature of Table 1.6 is the decline in the war period of the proportions of recruits with other than traditional skills, and the converse rise in the percentage of semi-skilled entrants. In part this reflects the decline in such non-essential, consumer oriented trades as motor mechanics, but it also points to the fact that the wartime explosion of entrants meant that the union had to concentrate its resources on organising the traditional trades and the semi-skilled jobs which it always saw as the main potential threat to craftsmen members.

Another property of war and post-war entrants is that 14 and 12 per cent respectively failed to provide information about the industry in which they worked — which is more than double the pre-war average. The major reasons for this were a change in the application forms and the fact that 20 per cent of the 'dilutees', as adults entering crafts under the emergency schemes were known, were still attending technical school when they joined the union. Given the emphasis on the 'essential' defence industries and the tight government control on manpower we can be sure that at least the wartime proportion of recruits engaged in the metal trades is understated in the table. As it is, the table indicates that, apart from the Depression years, the proportion of entrants employed outside the metal industries ranged from one quarter to one third of the total. In most years manufacturing industries (including heat, light and power generation) combined to account for some 80 per cent of entrants, but A.E.U. recruits were also employed in every conceivable part of the primary and tertiary sectors of the economy, from hospitals to sewage farms and from pastoral properties to Chinese laundries. Since there is no reason to assume that there would be any great disparity between the turnover of members engaged in the metal trades and elsewhere we can assume that a significant proportion of A.E.U. members in all years were employed outside the central metal sector. This dispersion of engineers

---

[31] W. K. Jones, Assistant Chief Industrial Officer of the Broken Hill Pty. Co. Ltd., ibid., p. 225.

throughout the economy helps explain why the fitter's margin was chosen by the arbitration tribunals as being representative of craftsmen's wages in every industry. It further points to the reason why all parties interested in the wage-cost structure of each industry attached such importance to the exact level at which the fitter's rate was set.

2

The structure, policy, and outlook of the A.E.U.

One other important British craft union, the Amalgamated Society of Carpenters and Joiners (A.S.C.J.), established branches in Australia during the nineteenth century. Like all the British 'New Model' unions of the period the carpenters when forming their union had based its rule-book on that of the Amalgamated Society of Engineers. Thus until 1923 the Australian section of the A.S.C.J. was governed by a constitution similar in all important respects to that of the engineers. However, when they separated from the British union in that year the carpenters took advantage of the break completely to remould their constitution along lines more typical of modern Australian unions.[1] This left the A.E.U. alone in retaining a structure which, originally adopted in an effort to solve some of the problems of organising engineering workers in mid-nineteenth century Britain, was amended only when changing circumstances in the United Kingdom demanded it. Between 1920 and 1959 it was only very rarely, and then in a limited manner, that the A.E.U. rules were altered to provide for diverging Australian conditions. The union's structure was thus a British transplantation. For the first 35 years of its existence in Australia the branches were governed directly by the British Executive Council. A local inter-colonial executive was provided in 1887 in the form of the part-time Australasian Council which was replaced in 1917 by a full-time Commonwealth Council. These bodies were the direct representatives of the Executive Council in Australia, and thus firm control was retained over branches of the union in all States. The Executive, the Australasian, and the Commonwealth Councils in turn supervised the actual establishment of new branches in

---

[1] S. Higenbottam, *Our Society's History*, Manchester 1939, pp. 108, 286, 289–90; Brian Fitzpatrick, *A Short History of the Australian Labour Movement*, Melbourne 1944, p. 30; *Rules of Australian District Amalgamated Society of Carpenters and Joiners*, December 1911; *Amalgamated Society of Carpenters and Joiners of Australia. Rules Operating from 1st May 1929.*

Australia. The branches were given a certain degree of freedom of action in negotiating local working conditions but overall control remained in the hands of the central executive.

  In contrast to the A.E.U., most federal unions were formed by the merging of societies which had grown spontaneously in the various industrial centres of the Commonwealth. Locally based organisations of manufacturing workers drew together for various reasons. Among craft unions the movement towards federation often began because of a need, emerging in the late nineteenth century, to help members travelling interstate in search of employment.[2] Among weaker unions, often organising less skilled workers, the stimulus was sometimes provided by a desire to obtain in the Commonwealth Arbitration Court an award which they hoped would prove more favourable than those currently handed down by the state tribunals.[3] But whatever the actual causes of federation, the existence of previously autonomous local branches militated against the formation of a powerful central executive in the new unions. The typical structure was a loose grouping of large state, city, or perhaps single suburban branches controlled federally by a conference of branch delegates meeting once a year.[4] When the conference is not sitting a smaller executive body, including representatives from each state, can be summoned to deal with matters considered sufficiently important to require federal attention. Routine federal affairs are attended to by one or two full-time officials. Within the framework of the general rules the branches run their own affairs with a minimum of interference from federal officials. Most unions allow the branches to pass by-laws to meet regional conditions. Usually only a relatively small proportion of branch income is forwarded to national headquarters, leaving the bulk of the unions' funds to be administered locally. General branch meetings are held quarterly or, at most, once a month. Branch affairs are supervised by a part-time management committee but day-to-day union business is in the

[2] E.g. the moulders and the printers. See W. J. Hargreaves, *History of the Federated Moulders' (Metals) Union of Australia 1858–1958.* (The Worker Print, n.d.) pp. 25–6, 31, 37; J. Hagan, *Printers & Politics* (Canberra, 1966), pp. 93–7.

[3] E.g. the F.I.A., See J. Merritt, 'A History of the Federated Ironworkers' Association of Australia, 1909–1952', Ph.D. thesis, Australian National University, 1967, Ch. 2.

[4] An important exception in some respects to this general picture is the F.I.A. This body consists of relatively few, large, branches but in the 1940s for a variety of reasons, federal executive control over the branches was greatly strengthened. ibid, Ch. 7. For details of union structures, see, P. W. D. Matthews, 'Trade Union Organization' in P. W. D. Matthews and G. W. Ford, *Australian Trade Unions*, op. cit., pp. 70–102; J. E. Isaac and G. W. Ford (Eds), *Australian Labour Relations: Readings* (Melbourne, 1966), pp. 79–84.

hands of full-time secretaries assisted by organisers. As far as benefits are concerned some unions provide a funeral fund, others also insure members against accident or loss of tools. Commonly there are also funds available for the purpose of alleviating, at the discretion of the local executive, general distress among members caused by sickness or unemployment. But only very exceptionally is specific statutory provision made for unemployment benefit or superannuation allowances.[5]

Alongside such union constitutions that of the A.E.U. appeared involved and cumbersome. All A.E.U. officials needed to have an extensive knowledge of what appears to have been the lengthiest union rule book in Australia: the 1942 edition, for example, consisted of 196 pages containing 47 principal rules and a multitude of sub-clauses. The Figure overleaf illustrates the structural complexity of the union. In order to follow the course of the complicated bitter public controversies which arose within the union in the 1950s and 1960s, and to judge allegations then made of 'control' and 'manipulation' of the union by outside bodies, it is of the first importance to clearly understand the working of this unusual constitution.

As with other unions, the primary unit of the A.E.U. was the branch but there were several important differences. In the first place the original importance of benefit payments imposed certain limitations on branch size and frequency of meetings. Membership of a branch was based on residence but the need to keep the task of handling contributions and benefit payments within proportions manageable for part-time officials resulted in branches being restricted to a total membership of 300 until 1933 and 500 thereafter. Once this number had been reached a new branch had to be formed. Consequently in 1966, for example, there were some 231 A.E.U. branches, including 53 in Sydney alone. All branches continued to meet fortnightly although the original necessity for such frequent meetings largely disappeared with the decline in the proportion of members eligible for benefits and the advent of full employment in the 1940s. The powers of these numerous small branches were in the main limited to the receipt of contributions, disbursement of benefits, induction of new members and discussions of matters (other than religion) of general interest to members. The branches usually raised a 'Local Purposes Fund' by small annual levy to assist distressed members or to support the local interests of the trade. Branch officers performed all their duties in their spare time, the

---

[5] The printing unions provide statutory unemployment benefit but these rules were a continual source of controversy until the advent of continual full employment in the 1940s. See Hagan, op. cit., pp. 20, 35, 49, 243–4.

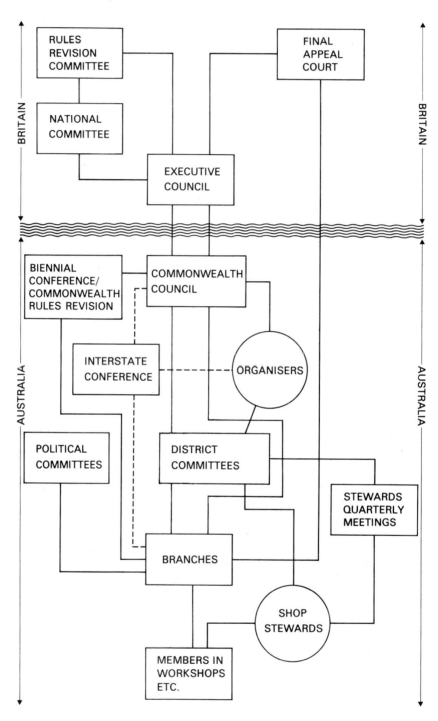

most important of them being the secretary who kept the Commonwealth Council informed of the state of trade in his area by means of a monthly report. His small emolument varied with the number of members on his books. All financial transactions of the branches were closely scrutinised by the Commonwealth Council when quarterly or half-yearly branch returns were sent to the federal office. Decisions to open new branches were ultimately made by Council and if an existing branch did not conduct its affairs in the approved manner it could be dissolved by the federal executive.[6] The relationship was far from one sided however, for the number of branches and the frequency of the meetings meant that there was in total an exceedingly large number of branch officials who naturally followed the affairs of the union closely and who had every opportunity of making their views known within internal channels. Throughout its history it proved a foolhardy and short-serving A.E.U. full-time official who neglected to nurse the branches within his electorate.

Next in the organisational hierarchy came the District Committee consisting of delegates elected from branches within the 'district' which until 1938 included all branches within a radius of 25 miles, although the Commonwealth Council had the discretion to create a new district if sufficient members lived outside a 15 mile radius. After 1938 Council could group branches solely according to convenience but in fact no major change was made in existing arrangements. The number of branch delegates was limited to 25. Shop stewards also elected representatives whose number was set at 1 per 10,000 district members until 1933 and 1 per 5,000 thereafter. In some senses these committees are comparable with the branch management committees of other federal unions. Subject to the approval of the Commonwealth Council, the District Committees were the local executive arms of the A.E.U., regulating ' . . . the rate of wages, hours of labour, terms of overtime, and general conditions affecting the interests of the trade in their respective districts'.[7] They were empowered to conduct negotiations with employers and controlled local disputes. During a strike or lockout the Committee could ballot unaffected members on whether to pay a supporting levy and other districts could be appealed to for help. Votes could also be taken for the purpose of striking levies to support A.E.U. members upon local bodies such as Labour Councils and metal-trades associations. District Committees in the larger industrial

---

[6] The Darwin branch was dealt with in this fashion in 1923 because its members *inter alia* used the union's funds 'in fighting each other at law', *M.R.*, September 1923, p. 4.

[7] *A.E.U. (Australian Section) Rules 1928*, Rule 13, Clause 4.

centres also supervised locally the work of the full-time, elected organisers based in these areas. The District Secretaries in Sydney, Melbourne and, after 1956, Adelaide were full-time officials. All other Committee members were part-timers receiving small fees for attendance at meetings and on delegations. For certain purposes such as complying with state legislation or participating in the activities of state based organisations such as branches of the A.C.T.U., the capital city District Committees were empowered to act as the state authority of the union.[8] In Britain the role of regional co-ordination was catered for in the rules by a grouping of District Committees to elect representatives to form a Divisional Committee which in turn elected delegates to the supreme policy-making body of the union, the rank and file National Committee. The latter met annually and was empowered, at certain fixed intervals,[9] to consider suggestions and decide on alterations to the rules. On these occasions the National Committee changed its title to that of General Rules Revision Meeting. The Australian branches were not represented on these bodies until 1945[10] but thereafter Commonwealth delegates attended the quinquennial General Rules Revision Meetings and any recalled meetings in between.

The general internal affairs of the A.E.U. were conducted by the full-time Executive Council situated in London and composed of a President and seven council members assisted by a General Secretary and two Assistant General Secretaries. The Council members were elected by the British members alone but overseas members participated in the voting for President and Secretaries. Standing outside the administrative framework was the supreme judiciary of the union, the Final Appeal Court. All A.E.U. members dissatisfied with executive decisions had ultimate re-course to this annual tribunal which consisted of elected rank and file delegates and which, as its name suggests, gave final decisions on all matters brought before it.

In order to meet the need for on-the-spot administration of affairs in Australia, two further bodies were added to the structure of the A.E.U.

[8] In Western Australia the situation was formally different from that elsewhere, for the state arbitration act required unions to have full power over their own rules and funds. Thus the A.E.U. rules registered there omitted reference to the higher echelons outside Western Australia. In reality the Coastal (Perth) and other District Committees in the state functioned in exactly the same way as elsewhere.
[9] Until 1937 the General Rules Revision Meeting met every four years. There-after it sat quinquennially.
[10] The rules of the old Amalgamated Society of Engineers had made provision for overseas representation at Delegate Meetings (the forerunner of the A.E.U. National Committee) and Final Appeal Court.

Until 1933 a Biennial Conference, composed of working members represent-ing each state, had the power to amend the General Rules in order to bring them '. . . into conformity with Labour legislation and conditions prevailing in the Commonwealth'.[11] After 1933 the name of this body was changed to that of Commonwealth Rules Revision Meeting and it could henceforth meet only within the twelve months after the quinquennial (after 1937) General Rules Revision Meeting had been held in Britain.

The other body unique to the Australian section was the Common-wealth Council which, as the direct representative of the Executive Council, constituted the supreme executive in this country. The Council consisted of a Chairman and three Councilmen assisted by a Secretary. Each member was elected for a renewable term of three years, the Chairman and Secretary by the whole membership of the Commonwealth, the Councilmen by the divisions which they represented. The geographical boundaries of these electoral divisions altered slightly over time but for most of the period Division 1 consisted of branches in South Australia, Victoria, Tasmania, and Broken Hill, Division 2 of branches represented on the Sydney and New-castle District Committees, Division 3 of branches in West Australia, Queensland, Northern Territory, and all remaining branches in New South Wales. All members of the A.E.U. federal executive, upon taking office, had usually received a thorough training in union affairs in the lower echelons of the organisation. The normal progress was for the future Council member to begin with five or ten years in an unpaid capacity at the branch or district level. Next might come a period of full-time service as an organiser before entering the Commonwealth Council. The A.E.U.'s com-plex structure and in particular its multi-branch system served this very important purpose: there was always a plentitude of members capable of taking up all full-time positions — and indeed until the polarisation of activists into two camps in the 1950s A.E.U. elections were renowned for their large fields. Other unions were not always so fortunate. After the F.I.A., for example, had voted out its communist leaders in 1952 it had difficulty in finding members with even the slightest administrative ex-perience to replace the defeated officials.[12]

Issues coming before Commonwealth Council were theoretically decided by a vote of the Councilmen only — although the Chairman was allowed a casting vote if a Councilman was absent. In fact all Council members participated in the discussion and on most matters a sufficient

---

[11] *1928 Rules*, op. cit., Rule 16, Clause 4.
[12] Merritt, op. cit., p. 454.

measure of agreement was reached to render a vote unnecessary. Until the 1950s, aided by the integrity of certain long-serving individuals, membership of the Council acquired a considerable patina of respect within the A.E.U. Despite their lack of formal voting power, the position of Chairman and Secretary usually carried a higher status than that of Councilman. The Chairman, as well as presiding over all meetings, always represented the union in the most prestigious dealings with employers, government and other trade unions. The Secretary, on the other hand, devoted most of his time to administration and because of his constant intercourse with branch and district officials he wielded great influence among rank and file members.

With the conspicuous exception of certain short periods in the 1920s, 1950s and 1960s the executive worked as a team whose members were imbued with a strong sense of collective responsibility. The composition of the Council prevented any single official from concentrating too much power in his own hands. Individuals could exert considerable influence at the Council-table by virtue of their personalities but it was impossible for them to determine A.E.U. policy in the almost dictatorial fashion alleged of the leaders of some other unions. The collective nature of Commonwealth Council decisions and the absence of a clearly distinguishable leader meant that, with rare exceptions, its members were seldom in the public eye until the politically based internal controversies of the 1950s. Policy formulated by five men and often couched in legalistic phrases seldom made good copy for newspaper reporters.

As well as its relative anonymity, the federal executive of the A.E.U., with five full-time members, was heavily staffed in comparison with most other Australian unions and its powers were far greater. Commonwealth Council was vested with 'absolute powers in connection with all matters pertaining to the functions of the Union as an Industrial Union of workers in the Commonwealth'.[13] All A.E.U. activities, whether conducted at the branch or district level, and ranging from wage negotiations with employers to expenditure on stationery were, in the final reckoning, controlled by the Commonwealth Council. Given the concentration of power in the hands of the Council it becomes clear that the outward similarities between A.E.U. District Committees and the branch executives of other federal unions were more apparent than real. The District Committees had no power to amend rules to meet local conditions. Nor had they any control over union finances in their areas. The expenses which the District Committees incurred

---

[13] *1928 Rules*, op. cit., Rule 16, Clause 1.

were covered by periodic transfers of the necessary sums from the branches at the direction of the Commonwealth Council. Organisers, while supervised by the Committees were, in the final analysis, answerable to the Council. District Committee decisions were not binding on members until the Committee minutes had been approved by the Council. If the Council considered the Committee to be acting *ultra vires* the latter would be reprimanded. If a Committee disregarded such warnings the Council had the power to cut off its income from the branches or, in the last resort, to dissolve the Committee and call for a new election.

A further contrast with other Australian unions was provided by the Commonwealth Council's control over A.E.U. funds in Australia. There were three main funds; the General Fund, the Superannuation Reserve Fund, and the Supplementary Fund. All contributions were paid into the General Fund and from it were paid all statutory benefits and general running expenses of the union. Any surplus of income over expenditure was invested in government and municipal bonds. The income of the Superannuation Reserve Fund was derived from a quarterly 2s. levy paid by Benefit members only and was invested in bonds or on mortgages of houses owned by A.E.U. members. The interest accruing from these investments was paid into the General Fund to help cover the cost of superannuation payments. The fund was strictly a reserve but in the exceptional circumstances of the depression of the 1930s the Executive Council was empowered to transfer from the Superannuation Reserve Fund to the General Fund an amount equal to one third of the annual cost of superannuation until the General Fund was in a healthier position.[14] The Supplementary Fund was an Australian innovation and was originally raised by casual levy. In 1929 3d. per week was added to the contributions of all members increasing to 6d. in 1965. This fund paid for the salaries and expenses of those organisers engaged in Australia in addition to the number provided for in the General Rules,[15] supplemented the salaries of all officials to allow for the higher cost of living in the Commonwealth compared with Britain, and provided special grants for needy members. Thus Industrial members could receive payments when unemployed and the statutory dispute benefits paid to all sections were augmented provided the Supplementary Fund was in a sufficiently satisfactory state. In addition the Commonwealth Council could, at its discretion, make special grants from the fund to alleviate distress caused, for example, by lengthy sickness. Any surplus was invested or kept on Deposit Account in the bank.

[14] Jefferys, op. cit., p. 240.
[15] See below, p. 38.

As well as the three main funds there was, following the 1913 British Trade Union Act, a small Political Fund raised by voluntary levy and used for the support of Labor candidates and payment of affiliation fees to the A.L.P. For the greater part of our period the exact size of A.E.U. affiliation to state A.L.P. branches — which was always less than the number paying the levy — was in effect determined by members of Political Committees established in the capital city districts. Only in 1959 did the rules set out a formal structure for these committees almost identical to the District Committees. Previously Commonwealth Council could vary their structure, but in fact they always consisted of delegates elected by the branches.

Both the General Fund (to which for this purpose the Supplementary Fund was added) and the Superannuation Reserve Fund held in Australia were part of the greater equivalents administered by the Executive Council in London and transfers of money between the two countries were possible. In practice this was rarely necessary and took place only in times of great industrial disputes, such as the 1922 lock-outs in Britain (£15,000), and the Victorian and Queensland disputes between 1946 and 1948 (£25,000), or when benefits proved too onerous a burden, as did unemployment payments in Britain in 1928 (£25,000) and in Australia in 1931 (£20,000), and superannuation payments in Australia in 1959 (£82,000).

The total General Fund belonged to all members and the Superannuation Reserve Fund to all Benefit members. Hence if the Australian section of the A.E.U. were to separate from the British union it would be entitled to a fixed proportion of these total funds. Such a break would entail a net transfer of money either way between Sydney and London with the direction of the flow being determined by the differences in recent rates of fund accumulation or dispersion in the two countries. In 1927, for 'example, it was estimated that Australian autonomy would involve a remittance of £23,000 to Britain.[16] The 1968 separation saw a transfer of $A370,000 to Australia.

Given the essential unity of the international A.E.U. funds and subject to supervision from the British Head Office and regular audits, the Commonwealth Council had complete *de facto* control of union finances in Australia. A further check was provided by the fact that decisions on investments had to be made by a separate Investment Committee, but since this body consisted of the Commonwealth Council plus five trustees elected from among working members in the Sydney District the views of the Council inevitably held sway.

[16] *M.R.*, July 1927, pp. 32–5.

All expenditure by the lower echelons of the union was minutely scrutinised by Council. A branch could not buy a table nor could an organiser hire a clerical assistant without Council approval. As an actual working arrangement until the late 1950s the branches at any one time held between them the major part of the A.E.U.'s cash accounts, but these moneys always remained under Council's control. When necessary the Council would order an 'equalisation' of accounts which involved the movement of funds from branches with high net income to those with high net expenditure. Surplus cash was remitted to Commonwealth Council in Sydney.

The A.E.U.'s centralised structure, whereby all activities had to be approved by the federal executive meant that at least two days a week of the Commonwealth Council's time were taken up by routine paperwork. In times of exceptionally rapid growth in branch and district correspondence, such as during World War II, the Council was forced to spend six or seven days per week, as well as most evenings, in ensuring that local union business was being conducted according to rule. Council members inevitably acquired a bureaucratic outlook and, given the importance attached to the complicated rule book at all levels, the union generally was open to the charge of wrapping even the simplest of transactions in too much red tape. Entries such as the following were not too uncommon in the Council's minutes,

In the matter of providing convenient communication between the D.C. [District Committee] and C.C. [Commonwealth Council] rooms — Decided — That a small doorway be made in partition, the Sydney D.C. be written asking for its agreement to proposal [sic].[17]

Branches and District Committees also tended to display a sometimes incongruous fondness for detail. Another Council minute reads 'Townsville Branch re Bro. W. Dunn's contributions whilst imprisoned for opium smuggling — To be advised — That same may remain in abeyance'.[18]

II

Because of the serious and widely publicised allegations made about minority 'control' of the union in the 1950s and 1960s, it is necessary to consider the degree to which A.E.U. members participated in their union's internal affairs. Unfortunately discussion of this topic must be couched in rather general terms both because of a relative lack of quantitative evidence

---

[17] 'Commonwealth Council Minutes', 29/7/18. (Hereafter abbreviated to 'C.C.M.').
[18] 2/10/23.

concerning membership participation within the A.E.U. and the virtual absence of any other Australian studies on this aspect of trade union affairs.[19]

Today the major point of formal contact between rank and file members and their union is the workshop. This is, however, a fairly recent development. The A.E.U. constitution always paid more attention to shop stewards and shop committees than virtually any other union.[20] The rules encouraged District Committees to appoint stewards and create shop committees. Stewards were expected to report back regularly and to attend quarterly stewards' meetings. But although the first appearance of stewards in Australia during World War I helped create a furore within the union,[21] the emphasis laid on them in the rules is largely a reflection of their significance in the much larger-scale British metals industry.[22] For many years in Australia shop stewards were important only in the relatively few larger plants, notably in the government railway workshops which long remained the largest single source of employment for engineers. Quarterly stewards meetings were certainly held in the main centres and, after the initial controversy, A.E.U. officials were generally unanimous in encouraging the spread of the steward movement and the establishment of shop committees. Yet it was not until the late 1950s that they really began to have an impact in the general metals scene — and drew criticism from leaders of certain other unions who disapproved of some of the implications of this form of rank and file participation.[23]

Thus it was the branch which for long remained the main avenue by which A.E.U. members could take an active part in their union's affairs. And given the relatively personal nature of relationships within the atomistic A.E.U. branch it also often presented certain extra-mural attractions including social evenings, debates, outings, children's parties and the like. Nevertheless, allowing for considerable variance between individual branches, most evidence points to the fact that only a minority of members regularly participated in branch affairs. One way of retrospectively estimating

[19] For a recent discussion of participation based on personal interviews with 50 skilled metal workers see, N. F. Dufty, *Industrial Relations in the Australian Metal Industries* (Sydney, 1972), pp. 104–11; see also Lloyd Ross, 'Problems of Participation of Members in the Administration and Activities of Trade Unions (with special reference to the Australian Railways Union, New South Wales State Branch)', in Australian Political Studies Association, *Proceedings of Fourth Conference, Canberra, 8–10 August 1962*; Matthews, op. cit. pp. 99–100.
[20] Matthews, op. cit., pp. 88–9.
[21] Below, pp. 41–4.
[22] Although the depressed economic conditions between 1921 and the late 1930s saw the British steward movement lose some ground, J. F. B. Goodman and T. G. Whittingham, *Shop Stewards in British Industry* (London, 1969), p. 34.
[23] Below, p. 280.

participation is to calculate the percentage voting in union elections. There are obvious weaknesses in this method. Until the supervision of certain ballots by the Commonwealth Electoral Office from 1953 onwards all A.E.U. elections were conducted at branch meetings held on one of the quarterly 'Star Nights'.[24] Ballots for full-time posts did not occur simultaneously in neat bunches but were staggered depending on the date at which individual three year terms expired, or retirement or death intervened. Thus it is unlikely that in any one time period exactly the same members participated in the frequent A.E.U. elections — and so we might expect a larger number of regular branch attenders than the voting figures suggest. On the other hand we cannot assume that all voters were necessarily regular attenders. Nevertheless if we take voting for Commonwealth Council positions as a rough yardstick we find that before 1953 the poll never rose above 27 per cent. Participation fell markedly during the war because of the membership explosion and exceptionally long hours of work, and the overall average poll between 1920 and 1953 was only 18 per cent. Comparable time-series are not available for other Australian unions so it is impossible to say whether or not the engineers were more or less apathetic in this sense than workers in other trades. British unions approximate closely to the Australian A.E.U. performance.[25] The British A.E.U. has even smaller post-war voting rates. One explanation offered for the British engineers' lower than national average participation in ballots is the greater frequency with which elections occur in the A.E.U. The same factor would apply to the union in Australia. Apart from the staggered triennial elections for President, General Secretary, Assistant General Secretaries, five Commonwealth Council members, up to eleven organisers (to 1953) and, in Sydney and Melbourne, permanent district secretaries, there were also annual elections for all Branch officers, delegates and substitutes to, and president and secretary[26] of, the District Committees. In addition there were elections for delegates to Political Committees, Biennial Conferences, Rules Revision Meetings, Interstate Conferences, and A.C.T.U. Congresses. As well as elections, members were often called upon to vote on particular

---

[24] Postal voting was possible upon application to the branch secretary but only a tiny proportion of members appear to have taken advantage of this provision.

[25] B. C. Roberts, *Trade Union Government and Administration in Great Britain* (London, 1956), pp. 227–8; Joseph Goldstein, *The Government of British Trade Unions* (London 1952); Political and Economic Planning, *British Trade Unionism* New and Revised Edition (London 1955), Ch. iii.

[26] From 1951 onwards part-time as well as full-time district secretaries were elected triennially.

issues such as levies, autonomy, arbitration policy, amalgamation and many others. Thus the statements that

many members of the union [A.E.U.] must have been called upon to vote on something or another at almost every occasion on which they attended a branch meeting. A ballot is, therefore, almost a normal feature of a branch meeting and must become something of a habit which does not arouse any very special interest unless the circumstances are exceptional.[27]

are as applicable to the A.E.U. in Australia as in the United Kingdom.

Over the years A.E.U. officials continually expressed concern about small branch attendances and often attached the blame to the dullness of the typical meeting,[28] but this was more of a rationalisation than an explanation. Nor are there any indications that older members were correct in claiming throughout the period that branches had been much better attended in their younger days. Yet when we translate the low percentages into absolute numbers a slightly different perspective appears. If we arbitrarily accept the average Council poll of 18 per cent as a measure of branch attendance then we are considering something of the order of 3,000 to 4,000 members in the 1920s and 12,000 to 13,000 in the early 1950s. These are obviously not inconsiderable figures and all the literary evidence points to the fact that A.E.U. branch activists were particularly articulate, independent-minded, and even less likely than most Australian workers to stand being dictated to by their full-time officials. Even the most cursory glance at the union's impressive monthly journal will help substantiate this view. By the very nature of their job and the workshop status attached thereto, craftsmen engineers tended to be proud men, more than aware of their own worth. Whether they came initially from Britain or not — and in the early years a significant proportion of them did — the activists were steeped in the history of their union and the rank and file tradition in the old country of not giving paid officials too much freedom.[29] Their pride in their union and its independence was enormous — and the course of the controversial internal events of the 1950s and 1960s may only be properly interpreted in this light. Memories were long — in 1959, for example, at

[27] Roberts, op. cit., pp. 228–9.
[28] In 1925 a meeting of the Melbourne District Committee and representatives of the branches in the district concluded that the causes of low attendance at branch meetings were; the unattractiveness of routine branch business, uncomfortable branch rooms, too many 'jazz palaces', too much interest in sport, the affluence of members, the centralisation of wage fixing in the Commonwealth Arbitration Court, and the inability of Commonwealth members to make rules to govern Australian conditions. 'A.E.U. Melbourne District Committee Minutes', 30/6/25. (Hereafter abbreviated to 'M.D.C.M.'
[29] See below, pp. 38–9.

the funeral service of a Sydney activist who had never held paid office, the A.E.U. Commonwealth Council Chairman laid a single white lily on the coffin to mark the deceased's role as a 'lily white' during the New South Wales strike 42 years previously.[30] The oral tradition was constantly fortified by the celebration of anniversaries of different sections of the union, including the first establishment of branches in various centres. The tradition of son following father in his trade extended also in many cases to interest in the A.E.U. The union was often familiarly referred to as 'the club' in the nineteenth century and such it continued to be in the twentieth century for many engineers who devoted a great part of their spare time to local branch affairs, often without ever seeking office in higher echelons of the union. An A.E.U. 'Award of Merit' was available to the many who thus gave long service. Contact was maintained after retirement through regular meetings of superannuated members in the major centres — 260 sat down to the 1959 Labour Day dinner in Melbourne, for example.

As might be expected the Benefit Sections were relatively over-represented among the active minority. For a start there was always a greater likelihood of them attending branch meetings if only to receive benefit payments. More importantly these members had a greater vested interest than Industrial members in seeing that union funds were efficiently administered. This tended to make Benefit members more aware of the activities of A.E.U. federal and district executives and more likely to attend their branches in order to check up on the capabilities of officials there. For similar reasons Benefit members were more likely to stand for office than members of the Industrial Section whom the British-made rules actually barred from becoming full-time District Secretaries, members of Commonwealth Council or delegates to Commonwealth Rules Revision Meetings for much of our period. Until 1925 the position of organiser was similarly restricted. Both the early existence of workshop committees and the fact that it was generally easier for government employees to obtain time off work for union affairs meant that railway members also tended to be disproportionately represented among A.E.U. activists.

The fact that A.E.U. rules were basically made in Britain had one other effect which fortified the independent spirit of the rank and file and made it even less easy for officials to dictate to working members. British delegates to General Rules Revision Meetings continued to insist that the ratio of organisers to working members should remain the same in both countries. This meant, in 1964 for example, that the Australian Section with 80,000

[30] *M.J.*, June 1959, p. 8.

members was entitled to pay only eight organisers from the General Fund. The British attitude rested on an inability to comprehend either the implications of small-scale plants scattered throughout the Australian urban sprawl, the distance between industrial centres, or the effects of not having an extensive shop steward network. The Australian Section was able to get round the problem to a certain degree by financing additional organisers out of the Supplementary Fund (e.g. six in 1964). Nevertheless, A.E.U. working members saw less of their official union representatives, whether stewards or organisers, than in Britain or, at least as far as organisers were concerned in the post-war years, than many other Australian unionists. Fortified of course by their relatively strong bargaining position, A.E.U. members, often working in mere handfuls in the smaller shops, thus became accustomed to acting independently as the situation seemed to demand. The union's history abounds in examples not merely of members deciding to 'go out on the grass' of their own accord, but of staying there despite the exhortations from their officials for a tactical return to work. This independence of thought and action was naturally carried over to internal A.E.U. affairs by the branch activists. What is more, the A.E.U. constitution deliberately encouraged them in this trait. The history of the British union was marked by frequent clashes between executive officers and rank and file members. The most notable examples took place between 1910 and 1919. The peak of animosity was reached in 1913 when, after being dismissed by the annual conference, the Executive Council stocked up with siege provisions and barricaded itself in the Peckham Road Offices. The officials only succumbed after rank and file members effected a breach in the wall of an adjoining house and threw them bodily into the street after an 'undignified skirmish'.[31]

The union's intricate constitution was the visible outcome of many attempts to reconcile the necessity for a strong and efficient executive with the democratic desire to ensure that policy was ultimately formulated by the union's working members.[32] The 1920 amalgamation constitution was drawn up with these conflicting considerations very much in mind.[33] Over the succeeding decades the British rank and file were largely able to impose their will on the union's full-time officials. Important elements in this process were use of the Final Appeal Court as a check on executive authority and the integration of the shop steward into a position of import-

---

[31] Jefferys, op. cit., pp. 169–71, 174–91.
[32] For comments on the constant elaboration of the rules of several British unions resulting from rank and file attempts to control salaried officials see Webbs, *Industrial Democracy*, p. 18.
[33] Jefferys, op. cit., pp. 193–4.

ance in the A.E.U. infrastructure. But the most important factor was the emergence of the National Committee as a forum in which the executive was both directed regarding future policy and censured for deviations from past instructions. So far did the control of the National Committee over A.E.U. policy grow that, in the view of·one observer, '. . . central authority has been dispersed to a point at which it sometimes seems to disappear.'[34]

The situation never reached this point in Australia for a variety of reasons, including of course the absence of an Australian equivalent of the National Committee – the Biennial Conferences/Commonwealth Rules Revision Meetings being limited to altering rules to meet local conditions. Just as importantly, the Commonwealth Council, with rare exceptions, wielded its considerable constitutional powers very diplomatically, keeping in close touch with grassroots activist sentiments. When necessary it made use of its power to convene Interstate Conferences of rank and file delegates and usually accepted the advice thus offered. The District Committees were allowed considerable freedom in their efforts to improve local wages and conditions of work – and this despite the fact that, because of the automatic implications for the A.E.U.'s federal arbitration award, the Commonwealth Council did not, in most districts, have to wait for an invitation to intervene in a dispute as did the Executive Council in Britain. Diplomatic or not, the activists watched and weighed every move the federal executive made – just as they also minutely scrutinised the activities of branch and district officials. The A.E.U.'s complex constitution placed a premium on knowledge of the rule book and consequently tended to breed some redoubtable bush lawyers who would launch appeals on the most technical of pretexts. Whatever the motive, there was always a steady stream of objections ascending the A.E.U.'s internal appeals ladder. A typical communication between London and Sydney concerned the,

Appeal of Rockdale Branch against the decision of E.C. [Executive Council] in upholding the decision of Commonwealth Council in dismissing the appeal of that Branch against the Sydney District Political Committee's right to discuss the question of a grant being made by the Commonwealth Government to Denominational Schools.[35]

There was absolutely no way A.E.U. officials could prevent appeals going to London and, if necessary, on to the wholly rank and file Appeals Court.

---

[34] H. A. Turner, *Trade Union Growth, Structure and Policy: A Comparative Study of the Cotton Unions* (London, 1962), p. 225. For further comment on the National Committee's policy-making activities see Roberts, op. cit., pp. 155–6, 220.

[35] *M. J.*, June 1957, p. 4.

As we shall see the final verdicts on several occasions represented important checks to the federal A.E.U. executive.

In addition to the appeals system, the rank and file members always had an ultimate weapon to level at the Commonwealth Council. If the latter acted in a sufficiently unpopular manner then Council members could be removed from office at the triennial elections. That this rarely happened until the left—right split in the 1950s bears witness to the relatively harmonious nature of the relationship between federal executive and the working members. From its foundation in 1917 to its dissolution in 1968 no Council Chairman or Secretary was ever defeated when contesting re-election. In the 28 separate elections for individual Councilmen in the shorter period of 1920—51 the current occupant of the position was defeated on only five occasions.

III

The A.E.U. ceased to be unique in 1968 when it cut the links with Britain and changed its constitution to one more typical of Australian unions. Yet half a century earlier when the title A.E.U. first came into existence it seemed likely that the international ties might be severed in the very near future. The failure rested on a bitter internal controversy which was one occasion when serious strains were placed on the A.E.U.'s internal machinery by a head-on collision between the Commonwealth Council and an important section of branch activists. The underlying causes of the rift were complex but several basic factors may be discerned. Firstly, the domestic political and industrial events of World War I created a ferment within the labour movement. The setbacks experienced in this period led many trade unionists, including members of the Amalgamated Society of Engineers, to urge the formation of One Big Union covering all industries and occupations. It was against this background that the full-time Commonwealth Council was established in 1917. The event was hailed by certain sections of the rank and file as representing the first major step towards separation from Britain and a reform of the union's structure which would make possible amalgamation with other metal trade unions. Such enthusiasm largely dissipated when it was seen that the infant body ushered in no great changes in internal organisation. In some quarters resentment appeared when the new executive proved more efficient than its over-burdened part-time predecessor in close supervision of branch and district activities.

Rank and file engineers were also affected by the upheaval in the British A.E.U. caused by the recent rapid rise in importance of the engineering shop steward. The power to appoint stewards had been vested in the District Committees since 1896, their functions being '. . . limited to ensuring that members remained in benefit and that newcomers were Society men'.[36] In Britain they were at first unknown outside Scotland and Northern Ireland, but by 1914 they were important in most of the major engineering centres. During World War I shop stewards emerged as the representatives of the dynamic radical forces within the parent society, leading, by means of their interlocking committees, the wages campaign against employers and Government, and challenging the authority of the more conservative Executive Council.[37] In Australia the growth in the numbers and importance of shop stewards lagged behind the movement in Britain and it was not until towards the end of the war that stewards and shop committees began to acquire any real prominence. Awareness of British developments was heightened both by the gradual return of some 800 Australian members who had worked in British munitions factories during the war and later by the gradual re-commencement of immigration of A.E.U. members from the United Kingdom.

The importance of the shop stewards grew in the early postwar years but an important divergence in opinion soon emerged as to the exact role to be played by those holding the position. The Commonwealth Council in urging the formation of Shop Committees on the U.K. model, and in sanctioning the holding of meetings of stewards and the payment of fares and attendance fees for those participating, saw the shop steward largely as an instrument for reducing the number of 'unfinancial' members (i.e. those in arrears) and bringing about the one hundred per cent union shop. A secondary function of the steward would be the fostering of closer ties with kindred unions with a view to eventual amalgamation or federation.[38] The other and syndicalist school of thought upheld by radical sections of the A.E.U. rank and file envisaged the shop stewards acting as the mainspring of any advances in working class conditions as in war-time Britain. The work of the stewards must not be circumscribed by union rules. In the past the A.E.U. steward had been little more than a conciliator between employer and employees. In the future he must act as '. . . the stormy petrel who goes before the storm'.[39] As against the successes of the steward movement in Britain the militants held up for comparison the current situation in Australia. Many members' real wages were declining and the

[36] Jefferys, op. cit., p. 165.
[37] Ibid., pp. 181–90.
[38] *M.R.*, March 1919, pp. 4–6; May 1919, pp. 8–11; *M.R.*, July 1919, p. 6.
[39] *M.R.*, April 1919, p. 26.

Commonwealth Council had failed to reverse the trend. In fact, it was argued, the formation of a full-time federal executive had been a waste of time and Council members had proved themselves inept, bureaucratic and overpaid. Some rank and file spokesmen went so far as to claim that the Council had been established by the machiavellian tactics of the second Chairman, John Smith (1918–1923), who had seen an opportunity for his own personal advancement.[40] Fuel was added to the flames by working members' widespread opposition to the first A.E.U. Rulebook which ensured eight years uncontested continuance in office to all officials of the unions party to the British amalgamation of 1920. This provision applied to the Australian Section also and although the Commonwealth members had voted in favour of the amalgamation by 4,299 to 774 many felt that the members of the Commonwealth Council were taking advantage of a technicality in not offering themselves for re-election.

The first formal moves by the branches took the shape of general 'Indictments' against the Commonwealth Council issued separately in May 1919 by the Lithgow 2nd and Portland branches and circularised to all other branches. This was followed by a more constructive programme of reform being drawn up by the Sydney 2nd Branch which, as well as stressing the superfluity of the Council's existence, was concerned with the need to make shop stewards and shop committees the basis for union action.[41] Sydney 2nd's sixteen point charter had been endorsed by 32 of the 98 Australian branches by October 1920. A major part of the support for this platform seems, however, to have been due to the resentment of the Commonwealth Council's acceptance of the eight years tenure provision of the British amalgamation agreement. The Adelaide 2nd Branch, for example, had rejected the Lithgow Indictment but made 'emphatic protest' against holding eight year office in C.C. [sic] Council.[42] The usual method of recording dissatisfaction was for the branches to pass resolutions in favour of 'recalling' the Council Chairman and Secretary together with the Councilman representing their respective divisions in the hopes that the federal officers would be forced to hold elections. The Commonwealth Council, however, refused to be moved.

The climax came in June 1921 when the 1920 Biennial Conference was recalled to make the necessary amendments to the Australian rule-book

[40] *M.R.*, June 1919, pp. 28–9, September 1919, pp. 19–21, November 1920, pp. 38–9.
[41] Details of the reform programme may be found in *M.R.* November 1920, pp. 35–7.
[42] 'Adelaide 2nd Branch Minutes', 1/5/19, 16/9/20.

to bring it into line with the new A.E.U. General Rules. After refusing an offer by Chairman Smith to preside over the meeting, the Conference made major rule alterations including abolition of the eight-year provision. All full-time officials were ordered to stand for re-election during the current year. Commonwealth Council immediately rejected these amendments as illegal and was firmly supported by the Executive Council. The major spokesmen for the Biennial Conference were the future New South Wales Labor Premier, J. J. Cahill of Sydney, and H. Taylor of Broken Hill who had been the Australian representative at the 1919 British Delegate Meeting (predecessor of the National Committee). One of their major supporters was E. H. Barker, A.E.U. federal arbitration agent to 1922 and subsequently the West Australian organiser. These members countered Commonwealth Council charges by claiming that the 1916 Biennial Conference had similarly acted *ultra vires* in creating the Council itself. Yet the current Council members had, without any qualms, accepted their illegal office until the 1919 Delegate Meeting had recognised their position *de facto*. More importantly no Council member had stood for election since the Council was thus legally established within the union's constitution in 1919.

Commonwealth Council recalled the Conference in December 1921 but no settlement was reached. The Conference decided to have its new rules printed and filed with the Industrial Registrar and instructed Council Secretary, J. McCallum, to take the necessary steps. The Council forbade this and, with McCallum and the A.E.U. trustees supporting the Conference, Taylor and Cahill proceeded into the Court of Equity to obtain a declaration that the Council was illegally in office and to restrain it from blocking the printing of the new rule-book. With full backing from the Executive Council the Commonwealth Council took over certain financial duties hitherto performed by the Secretary despite strenuous opposition from McCallum. It also banned the distribution of circular letters by any branch which had not first obtained Council approval. In the midst of these controversies Smith and McCallum reached retiring age and in the ensuing elections A. S. Evernden and L. N. Wickham were returned as Chairman and Secretary respectively. Taylor, however, finished a fairly close runner-up in the ballot for Chairman.[43]

Taylor and Cahill's legal suit failed on a technicality and although the plaint was resubmitted lack of finance hampered their efforts. The Council refused to consider branch appeals to pay its opponents' legal expenses until

---

[43] The voting figures were Evernden 1,984, Taylor 1,520, Perrott 974. At this date the rules did not provide for preferential voting.

the claims were withdrawn. In fact the Council moved to recover costs from the initial case and obtained a Court order which necessitated Taylor putting his house and personal effects up for sale in Broken Hill. However the enforced sale was not proceeded with and upon the two dissidents agreeing to drop their court action the Council paid the costs. It was not until mid-1925, however, that the Council withdrew its embargo on Taylor or Cahill holding office in the union.

The Commonwealth Council emerged the victor of this prolonged struggle largely because it controlled the A.E.U.'s purse-strings. One result was that all three Councilmen[44] enjoyed the eight year tenure in office. By the time they did stand for re-election in 1928 their constituents had largely rid themselves of any earlier ill-feeling. The representatives of Divisions 1 and 3, J. J. Scoffin and W. R. Potter, were returned to office with comfortable majorities. Only H. Pickard of Sydney was defeated — and although taking the same legalistic stance on the eight years tenure as his colleagues he was definitely the Council member most in tune with the militants' general programme.[45]

IV

The most important effect of the internal warfare of 1919—25 was not the length of time the Councilmen remained in office; it was rather that in the general confusion and name-calling the possibility of separation from the British A.E.U. was lost. Initially Taylor, Cahill, and their supporters, apart from wishing to alter the structure of the A.E.U. to provide for more rank and file control, fervently desired complete Australian autonomy in order to make amalgamation with other metal unions possible. In this they were whole-heartedly supported by all Commonwealth Council members save Scoffin. But clashes of personality destroyed all chances of a united approach to the issue.

It is safe to say that the question of amalgamation never loomed larger before the general trade union movement than in the period between 1917 and 1925. In an atmosphere charged with contemporary discussions on the One Big Union (O.B.U.) the A.E.U. entered into amalgamation discussions with many other unions and in a few instances was successful in absorbing

---

[44] The 8 year rule provision did not apply to Wickham or Evernden since they were first elected after 1920. As a result there were elections for their positions in 1924 and 1927 when they both returned to office. Only three organisers came under the 8 year provision but all volunteered to stand for re-election. However, the Commonwealth Council forbade them from doing so.

[45] Below, pp. 95—6.

a few small sectional societies.[46] In Broken Hill an Amalgamation Committee was formed in 1917 and the local A.E.U. branch became the driving force of one of its subdivisions, the Metal Unions' Amalgamation Committee. H. Taylor was a prominent figure on the Committee and the Broken Hill Branch circularised all other A.E.U. branches urging them to work actively towards the merging of kindred metal unions as a first step towards the formation of the O.B.U. This campaign attracted a fair amount of support within the A.E.U. but both the Commonwealth Council and a sizeable proportion of activists, while supporting amalgamation, rejected the O.B.U. scheme. The latter was seen by them as an unrealistic plan formulated by visionaries and advocated by those who were jealous of the strength of craft unions and who sought to impose on skilled workers the same weaknesses of organisation that had always plagued unions catering for less skilled employees.[47] In 1924 the A.E.U. was one of the 24 unions to oppose the application for federal registration of the O.B.U..[48] Not the least important reason for Council's drive for amalgamation was the need for the craft metal unions to form a common front against the 'poaching' of their members by the 'industrial' unions such as the railway workers', coalminers', and meat employees' organisations which theoretically formed the basis of O.B.U. This point was made explicit at the conferences of metal unions convened by the Boilermakers' Society in 1922.[49] But whatever the differing reasons behind A.E.U. members' enthusiasm, the first prerequisite for amalgamation was complete local autonomy for the Australian Section of the union. Until Commonwealth members obtained the power to alter the union rules not merely to meet the requirements of local industrial

[46] In addition to the Melbourne and Queensland branches of the Steam Engine Makers Society which was one of the small unions taking part in the 1920 British amalgamation to form the A.E.U., the Australian Section also absorbed the following societies between 1915 and 1923: the West Australian branch of the F.I.A. (1915), the West Australian goldfields branch of the E.T.U. (1915), Mount Morgan Electrical Workers' Association (1915), Sydney Motor Mechanics Union (1919), Launceston Branch of the A.S.E. (1920), Sydney Typewriter Mechanics' Union (1920), Melbourne Cycle Trades Union (1923).
　　In the same period unsuccessful discussions on amalgamation were conducted with the South Sydney Branch of the A.S.E. (1918), Moulders' and Boilermakers' Societies (1918 and 1921), Agricultural Implement Workers (1920), South Australian Electricians' Union (1921), B.S.A. (1921), Stovemakers (1922), South Australian branch of the F.I.A. (1923).

[47] 'C.C.M.', 14/4/19, 16/10/19. That such views were not restricted to the Council see, for example, the letter by a working member, J. Nimmo, in *M.R.*, September 1920, pp. 32—4.

[48] Even some of the O.B.U.'s most enthusiastic supporters were against this ill-fated tactic, E. Ross, *A History of The Miners' Federation of Australia* (Sydney, 1970), pp. 306—7.

[49] *M.R.*, April 1922, p. 7.

and labour legislation, but also to meet any conditions agreed on after discussions with other Australian unions, amalgamation would be out of the question. Without autonomy, the only possible merger between the A.E.U. and any other organisation would be an absorption by the former of the latter. Few unions were prepared to contemplate such an unconditional surrender of their identity.

The first move towards securing autonomy was made in 1920, when the Biennial Conference supported a sub-committee's recommendations that autonomy should be based on three main points.[50] First, the Biennial Conference to be given the same powers in Australia as those which the National Committee exercised in Britain. Second, the Australian Section should be credited with three-quarters of its 'total worth' of the A.E.U.'s funds. Arrangements should be made for a *per capita* transfer on the same basis when British members transferred to Australia. The Biennial Conference should have full control of all payments except Funeral and Superannuation. Third, an Australian Final Appeal Court should be set up to hear all matters except those connected with Funeral or Superannuation benefits. In the ensuing ballot Commonwealth members accepted these proposals by 3,717 votes to 770.

The significant point was that the Australian members were anxious that the parent union should continue to be responsible for Superannuation benefits because they feared that actuarily this fund might become too great a burden if separately administered in the Commonwealth. This, together with the desire for a *per capita* clearance for A.E.U. members migrating from Britain, became the stumbling blocks during subsequent negotiations between Sydney and London. The Executive Council was quite willing to cut the ties between the two countries, in fact it saw positive advantages in the break. In 1921 A. H. Smethurst, A.E.U. General Secretary, wrote from London,

The E.C. [Executive Council] believe that it is absolutely essential for the well-being of our members in Australia that the Commonwealth Council should have complete jurisdiction in that country, in view of the varying laws, local conditions and long distances between the two countries.[51]

---

[50] *M.R.*, April 1920, p. 47. The North American A.E.U. separated from Britain and merged with a larger union in 1920. The South African and New Zealand Sections made moves to gain autonomy at roughly the same time as Australia. New Zealand separated in 1923 but South Africa remained linked to Britain until 1957.

[51] Quoted by J. Smith in *M.R.*, July 1927, p. 32; See also 'Minutes of Special Meeting of the Executive Council, 9 November 1920'.

But the Executive Council's condition for separation was that the break should be complete. The Australian section must take full responsibility for its own financial management — including superannuation. Hence the London office was unable to accept the 1920 ballot as an indicator of Commonwealth members' views since the proposals put before them had not set out the true implications of separation. Despite the fact that the British union did not adopt the strict actuarial approach of a Friendly Society,[52] it seems possible that, in addition to all other factors the Executive Council was concerned about the future of Australian Superannuation benefits. The Australian Section had been financially self-supporting in all respects since the 1890s, but certainly by 1925 Executive Council was commenting critically on the rising proportion of Industrial members and the possibility that the Australian Benefit membership might not be sufficient to cover Superannuation payments.[53] In fact this spectre was only to materialise after the depletion of the Australian funds in the great disputes of 1946—8.[54]

At all events a second ballot was held in 1922 on the Executive Council's proposals. In the interim period lengthy debates were conducted in the branches, District Committees and the union journal. All members of the Commonwealth Council except Councilman Scoffin were in favour of breaking the British connection, but many Benefit members who had originally supported autonomy now became fearful that complete separation would jeopardise the union's financial stability. The decision of the Commonwealth Council to allow Industrial members to vote was queried on the grounds that they had no interest in the benefits question.[55] More significantly the issue was confounded by the concurrent strife between the 1921 Biennial Conference and the Commonwealth Council. Taylor, for example, who had always been one of the most ardent supporters of autonomy stated that in the circumstances separation would mean that the Australian A.E.U. would be saddled with the eight year tenure of office provision beyond any hope of redemption. Therefore he gave his support to the opponents of separation.[56]

The ballot, conducted by post, resulted in an above-average poll of 40 per cent in which 3,912 members voted for separation and 3,809 against. Despite the tiny majority Commonwealth Council forwarded the result to

[52] Webbs, *Industrial Democracy*, pp. 155—7.
[53] 'Report to Executive Council on the Australian Rules by B. Gardner, June 1951'.
[54] Below, p. 296.
[55] For examples of arguments used see *M.R.*, September 1921, p. 3; January 1922; p. 6; February 1922, p. 31; April 1922, pp. 35—8, 'M.D.C.M.', 15/3/22.
[56] *M.R.*, March 1922, pp. 35—6.

London with the recommendation that the vote should be accepted as an indicator of Australia's desire for autonomy. However, since the British lock-out of 1922 had led to an overall deficit in the General Fund, Commonwealth Council suggested that actual negotiations should be delayed until after the deficit had been liquidated. Councilman Scoffin dissented completely from these decisions.

Opponents of separation had the last say, however, when the 1923 Final Appeal Court upheld an appeal objecting to apprentices taking part in the ballot.[57] The Executive Council then decided that the decision on separation should be made by Benefit members only. After further delay a second postal vote was taken in 1925 in which Benefit and Industrial members voted separately. The result again favoured separation with the former voting in favour by 2,093 votes to 546, and the latter by 1,009 votes to 158. Both the greater majority and the smaller poll on this occasion were, however, due to the fact that the proposals submitted to members departed from those set out by the Executive Council in 1921. No details are available but it seems that at least one of the conditions set out on the ballot paper was that financial membership should be transferable between Britain and Australia. Thus once again the Executive Council was unable to accept the ballot result. There the matter rested.

The various crusades to alter the A.E.U.'s structure, to lend greater weight to the shop steward movement, to form One Big Union, all lost momentum as the attention of the A.E.U. and the general labour movement was drawn to other matters. In turn the campaign for a 44 hour week, the controversies over the future of federal arbitration, and the onset of economic depression, diverted the thoughts and energies of A.E.U. members. Smith, the ex-Chairman, and a few others continued to urge the necessity of separation in the A.E.U. journal but though the majority of Commonwealth Council members favoured the principle of autonomy they were not prepared to take the financial risks of complete separation. In this the Council re-presented the view of the majority of members. Among the suggestions which were forwarded to the 1926 General Rules Revision Meeting, that which received endorsement from the greatest number of branches expressed the desire for the Australian Section to enjoy autonomy without separation.

Following on the re-opening of negotiations on amalgamation of the metal unions in 1927, the Biennial Conference of that year did call for another ballot on the Executive Council proposals of 1921. Upon the Commonwealth Council cabling London for details of procedure it was given the confusing

[57] A.E.U. rules only permitted apprentices to vote for branch and general officers.

ruling that the rules now made no provision for ballots on the issue. Autonomy could come about only after negotiations between the Executive and Commonwealth Council which could take place at any time. Commonwealth Council was content to take refuge in the declaration that it could not enter into such negotiations without a mandate from members. No action could be taken until after the 1930 General Rules Revision Meeting had considered a suggested rule amendment allowing Australian members to take the requisite ballot. The amendment was not adopted but by the time the negative decision was reached the union's members were struggling against the effects of the world-wide economic depression. During this period of high unemployment, A.E.U. members were primarily concerned with the stability of their union's finances and its ability to afford them some monetary relief. Hence in 1931 a planned amalgamation of the metal unions initiated by the F.I.A. and supported by the A.C.T.U. was rejected by A.E.U. members after the Commonwealth Council had vigorously attacked the scheme for what Council regarded as its unsound financial proposals.[58] While the ballot was actually taking place the Executive Council made known its disapproval and ordered the Commonwealth Council to withdraw from all discussions immediately. The latter's cabled reply was significant, 'Proposals defeated. Best interest of our union that results be known and published'.[59]

After this the Commonwealth Council refused to be associated with further amalgamation schemes during the depression, tersely informing the A.C.T.U. that it was 'not prepared to take part in proposed conference on account of the expense entailed — and the lack of sincerity of other unions'.[60] Only absorption of other organisations without changing A.E.U. rules was possible. In 1935 it seemed likely that the F.I.A. would adopt this course. However, while the A.E.U. executives in London and Sydney were still debating the legality of guaranteeing three years continuance in office to the F.I.A. full-time officials, the Ironworkers themselves rejected the proposals. Further discussions between the two unions lapsed in 1937.

During World War II, after spontaneous agitation by the rank and file of both engineering unions, the A.C.T.U. sponsored amalgamation discussions between the A.E.U. and A.S.E. These continued until 1946 and came

---

[58] *M.R.*, September 1931, pp. 6, 18–21.
[59] 'C.C.M.', 6/11/31. Actual voting figures in the 41 per cent poll were 5,964 votes against amalgamation and 2,215 in favour. The scheme was rejected by most trade unions concerned but the only other figures available are those of the Boilermakers' Society which turned down the proposals by 1,455 votes to 304 ('C.C.M.', 13/11/31).
[60] 'C.C.M.', 18/10/32.

to include the B.S.A. Eventually, however, the question of the A.E.U.'s ties
with Britain proved an insurmountable obstacle for the A.S.E. and it withdrew from the negotiations. Amalgamation with other unions continued to
be regarded by A.E.U. officials as an ideal development but it was tacitly
accepted that until the union completely separated itself from Britain a
merging of metal unions would never take place. For a variety of reasons
it was not until the 1960s that A.E.U. members considered the breaking of
the century-old ties worthwhile.

Over the years the link with Britain had three main disadvantages for
Australian members: amalgamation was prevented; Australian members
were unable to alter the union structure; and the British Rules Revision
Meetings were unable to appreciate the very different circumstances under
which the Australian section operated. On the first point, it is debatable
that amalgamation would have occurred if the A.E.U. had been a completely
free agent. Merger proposals were often rejected by the members of other
unions. In fact only two amalgamations between important metal unions
took place between 1920 and the formation of the A.M.W.U. in 1972 – that
which resulted in the formation of the S.M.W.I.U. in 1946, and the merging
of the Boilermakers and B.S.A. in 1966.[61] Other factors than the A.E.U.
constitution militated against the formation of new metal unions including
the vested interest of union officials in continued separate existence and
the fear of small organisations that their members' interests would be sub-
merged within the proposed larger body.

The inability of Australian A.E.U. members to alter the structure of their
union as they wished was an obvious drawback of the continued connection
with Britain, but they only rarely expressed the desire to do so between
the early 1920s and the late 1950s. The relatively pacific acceptance of a
constitution formulated to meet British circumstances was aided by the
provision allowing for Australian members to amend the rule-book to bring
it into line with local labour legislation. The alterations thus made were
usually marginal but the Australian section was able, for example, to begin
recruiting Industrial members twenty years before the British A.E.U. opened
its ranks to engineering workers who, although eligible, were not interested
in the benefits aspect of the union. On the other hand the British A.E.U.

---

[61] There was one other metal union amalgamation of note – that between the
F.I.A. and the Munition Workers' Union in 1943. However, the latter body,
although enjoying a great mushroom growth in membership during the war
had previously catered for only a small number of workers. It was obvious
that after the war employment in the munitions industry would again shrink
to fairly insignificant proportions.

refused to allow women to join the union until 1943. The majority of female workers left the industry within a year or so of the end of the war but the British shortsightedness handicapped the Australian Section for two years in its endeavour to organise all wartime newcomers to the engineering trades.[62]

The lack of understanding displayed by British delegates at the General Rules Revision Meetings to Australian requests for more organisers was undoubtedly a continual irritant, although the Australian Section was able to get round this parochial outlook by financing them from the Supplementary Fund. The refusal of the British union to accept that both the cost and the standard of living were higher in Australia was similarly nullified by subsidising the salaries of all full-time officials from this fund.

On the credit side the link with Britain was important both 'spiritually' and financially. As part of a truly international union, the Australian A.E.U. was always conscious of being an integral part of the world-wide labour movement. More tangibly its members were always aware of industrial developments abroad and were often able to learn important lessons from the experience of engineers in Britain, Europe and America through the regular reporting of such events in their journal. The A.E.U.'s acceptance of 'dilution' of skill in World War II in advance of other Australian metal unions was largely based on conclusions drawn from the British Section's experience during the First War, and a study of schemes currently being agreed to in the United Kingdom.

Financially the British link meant that the A.E.U. could draw on considerable funds held in the United Kingdom. This was of great practical importance during the depression of the 1930s when the A.E.U. never failed to meet its heavy benefit commitments. In contrast the printing unions, catering for equally skilled and even more highly paid workers, were unable to stand the strain and ceased unemployment payments in all states save New South Wales.[63] During the post-war strikes, apart from the actual remission of £25,000 from Britain, the very existence of such large financial resources at the union's call weighed heavily on employers' minds. At the end of our period when the Australian Section's rivals were making it acutely aware of the organisational restrictions imposed by British rule makers, the need for British financial assistance outweighed the advantages of structural reform in the view of practically all Australian officials. Thus

---

[62] Below, pp. 160—2.
[63] Hagan, op. cit., pp. 243—4.

the moves towards final separation did not commence until British aid had helped ensure Australian financial stability.

V

Before going on to consider the chronology of the A.E.U.'s experience in Australia it will be useful to establish the basic policies to which the union adhered. These remained remarkably consistent over the 50 year period despite quite radical changes in the constancy of employment, in productive techniques, in the supply of engineering labour and in the value of money. As with all other unions, the A.E.U.'s *raison d'être* was to guard and improve its members' conditions of work. Within the policy structure erected on that premise, the major influence was the fear of unemployment. Although craftsmen had fared better than less skilled metal workers, their long experience of the cruel trade cycle naturally made them hesitate for a considerable period before finally accepting that the 1940s had ushered in a new era of full employment. Most engineers' doubts disappeared only in the late 1950s and their long conditioning has continued to call forth most of the old automatic reflexes into the seventies.

The fear of unemployment shaped A.E.U. policy in two broad ways. The unions always desired to increase its members' employment opportunities and concurrently attempted to spread such work as was available among as many members as possible. In the first direction the A.E.U. co-operated wholeheartedly with employers in campaigning for increased protection for domestic producers. The pressure for higher tariffs seldom slackened until the sixties and, like employers, the union was never much concerned about arguments that protection entailed higher costs to consumers. Similarly the A.E.U. combined with employers and other unions in urging preference for domestic tenders for government contracts no matter what the price difference of overseas tenders.

While doing all in its power to assist in the creation of more work opportunities, the A.E.U. never compromised its other principles in the process. Thus employers sometimes accused it and other unions of hampering the establishment of new firms and industries by, for example, a persistent refusal to consider experimenting with incentive schemes. Likewise A.E.U. policy in endeavouring to limit the entry of new craftsmen into the trade to the inflow from the apprenticeship system was said to hold back engineering expansion. The union also did what it could to limit the inflow of craftsmen from abroad for it was ever keener to attract foreign capital than foreign labour. A.E.U. officials continually protested to the government that immigration should not be encouraged while Australians were unemployed.

On numerous occasions through to the 1960s Commonwealth Council appealed to the Executive Council to tell British members the 'true' facts about Australian conditions in the British *Monthly Journal* and thus counter the roseate picture painted by Immigration authorities and private employers.

In addition to attempting to widen the demand for engineering labour the A.E.U. sought to ensure continuity of its members' employment by spreading existing work opportunities as widely as possible. The union's policy in this direction was largely aimed at securing a reduction in hours worked but it occasionally made use of several other ploys. When economic activity was low the A.E.U. always preferred that work should be rationed among all rather than that a few members should be fully employed while their colleagues walked the streets. Overtime bans were often used to good effect in ensuring the absorption of out-of-work engineers during the up-swing of the trade cycle and A.E.U. organisers always counted it an important victory when employers could be persuaded to start an extra shift as a result of these tactics. Because of the continually changing variety of their work the engineers were never able to restrict their daily output as the coalminers did under the traditional 'darg' system. The only areas of the metal trades in which this proved possible were among jobbing moulders and sheet metal tinsmiths who operated a 'task' system. There are one or two isolated instances of A.E.U. members attempting to 'go slow'.[64] In general, however, engineers realised that their employment would be in jeopardy if they attempted to spin out their work and management's right to dismiss 'inefficient' workers was one province in which the union seldom attempted to interfere.

With other unions, the A.E.U. saw four major advantages in a reduction of hours: members secured increased leisure; a gain in this direction was permanent and, unlike an increase in wages, could not be nullified by an increase in prices; in times of buoyant demand for labour it acted as a disguised pay rise since employees often worked the same number of hours as before and pocketed extra overtime earnings; in slack periods it spread the available employment among more workers. The gain in leisure was a permanent attraction of shorter hours, the second and third factors were particularly important in the post-1945 period, and the fourth was the major reason underlying the union campaigns of the inter-war period. The A.E.U.

---

[64] On one occasion during the 1921–2 recession organiser R. J. Carroll actually urged members to slow down their work in order to provide jobs for out of work engineers. *M.R.*, April 1921, p. 15.

always felt particularly strongly about the shorter working week. In the early 1930s it regarded a reduction in hours as the most feasible method of reabsorbing the unemployed and unsuccessfully attempted to persuade other unions to give the hours campaign priority over the restoration of wage-cuts.

Despite its constant efforts to obtain pay rises A.E.U members always refused to accept one means by which, on employers' arguments, they could have greatly increased their earnings. Debates between employers and unions on the merits or otherwise of systems of payments by results have continued almost since the inception of manufacturing industry in Australia. The A.E.U.'s refusal to consider the introduction of incentive schemes was based on many factors including the personal experience of migrant members of the evils of unregulated piece-working in Britain and elsewhere. In return for the prospect of initially higher wages the union argued that piece-workers faced harder and faster work, the possibility of rate-cutting by unscrupulous employers and deterioration of shop floor 'mateship' as a result of an 'every man for himself' attitude arising among fellow workers. In certain circumstances, those time workers 'feeding' the piece-workers with materials might well experience a 'speed-up' of their work without any compensatory rise in earnings. An increase in output under incentive schemes could result in employers who still operated their plants under time-work demanding similar increases in output from their employees — again without a compensatory rise in earnings.

The main reasons for A.E.U. opposition to incentive schemes were, however, that their introduction might lead to the redundancy of some workers and, above all, that members' bargaining position might be weakened. Trade unions exist in order to apply the collective strength of their members to negotiations with employers. The A.E.U. had no objection to workers individually obtaining concessions from management above the rates and conditions set out in collective bargains or arbitration awards, but it always strenuously resisted any tendency towards its members being forced to negotiate their individual *basic* conditions of work with their respective employers. As the union's advocate put it to the New South Wales Arbitration Court, 'they [the union's members] believe in collective bargaining and when mutual arrangement comes in it means the strong employer and the weak employee'.[65]

---

[65] New South Wales Arbitration Court, *Amalgamated Society of Engineers (N.S.W.) and the Iron Trades Employers' Association 1908*, Transcripts of Evidence, p. 30. (Hereafter references to this case will be abbreviated to *1908 N.S.W. Arbitration Case*).

In some trades, such as the clothing, coalmining, meat and footwear industries, where there existed a certain degree of standardisation of product, it was possible for unions to negotiate piece rates for their members. In the metal trades, before 1939, such circumstances prevailed only in limited areas, for example machine moulding, holloware manufacture, and agricultural implement making. The unions catering for workers in these sectors had historically been forced to accept incentive schemes because of initial organization weakness.[66] The work performed by A.E.U. members, however, was uniquely unsuitable for collective rate bargaining.[67] In fact the A.E.U. argued that the employers' demands to be allowed to introduce payment by results into the engineering industry were completely unfeasible. At least until World War II the vast majority of engineering work was of a jobbing and repair nature, with each task different from the next. Hence it would prove impossible for unions or arbitration tribunals to efficiently supervise the process of rate setting. The union claimed therefore, that the employers were not so much desirous of increasing productivity but of securing a general lowering in wages by means of removing the A.E.U. from the bargaining framework. At best, from the union's viewpoint, plant committees would be the largest feasible unit able to negotiate with the employers. At worst, the individual engineer would be left to strike the best bargain he could with his shop foreman or manager. In the place of the strong nationwide union there would be substituted a variety of much weaker bodies which would be at an overwhelming disadvantage when dealing with employers. Statements made at various times by employers, extolling the virtues of individual, as against collective, bargaining did nothing to allay this fear. Thus A.E.U. officials, fully supported by the vast majority of rank and file members, remained opponents of payment by

---

[66] The union organising stove and holloware workers in N.S.W., the Stovemakers' Union, was actually formed by the employees of Fred Metters, Sydney, in order to combat the attempted introduction of piece-working by that firm in 1906. However, the organisation proved too weak to withstand the pressure applied by the employers and in 1911 was forced to accept a Wage Board decision to make provision for piece work. See 'The Stove and Piano Frame Moulders and Stovemakers Employees Union. Minutes of Meetings', 4 April 1906—22 September 1924.

The Agricultural Implement Makers' Society was very weak in its early years. When it did gain a footing in the most important firm in the industry, H. V. McKay, incentive schemes were well established. See P. G. Macarthy, 'The Harvester Judgement — An Historical Assessment', Ph.D. Thesis, A.N.U., February 1967, pp. 483—7.

[67] For a discussion of the difficulties involved in introducing piece-work into the engineering industry see Webbs, *Industrial Democracy*, pp. 291—7.

results even after 1945 when the system became more obviously feasible in certain sectors of the industry and when some of the other craft unions, particularly the E.T.U., began to look more favourably at the employers' inducements.

VI

As far as A.E.U. methods of pursuing its general, positive aim of improving members' wages and conditions were concerned, the first and essential point to grasp is that the A.E.U. was always an industrially aggressive union. This statement will come as no surprise to any student of the industrial scene in recent years, for the A.E.U.'s name was synonymous in many people's minds with industrial militancy prior to the 1972 amalgamation. Yet the common view of the earlier decades of this century does not often encompass the notion of industrially aggressive craft unions. Rather it would more likely be summarised in the statement that, '. . . once they are organised, unskilled workers tend to be more militant and to rely more on their industrial strength than skilled workers'.[68] It is therefore necessary to stress that, whatever may have been the case in other industries, this was never true in the metal trades. We will be tracking the A.E.U.'s own pugnacious career in the remainder of this book but, to take a popular indicator of 'militancy', the engineers' propensity to strike seems to have been rivalled only by the other craft unions, particularly the Boilermakers and Moulders. On the other hand, prior to the advent of full employment during World War II, the unskilled members of the F.I.A., for example, appear to have resorted to direct action only in the wake of the skilled unions or when forced to by the overt aggression of their employers.[69]

Attempts to classify the attitudes of metal craftsmen in these earlier years inevitably run into definitional problems and it is easy to confuse the A.E.U.'s industrial stance with its members' craft outlook. Some of the prominent leaders of the early twentieth century socialist groundswell were A.E.U. men. To name but a few: Tom Mann, in addition to his renowned British activities, was an organiser for the new mass unionism in Australia and was A.E.U. General Secretary at the time of the 1920 amalgamation; W. P. Earsman, a Melbourne activist, was one of the founder members and first secretary of the Communist Party of Australia (C.P.A.) established in 1920; and A.E.U. Queensland organiser R. J. Carroll, was a leading left winger,

---

[68] Ian Turner, *Industrial Labour and Politics* (Canberra, 1965), p. 6.
[69] For confirmation of this view see Merritt, 'A History of the F.I.A.', Chs. 2—5 *passim*.

who, *inter alia*, was imprisoned in 1919 for participating in the 'Red Flag' demonstration in Brisbane. Nevertheless, most A.E.U. members lacked the sweeping class consciousness that Professor Turner points to in other sections of the early twentieth century union movement.[70] Indeed throughout their history they never extended fraternal principles as far as to allow unskilled workers easy access to craftsmen's work. But to agree that A.E.U. men ruthlessly opposed 'handymen', were suspicious of the One Big Union, and were always open to the charge of undeviating pursuit of their own (skilled) interests regardless of what anyone else in the labour movement thought – from fellow unionists to A.L.P. Prime Ministers – is not the same thing as saying they were industrially passive. In pre-war years A.E.U. members were proud – sometimes arrogant; they were sectional – sometimes selfish; but while the demand for skill was high they were never pacific. Here the engineers' relatively strong bargaining position may also cloud the issue. Because the skilled labour market was tighter in brisk trading years than that for other workers, employers were more likely to concede craftsmen's demands without resorting to a direct trial of industrial strength. Conversely the A.E.U. and other skilled metal unions were somewhat less open to attack by employers in times of declining economic activity. As a result less attention was paid to the activities of such craft unions than to the more dramatic events on the wharves and coalfields and in the maritime and transport industries. However, it by no means automatically follows that relatively unskilled employees engaged in these industries were more industrially aggressive simply because of their greater susceptibility to economic fluctuations – although the latter might well have made them more class-conscious and more socialistically inclined.

So, in fact, the A.E.U. was one craft union which relied more on its industrial strength than on anything else, including 'self help' and political action. It certainly used the arbitration system, but in brisk trading years it never ceased to push for over-award payments and other improvements in conditions of work. This was the case in the 1920s when a relatively conservative Commonwealth Council was particularly favourably disposed towards arbitration. If labour market conditions were propitious and the federal leadership hesitated, the districts and the independent-minded rank and file acted of their own accord. The existence of friendly-benefits certainly never kept them quiet in the manner of British craft unions in the nineteenth century.[71] The steady decline in the statistical importance of the A.E.U.

[70] *Industrial Labour and Politics*, op. cit.
[71] Webbs, *Industrial Democracy*, op. cit., pp. 159–60.

Benefit Sections has already been noted — although actually the most active and aggressive A.E.U. leaders were usually themselves Benefit members. Employers were naturally well aware of the A.E.U.'s aggression. One of their representatives described it in 1921 to the Commonwealth Arbitration Court, as,

a union that we do not trust, they have caused us a great deal of trouble. The biggest upheaval we have had was from the A[malgamated] S[ociety of] E[ngineers]. We have had trouble with them while this case has been on ... They have taken men out of every shop ... If they had full strength and every worker in their organisation we could not possibly carry on. It is only the fact that we have some workmen who are outside the organisation that keeps the balance in the trade at all.[72]

In turn of course the employers handed out some rude knocks to the A.E.U., particularly on the downswings of the pre-war trade cycle in 1921–2 and 1928–33.

The emphasis placed by the A.E.U. on the industrial side of things did not, of course, prevent it being one of the largest affiliates to the various state branches of the Australian Labor Party (A.L.P.), or providing from its ranks leading politicians in the federal and state spheres such as N. J. O. Makin or J. J. Cahill. Yet while the union always endeavoured to gain full mileage out of such political contacts, its industrial activity was seldom inhibited by them. The presence of A.E.U. members in both the federal and Victorian A.L.P. Cabinets in 1946–7, for example, in no way restricted its course of action in the great industrial upheavals of that period.

While stressing the A.E.U.'s aggression and independence it is important to recall the discussion of A.E.U. recruiting in Chapter 1, which indicates that the A.E.U. was never a 'closed' union turning its face away from semi- and unskilled workers in the industry. Craft opposition to handymen and industrial unionism did not mean that the A.E.U. was shortsighted. The often bitter experience of the parent union in technologically advanced Britain served as a stern forewarning to Australian members. In the British engineering industry twentieth century technology clashed head-on with the craftsmens' nineteenth-century pride and status. In the view of E. J. Hobsbawm it made metal manufacturing, particularly after 1914, 'a frontline of class battle' with the result that, 'for most of the twentieth century [the] radicalism of the threatened labour aristocrat was a major factor in industrial relations'.[73] The Australian A.E.U.'s approach was to seek to

---

[72] W. B. Hipsley, *1920–1 Arbitration Case*, op. cit., p. 3160. See also evidence of H. A. Mitchell, B. H. P. Ltd. representative, p. 2770.
[73] *Industry and Empire* (London, 1969), pp. 289–90.

control the new processes as they slowly seeped into the small-scale Australian industry and it was hampered neither by blind opposition to technical change *per se* nor by enmity to those employed on the new machines and new processes. In its simplest sense technological change took the form of the introduction of new machinery — and by definition engineers depended for their livelihood on making, assembling, maintaining, or repairing machines. Consequently the union always recognised that opposition to new methods was not merely futile but inimical to its members' interests.

The A.E.U.'s whole approach to this question was much more flexible and practical than, for example, that of the moulders' union.[74] This body, representing highly skilled craftsmen employed in a key sector of industry, simply refused to have anything to do with the new method of machine moulding when it first appeared in Australia at the end of the nineteenth century. Scorning the simplicity of such repetition work the union originally refused to organise machine and plate moulders and restricted its member-ship to the ranks of fully qualified 'jobbing' moulders. As a result other unions, such as the Agricultural Implement Workers and the Stovemakers began to recruit the semi-skilled machine operatives. When, in 1920, the skilled moulders did deign to open their ranks to the machine men, payment by results had become the normal wage system on this repetitive class of work. Since the craftsmen were strongly opposed to piece-work they were unable to accept the great majority of machine moulders as members. Thus the Federated Moulders' Union remained a small and exclusive body which, although powerful in relation to its size, was restricted in its coverage to a declining proportion of the total foundry workforce.

In contrast the A.E.U. set out to ensure that practically every new engineering process came within its control. As soon as a machine or method of work was seen to be assuming any degree of importance within the engineering industry, A.E.U. officials made every effort either to organise the new workers concerned or to see that current union members obtained the new jobs offering. The A.E.U.'s effort to organise the new processes primarily aimed to ensure that skilled wage levels should be maintained. The union's fear was that with the growing specialisation of the various elements of the craftsman's work his wages would be reduced to the level of the relatively inexperienced workers called upon to operate the new

[74] The following brief outline of the moulders' attitude to technical change is based on W. J. Hargreaves, *A History of the Federated Moulders*, op. cit. and 'Minutes of the Executive Committee, Victorian District, Federated Moulders (Metal) Union of Australasia', 30 October, 1882–8; January, 1890; 7 December 1906–9; January 1934. 'Minutes of General Meetings', 18 January 1912–16; December 1920.

single-purpose machines. Hence the union fought to boost the rates of pay of all semi-skilled machine operators. Although unable to attain the ideal of having all of them paid the craftsman's rate the A.E.U., in conjunction with the other metal unions, was able to gain them relatively substantial margins.

An early example of the A.E.U. outlook is provided by the Coastal (Perth) District Committee in 1911 when it urged general consideration of the unanimous resolutions passed by the branches in its area,

(a) That having regard to the introduction of labour-saving machinery, it is essential that a system of apprenticeship for machinists be introduced.
(b) That the elevation of machinists to the same position as fitters and turners, as regards rates and conditions, be secured.
(c) That efforts be made to secure the insertion of the foregoing clauses in all future agreements and awards.
This question must be regarded from the aspect of self-preservation; we as a progressive society, cannot object to the introduction of labour-saving machinery, yet our mechanics are being displaced by a gradual but no less insidious process, which increases the employers' profits, and depletes our ranks.[75]

However, while always striving to implement the second and third points in this programme, it was only during the depression of the 1930s that A.E.U. leaders temporarily subscribed to the view that technological change *per se* contributed to engineering unemployment. In fact the new machines and processes were never introduced in sufficient quantity to result in redundancy among craftsmen before World War II. Repetition work increased in certain fields but never on a sufficient scale seriously to threaten the demand for skill. Hence the number of machines which one worker could operate never became a serious bone of contention in Australia. Process working was most common in the new industries such as electrical goods manufacture and here the craftsman was always required to set up the new machines and man the tool-room. By the time the first real mass production techniques appeared in Australia during and after World War II conditions of full employment existed and far from being thrown out of work skilled engineers were more in demand than ever.

The A.E.U.'s aim to control new machines and processes naturally sometimes involved clashes with other unions similarly concerned for their members' employment opportunities. Many demarcation disputes stemmed from technical change. Thus the introduction of oxy-welding and

[75] *M.R.*, August 1911, p. 15.

cutting techniques, for example, affected both boilermakers who had hitherto undertaken rivetting, and engineers who had previously dismantled obsolete machinery. The A.E.U. was involved in demarcation disputes with practically all other metal unions together with bodies such as the carpenters', plumbers', and shipwrights' unions. Friction was most common in ship building and repairing and the construction of railway rolling stock. As with the specialist machines, although the A.E.U. fought stubbornly to maintain and extend its members' sphere of work, they were never seriously threatened by new techniques. Engineers never experienced a change such as did the boiler-makers whose main livelihood switched from rivetting to structural steel working over a period of two or three decades. In most years A.E.U. officials were more anxious to preserve the union's job territory than the rank and file who were usually in the happy position of being able to disdain repetitive or rough work. Craftsmen's attitudes to work satisfaction could prove exasperating to their officials. A Queensland organiser gave vent to his feelings during a squabble with the F.E.D.F.A. by emphatically declaring,

It is the old story of our tradesmen members neglecting to do the rough fitting work as being beneath their dignity, and now, it commences to get out of hand and certain practices have become established. Our members must take the rough work with the fine work, if they want to protect their trade rights for the future.[76] [Emphasis in original].

Thus far the discussion has stressed the A.E.U.'s independence and assertiveness — but there were of course important areas of activity in which the engineers found it impossible to go it alone. For a start, given the existence of rival bodies organising engineering workers, it was always preferable to have the support of the A.S.E., B.S.A. or other relevant unions even on the most minor of issues. We will take up the A.E.U.'s industrial story in the next chapter at a time when it learnt by bitter experience not to act too far ahead of other unions, particularly in an economic downturn. Over the 50 year period as a whole the A.E.U. probably grasped earlier than most unions the importance of both demonstrating to arbitrators that specific items claimed in its log had already been implemented by collective bar-gaining, and simultaneously impressing them that their refusal to standardise or extend the concession would lead to considerable industrial unrest. With the growing national concentration on the Metal Trades Award, and particularly after the important changes in the legal setting following the great post-war industrial upheavals, the A.E.U. found it increasingly

[76] R. Leggatt, *M.J.R.*, March 1946, p. 14.

necessary to gain the co-operation of all other metal unions in its industrial campaigns. It was convenient, too, if the A.C.T.U. and the state Labour Councils could be persuaded to endorse A.E.U. policy. Although other bodies were sometimes responsible for a particular initiative, the A.E.U.'s size, strength, wealth and inclination made it a natural leader among the metal unions both inside and outside the arbitration tribunals. In the main cases before the federal arbitration tribunal the A.E.U. advocate traditionally led for the unions and when, in the 1950s, national recognition of the fitter's rate as the key to the margins pyramid resulted in A.C.T.U. intervention in the main metal trades cases, the A.E.U. remained prominent on the small panel of advocates. In important litigation over the function and role of the tribunal the A.E.U. was the organisation concerned in most test cases. In the state arbitration arena, particularly in Queensland and Western Australia, A.E.U. organisers often found themselves spending most of their time in court acting as metal-unions' advocate and consequently restricted in fulfilling the normal organisers' role. This, together with A.E.U. officials' leadership in direct negotiations with employers, meant that the A.E.U. rank and file saw even less of their union officials. Their tendency to act of their own accord was consequently fortified but A.E.U. officers often ruefully complained that while they were gaining better conditions for all metal workers in their area, the organisers of rival unions were out in the field concentrating on recruitment and taking any credit that was going.

3

The early 'twenties: the fitter's margin and the 44 Hour Week

The A.E.U. adopted its new name in July 1920[1] on the upsurge of the post-war boom and after a five year period which had witnessed considerable industrial unrest caused largely by inflation and the associated decline in the real value of wages. Inflation began in 1910 and between the second quarter of 1917 and the end of 1920 prices as measured retrospectively by the 'C Series' index (six capitals) rose by 37 per cent, with marked accelera-tion occurring in 1919 and 1920. The A.E.U. had been involved in wage campaigns and disputes in all districts and the result had forced employers to make over award payments proportionately higher than any gained until World War II. No measurement of their exact extent or size is possible, but for example, those reported in Sydney in 1918 ranged between $7\frac{1}{2}$ and 22 per cent of award rates.[2] Yet so far behind did state award rates lag because of the tribunals' reluctance to yield to union pressure or industrial reality that these large over-award payments need to be viewed in different perspective. The 'A Series' index, which underestimated price rises,[3] indicates that, in order simply to maintain 1911 wage rates, over-award payments of 11 and 18 per cent were required in Sydney and Melbourne respectively in 1920. These orders of magnitude support literary evidence that the earnings of an unknown but sizeable proportion of engineers were failing to keep pace in the contest with inflation.

The A.E.U. districts in each state although viewing arbitration more sceptically than unions of less skilled workers, had originally decided to

---

[1] The title A.E.U. will be used consistently throughout this chapter even when referring to the union's activities before July 1920 — greater details of which may be found in Sheridan, 'A History of the A.E.U.', Ch. 4, and Buckley, *The Amalgamated Engineers*, pp. 167ff.

[2] *M.R.*, September, November 1918.

[3] Below, p. 72. The superior 'C Series' Index cannot be extended back beyond 1914.

apply for their separate awards because of the possibility of increased recruitment and an associated fear that the A.S.E. and B.S.A. might steal a march. Once enmeshed in the six state systems, the union discovered their many drawbacks, above all the aforementioned reluctance of the tribunals to maintain the real value of wage rates. The president of the Commonwealth Court of Conciliation and Arbitration, Mr Justice Higgins, seemed rather more sympathetic, and kindred bodies such as the F.E.D.F.A. and the Australian Institute of Marine Engineers obtained relatively favourable federal awards. In a ballot held in September 1916 A.E.U. members decided by 2,184 votes to 705, and by a majority in all states, to apply for a federal award.

The A.E.U.'s decision was of great significance. As the largest and strongest manufacturing trade union its application for an award would represent an obvious and immediate accretion of importance to the federal tribunal. The court's decision would constitute the first major federal attempt to standardise conditions of employment in the metal industries which were a key component of national industrial expansion. Further, any conditions of employment awarded to the union would have immediate ramifications throughout the economy because its members were engaged in practically all industries. Yet at times it seemed as if the A.E.U. would never get into court. Almost unbelievably lengthy delays occurred before the actual commencement of hearings. To start with, it took the best part of two years to collect and assess the claims from the various districts. By this time Queensland members had decided to stick to state arbitration because of changes effected by their state A.L.P. government. It took a further year to coordinate the claims and follow the intricate legal steps involved in serving the log — which at this date included having an Authorisation signed by members employed in each of the 700 firms cited. In March 1920 the union finally obtained from the High Court the requisite certificate declaring that an official dispute existed. Even then the A.E.U. had to wait in a queue because the court was congested with business, and the pleas of Mr Justice Higgins and his deputy, Mr Justice Powers, for the appointment of additional judges to clear up the backlog were ignored by the Commonwealth government.

One factor behind the refusal of the government to act was the mounting personal antipathy between Higgins and Prime Minister W. M. Hughes.[4] This

---

[4] For a summary of the division between Higgins and the Prime Minister and its consequences see E. Scott, *Australia During the War, Official History of Australia in the War of 1914–1918*, Vol. XI (Sydney, 1937), pp. 668–77; H. B. Higgins, *A New Province of Law and Order* (London, 1922), pp. 172–6; G. Sawer, *Australian Federal Politics and Law, 1901–1929* (Melbourne, 1956), pp. 196–9.

stemmed originally from Hughes' actions during the war when, in order to secure speedy settlements, he intervened in several important industrial disputes which came within Higgins' jurisdiction. The Prime Minister's methods often meant that the federal arbitration court was bypassed and its precedents ignored. The dispute between Hughes and Higgins reached its climax in April 1920 when the latter adjourned current hearings on the timber workers' log of claims in order to conduct an inquiry into standard hours of work. Employers and unions in all industries were invited to submit evidence and it soon became clear that Higgins was favourably inclined towards a reduction of weekly hours from 48 to 44. Before the President announced his decision, however, Hughes amended the Conciliation and Arbitration Act, establishing special conciliation tribunals and appointing two new judges to the court. Standard hours could only be varied in future by a 'Full Court' constituted by at least three judges sitting together. This did not affect the cases currently in the court but Higgins

1920 he announced his intention of resigning when his current term in office expired in September 1921.

The A.E.U. had been involved in a particularly invective-laden clash with Hughes over its refusal to accept incentive schemes in the government's wartime shipbuilding programme and, when appealed to, Higgins had sided with the union and questioned Hughes' motives.[5] Thus in 1920 the A.E.U. had little difficulty in deciding how to apportion the blame for the bottle-neck in the work of the federal tribunal,

It is hard to express in printable terms the feelings of members who have waited with so much patience since our plaint was lodged, and arbitration as a means of settlement of disputes has never been spoken of so disparagingly as at present, and all because the powers that be — the Prime Minister — so flagrantly causes delay, and does many other things, obviously to belittle the Court and its President.[6]

Strongly worded protests were forwarded to the Industrial Registrar and deputations waited upon Hughes but the delay continued with the engineers themselves adding to it by citing as a respondent the West Australian government which operated large implement and engineering works and sawmills. Higgins, therefore, submitted a case for the High Court's consideration as to whether such state instrumentalities were justiciable before the federal arbitration court. The hearing of the *Engineers' Case*, as it became

---

[5] 12 *C.A.R.* 386.
[6] *M.R.*, June 1920, p. 5.

known, necessitated Higgins' attendance at the High Court. The union was then appalled to find that he had to preside at compulsory conferences in connection with disputes involving the gas workers' and engine drivers' unions.

The continued delay, followed by Higgins' decision to retire, forced the A.E.U. seriously to consider abandoning its long drawn-out efforts to obtain a federal award. The Melbourne and West Australian branches favoured withdrawal but after a two-day conference between the Commonwealth Council and district organisers it was decided to press on. One important factor behind the decision was that a federal award would be of particular value to members in South Australia 'where the narrow scope of the State industrial legislation restricted [*sic*] very much the activities of our organisation.'[7] However, the conference decided to serve notice on all employers to the effect that if the federal claims were not met by 2 October then the employers would be responsible for any actions members might take. The threat of direct action was never implemented because Higgins was able, at long last, to commence hearing the case on 4 October 1920.

II

An important aspect of the engineers' contemporary campaigns for better employment conditions was a growing demand for a shorter working week. Rank and file calls for a 44 hour week began during the early years of the war and a claim for a reduction was included in the federal log. The demand for shorter hours had been one of the central issues in the mining strikes of 1916 when the coalminers had gained an eight hour day 'bank to bank', and the metal miners at Broken Hill a 44 hour week. In 1919–20 the Barrier workers, after a 16 month stoppage, withstood employers' attempts to impose a reversion to longer hours. For manufacturing employees the greatest advances had been made in Queensland where, largely because of the enervating effect of northern temperatures, the arbitration tribunals had been gradually introducing a 44 hour week. The A.E.U. had secured this reduction for Brisbane engineers early in the century by agreement although members initially forfeited four hours pay for the privilege. By 1920 it was standard throughout the Queensland metal trades.

In West Australia also the arbitration tribunal was moving towards establishing a 44 hour week. The railway unions, including the A.E.U., became the first to obtain the desired award in November 1919. During their wage campaigns of 1919 and 1920 the Victorian metal unions had

[7] *M.R.*, September 1920, p. 5.

unsuccessfully demanded a 40 hour week from employers. Indeed the unions attached primary importance to this aspect of their claims because they believed, 'increased wages will only be a temporary benefit which the increased price of commodities will soon nullify, and until the present system is altered, a reduction in hours is our only hope of obtaining a material benefit'.[8] In New South Wales agitation for a shorter week came to a head in 1920. The moves were here led initially by the building workers who in March began to refuse to work on Saturday mornings. In September, the A.E.U., boilermakers, sheet-metal workers and stovemakers followed suit.[9] The state government bowed to this pressure and commissioned the President of the Board of Trade, Mr Justice Beeby, to conduct a speedy investigation into the hours question. His recommendations, made known towards the end of November, were for an immediate reduction of hours for building workers and in six months time for metal workers.

Beeby's pronouncement, however, had already been overshadowed by events in the federal arbitration arena where Higgins had just concluded the hours inquiry arising out of the timber workers' log. He had decided on a 44 hour week and in his judgments he quoted extensively from evidence submitted by the A.E.U.[10] Upon recommencing the now month-old hearings into the engineers' federal claims Higgins declared 'the parties should know that the proving should now rest on the respondents [i.e. the employers] to show that 44 hours should not apply'.[11] In view of this A.E.U. members in the five states joined to the log felt confident that they all would soon be enjoying the long sought for reduction in hours.

A concurrent development of great significance was the High Court's decision in the 'Engineers Case'.[12] With one dissension the court ruled that employees in state government instrumentalities were justiciable in the Commonwealth Arbitration Court. This decision was of the greatest importance to the constitutional extension of federal industrial authority.[13] More immediately, the High Court judgment meant that the large proportion of A.E.U. members employed in railway workshops could now apply for a federal award. Steps were at once taken to compile a federal railway log although it did not enter court until after the general case had been dealt with.

---

[8] *M.R.*, March 1920, p. 21.
[9] A.S.E. and B.S.A. members remained in work. *M.R.*, September 1920, p. 7.
[10] 14 *C.A.R.* 811 at 847, 859, 861. See also *M.R.*, December 1920, p. 7.
[11] Quoted in *M.R.*, December 1920, p. 2.
[12] 28 *C.L.R.* 129.
[13] Sawer op. cit., pp. 216–17; O. de R. Foenander, *Towards Industrial Peace In Australia* (Melbourne, 1937), pp. 25–6, 194–6.

In the general case itself the A.E.U. had every right to be optimistic about its margins claims, for Higgins had already given ample indication of the probable basis of his judgment. In this, his last arbitration case, he was to revert to the wage ratios established in his first, the historic 1907 Harvester Judgment. Higgins had then not only set the 'living wage' for unskilled workers at 7s. per day, but also, on the basis of rates ruling in other engineering establishments where the employees were organised in trade unions, he had awarded craftsmen a 3s. margin or a total of 10s. per day. Higgins' written judgment shows that he tended to take the fitter as the representative skilled artisan and to base other tradesmen's rates on the going fitter's wage. Referring to moulders for example, Higgins declared 'I see, moreover, no sufficient reason why, if 10s. is a fair and reasonable rate for the average journeyman fitter, it should not be fair and reasonable for the average journeyman moulder.'[14] In addition, when fixing suitable wage-rates for blacksmiths and turners and other engineering machinists, he quoted in support of his decisions the fact that they coincided with the approved minima set by the A.E.U.

Price inflation commenced soon after Higgins had begun to extend the 7s. Basic Wage for labourers to all cases brought before him. It was not until 1913 that the President began to make use of the new 'A Series' price index in order to estimate the readjustment necessary to maintain the real value of the Harvester equivalent. Even so the Court erred 'on the side of delay and caution' and the money Basic Wage lagged behind the rising cost of living until 1921.[15] No attempt at all was made to maintain real margins. Higgins sympathised with skilled workers' concern at the deterioration of their real income, but in view of the abnormal wartime conditions he did not think it advisable 'to push principles to an extreme'.[16] Compared with the expenditure of labourers, the extra expenditure of margin earners was 'not so absolutely essential' and they must be prepared to make temporary sacrifices. The President did make it clear, however, that 'if we should hereafter reach the haven of settled times, their [margin earners] claims will have to be further considered'.[17]

In 1919 the A.E.U. and three other craft unions were caught up in the general discontent over conditions of employment at Broken Hill and Port Pirie and applied to the Commonwealth Court for a settlement. Higgins

[14] 2 *C.A.R.* 1 at p. 10.
[15] For a detailed analysis of the aftermath and ramifications of the Harvester Judgment see Macarthy, op. cit.
[16] 10 *C.A.R.* 214 at p. 226.
[17] Ibid. at p. 227.

gave judgment in February 1920. After reviewing the reasons for his war-time procedure in holding money margins constant, the President made it clear that he considered that the time had arrived for revision. The A.E.U. asked for a rise in margins from 3s. per day to 5/6d., and Higgins declared that his mind was 'strongly inclined in favour of now granting the relief which these highly skilled artisans seek',[18] at least to the extent of a 1s. per day increase. If he did so, however, he felt that this would be a precedent for margins increases throughout Australia. Therefore he postponed making an award until after the engineers' general case had been dealt with so as to allow employers from all parts of the Commonwealth to submit their counter-arguments. Any rates fixed in the general award would be back-dated to 19 December 1919 for engineers at Broken Hill and Port Pirie. The claims of the carpenters and engine-drivers were similarly set aside until these unions' impending general federal cases had been heard.[19] All now depended on the engineers' case, which was the first of the three on the court's list, and the issue was never in doubt. In September 1920 the President gave judgment in a case concerning ships' officers in which he reverted un-reservedly to the Harvester ratio of 10:7 between skilled and unskilled wages.[20] When the A.E.U. case began in the following month it soon became apparent that Higgins could see little reason why this ratio should not be re-applied to metal craftsmen also.

The employers' interests during the case were handled by 19 re-presentatives including those of three separate employers' associations. Deliberate[21] veils of secrecy surround the activities of employers' associa-tions in these early days but undoubtedly the most influential and dynamic body was the New South Wales Iron Trade Employers' Association (I.T.E.A.) which had a history almost as long as the A.E.U. and, throughout our period, was to mirror the A.E.U.'s role among metal unions on the employers' side of the fence.[22] Formed originally in 1873 as a loose knit organisation of the larger Sydney firms, the I.T.E.A. began formalising its structure with the advent of arbitration in 1901. In 1912 it appointed a full-time

[18] 14 *C.A.R.* 22 at p. 26.
[19] The fourth Broken Hill craft union involved was the Boilermakers' Society. This organisation had no plans afoot to apply for a Commonwealth award, but Higgins postponed a decision on its demands also in order that wider evidence on margins could be considered.
[20] 14 *C.A.R.* 459, particularly pp. 464—6.
[21] See e.g. Employers' Federation of New South Wales, *Report of Annual Meeting,* 24 September 1908.
[22] For further details of the I.T.E.A.'s history and role before 1920 see 'Brochure to Commemorate the New Building', M.T.E.A., 1958; *Metal Trades Journal* 15/2/1954; Sheridan, 'A History of the A.E.U.', pp. 177—80.

secretary and severed its link with the N.S.W. Employers' Federation which it had helped form in 1903. In 1917 it established a branch in Newcastle and in 1921 changed its name to that of Metal Trades Employers' Association (M.T.E.A.), indicating the broadening both of its coverage and its sphere of activities. The members of the M.T.E.A. while only a fraction of all the N.S.W. metal firms were the largest, the most influential and the most aggressive towards unions.

Employers in other states were not offered the same degree of efficient co-ordination provided by the M.T.E.A. Independent metal employers' associations enjoyed continuous existence only in West Australia and Queensland. The Metropolitan Ironmasters' Association was the body with which the A.E.U. conducted negotiations concerning basic conditions of work in private shops in Perth. The Queensland Ironmasters' Association which acted as a leader for private employers in that state's metal industry, is first mentioned towards the end of the nineteenth century but was apparently established on a formal basis in 1905 to protect employers' interests under the federal Arbitration Act.[23] At this time if Victorian and South Australian employers chose to negotiate collectively with unions, they did so through the iron and steel section of their local Chambers of Manufactures.

Before Higgins, the employers' main defence rested on claims that margins throughout the Commonwealth had long remained constant at approximately 3s. per day for a fitter. They endeavoured to show that a 4s. margin was a very recent innovation. The union, however, was able to prove that this was true only in South Australia and Broken Hill and that 4s. and above had been the norm in the other four states before the inflation. The employers' secondary line of argument acknowledged the logic of a reversion to the Harvester ratio which would give a 6s. margin to the fitter. They urged, however, that such a 'drastic' step should be postponed for five or ten years. Unlike the Basic Wage earner, whose income they accepted as inviolable, the employers considered that tradesmen should contribute to the 'restoration of the country'.[24] One representative of New South Wales manufacturers declared that it was impossible for employers to see how the world's debts were to be paid if every man,

be considered entitled to have the same money, and have the same privileges and to live in exactly the same style now when costs are high as they did before the world accumulated its load of debt.[25]

[23] *Metal Trades Journal*, 2/1/57.
[24] *1920—21 Arbitration Case*. Evidence of A. W. Tournay-Hinde, p. 2392.
[25] Ibid. Comments on the minutes of the award by W. B. Hipsley, p. 4009.

All such remonstrations were in vain. In his final judgment,[26] issued on 4 May and confirmed on 14 June 1921, Higgins declared that since the uncertainty of the war years had passed it was now time to compensate skilled workers in accordance with their real value. No evidence had been submitted by employers to show that they were financially unable to bear an increase in the cost of skilled labour. The fitter's margin was set at 6s. per day, or 43 per cent above the labourers' rate, as in the original Harvester case. This represented increases in skilled nominal wage rates ranging from 6 per cent in Perth to 28 per cent in Hobart.[27] In addition the President extended the 44 hour week to A.E.U. members. This meant that their hourly rates of pay rose by yet another 9 per cent. Higgins also accepted the union's arguments in favour of introducing weekly hiring to replace the system whereby employers hired men by the hour or the day. Engineers could not now be dismissed without a week's notice. The only exceptions were to be members employed in ship repair shops where the casual nature of the work militated against weekly tenure but these employees were compensated by a daily wage 10 per cent higher than the general rate.

Eight days holiday per year were granted on full pay. Higgins followed the state tribunals' practice of limiting the number of apprentices in a workshop to a ratio of one to every three craftsmen, but he stipulated that each apprentice was to attend a technical school for four hours per week at his employer's expense. Apprentices were to be paid the full craftsmen's rate for overtime worked, and Higgins stated that he would have been prepared to prohibit such overtime completely had the union so claimed. Finally, in dealing with the question of payment by results which the A.E.U. wanted the court to prohibit, Higgins sympathised with engineers' suspicions and fears and ruled that incentive schemes were not to operate unless sanctioned either by the union or by a Board of Reference. These Boards, consisting of three representatives from each side, were established in the 14 main industrial areas to deal with any dispute arising out of the award. All in all, the impatient months of waiting seemed, in retrospect, not to have been wasted for the engineers had won the most favourable award ever granted to any union. It remained to be seen whether they could hold on to it.

In the background to the A.E.U.'s first federal margins case, certain changes were being made in the mechanics of Basic Wage adjustment to price changes which were to remain a feature of the system until 1953. During the rapid

---

[26] 15 *C.A.R.* 297 at pp. 306–8.
[27] The increases for fitters in other capital cities were: Melbourne 12 per cent, Sydney 14 per cent, Adelaide 18 per cent.

inflation from 1917 onwards the unions began to argue that the 'A Series' index was not a fair indicator of the rising cost of living. The Index was based on food, groceries, and housing. Items excluded from the regimen were estimated to account for 40 per cent of workers' total expenditure. The court assumed that the prices of these residual items varied in the same ratio as food, groceries, and housing. The unions claimed that the prices of clothing and other necessities were rising at a faster rate. The 'C Series' index compiled from 1921 onwards supported this assertion.[28]

In 1919 a Commonwealth Royal Commission was appointed to examine the relationship of the Basic Wage to the cost of living. Its Report, issued in November 1920, found that in order to maintain a family of five 'according to reasonable standards of comfort' the minimum average income required in the six capital cities was £5.15.8 per week, or 31 per cent more than the Harvester equivalent. The unions immediately asked the federal court to adopt the Commission's cost of living figures as a basis for wage fixation. The A.E.U. made an application in these terms during the course of the hearings on its general log of claims and a more formal approach was made to Higgins' successor, Mr Justice Powers, by the gasworkers. Both judges refused to depart from the principle of the Harvester judgment on the grounds that the Commission had ascertained the needs of an 'average' worker rather than those of an unskilled labourer.[29]

However, it was demonstrable that during the inflation workers were not even receiving the Harvester equivalent because of the time-lags which occurred before the Basic Wage was adjusted in accordance with price rises. In assessing the cost of living in any particular case, the court had at first referred to the 'A Series' index number for the previous calendar year. From 1918 it began to use the figure for the preceding 12 months. The final step was taken in 1921 when the court began to make provision in awards for the automatic adjustment of the Basic Wage every quarter. In addition, Powers compensated wage earners for the time lag by adding a fixed sum of 3s. per week to the Basic Wage. Ironically, these safeguards against inflation were granted at the very end of the long period of increasing cost of living. During 1921 retail prices, as measured by the 'C Series' index, fell by 13 per cent. For the remainder of the decade the cost of living remained relatively constant.

The reason for the sharp fall in prices in 1921 was that Australia was touched by the world-wide post-war slump and, although not as adversely

[28] G. Anderson, *Fixation of Wages in Australia* (Melbourne 1929), pp. 241–5.
[29] 15 *C.A.R.* 297 at p. 303, 15 *C.A.R.* 838 at p. 839.

affected as many other countries, unemployment through lack of work among A.E.U. members rose above 3 per cent for the first time since 1906 (see Table 3.1). In the metal trades as a whole the percentage rose from 3.8 in 1920 to 15.3 in 1922, with the unskilled workers as usual bearing the brunt. In this depressed state of trade, metal employers were particularly loath to concede the new liberal provisions of the engineers' award. Their opposition was strengthened by the court's rejection of applications made by other unions for an extension of similar conditions to their members.

While the engineering case was still in its final stages, Powers commenced hearing the carpenters' log of claims. Encouraged by Higgins' remarks in the Broken Hill case[30] and the favourable consideration he was currently giving to A.E.U. arguments in another court-room, the carpenters asked for an increase in margins which would compensate for the rise in the cost of living during the preceding decade. Powers gave his decision before Higgins announced his new engineering margins. The Deputy President dismissed the margins application, apparently on the grounds that the time had not yet arrived for a re-assessment of wage differentials for skill. He declared, somewhat ambiguously, that to allow such a proportionate increase in margins as well as the Basic Wage,

Table 3.1: Unemployment in the Metal Trades, 1920–9[a]

	Percentage of A.E.U. members unemployed	Percentage of all metal unionists unemployed
1920	1.5	3.8
1921	4.4	8.9
1922	4.9	15.3
1923	2.6	8.4
1924	2.1	10.3
1925	2.1	10.6
1926	1.9	4.1
1927	2.5	4.9
1928	4.7	12.0
1929	5.3	11.5

Sources: N. G. Butlin, 'An Index of Engineering Unemployment, 1852–1943', *Economic Record*, xxii, 43, 1946, pp. 241–60; *Labour Reports* Nos. 10–20.

[a]Unemployment because of sickness and accident etc. is not included in either column.

---

[30] Above, p. 69.

has not been the practice of the Court and it has rarely been granted by the President. I think the full rate allowed at any time for skill should be awarded, and I propose to grant it; but in the troublous times about us and ahead of us I do not think I would be justified in the public interests in granting that claim. The skill is not greater than in 1913 and the basic wage has only been increased as a living wage not on the value of work in every case.[31]

Despite his reference to Higgins' war time refusal to increase margins there can be no doubt that Powers was fully aware of the President's intention to restore the Harvester ratio in the engineers' case. Thus Powers was here indicating that in fact he fundamentally disagreed with Higgins' line of thought. Upon becoming President he revealed this divergence of opinion more clearly.

In October 1921 Powers gave preliminary judgment on the log of claims of the F.E.D.F.A. which had also been joined to the Broken Hill Case and which was able to base its margins arguments on the recently issued Higgins' engineering award. Powers refused to accept Higgins' decision as a precedent for a general restoration of real margins to pre-inflation levels. Ignoring the whole tenor of his predecessor's written judgment, the new President declared that he did not think that Higgins had based his award 'on anything but the value of skill at the date of the award under 1921 conditions'. Even if the F.E.D.F.A. was correct in claiming that Higgins had simply concluded that it was due time for a reversion to the Harvester ratio Powers still felt himself unable 'to admit the decision as a guide in this Court'.[32] The 'whole industrial position' had altered since the Harvester Judgment,

In numerous ... ways skill and duties required in 1921 are not the same as in 1907, and the marginal rates are not necessarily the same ...

I cannot under the circumstances see how this Court can, in fixing margins for skill, take into consideration anything but the question — what amount should be allowed for skill at the time the award is made on the evidence submitted to the Court in support of the claim.[33]

Thus, within four months of the issuance of the engineers' award, Higgins' attempt to restore skilled wages to their pre-inflation real value had been repudiated by his successor.

Higgins' other major innovation was similarly rejected. Five unions, the Federated Gas Employees Industrial Union, the F.E.D.F.A., the A.S.E., the

---

[31] 15 *C.A.R.* 239 at p. 248.
[32] 15 *C.A.R.* 883 at p. 898.
[33] Ibid., pp. 900–1.

Australian Workers' Union (A.W.U.) — Pastoral[34] and Mining Divisions, applied to the Court for the extension of the 44 hour week to their members. Their case was heard by Powers and two High Court judges, Duffy and Rich, who had been temporarily seconded to the Arbitration Court to deal with outstanding hours claims.[35] In their judgment of November 1921[36] all applications were refused on the grounds that even if Higgins had been justified in breaking with precedent in varying standard hours, the economy could no longer afford a reduction in the working week. This unanimous finding of the Full Court made it obvious that any future application on behalf of the engineering and timber employers to vary the two Higgins' awards would be favourably received by the Bench.

It was in this gloomy setting that the A.E.U. attempted to enforce the implementation of its federal award. The task proved arduous.[37] Provisions had been made for the new wage rates to apply retrospectively from 1 January 1921, but in a period of growing unemployment the union organisers found it very difficult to collect back-pay owing to members. Further, since the federal court had no power to make its awards the 'Common Rule' in industry and Higgins had refused to give A.E.U. members job preference,[38] the employers were able to discriminate against them. Wherever feasible, A.E.U. men were replaced on engineering work by non-unionists and members of the A.S.E. and the B.S.A. In those jobs which lay on the fringe between engineering and other metal trades the disparity in wage rates resulted in other metal unions being favoured by management so that, for example, boilermakers were given work which had long been performed by A.E.U. coppersmiths. Other methods used to minimise the effects of the award included discharging A.E.U. members just before Christmas in order to avoid payment of their three days holiday money, and sacking A.E.U. members and inducing them to resign from the union and return to their jobs at lower rates of pay for a 48 hour week. The union consequently found that, because of the currently declining demand for engineering skill, the award did not act as the envisaged spur to recruitment. On the contrary

[34] The A.W.U. had in fact already gained a reduction in hours in the pastoral industry by direct action during 1920. Turner, *Industrial Labour and Politics*, p. 200.

[35] Duffy and Rich resigned after dealing with the 'Five Trade Unions' Case' and were officially succeeded in June 1922 by Sir John Quick and Mr N. A. Webb.

[36] 15 *C.A.R.* 1044.

[37] Details of the A.E.U.'s experience may be found in the *M.R.*s September 1921 to December 1922.

[38] This was in line with the court's usual practice. Before World War II preference was granted only twice — to the Australian Tramways Employees Union in 1912 and to the female members of the Clothing and Allied Trades Union in 1931. Foenander, op. cit., p. 178.

it contributed to a decrease in membership from 19,630 in December 1921 to 18,568 in December 1922.

Even while attempting to evade the provisions of the award, the employers were moving to have it varied in the direction of lower wages, longer hours and the withdrawal of the remaining innovations. The A.E.U. was to contrast bitterly the speed with which the employers' log was dealt with to the lengthy period of delay which the engineers had been forced to endure before obtaining the original award. The claim was lodged in the court in November 1921, hearings commenced before Powers in March 1922, and judgment was announced in June 1922. The A.S.E. and the B.S.A. had separately applied to have the provisions of the Higgins' award extended to their members and the three cases were dealt with simultaneously. Powers, as a single judge, was unable to settle the question of hours and this was left for the Full Court. In all other respects his variation was favourable to employers' claims. Margins were reduced to the pre-Higgins level of 4s. per day, full overtime rates for apprentices were abolished, general overtime rates were reduced, the number of days for which engineers could claim sick pay was reduced and the A.E.U. claim that 300 extra respondents be attached retrospectively to the award was refused.[39] In his judgment the President stressed that the basic factor behind his decision was the depressed state of the industry. He regarded his duty as unpleasant but expected that the lowering of wage costs would stimulate the engineering trades and thus aid unemployed workers to regain their jobs. Powers felt sure that even Higgins would have acted similarly in the circumstances of 1922.

Regarding the general principles upon which margins should be set, he declared,

I have no hesitation in holding that I am bound to deal with this and other applications on the principles and practices laid down for the guidance of unions and employers and acted upon for so many years, except where they have been proved to be erroneous, and not on any new practice in an award made just before the late President's resignation in special circumstances, and in exceptional and prosperous times.[40]

His judgment therefore followed the lines he had set out in the F.E.D.F.A. case. He dismissed all consideration of maintaining margins at the Higgins' level because of changes in the cost of living during the preceding decade

---

[39] 16 *C.A.R.* 231. Only approximately 400 employers had been bound by the original award because the union had failed to observe the correct legal procedure in serving the log on some 300 others. 15 *C.A.R.* 297 at p. 331; 16 *C.A.R.* 231 at pp. 234–5.
[40] Ibid. at p. 233.

and indicated that the determining factor must be the current market value of skill. This he assessed at 4s. per day for a fitter, or 31 per cent more than a labourer's rate.

Powers was anxious to show that his wage reductions did not represent too great a setback for engineering workers, yet failed to point out that, because of the fall in the cost of living, the new margins had a higher real value than their money equivalents in 1921. Rather he erroneously argued that prior to the Higgins' award the generally accepted margin for fitters had been only 3s. per day. Powers compounded his error by claiming that the engineers had been content with the supposed 3s. margin. In support he resorted to sophistry,

The claimant organisation [A.E.U.] was so satisfied with its margins for skill up to 1921 and the classifications and rates it was strong enough to enforce that it never applied to this Court for an award before the present one.[41]

The President also stressed that the A.E.U. in its original log had asked that £7.10.0 be awarded to a fitter and £6.6.0 to a labourer. Since the difference between the two rates was £1.4.0, or 4s. per day, Powers claimed that by fixing the fitter's margin at 4s. he was granting the union's original demand in full. In fact, the difference between the skilled and unskilled rates in the 1920 log did not represent any limit either to the A.E.U.'s expectations or to Higgins' freedom to award a larger amount. All federal awards at this time were issued for a three year period and any application for variation during the triennium had to be based on the original log. Hence, in order to have some leeway for possible upward re-adjustments, unions always claimed much higher *total* wage rates than those they expected the Court to grant in the initial award. Thus the A.E.U.'s 1920 wage claims for fitters, labourers, and all other classifications merely represented upper limits below which the President could set rates incorporating any margins he considered just. During the case the union's advocacy was always directed towards gaining as large a margin as possible and the employers' representatives never argued that the A.E.U.'s log had in any way restricted its margins claims. The A.E.U. was therefore far from convinced by Powers' reasoning. 'To express ourselves mildly', the Commonwealth Council wrote, 'it can be definitely stated that we are thoroughly disgusted with the variations made, and consider same are unreasonable and unjust.'[42]

The feeling that Powers had displayed prejudice was strengthened by the manner in which he arrived at his conclusions concerning the grading

[41] Ibid. at p. 270.
[42] *M.R.*, July 1922, p. 5.

of the many engineering job classifications. To ascertain the skill required to perform each task, the judge had appointed two assessors, one nominated by each side. However, in those cases where the measure of disagreement between them was most marked, Powers obtained the opinion of an unnamed 'competent expert – not interested in any engineering business – who has worked through all the classes in question from improver to the top of the tree, and who has now retired'.[43] The A.E.U. was able to discover that this third person was an ex-employer and hence considered that the views of its own assessor had been unfairly outweighted.[44]

It was thus with feelings of outrage against what they considered to be the manifest bias of the Court that A.E.U. members joined in nationwide stop-work meetings of protest. The immediate problem, however, was the imminent increase in hours – for the union did not expect any better hearing of its arguments on the profitability of industry from the Full Court than it had received from Powers. In an attempt to arrive at a national policy, an interstate conference was held in August at Melbourne. The arbitration agent, all organisers, and representatives of the six major District Committees in the five states concerned were invited. The Commonwealth Council members also attended, Chairman Smith presiding, but they did not exercise a vote. The Council's lack leadership was made clear when it announced that it had no recommendations to place before the meeting but wished merely to hear the views of the different States. Councilman Pickard did declare himself a 'direct actionist' and urged the conference to resort to a general withdrawal of labour, but his fellow Council members were much more irresolute. Their attitude was influenced by the current state of the union's funds. During the first half of 1922 over 90,000 A.E.U. members in Britain were involved in a national lock-out, while a similar number were unemployed through lack of work.[45] The Commonwealth Council had therefore forwarded £15,000 to London to help ease the parent body's financial burden. This remittance together with increasing payment of unemployment benefits at home left Australian cash resources at a very low level. The union had assets in the form of £15,000 invested in war loans but the Commonwealth Bank, without giving reasons, refused to provide a cash loan on this security. Eventually at the end of 1922 the A.E.U. was able

[43] 16 *C.A.R.* 231 at p. 254.
[44] The A.E.U. was never explicitly informed of the identity of this 'competent expert'. The union's arbitration agent claimed that Powers' procedure in this direction surprised the employers equally as much. He hazarded that the anonymous ex-employer might have been the former Manager of the Austral-Otis Company. See *Minutes of 1922 A.E.U. Interstate Industrial Conference*, p. 31.
[45] Jefferys, op. cit., p. 224.

to borrow £6,000 from the A.W.U. in order to meet its temporary shortage of ready money. This internal liquidity crisis alone could well have provided sufficient reason for avoiding direct action over the hours question. Yet the Commonwealth Council refused to assert its constitutional authority and make a decision either way. It seems certain that the Council feared that a recommendation against strike action would increase its current unpopularity among the branches which were already agitating in support of the 1921 Biennial Conference.[46]

The Council's lack of direction resulted in a profitless exchange of conflicting opinion among the delegates. West Australia stood for immediate strike action and withdrawal from the Commonwealth Court. At the other extreme, Sydney, in the light of the deteriorating labour market, urged caution and a retention of the federal award at all costs. The remaining delegates placed themselves between these two poles. It was finally agreed that the West Australian branches should be allowed to revert to state arbitration at the termination of the current award, and that a ballot should be taken of members' views on giving a mandate to their District Committees to take any action deemed necessary to retain the 44 hour week. In September 1922 the Full Court's decision to restore the 48 hour week in the timber and engineering industries was announced[47] but the A.E.U.'s attempts to prevent its implementation proved completely ineffective.

The mood of the rank and file activists was revealed in the ballot, with 2,407 voting in favour of direct action and 649 against in a 16 per cent poll. Hence the Commonwealth Council issued directions to all districts that members were to continue working only 44 hours in those firms covered by the federal award. In a slackening labour market, and bereft of co-ordinating federal leadership, the result was a debâcle. In Melbourne the District Committee failed to secure any promises of co-operation from kindred unions because of the general level of unemployment. Consequently a mass meeting of A.E.U. members had to accept that resistance would be futile. The Adelaide Committee instructed all members, wherever employed, to work only 44 hours but the financially fearful Commonwealth Council prohibited this extension of the dispute to firms not covered by the federal award. This weakened the resistance of members sufficiently for a mass meeting to agree to work 48 hours throughout the district. In New South Wales the hours question involved unions other than the A.E.U. The state Labor government in office from March 1920 to March 1922, had implemented the Beeby

[46] See above, pp. 41–4.
[47] 16 *C.A.R.* 649.

Commission's recommendations by Act of Parliament. The Nationalist ministry which succeeded it immediately repealed this legislation. Employers followed this up by successfully applying to the state court for variation of several awards to restore the 48 hour week which was to operate from 10 November 1922. Since all unions were affected by these variations the 'Emergency Council of Action'[48] was invited to co-ordinate industrial action to resist the extension of hours. The Council was unable to promote unity among its constituent members and the unions, including the A.E.U., separately accepted the longer week. Only in West Australia was direct action taken and members in that state 'with apparent relish' promptly declared their intention of maintaining the 44 hour week.[49] Large numbers were immediately locked out, together with members of the A.S.E., Moulders' and Boilermakers' Societies. The stoppage lasted seven months before a return to work took place on the employers' terms.

The Commonwealth Council adopted an ambivalent attitude throughout. After issuing instructions in accord with the mandate received from members in the ballot the Council, ignoring its critics,[50] stood to one side and acted as a commentator on the flurry of events, deploring the 'volte-face' in Adelaide[51] and the lack of resolution in Melbourne.[52] Yet it is certain that the federal leaders would not have welcomed a more determined stand – for as soon as it became apparent that the West Australian stoppage might endanger the award in the rest of the Commonwealth, the Council began to urge the striking members to return to work. It did not use its power actually to order an end to the stoppage, but Councilman Potter was sent to explain the Council's views to his western constituents. His pleas had little effect, however, and the dispute continued until April 1923.

Basically the Council felt that, despite the rapid retraction of the major gains of the Higgins' award, arbitration still provided the best means of improving conditions of employment. Chairman Smith made this clear soon after the full implications of the Powers' variation were realised. In the *Monthly Report* of August 1922[53] he had urged members not to be 'recklessly despondent' because of the current state of affairs '. . . which is more the result of the President of the Court than the principle he is expected to

---

[48] Councils of Action were set up in each state following the decision of the 1921 All-Australian Trade Union Congress to work towards the establishment of the One Big Union. *Official Report of 1921 Congress.*

[49] *M.R.*, October 1922, p. 8.

[50] E.g. *M.R.*, December 1922, p. 29.

[51] *M.R.*, November 1922, p. 4.

[52] *M.R.*, October 1922, p. 9.

[53] pp. 10–13. See also *M.R.*, June 1923, p. 3.

administer'. Unfavourable though the Powers' variation had been it still preserved eight days paid public holidays, weekly job tenure and uniform regulation of the apprenticeship system. The Council was also still attracted to the federal tribunal because it felt that its apparent bias need not be permanent. A.E.U. members believed that Prime Minister Hughes had deliberately forced Higgins to retire in order to replace him with men less sympathetic to employees.[54] A future A.L.P. government could reverse the process by re-constituting the Court with personnel favourably inclined towards the unions.

This sudden appreciation of the utility of political action was accompanied by a determination that when a Labor government was returned to power the A.E.U. should have as big an influence as possible in its counsels. Hitherto affiliation to the A.L.P. had rested on the initiative of the various districts. Although sections of the unions were affiliated in most states, nothing like the true numerical weight of A.E.U. membership had been brought to bear at conferences and in pre-selection ballots, and the chances of A.E.U. members winning important posts in the party had been correspondingly small. The Commonwealth Council therefore decided to hold a national ballot on the question of putting into universal practice the provisions in the rules for payment of a political levy, leaving it to individual members to opt out if they so wished. In a 14 per cent poll the majority decided in June 1923 in favour of affiliation.[55] Political Committees were set up and affiliation on the new larger basis took effect on 1 January 1924. Even so, in common with other unions, the A.E.U. did not affiliate on behalf of all its levy-paying members. In N.S.W. for example the number for which the first fees were paid was 4,020 out of a reported total membership of 7,623.[56] The new numbers were, however, sufficient to increase greatly the union's influence within the A.L.P.

Political action could be expected to bear fruit only in the long-run. The

---

[54] For an example of A.E.U. convictions concerning Hughes see the comments of its former arbitration agent, E. H. Barker, in *M. R.*, December 1922, p. 26. Barker went so far as to claim that anonymous employers made a gift of £25,000 to Hughes as a reward for his services in ousting Higgins and preventing an extension of the 44 hour week by means of the 1920 amendments to the Arbitration Act. Similar charges were prevalent among all unionists at the time. See, for example, *The Australian Worker*, 1/11/22, 8/11/22, 22/11/22, 6/12/22, 13/12/22. A censure motion was unsuccessfully moved in the House of Representatives against Hughes' acceptance of the gift. Sawer, op. cit., p. 215.

[55] The full figures were: for affiliation 1,609, against 1,019. *M.R.*, July 1923, p. 27. These totals do not include 'several belated returns' mentioned in *M.R.*, August 1923, p. 4.

[56] 'C.C.M.', 11/12/23.

immediate question in 1922–3 remained that of how best to use the current imperfect federal Arbitration Court. One very apparent defect in the A.E.U.'s previous approach had been that in applying for its original award in advance of the other metal trade unions it had exposed its members to the employers' tactics of discrimination. Thus when the A.E.U. came to draw up its new log in 1923 it conferred closely with the other two engineering unions, the A.S.E. and the B.S.A., and the three parties agreed to present identical claims to the court and share all costs on a proportionate basis.[57]

The next step was to sound out the Moulders', Boilermakers', and Iron-workers' unions on their attitude towards applying for a federal award. The F.I.A. had long been endeavouring to secure an award and continued with a separate application[58] but the two skilled unions adopted the basic A.E.U. log regarding margins, holidays, hiring and other conditions of work applicable to their members.[59] Thus the A.E.U. was a prime mover in bringing the metal unions into the federal court. Although the separate claims were not formally combined into one overall log until the next metal trades hearing, the three cases were in practice treated as a single entity in 1924 for Sir J. Quick's judgments in the boilermakers' and moulders' cases[60] were based on Powers' decisions in the engineers' hearing.

The combined engineers' case[61] commenced on 6 May 1924 and the boilermakers' and moulders' separately five months later. The A.E.U. was hopeful that its second federal log, which was largely based on the original Higgins' award, would be favourably received. Its sanguine views rested not only on the unity of claims submitted by the five craft metal unions but also on the great improvement in the state of the industry. Powers had issued his 1922 variation at a time when demand for metal products was diminishing. Later in the same year, however, trade began to improve and the general expansion of the economy rapidly reduced unemployment among skilled workers (see Table 3.1). Thus, when Powers was considering the 1924 claims, engineers were profiting from a tight labour market for skill and it was believed that this would induce the President to grant some increase in margins.

In fact Powers' findings, issued on 27 October 1924,[62] were largely a simple

---

[57] *M.R.*, August 1923, p. 4.
[58] The F.I.A. obtained its first federal award (by consent) in 1925 (22 *C.A.R.* 378 and 399).
[59] *M.R.*, September 1923, p. 4.
[60] 20 *C.A.R.* 770. 20 *C.A.R.* 890.
[61] The West Australian branches of the A.E.U. were not included in the log. In accordance with the 1922 Interstate Conference decision they had been removed from the original award on its termination date of 31/12/23.
[62] 20 *C.A.R.* 1134. The award is given in 20 *C.A.R.* 982.

repetition of the 1922 variation. The Basic Wage and margins were left unchanged although the award was extended to several more engineering occupations and the definition of a fitter was widened. The weekly hiring clauses were tightened in favour of employers who had complained that engineers had been taking advantage of the provisions by feigning sickness. The overtime and apprenticeship clauses were unaltered. The only concessions to the unions were the increase in the number of public holidays granted on full pay from eight to ten and the provision for extra rates for work performed under hot or wet conditions, or in confined spaces.

The unions had, for the first time, cited the governments of the four southern states as respondents. However, because prevailing conditions of work in the New South Wales and Victorian railway workshops were superior to those which the President was prepared to grant to the industry in general, he exempted them from the relevant section of the award. For similar reasons the New South Wales railways were also exempted from the wages clauses.

On the important question of margins, Powers re-iterated his 1922 declaration that the changes in the cost of living since 1907 were immaterial to the issue. He referred back to his F.E.D.F.A. judgment and made it clear that as far as he was concerned the only relevant criterion was the current market value of skill. In his view this value had apparently not increased since the depressed days of 1922. He ignored the fact that engineers were beginning to regain over-award payments and that agreements had been reached with employers not covered by awards for the payment of amounts in excess of 4s. per day for fitters.[63] The unions showed that the lowest margins paid in the New South Wales railway workshops were above 4s. per day: the President dismissed the illustration as a special case because he considered railway work 'worth on an average more than that done by fitters outside'.[64]

Powers had made a further contribution to the concept that the capacity of the economy to pay should determine margins rather than the prosperity of individual industries. After the war Higgins had been prepared to restore

[63] In fact some employers paid over-award rates from the inception of the 1922 variation because they considered Powers' wage-cuts were 'too drastic'. (M. R., August 1922, p. 33). For examples of over-award payments and agreements see M. R., July 1923, p. 22, October 1923, p. 22, November 1923, p. 25, January 1924, p. 15, April 1924, p. 21, May 1924, p. 21, October 1924, p. 24.

[64] 20 C.A.R. 1134 at p. 1166. This view contrasts with the statement of Judge Drake-Brockman on the next occasion that N.S.W. railway members applied for a federal award, 'It is not disputed that the class of work upon which such [tradesmen] fitters are employed both inside and outside the Railway Department is substantially alike', 34 C.A.R. 702 at p. 704.

pre-war differentials because he had been satisfied that employers in the shipping and engineering industries could afford to meet the increase in wage costs.[65] Powers, however, had indicated in his 1921 judgment on the carpenters' case that he did not consider the *economy* was yet ready for an alteration in margins — times were still 'troublous'. The onset of the 1921–2 economic recession appeared to vindicate this view. When varying the engineers' award in 1922 he was able to refer justifiably to the precedent set by Higgins and himself of cutting back margins (in real terms) during periods of uncertainty. In 1924 the uncertainty had passed. Powers' main reason for still refusing to increase margins appears to have been that he was fully aware that such an adjustment would not be restricted to the engineering trades. The fitter's margin was becoming the basis upon which the Court was setting wages for other skilled workers. In several war-time judgments Higgins followed the practice which he had first adopted in the Harvester case of using the fitter's rate as the skilled yardstick.[66] The practice of referring to the fitter's margin grew after the A.E.U. obtained a federal award. In 1923, for example, Deputy President Webb based his clothing trades award on the 1922 Powers' variation. He noted that,

In a great many recent awards, 'skilled artisans fully trained', who have served a five years' apprenticeship to their trade have been awarded a margin of 4s. per day, or 24s. a week. It appears to me that the claim of the artisan in this industry to have his margin for skill adjusted is irresistible.[67]

Hitherto margins in the clothing industry had been below the fitter's rate. If engineering margins were to be increased by Powers, workers in other trades, such as clothing, would regard his action as an indication that all skilled wages would be similarly raised. Powers never explicitly stated in the 1924 case that he was taking into consideration factors other than the ability of engineering firms to pay their skilled employees higher wages. He did, however, attack the engineering unions' claims that margins should be adjusted according to changes in the cost of living on the grounds that if granted 'it would only be just to give the same to all other persons in the Commonwealth'.[68]

In the boilermakers' and moulders' cases Deputy President Sir J. Quick based craft rates in these occupations directly on the rate determined by

[65] 14 *C.A.R.* 459 at p. 465, 15 *C.A.R.* 297 at p. 307.
[66] See e.g. 10 *C.A.R.* 155, 11 *C.A.R.* 267, 12 *C.A.R.* 427.
[67] 18 *C.A.R.* 1033 at p. 1047. See also Webb's comments in the 1922 carpenters' case, 16 *C.A.R.* 1136.
[68] 20 *C.A.R.* 1134 at p. 1151.

Powers for the fitter.[69] The fact that the fitter's margin had become the standard secondary wage rate was made even more explicit in succeeding years. In dealing with the printing union's first federal log of claims in 1925, Webb directly related printers' skills with those of a fitter and set margins accordingly.[70] Coopers' rates were similarly assessed by Powers.[71] Even butchers' margins were determined by comparisons with the skill required by a fitter.[72]

III

Although the A.E.U.'s prospects of obtaining higher award rates for skill declined with the increasing importance of the fitter's margin, its members' earnings were not subject to a similar petrifaction. Between 1922 and 1927–8 demand for skill was as high as it had ever been and the A.E.U. took advantage of the fact. It is impossible to measure the degree or extent to which over-award payments were made to engineers in these years.[73] They do not appear to have been quite so common as they were in the inflationary period between 1917 and 1921 but a substantial proportion of A.E.U. members were still able to profit from the general shortage of skill.[74]

The industrial expansion of the 1920s was based on growth of the domestic market combined with import replacement in certain manufacturing fields. Population increased from 5.4 millions in 1921 to 6.4 millions at the end of 1929. The tariff reconstructions of 1920 and 1921 were specifically designed to encourage development in secondary industries. In succeeding years the newly created Tariff Board generally proved sympathetic towards calls for further increases in the level of protection. It is difficult to discuss the level of tariff protection enjoyed by the engineering industry because of the multiplicity of items produced. However the 1921 tariff on Motive Power Machinery and Appliances, for example, lifted duties from 25 per cent (British Preferential Tariff) and 30 per cent (General Tariff) to $27\frac{1}{2}$ and 40 per cent respectively. In 1925 these rates were increased to 45 and 60 per

[69] See 20 *C.A.R.* 770 at p. 778, 20 *C.A.R.* 890 at p. 897.
[70] 22 *C.A.R.* 247. See particularly pp. 251–3, 261–6.
[71] 22 *C.A.R.* 141 at p. 144.
[72] 22 *C.A.R.* 794 at pp. 803–804.
[73] The N.S.W. state secretary of the moulders' union produced statistics in 1924 which indicated that over-award payments to his 1,079 N.S.W. members ranged from 5 per cent to 17 per cent of the state award rate. The weighted average was 7 per cent. Commonwealth Arbitration Court, *The Federated Moulders' (Metals) Union of Australasia and The Adelaide Steamship Co. Ltd., and Others*, 1924. Transcripts of Evidence, p. 87; See also, Sheridan, 'A History of the A.E.U.', p. 259n.
[74] See e.g. *M.R.*, February 1925, p. 5, September 1925, p. 19, October 1925, p. 26, November 1926, p. 31, April 1928, p. 30. 'M.D.C.M.', 11/3/25, 13/2/27.

cent.[75] This order of protection encouraged Australian metal manufacturers to undertake the production of many new commodities. In addition a number of foreign firms established plants behind the rising tariff wall. Employment in the metal trades increased from 85,000 in 1919–20 to a peak of 131,000 in 1926–7. Growth was particularly marked in sectors producing the new consumer durables. Employment in establishments manufacturing electrical machinery and appliances expanded from 1,890 in 1919–20 to 5,635 by 1929–30.[76] Firms associated with the assembly and maintenance of motor vehicles and acessories provided jobs for 27,373 workers in 1926–7, an increase of 85 per cent over the 1919–20 figure. The establishment of large vehicle assembly plants by the Australian firm of Holdens and foreign companies such as General Motors and Fords led to a great increase in demand for standardised components. One result was that the manufacture of screws was begun on a large scale for the first time in Australia by Nettle-folds, a British company which had formerly been the main foreign supplier.

Yet the degree to which the industrial base was widened and import replacement occurred in the metal trades should not be exaggerated. During the decade an estimated 59 per cent of gross additions to factory equipment was supplied from abroad despite the high level of protection.[77] Even in the rapidly growing electrical machinery and appliance sector Australian producers provided only 21 per cent of total consumption of these goods in 1926–27.[78] Over one fifth of metal workers were still engaged in railway and tramway workshops. Of the remainder, practically half of the employees in general engineering continued to work in establishments with less than 100 hands on the payroll. Arm in arm with small scale and high tariffs went the inefficiency stressed by the unions in arbitration cases and commented on by neutral observers.[79] To take but one example early in the decade, high-speed steel appeared in Australia at the turn of the century, but in 1921 one employer who claimed his works were up-to-date in every respect admitted

[75] For full details of the levels of engineering tariffs see, Nancy Windett, *Australia as Producer and Trader 1920–1932* (London, 1933), Ch. IX.
[76] C. Forster, *Industrial Development in Australia 1920–1930* (Canberra, 1964), p. 104.
[77] Ibid., p. 23.
[78] Ibid., p. 104.
[79] See e.g. Commonwealth Arbitration Court, *Amalgamated Engineering Union and J. Alderdice and others. Enquiry re, Standard Hours* (1926), Transcripts of Evidence, pp. 120, 656. (Hereafter reference to these transcripts will be shortened to *Standard Hours Case 1926*); *Report on the Productivity of Queensland and the Remuneration of Labour by A. B. Piddington K. C.* The Queensland Trade Union Economic Research Committee 1925; *The Australian Tariff — An Economic Enquiry*, Economic Series No. 6 (Melbourne, 1929), p. 6.

that he had not merely failed to introduce it to his establishment but had no idea what difference it could make to output.[80] Many sectors of the engineering industry were influenced by seasonal fluctuations in demand. A significant proportion of plants, particularly the larger ones — and including newer industries like auto assembly and radio manufacture — either cut back their staff during the slack periods or closed down completely for several weeks, usually over Christmas. In certain trades, notably ship repairing, production was largely on a casual basis with plant operating practically around the clock when demand was heavy but men being laid off at other times.[81]

The A.E.U. eagerly supported the expansion of industry and as overall employment in the metal trades increased, so too did union membership. A.E.U. growth resumed in 1924 and membership increased by 20 per cent to over 23,000 in 1928. A sample of entrants to the Industrial Section[82] suggests that welders, motor mechanics and other workers possessing newer engineering skills formed an increased proportion of A.E.U. recruits in the 1920s. Yet the gradual growth of product-standardisation and repetition work in the 1920s presented two main problems to the union: employers pressed harder for the introduction of incentive payment schemes; and the numbers of semi-skilled machinists and assemblers encroaching upon craftsmen's work increased. In the 1920s employers raised the issue of payment by results in virtually all arbitration hearings, relevant public inquiries and commissions, in the press and on the radio. One parliamentary advocate urged that incentive schemes should be an issue at the 1928 Federal elections.[83] Although perhaps spurred on by excess capacity installed in an over optimistic mood in the post-war boom,[84] the demands by private engineering employers were largely premature. The bulk of their output was still restricted to non-repetitive jobbing and repair work. Arbitration transcripts and press reports suggest that most employers saw incentive schemes as a panacea for all their business ailments but when questioned closely about the application of piece-work to their own particular establishments, their answers were usually couched in vague and very general terms. Some employers admitted that payment by results was possible only in limited areas of metal manu-

[80] *1920—21 Arbitration Case*, p. 2182.
[81] See e.g. ibid., pp. 1668, 2065, 2495; *M.R.*, June 1931, p. 18. *M.J.R.*, April 1939, p. 4.
[82] Sheridan, 'Partial Anatomy of a Union', Table 5.
[83] *Argus*, 2/4/28. For a small sample of employer arguments in favour of payment by results see *Report of Interstate Conference of Employers' Federations, October 1926. Australasian Manufacturer*, 9 July 1927, *Industrial Information*, 30 July 1928.
[84] Forster, op. cit., p. 13.

facturing[85] and management was never able to produce a concrete scheme for consideration by the unions despite the constant promptings of the federal arbitration bench. In 1927, for example, Judge Beeby expressed his disappointment that, although strongly urging him to provide for the introduction of payment by results in the metal trades, employers had not submitted to the Court 'some thought-out scheme as a basis for discussion'.[86]

Union fears that employers saw incentive schemes as a means of removing the union from the bargaining process seemed to be confirmed by the manner in which many representatives of management opposed the inclusion of union officials in any joint committees which the court might create for the purpose of setting piece rates. Employers frequently extolled the advantages of restricting negotiations to workers actually employed in their establishments and one could not see, 'why the Union should be brought into the matter at all. It is a matter between the employer and the workmen'.[87]

The possibility of peaceful alterations in work practice was minimised by the almost complete lack of contact between management and labour within the workshop. Employers jealously preserved what they considered to be the prerogatives of management from trade union 'interference', and organised employees remained instinctively mistrustful of every suggested innovation. Impartial observers such as Beeby and Higgins lamented the results.[88] The nature of the federal arbitration system tended to harden the rigid divisions between management and labour. Hearings before the court — particularly in metal trades cases — were widely publicised and advocates on both sides inevitably took the opportunity to play to the gallery. The fact that the parties to an industrial dispute were largely absolved from responsibility for reaching agreement once the case entered the court further militated against conciliation of the conflicting claims. Since courtroom discussions were always conducted on a national level, the problems and potentialities of altering work practice in individual plants were considered only if one side could quote to advantage concessions already made by the other.

In this atmosphere examples of co-operation between unions and management over the introduction of incentive schemes were practically non-existent in the metal industries. Acceptance of piece work was restricted to certain

---

[85] E.g. *Standard Hours Case 1926*, p. 4037.

[86] 25 *C.A.R.* 364 at p. 375.

[87] *1920—21 Arbitration Case*. Address of G. H. Boykett, p. 1975. See also ibid., pp. 1764, 2025, 2073, 2898.

[88] See e.g. *Report of the Royal Commission on Standard Hours*, N.S.W.P.P. 1920, Vol. 2, pp. 15—6; *1920—21 Arbitration Case*, op. cit., p. 3592; 25 *C.A.R.* 364 at pp. 382—3.

areas of holloware and agricultural implement manufacture, where relatively weak unions had long before been forced to accept incentive schemes.[89] The other metal unions constantly denounced payment by results. The boiler-makers, who had given piece work a trial during the Commonwealth ship-building scheme, were probably most antipathetic towards its introduction.[90] Employees engaged in non-metal trades also feared incentive schemes and the 1927 All-Australian Trade Union Congress declared its official opposition to their extension.[91] To many A.E.U. members the blocking of attempts to introduce piece work was even more important than securing a 44 hour week.[92] The large scale of operations common to certain sections of British engineering had forced the parent A.E.U. to accept the principle of incentive schemes in the late nineteenth century.[93] Feelings against payment by results among Australian members were such, however, that the 1924 Biennial Conference deleted from the Rule Book the clauses which allowed District Committees to make provision for piece work in their areas. In their place was substituted a rule prohibiting members, under pain of fines, from accepting payment by results in any part of the Commonwealth. In 1925, the Executive Council objected that the Conference had acted *ultra vires* in this and many other matters. Obediently, the Commonwealth Council recalled the two-member Rules Compilation Committee and instructed it to make the necessary modifications —but with two significant exceptions: one concerning clauses making the decision to affiliate with the A.L.P. a national rather than a district one, and the other regarding the prohibition of piece work. The Commonwealth Council's unusual disregard for Head Office instructions was carried a step further in 1927 when the Biennial Conference greatly increased the fines to be exacted from piece-working members.

Until 1927 the federal arbitration tribunal made no effort to force the engineering unions to accept piece work. Higgins indeed, had sympathised with A.E.U. fears. Only the Victorian brass manufacturers attempted to

[89] Above, p. 55.
[90] See for example, Commonwealth Arbitration Court, *The Amalgamated Engineering Union and Others v Metal Trades Employers' Association and others, 1928–30*, Transcripts of Evidence, pp. 3581–2, 4614–24. (Hereafter this case will be referred to as *Metal Trades Case 1930*).
[91] *All Australian Trade Union Congress. Official Report* 1927. Some unions in other industries which had accepted piece work in the past began to oppose it in the 1920s. See for example, the evidence of E. A. Painter, Federal Secretary of the Textile Workers Union, in *Standards Hours Case* 1926, p. 1037.
[92] See e.g. 'Minutes of Melbourne Shop-Stewards Meeting', 20/4/27, and 'M.D.C.M.', 28/4/27.
[93] Jefferys, op. cit., p. 137.

make use of the Boards of Reference provided for in the 1921 award. The equal representation of the two sides on the Board prevented these firms from securing legal permission to continue their traditional piece-work schemes. The A.E.U. was therefore able to extend its coverage among brass workers. Powers was not asked to make any determination concerning payment by results in 1924 although he attacked the unions' obstructive attitudes in his judgment.[94]

In the few areas of private engineering work where payments by results was feasible it was therefore left to individual employers to make the attempt to introduce it. Given the firm opposition presented by the unions the success of these efforts depended on the degree to which employees within the relevant plants were organised. Where the A.E.U. or other craft unions had a firm foothold, the moves usually failed. In addition the unions were able to end long-established piece work or bonus schemes as they increased their coverage of workers within individual firms. A.E.U. records reveal that only in the rarest of cases did members accept incentive schemes, and then often under duress.[95]

Accompanying the sporadic efforts of private employers to introduce piece work were attempts to engage cheaper semi-skilled labour on the simpler engineering tasks. Here too the A.E.U. was largely successful in ensuring in union shops that all machine operators received adult award rates but the picture on both scores was slightly different in government workshops and in plants where labour was unorganised.

The card and bonus systems were imposed in the New South Wales railways during the 1917 'general strike', and although agitation was maintained in the workshops the only way of removing them short of another major stoppage was by means of political action. Under the Nationalist government, the metal unions charged that the Commissioners' claim that the men were free to refuse to work under the bonus scheme was false. The state A.L.P. declared its opposition to the incentive system in November 1923 and the Labor government elected in 1925 fulfilled the pledge to remove it.[96]

In Victoria a running battle was maintained between Commissioners and unions over the bonus system which the former were anxious to introduce. At the main Newport shops the initial moves by management to implement the scheme were defeated by mass meetings of protest attended by all employees, and by agitation through shop committees. The Commissioners continued their campaign by increasing the monetary inducements to their employees

[94] 20 *C.A.R.* 1134 at pp. 1185—8.
[95] For details see Sheridan 'A History of the A.E.U.', pp. 269—70.
[96] 'A.E.U. Railway and Tramway Sub-Committee Minutes' 1925; *M.R.*, January 1926, p. 18.

and discriminating against those who persistently refused to co-operate. The Victorian unions, like their New South Wales colleagues, applied pressure in the parliamentary lobbies and the minority Hogan Labor governments were urged to prohibit payment by results in the railways.[97]

The new engineering shops of the 1920s were largely those connected with the growth industries, particularly motor cars and electrical goods. Equipped with up-to-date plant and machinery they were often designed to handle a fair amount of repetition work, produced on the simple single-process type of machine. Hence management was particularly keen both to introduce payment by results and to make use of the cheapest possible semi-skilled labour. As in the older establishments, the permanence of such innovations depended on whether or not the A.E.U. were able to gain an early foothold and organise the employees. This task was not always easy because the management of these new shops was often recruited in Britain and America where the restrictive practices of skilled unions were harder to implement.[98] The Ford motor plant at Geelong, for example, refused entry to union organisers even during the lunch hour.[99] The Victorian country organiser, G. Hargreaves, worked hard for the greater part of 1926 before he was able to persuade the majority of semi-skilled workers to join the A.E.U. The firm had been operating a bonus system but the basic rate for the semi-skilled had been up to 15s. below the A.E.U. award rate for machinists. On the other hand the fact that skill was in short supply was illustrated by the over-award rates paid to Ford's skilled employees.[100]

The A.E.U. experienced mixed fortunes in its dealings with other new industries and establishments. They included a clash with the Defence Department over conditions in the new federal munitions plants at Footscray and Maribyrnong. This dispute ended in A.E.U. victory after a short stoppage in March 1926.[101] Other samples of the union's activity were a successful recruiting campaign in the Westinghouse Brake Co., Sydney[102] and the limitation of payment by results to the non-mechanical engineering departments in the large-scale works of the Electricity Meter Manufacturing Company, Sydney.[103] The union was not always successful, and though recruitment in motor assembly and repair shops appears to have greatly expanded in the

[97] *M.R.*, May 1923, p. 25, September 1924, p. 22, May 1927, p. 19, *Argus*, 16/5/28, 27/3/29, 28/3/29, 8/5/29.
[98] For typical A.E.U. comments about foreign management see *M.R.*, September 1924, p. 18.
[99] *M. R.*, October 1926, p. 23.
[100] *M.R.*, November 1926, p. 31
[101] *M.R.*, March 1926, p. 17.
[102] *M.R.*, January 1926, p. 19.
[103] *M.R.*, June 1927, p. 19.

1920s, many of the small garages presented particularly difficult organisational problems.[104]

The rank and file A.E.U. members were less concerned than their officials about the existence of pools of unorganised workers in the new industries. In the tight labour market for skill, craftsmen were generally able to pick and choose between jobs. One of the results was that A.E.U. members often refused to tackle the more monotonous varieties of the new engineering work — sometimes despite the inducement of over-award payments.[105] The union's leaders worried lest the repetition jobs scorned by working members were secured either by lesser skilled men or by members of other metal unions. Hence members were urged and cajoled to undertake the repetitive work in question — wheel and tyre turning, tuning and testing, motor assembling, steel window-frame making, heating installation and oxy-acetyline and electric welding[106] — but it was to take the economic disaster of the depression to teach the rank and file the wisdom of such arguments.

The matter with which A.E.U. working members were most concerned in the mid-1920s was the campaign for a 44 hour week. Powers had indicated in his 1924 judgment that he considered a shorter working week would in fact be detrimental to the interests of workers.[107] This made it clear that the Arbitration Court as currently constituted was not likely to consider an application for a 44 hour week favourably. The alternative procedure was legislative action. Since anti-Labor governments remained in continuous office in the federal parliament[108] all the moves took place in the state legislatures where three Labor ministries, urged on by the unions, introduced 44 Hour Bills.

Queensland acted first in 1924 with legislation that provided for the shorter week for all workers from 1 July 1925. In New South Wales it came into operation on 4 January 1926. In 1926 also, the West Australian Labor-dominated Lower House passed a 44 Hour Bill but the conservative Legislative Council rejected it. The West Australian government had, however, already granted state employees the reduction[109] and the state Arbitration

---

[104] See e.g. *M.R.*, July 1923, p. 17, December 1923, p. 16, November 1927, p. 24.

[105] E.g. *M.R.*, December 1924, p. 23, June 1926, p. 26.

[106] *M.R.*, July 1924, p. 38, December 1924, p. 23, February 1926, p. 20, October 1927, p. 38, December 1927, p. 25; 'C.C.M.', 18/9/25.

[107] *C.A.R.* 1134 at p. 1164.

[108] In addition it was doubtful if the Commonwealth Government had the constitutional power to introduce such legislation. See Sawer, op. cit., p. 281. The 1926 referendum proposals, dealt with in the next chapter, would have given the government the requisite authority. However, the current Bruce—Page ministry would hardly have been likely to use it to introduce the 44 Hour Week. See below, pp. 97–9.

[109] This was a restoration by an administrative act of a privilege taken away by the state Arbitration Court in October 1923.

Court announced its intention of introducing 44 Hours as the standard working week. The only Labor governments to shirk the task were the South Australian Gunn and Hill ministries (April 1924–March 1927) which, despite the promptings of the unions made no move even to place state employees on a 44 hour week.

The A.E.U. greeted the legislative enactions of the shorter week with enthusiasm. Its pleasure was modified, however, when it was found that while the West Australian engineers were able to enjoy their extra leisure,[110] members in New South Wales were faced with the legal question of whether they were entitled to a 44 hour week in view of the fact that the majority of them came under the 48 hour provisions of the federal award. At a conference held between unions and employers at the end of 1925 it was decided that the men would work 44 hours for four hours less pay while the employers were sued for the difference in wages. In this way a legal decision could be obtained as to the validity of the state Act in regard to the federal award.

The A.E.U. represented the other unions in the ensuing litigation and the Sydney District Secretary gave his name to a High Court case which complemented the 1920 *Engineers' Case* by providing a further important extension of federal industrial authority. In the judgment in *Cowburns Case*[111] the majority of the court (Higgins and Powers dissenting) ruled that Commonwealth awards were paramount and that the, 'Commonwealth Court had full power to make a complete and permanent settlement of an industrial dispute by means of an order and award and no State measure could be effective to vary or disturb that order or award'.[112]

The federal unions were not, however, prepared to accept this unfavourable pronouncement. As a consequence of their refusal to attend work on Saturday morning 1 May, fifty of the five hundred members of the M.T.E.A. locked out some 7,000 unionists, including approximately 1,000 A.E.U. members. The unions decided to separate the wages and hours issues and concentrate in the first instance on the retention of shorter hours. After negotiations with the M.T.E.A. and the state government the men affected returned to work on 31 May on the basis of 44 hours work for 44 hours pay, until the federal Arbitration Court dealt with a general application for a reduction in hours. It was agreed that the settlement was not to prejudice the employers' future arguments before the Court in favour of the 48 hour week.[113]

---

[110] The Queensland engineers had enjoyed the 44 Hour Week since 1920. (See above p. 66). The 1924 Act extended the privilege to workers in all industries.
[111] 37 *C.L.R.* 466.
[112] Foenander, op. cit., p. 26.
[113] *M.R.*, May 1926, p. 2., June 1926, p. 4; M. Hade, *The Case for the Forty-Four Hours Working Week* (Pamphlet), Labour Council, Sydney, 1926.

But even as this dispute was being settled B.H.P. Ltd., Newcastle, notified the A.E.U. that, in return for a continuation of the 44 hour week on full pay, the engineers must agree to forfeit the federal award and accept the inferior conditions of work which applied to other employees in the steel works. When the union rejected the proposal B.H.P. and Rylands, an associated firm, dismissed over 400 A.E.U. members on 25 May. The dispute dragged on for fifteen months, for the engineers were able to find alternative work and the companies were prepared to incur the expense of sending work to Sydney rather than revert to federal award conditions.[114] Finally Judge Beeby settled the dispute by temporarily exempting the firms from the 1927 award.

In the meantime the focus of industrial attention had moved back to the federal Arbitration Court. Legislation in 1926 reconstituted the Court by appointing three new judges, Dethridge C. J., Beeby J. and Lukin J., who were to hold office for life on judicial tenure. The first task facing the new Bench was that of hearing the test case whereby the industrial labour movement throughout Australia hoped finally to achieve a reduction in standard hours. The A.E.U. was given the responsibility of convincing the Full Court that 44 hours should be granted. Hearings lasted four months and 145 witnesses were called. The judgment was delivered on 24 February 1927 and the union's application was granted by a majority decision,[115] Lukin J. dissenting. Dethridge and Beeby in their separate judgments considered that workers had every right to increased leisure provided national output was not adversely affected and both believed that the ending of the continued industrial friction over hours of work would stimulate productivity. A general note of caution was struck, however, and the union was informed that it must play its part in maintaining production. The best means of so doing was for the A.E.U. to accept payment by results which should — in the judges' view — be the corollary of reduced hours.

The 44 hour week was not actually implemented in the engineering industry until 14 July 1927 after Beeby had issued his general findings on the A.E.U.'s third federal log but the Full Court decision seemed to assure the application of the new standard hours not merely to the engineers but to all Australian workers. If the Bench could be persuaded to abandon its penchant for piece work, and if the economy continued to expand, the engineers felt they could look forward to the new Arbitration Court conceding further improvements in their working conditions.

---

[114] *M. R.*, January 1927, p. 21.
[115] 24 *C.A.R.* 755.

4

1926—34: Arbitration controversies and economic depression

I

During the 1920s the majority of the federal leaders of the A.E.U. remained firmly convinced that federal arbitration offered the best means of improving members' conditions of work. Although allowing and often encouraging rank and file members to resort to direct action, the Commonwealth Council was always anxious that strikes should never be so prolonged as to induce employers to apply to the court for a suspension of the federal award. At times the Council's fears in this direction drew criticism from the more militant district officials and working members. Charges that the Council's ambivalent policies hampered rank and file action were largely justified during the 44-hour disputes of 1922 and those following the 1927 Beeby award.[1] The Council, on the other hand, could point to the fact that the union's greatest gains had been secured under the auspices of the court. The 1926 hours-decision was the most notable of these but even the wage provisions of the original Higgins' award were not necessarily irretrievable.

The strongest and most conservative character among the A.E.U.'s federal officials was J. J. Scoffin, Councilman for Division 1 from 1917 until his death in 1930. Scoffin, an Englishman who had joined the Crewe branch in 1901 and emigrated to Australia in 1911, was a convinced supporter of arbitration. He had been the only Council member to oppose autonomy and the most fervent opponent of the 1921 Biennial Conference. On most issues he was supported by W. R. Potter who represented Division 3 from 1917 to 1940. Potter appears to have been essentially a middle of the road unionist who had a high regard for the arbitration process. The experience of the depression, however, led him to support different policies in the 1930s. The third Councilman was H. Pickard, the representative of Division 2 between 1919 and 1928. Pickard was in many ways the antithesis of Scoffin. Self-educated,

[1] Below, pp. 103—4.

his first industrial experience was gained at the age of 11 years when he worked a 56 hour week in a Yorkshire woollen mill for a wage of 4s. He later entered the skilled engineering ranks and emigrated to Australia in 1910. Although not a member of the C.P.A. he considered himself a Marxist, but when he urged the adoption of radical policies within the Council his arguments were seldom sufficiently well formulated to counter Scoffin's lucid conservatism. After expressing his views Pickard always accepted and supported the majority decision. L. N. Wickham, federal secretary from 1922 to 1944 also occasionally clashed with Scoffin whom he sometimes considered ultra-cautious on policy matters and too legalistic in interpreting the rule-book. A particularly capable administrator, Wickham was never as radical as Pickard and generally advocated the judicious use of arbitration. The highest A.E.U. office was held by A. S. Evernden, Chairman from 1923 to 1934. He was the third Englishman on the Council and had joined the London South branch in 1890, seven years before moving to Australia. Together with officials of six other unions, Evernden was arrested and charged with conspiracy in 1924 because of participation in attempts to prevent an allegedly unsafe ship, the 'Port Lyttleton', from putting to sea. He did not, however, allow the uncomfortable night he spent in Long Bay Gaol to influence his generally moderate attitudes towards political and industrial issues. Although more flexible than Scoffin he remained a supporter of federal arbitration throughout his period in office.

These, then, were the men who shaped A.E.U. federal policies during the second half of the 1920s when the problem of industrial peace and the associated question of how the arbitration system might best be altered to achieve this end came to the centre of political discussion. In 1925, 1929, and to a lesser extent in 1928, the major parties concentrated their federal General Election campaigns on these issues. The causes of the increasing concern with industrial matters were not to be found in any actual increase in either the number of disputes or the total working days lost through stoppages. Table 4.1 shows that the dislocation caused by strikes and lockouts remained well below the immediate post-war peak of 1919 and 1920 until the last year of the decade. The major factors underlying public awareness of industrial disturbances seem to have been the growth of importance of the Commonwealth Arbitration Court and the continuance in federal office of the Bruce–Page coalition government from February 1923 to September 1929.[2]

[2] The following account of arbitration policy under the Bruce–Page government is largely based on A.E.U. sources; Foenander, op. cit., Ch. III and passim; A. Wildavsky and D. Carboch, *Studies in Australian Politics* (Melbourne, 1958); Sawer, op. cit., pp. 267–8, 270.

Table 4.1: Industrial Disputes 1919—1929

	No. of industrial disputes	Working days lost ('000)
1919	460	4,303
1920	554	3,587
1921	624	1,286
1922	445	858
1923	274	1,145
1924	504	918
1925	499	1,128
1926	360	1,310
1927	441	1,713
1928	287	777
1929	259	4,671

Source: *Labour Report*, Nos. 6—21.

The jurisdiction of the federal court increased significantly after World War I until, by 1926, one-third of Australian trade unionists were governed by its awards. In addition the state tribunals came to be greatly influenced by its decisions. Two immediate effects of this expansion were that the court was inevitably drawn into a growing proportion of total disputes, and that the overlapping of federal and state awards increased with the consequent necessity for continual judicial interpretation of the meaning and extent of federal power granted under the Constitution. The High Court decisions in the 'Engineers' Case' and 'Cowburn's Case' contributed greatly to the extension of Commonwealth industrial authority but the unions were still open to the employers' charge that they tended to move between state and federal spheres in an attempt to 'pick the eyes' out of various awards.

The ruling Nationalist and Country Parties with their important bases of support among manufacturing, commercial, professional and rural interests, tended to view industrial disputes with much greater alarm than the A.L.P., but the Cabinet's interventions in the struggles between employers and unions aroused great distrust and hostility among the workers. In its attempts to tackle labour problems the Bruce—Page administration often bewildered even its own supporters by sudden switches of policy; the labour movement, governed principally by an instinctive suspicion of any governmental proposals, proved to be equally inconsistent. The federal government was originally favourably inclined towards the states' proposals that legislation should be passed to reverse the effects of the 'Engineers' Case'. However, negotiations at the 1923 Premiers' Conference proved abortive because of differences between the parties as to where the exact line of demarcation between federal and state jurisdiction should be drawn.

Following the Commonwealth Government's intervention in the seamen's dispute of 1925 and the amendment of the Immigration Act in an attempt to deport the two principal strike leaders, Bruce successfully fought the 1925 General Election on a platform of 'Law and Order'. With this fresh mandate he quickly introduced a stringent Crimes Act largely aimed at curbing the activities of the C.P.A. In 1926 the government moved to ensure that the federal court could enforce awards and impose penalties for breaches. It counteracted a 1918 High Court decision[3] by ending the old system of appointing arbitrators for a term of years and appointed separate arbitration judges (Dethridge, Beeby, Lukin) with life tenure.

In May 1926, almost simultaneously with the start of the New South Wales metal trades 44-hour stoppages, the Prime Minister announced his intention of appealing to the electorate to approve, by referendum, amendments to the Constitution which would give the federal Arbitration Court full unfettered control over industrial relations. This move left practically all major political groups internally divided. Although earlier Labor ministries had twice attempted to secure similar extensions of federal power,[4] large sections of the labour movement in 1926 feared that the amendments were designed to allow the court to filch from the workers the gains recently achieved by means of legislation passed by state Labor governments. The federal Parliamentary Labor Party, foreseeing its eventual return to power took the long-term view and supported Bruce's proposals. The Victorian A.L.P. and the Commonwealth Council of Federal Unions also urged a 'Yes' vote but the remaining state A.L.P. executives and Labour Councils were vehemently opposed.[5] The federal A.L.P. executive, threatened with a serious split in the party, hedged by advocating all Labor supporters to vote according to their own conscience.

On 4 September the voters rejected Bruce's proposals, and, thus rebuffed, the government turned to legislation as an alternative method of inducing industrial peace. In December 1927 a Bill was introduced to

---

[3] *Alexander's Case*, 25 C.L.R., 434.

[4] In 1911 and 1913. The Hughes Nationalist Government also made a similarly unsuccessful attempt in 1919.

[5] For an example of the divisions within the labour movement see *Official Report of Third All-Australian Trade Union Congress, 1926*, pp. 5—8. The Commonwealth Council of Federal Unions (C.C.F.U.) was the predecessor of the Australasian Council of Trade Unions (A.C.T.U.) formed in 1927. The A.E.U.'s arbitration agent, C. E. Mundy, was one of the first C.C.F.U. executive members and was President when in 1927 it was replaced by the A.C.T.U.

fulfil four main aims: to prevent duplication of state and federal authority; to mitigate the increasing legalism associated with the federal court; to encourage conciliation in the settlement of disputes; and to enforce rigorous observance of industrial law. Labor opposition to this 'leg-iron' Bill was spontaneous and united. Any merits inherent in other clauses passed unnoticed in the outburst of furious resentment directed towards those sections of the legislation that (i) instructed the court, when making awards, to consider 'economic realities' (ii) legalised employers' use of lock-outs to combat 'sectional' strikes (iii) enabled the court to intervene in unions' internal affairs (iv) increased the extent and effectiveness of penalties applicable to breaches of award. The measure was denounced by labour spokesmen as an attempt to crush active trade unionism in Australia, but despite their strenuous opposition in Parliament and outside it, the Bill became law in June 1928. Before the end of the same year the new penal provisions were used against the Waterside Workers' Federation. A Transport Workers' Act was also passed which broke the union's job control on the docks and resulted in violent clashes between strikers and non-unionist 'volunteers'. Industrial peace was an important issue at the general election in November 1928 when the coalition was returned to power with a reduced majority.

The new year witnessed the commencement of the greatest industrial upheavals of the decade: a strike in the timber industry and a lock-out in the New South Wales coalfields. These two disputes occurred against the sinister background of a steadily weakening national economy, engendering bitter partisanship on both sides. Labour supporters considered that the government showed open prejudice against the unions in prosecuting the striking timber workers but withdrawing similar proceedings against a prominent mine owner. In the midst of this unrest and suspicion, Bruce startled everyone, including his own supporters, by presenting the Premiers' Conference with an ultimatum that if the states did not surrender all industrial powers to the Commonwealth, then the Commonwealth would abdicate all its arbitration authority except with regard to the maritime industry. When the states refused to give up their powers Bruce proceeded to embody his decentralization proposals in the Maritime Industries Bill. Once again the labour movement united in opposition to his plans and it was joined on this occasion by several parliamentary supporters of the coalition. These members, led by W. M. Hughes, crossed the floor in the House of Representatives and brought down the government. At the ensuing General Election the A.L.P. enjoyed a landslide victory and in October 1929 the first Commonwealth Labor government since 1916 took office under J. H. Scullin, pledged to repeal the 1928 Acts and re-open the coal-mines.

The A.E.U. Commonwealth Council generally pursued a middle course during these stormy debates. As relations between organised labour and the Bruce—Page coalition worsened, A.E.U. attacks on the government in the columns of the *Monthly Report* portrayed an increasing radicalism, stressing the class bias of the coalition's policies. Nationalists were described as 'deceptive agents of bloated capital' and members were urged 'to sound the death knell of nefarious capitalist designs' at the polls by registering their vote for Labor.[6] But despite militant terminology the Council remained consistently in favour of retaining connection with the federal Court.

In 1926 the Council, although suspicious of Bruce's motives, did not take part in the campaigns against the referendum but followed the federal A.L.P. executive in advocating that individual members should use their own judgment when casting their votes. The A.E.U. fully supported the campaign against the 1928 Amendment Bill but did not adopt the newly formed A.C.T.U.'s recommendations that all unions should cancel their registrations with the Court. When the Act became law the Council refused to implement the decision of the 1928 All-Australian Trade Union Congress that affiliated unions should take a ballot on the A.C.T.U. suggestion. Scoffin was particularly opposed to the abandonment of arbitration. He saw the real issue before the unions as one of 'whether Arbitration should be attacked as a principle, or whether we should concentrate our attention on the prevention of application of the objectionable Amendments of the Act and the ultimate deletion thereof',[7] and argued that the second course was the only one worth pursuing. Abandonment of arbitration would neither prevent employers obtaining awards nor render unions immune from the penal provisions of the Arbitration and Crimes Acts. He further claimed that past experience had shown that the alternative of direct collective bargaining with employers usually ended in deadlock and ultimate resort to large-scale trials of industrial strength was a 'crude antediluvian mode of procedure' attended by 'privations, impoverishment and misery'.[8] Radicals might claim that use of the arbitration process destroyed working class militancy but Scoffin felt that working within the system did not rule out expeditious resort to selective strike action to obtain favourable variations of award. The only method of combating the current attacks on the unions was to concentrate all energy and resources towards ensuring that the A.L.P. won the forthcoming election.

Following the return to power of the Bruce Government in November

---

[6] *M.R.*, November 1928, p. 5.
[7] *M.R.*, August 1928, p. 5.
[8] *M.R.*, July 1928, p. 8.

1928 the question of mass withdrawals from the federal court again achieved great prominence. This time the Council supported a joint union application to Judge Beeby for a six week suspension of the current metal trades hearings. But this move can be more correctly interpreted as an attempt to apply pressure on Beeby because of his recent statements on piece-work and job classifications, than as a reversal of A.E.U. policy. When the judge refused the request the unions continued to participate in the case and no further mention was made of deregistration.

The timber and coal disputes affected some hundreds of A.E.U. members and the union was represented from the outset at all relevant conferences. Large sums were contributed by the engineers to the two unions chiefly affected. By March 1930 Chairman Evernden claimed that the mining stoppage had cost the A.E.U. £30,000 in addition to the widespread voluntary donations made by many branches and working members.[9] Important though the strikes were, the Council saw Bruce's proposals to destroy the federal court as a more crucial issue in 1929, and allied itself without reservation to the campaign against the Prime Minister. It contributed funds and propaganda and when the Government was defeated in Parliament the A.E.U. concentrated all its energies to ensure the return of the A.L.P. The Party's sweeping victory was greeted with enthusiasm. Scullin's ministry would, the Council was sure, finally settle the industrial peace question in accord with the unions' wishes, and federal arbitration would be properly safeguarded against future attacks. Yet by the time the new government took office the election issues were already being overshadowed by the threat of economic depression.

II

While controversies still raged over the future of federal arbitration Judge Beeby delivered his judgment on the counter claims put before him by the A.E.U., A.S.E., B.S.A. and the metal employers. His award of 1 July 1927[10] was intended to be of short duration, for it was to be re-considered in conjunction with the remaining metal trade cases in a single hearing covering all metal unions. Beeby, unlike his fellow arbitration judges, Dethridge and Lukin, had reached the federal bench after 20 years of close connection with industrial matters. A practicing solicitor, he had begun by representing trade unions in the New South Wales Arbitration Court in the early years of the century. Later he was a minister in the Holman state Labor governments but

[9] Robt. F. Davenport, *Report of All-Australian Trade Union Congress, 1930*, p. 110.
[10] 25 *C.A.R.* 364.

left the party with the Premier over the conscription issue. He then served as President of the Board of Trade and Royal Commissioner on labour problems before becoming a judge in the state arbitration tribunal. In 1926 he was appointed to the federal court. He had firm ideas concerning the solution of Australian industrial problems[11] and in his first federal engineering award he attempted to initiate the re-organisation which he considered to be a prerequisite for the industry's further expansion.

Beeby's 1927 award prescribed separate industrial conditions for the 'manufacturing' (repetitive process work) and 'general engineering' (jobbing and repair work) sections of the trade; the reclassification of labour; the adoption of 'properly safeguarded' systems of payment by results; the substitution for current apprenticeship provisions of the New South Wales scheme which abolished technical schooling in working hours and which permitted one apprentice to be employed for every one journeyman in the motor trade.[12] The major forms of re-organisation were to be dealt with by a committee of experts consisting of three representatives from each side under the chairmanship of Industrial Commissioner, A. M. Stewart. In the meantime employers were free to make arrangements with their workers for the introduction of any form of payment by results provided the returns to the employees amounted to 10 per cent over the minimum award rate. As long as the unions' rules continued to prohibit piece work, these agreements could remain secret. After 14 January 1928 any organised prohibition of incentive schemes was to be deemed a breach of the award. Beeby also gave employers the option of reverting to the daily hiring system and he even hedged the new 44 hour week by the proviso that normal rates of time and a half need not be paid for the first four hours overtime worked per week until six months after the inception of the award. This clause, inserted in order to assist any employers with unfinished contracts on hand, was particularly exasperating to engineers in New South Wales who had been forfeiting four hours pay since May 1926 in order to retain the 44 hour week.

Exemptions from the award included the Victorian Electricity Commission works at Yallourn, mines on the west coast of Tasmania, McKay's Sunshine Harvester Co., the Electrolytic Zinc Co. (Hobart), the Tasmanian Government railways, and motor body building and car-assembling firms in South

---

[11] Beeby foreshadowed two of his main innovations as federal arbitrator in an article written in 1915 in which he criticised arbitration tribunals for their failure to popularise payment by results and to expand the supply of skilled labour. See 'The Artificial Regulation of Wages in Australia', *Economic Journal*, xxv, 99, 1915, pp. 321–8.

[12] Beeby had introduced this system into N.S.W. in 1924 when President of the Board of Trade.

Australia. The B.H.P. steelworks, Newcastle, was exempted until it could be decided in the pending general metal trades case whether or not tradesmen should work under conditions applying to other employees in the industry. For the time being, engineers working for B.H.P. were granted the 44 hour week and their wages were based on the Sydney federal award rates.

The A.E.U. while officially denouncing the 'ambiguity and partisanship' [13] of the award, was not taken completely unaware by Beeby's provisions, for the Full Court's admonitions to the union on the matter of payment by results during the 1926 hours case had been duly noted. As a result, an Interstate Conference had been held in May 1927 to formulate policy in the event of an adverse award. The delegates determined both to establish the 44 hour week for all members and to resist the introduction of any form of incentive payments. A ballot was subsequently held in which members voted to pay a special levy in preparation for any future disputes on the hours issue. Thus, when members employed at firms exempted from the award refused to work more than 44 hours, the Commonwealth Council fully endorsed their action and, in addition, directed that no overtime be worked until the ambiguity of the relevant clauses was cleared up. In all cases the stoppages were relatively brief and resumptions of work were arranged pending a settlement by the Full Court of the hours question in the industries concerned. The speedy solution of these disputes meant that the Council was not faced with the possibility of being forced to forfeit the federal award in order to gain the shorter working week.

The rank and file A.E.U. members were, however, so incensed about the other provisions of the award that the Council was hard-pressed to persuade them that an immediate withdrawal from the federal arbitration system would be unwise.[14] Once again, as in 1922, the federal leaders wavered between their desire to retain the federal award and the need to make an all-out bid to maintain engineers' current conditions of employment. Although eventually swept along by the militancy of the rank and file, the Council at first sought to restrain them from direct action. With Pickard dissenting, it originally disapproved — albeit 'for the time being' — of the Sydney and Newcastle District Committees' proposals to withdraw members in certain shops in the event of employers refusing to continue weekly hiring.[15] The federal executive questioned Melbourne organiser, N. Roberts, about stoppages in his district and displayed its pacific outlook by resolving 'That the

[13] *M.R.*, July 1927, p. 14.
[14] See e.g. 'C.C.M.', 29/7/27, *M.R.*, December 1927, p. 6.
[15] 'C.C.M.', 15/7/27.

Organisers operating in all Districts covered by provisions of the Federal Award be specially directed not to advise or encourage members to cease working under the award of Judge Beeby.'[16] By this time, however, the working members had already taken matters into their own hands.

As soon as Beeby's major decisions became known mass meetings of protest, accompanied by minor stoppages of work, were held in all states concerned. In Sydney it was reported that it 'was only the efforts of the respective executives [A.E.U., A.S.E., B.S.A.] that prevented an upheaval of the first magnitude.'[17] Perhaps sensing the mood of their employees, Victorian firms largely ignored the new overtime and hiring clauses but in New South Wales the M.T.E.A. resolved to fully implement the award. Immediately the reversion to daily hiring was announced, 22 engineers, employed at the three Sydney firms initially affected, downed tools.[18] Militant feeling ran high throughout the district. A general stoppage of work seemed imminent when, after the M.T.E.A. had summoned the strikers and the A.E.U. Council to show cause why they should not be fined or imprisoned for breach of the award, some 2,000 A.E.U. members marched to the court as a demonstration of protest. At this point Industrial Commissioner Stewart intervened and secured an adjournment of the case until Beeby could preside over a conference between the two parties.

Alarmed by the possibility of a widespread and bitter dispute, Beeby readily indicated his willingness to hear the union's application to vary the award immediately after a resumption of work. The union was also able to extract an agreement from the employers that they would leave the matter of payment by results in abeyance for a period of three months. The A.E.U. officials had a difficult task in convincing the rank and file that no more concessions could be obtained but eventually the return to work was accepted. Within a fortnight Beeby had made the desired variation. The working members' spontaneous action, against the instructions of their leaders, thus resulted in an immediate mitigation of an important section of the award and gave the employers good cause to reconsider their intentions of implementing the remaining clauses.

Industrial friction in the engineering industry declined markedly in the months following the variation despite the retention of the piece-work and reclassification clauses. The committees which were to deal with these issues were unable to function because of the obdurate attitude of the union

16 'C.C.M.', 25/7/27.
17 *M.R.*, August 1927, p. 21.
18 For details see *M.R.*, September 1927, pp. 3—7.

representatives. The problem of reclassification of labour was left to Judge Beeby who commenced hearing evidence in the general Metal Trades Case in September 1928, and the onus of introducing incentive schemes was left, as in the past, with individual employers. A.E.U. organisers did not report any increase in the number of attempts to introduce piece-work and the court made no effort to penalise the union for its continued proscription of payment by results.

The A.E.U. was not so successful in its attempts to ensure, through the medium of the court, the extension of the 44 hour week to all members. In October 1927 it was estimated that approximately 1,000 members out of a total of 23,000 were still working 48 hours,[19] and practically all of them were employed in 'mixed' industries. Unfortunately for this minority the attitude of the Full Court towards standard hours began to alter as trade slackened towards the end of 1927. After extending the 44 hour week to the other metal trades, the gas and printing industries, and the engineering departments of railway workshops, all subsequent applications were refused — including those by workers in the agricultural implement and automobile assembling industries.

Influenced by the small proportion of members affected and the gloomy economic outlook, the Commonwealth Council dropped its original insistence on the universal application of the shorter week. Despite protests against this abdication of its responsibilities,[20] the Council instructed the individual districts to act in the matter at their own discretion. It would seem that the Council's assessment on this occasion was more realistic than that of the activists. In January 1929, for example, the Melbourne District Committee attempted to take advantage of the current busy season for jam-making firms in order to gain the 44 hour week for A.E.U. men employed in the industry. A meeting of members working at the Rosella Jam factory made it clear that they would have nothing to do with any proposed withdrawal of labour. The Committee considered their attitude 'deplorable' but one of the Rosella men probably spoke for many of the A.E.U. rank and file in 1929 when he declared that 'His job was worth more than the four hours'.[21] Thus, in the uncertain months as the economy paused before plunging into the depression of the 1930s, the campaign for shorter hours was temporarily relegated from the forefront of union agitation. It was shortly to reappear attended by a new sense of urgency.

[19] *M.R.*, October 1927, p. 3.
[20] E.g. 'M.D.C.M.', 24/4/28.
[21] 'M.D.C.M.', 15/1/29.

III

The boom in Australian manufacturing reached its peak in the mid-1920s, several years before the world economy commenced its downward plunge into the depression of the 1930s. The annual rate of growth of capital equipment in the secondary sector halved in 1925—6, from between 10 and 11 per cent to between 5 and 6 per cent, and it continued to fall for the remainder of the decade.[22] Employment in manufacturing was at its peak in 1926—7, but 1928 witnessed the highest unemployment rates among union members since 1921. After a slight recovery in early 1929 the Australian economy was hit by the onset of world depression and the proportion of unemployed continued to increase reaching a peak of nearly 30 per cent in 1932. Within the metal trades the overall trend was the same, although the percentage of union members out of work in the industry was even higher than the national average. Unemployment amongst A.E.U. members was greatest in late 1931 and early 1932 and the annual average figure remained above 5 per cent until 1936 (Table 4.2). Trade union membership fell generally and the A.E.U.'s declined by 20 per cent to a low point of 18,400 in May 1933, although recovery was rapid thereafter.

Table 4.2:　Trade Union Unemployment 1926—36

	Australia %	Metal Trades %	A.E.U. %
1926	6.3	4.1	1.9
1927	6.3	4.9	2.5
1928	10.0	12.0	4.7
1929	10.2	11.5	5.3
1930	18.6	20.2	14.4
1931	26.5	29.3	25.7
1932	28.1	31.5	25.5
1933	24.2	27.7	19.7
1934	19.6	22.3	13.5
1935	15.6	16.1	7.2
1936	11.3	8.8	4.4

SOURCES: *Labour Report* Nos. 17—28; Butlin, op. cit. Unemployment through sickness, accident and 'other causes' has been deducted.

It was against this background that the A.E.U. was a party to two important arbitration awards: Beeby's Metal Trades Award of 1930, and the Full Court's 1931 decision to reduce wages by 10 per cent.

[22] Forster, op. cit., p. 11.

The precedent of the 1927 interim engineering award combined with Beeby's remarks throughout the fifteen months of the metal trades hearings did not inspire optimism among the eight unions concerned. In his judgment[23] Beeby reiterated his view that the metal trades had reached a stage at which, in order successfully to compete with imported products, the industry must be reorganised in a manner that would enable employers to take full advantage of mass production methods. The draft proposals of December 1929 were eventually watered down in the face of the vehement union outcries, but the final award split the industry into the 1927 'general' and 'manufacturing' divisions. Margins were largely retained at the customary levels in the first section but in 'manufacturing' provision was made for 'Process Workers' who were defined as adult employees '... engaged on repetition work or any automatic, semi-automatic, or single purpose machine, or any machine fitted with jigs, gauges or other tools rendering operations mechanical, or in assembling parts of mechanical appliances so made, or in repetitive processes'. These workers were to receive a weekly margin of 6s. as compared with the fitter's unchanged 24s. Engineers classified as 'Assembler and Fitter' in window-frame making were awarded margins of only 15s. and further dangers to A.E.U. members were seen in the classification of 'Machinists not otherwise provided for' at a margin of 6s. per week in the ironworking section. Other clauses reduced shift rates, authorised employers to introduce incentive schemes into their establishments, enabled females to be employed on lighter engineering work, made weekly hiring again optional, and permitted the induction of male junior labour into all occupations for which apprenticeship was not provided.

Until 1930 metal employers had been among the most strident critics of the Commonwealth Court. They had regarded the introduction of the 44 hour week as a particularly unrealistic decision and had therefore generally supported Bruce's attempts to amend the federal arbitration system. The reduction in hours and consequent increase in wage costs had also added new urgency to their campaign for the freedom of management to utilise the cheapest possible semi-skilled labour.[24] The 1930 award seemed to meet most of their demands and they greeted it with enthusiasm. The M.T.E.A. had led the employers' case and much of the credit for Beeby's acceptance of their arguments was given to its president, J. Heine, who had been an energetic advocate of reclassification for a number of years. Ironically, Beeby's decision

---

[23] 28 *C.A.R.* p. 923.
[24] See e.g. *Report of Interstate Conference of Employers' Federations*, October 1926, October 1929; *Industrial Information*, 10/7/28; *Tariff and Industrial Information*, 15/11/28, 1/3/29, 13/9/29.

induced many employers to give job preference to union members because non-unionists were still governed by the 'common rule' provisions of state awards which were not now as advantageous to most firms[25].

The new conditions came into effect in May 1930 without causing any major stoppage of work. A.E.U. members, however, were more militant than most other metal workers and engaged in several single-plant strikes, the most important of which occurred at Brady and Franks, Sydney, Mort's Dock, Sydney, and the Victorian Electricity Commissioners' plant at Yallourn — the last being apparently the only instance during 1930 of any Victorian workers taking direct industrial action to defend their conditions of work.[26] Only in the Brady and Franks dispute were the strikers successful, but their victory was important since it prevented the application of the 'Assembler and Fitter' classification and full craftsmen's rates continued to be paid for window-frame work in New South Wales.

The reasons behind the relatively peaceful inception of the award included the great improvement which the final provisions represented over the draft award and the fact that the most sweeping of Beeby's decisions were applicable only to the relatively small 'manufacturing' sector of the industry. But the main factor was of course the falling demand for engineering labour. In 1927 the bargaining position of A.E.U. members had been strong enough to defeat the M.T.E.A.'s attempt to fully implement Beeby's interim award. In 1930 successful widespread resistance was impossible.

Paradoxically, worsening economic conditions lessened the immediate impact of the more controversial aspects of the award. South Australian employers reverted to daily hiring and some firms took the opportunity to end the payment of over-award rates, but in most cases such wage cuts were rather the result of the deepening depression than of Beeby's findings. In the longer run, employers took advantage of the provisions relating to juniors by increasing the number of youths in their employ to the detriment of adult union members. The evidence is too scanty to allow any estimates of the extent of this dilution during the depression but A.E.U. officials were increasingly concerned by the employers' moves in this direction.[27]

The apprenticeship system also came in for continual attack from the representatives of management before the federal and state tribunals. Despite A.E.U. protests 'rationing' of apprentices became common, particularly in

---

[25] The M.T.E.A. went to great pains to point this out to its members in a special Beeby Award news-sheet. See *Special Industrial Information*, 29/4/30.

[26] L. J. Louis, *Trade Unions and the Depression. A Study of Victoria 1930–1932* (Canberra, 1968), p. 67.

[27] E.g. 'C.C.M.', 24/3/31; *M.R.*, August 1933, p. 16.

New South Wales. The employers' main aim, however, was to completely abolish the indenture system.[28] The Full Court in 1932 rejected attempts by the M.T.E.A. to vary the relevant clauses in order to allow for 'unapprenticed learners' who, unlike indentured youths, could be laid off work during periods of slack trade.[29] The N.S.W. Apprenticeship Commissioner was more amenable to the suggestion and the M.T.E.A. application was granted in September 1933. In the expansionary period of the 1920s management had complained of a shortage of skilled metal tradesmen. Now, during the years of contraction, in order to cut the cost entailed in retaining an apprentice when there was no work for him, employers successfully reduced the numbers of newly trained engineers. The effects of this understandable policy of expedience were to become apparent in later years.

The second important Arbitration Court decision of the depression period was that in which the Full Bench, acting in the interests of the nation as it understood them, reversed the precedent of twenty years and made an arbitrary 10 per cent cut in the basic wage.[30] The Court issued its verdict on 22 January 1931 and over the ensuing eighteen months the state tribunals imitated its action, New South Wales being the last to fall into line in August 1932. The result was that the level of money wages fell more rapidly and more steeply in Australia than in most European and American economies during the depression.[31] Originally imposed for twelve months, the 10 per cent reduction remained in force until April 1934 despite union applications for its removal in 1932 and 1933. Even the 1934 decision[32] did not completely restore pre-1931 real wages because the 'Powers 3s.' was abolished and the 'C Series' price index replaced the 'A Series' as the basis for wage calculation. In fact the full Harvester equivalent was not to be regained until 1937.

Wage reductions, apart from their immediate effect on working members, represented the complete antithesis of the unions' views on how the depression should be fought. Industrial labour's policies largely rested on a combination of economic nationalism and under-consumption theory. The first essential was seen to be the export of domestic unemployment through greater tariff protection and absolute preference for Australian manufacturers when tendering for government contracts. This policy had always been pressed on the authorities in prosperous years, but, with the alarming rise

---

[28] See e.g., *Tariff and Industrial Information*, 2/7/31; *Metal Trades Journal*, 14/10/32, 17/11/32, 17/5/33, 13/6/33, 3/7/33.
[29] 32 *C.A.R.* p. 258.
[30] 30 *C.A.R.* p. 2.
[31] J. E. Isaac, 'Economic Analysis of Wage Regulation in Australia 1920—1947', Ph.D. thesis (University of London, June 1949), p. 59 and Chart 2.
[32] 33 *C.A.R.* p. 144.

in unemployment after 1927, the petitions of the A.E.U. and other unions assumed a new pitch of urgency. On this matter at least, organised labour and manufacturing employers spoke with one voice.[33]

Upon the A.L.P. assuming federal office the pleas for higher tariffs were quickly acceded to[34] but the Cabinet continued to be overwhelmed with requests from all sides to 'keep work in Australia'. In addition the unions began to urge their first inflationary policies on the government, including the necessity of operating its establishments at full capacity and of instituting extensive public works programmes. As the downward economic trend continued, the unions stressed the importance of maintaining consumer purchasing power and called for even bolder policies. The 1930 A.C.T.U. conference demanded the declaration of a state of national emergency, federal control of all natural resources, the nationalisation of banking and means of exchange, a maximum working week of 40 hours, an immediate increase of at least 24 per cent in the basic wage, and the abolition of state parliaments.

Along with other unions the A.E.U. was bitterly disillusioned as the Scullin ministry moved towards acceptance of the deflationary policies urged on it by commercial and financial interests backed by current orthodox economic theory. Although it officially continued to support Labor politicians at the polls, and after the disastrous splits became a staunch advocate of party unity, the failure in the political sphere left the union with the dubious choice of using either direct industrial action or the arbitration process to alleviate its members' worsening economic position.

The first alternative was never really a starter. Of the A.E.U. delegates to the 1931 All Australian Trade Union Congress only the Queensland delegate arrived in Sydney with a mandate to support a general strike if necessary, although a mass meeting of Adelaide members had voted in favour of a stoppage if a ballot of all Commonwealth members also approved. After discussion of the alarming state of the union's finances and the continuing deterioration of the labour market the delegates went on unanimously to oppose a general strike at the congress.

In the arbitration sphere a prime objective of most unions was the restor-

---

[33] The employers' increasing concern about the level of protection is illustrated by the M.T.E.A.'s appointment in 1928 of its first 'Tariff Officer' and the change in the title of the association's bulletin from *Industrial Information* to *Tariff and Industrial Information* on 7/9/28. For an example of co-operation between unions and employers' organisations see *M.R.*, February 1929, p. 7.

[34] See Louis, op. cit., pp. 26–7, 88, for evidence of unions being angrily disappointed by employers who benefited from tariff increases but who still imposed wage-cuts on their employees.

ation of the 10 per cent cut. The A.E.U. was associated with all the restoration campaigns and some of its members recovered the 10 per cent, six months before the 1934 judgment, by means of agreements with employers in the glass, paper and oil industries where trade picked up in advance of the economy as a whole. Of equal importance, however, were the demands for a reduction in the working week. To organised labour, casting around for explanations of the unprecedented high levels of unemployment, it seemed that apart from the obvious failure of the capitalist system efficiently to allocate resources, the factor aggravating the current economic catastrophe was the displacement of labour by machinery. Unions began to doubt that industry would ever be able to reabsorb completely the army of unemployed even when the pre-1928 levels of production were regained. Hence the work available must be spread amongst as many employees as possible by a drastic reduction in hours.

The 'Key Industry Conference', convened by the A.C.T.U. in September 1930, emphasised the contribution of mechanisation to the current distress, and, as we have seen, along with other measures, it urged the Scullin government to introduce a 40 hour week. From this date on all sections of the industrial labour movement campaigned for work spreading through a shorter working week and attempted to support their arguments by pointing to actual instances of technological displacement. In some industries, such as glass and bottlemaking,[35] such examples could be easily found, but in the metal trades it was difficult to prove that technical innovations had detrimentally affected employment during the thirty years of expansion preceding the depression. As we have seen, far from displacing large numbers of members, A.E.U. officials had experienced difficulties in persuading the rank and file to accept work on the more monotonous new jobs. Nevertheless, faced in the early 1930s with massive unemployment, the engineers were unable either objectively to recall the past or to think in terms of a future expanding market which would provide a rising demand for skilled labour.

The A.E.U. campaigned strenuously for shorter hours until the end of the decade. Whereas the 1930 'Key Industry Conference' had recommended a 40 hour week and an increase in wages, the A.E.U. originally called for a 35 hour week with no reduction in wages. The fact that thousands of members were being 'rationed' one in every five weeks was adduced in support of the claims. A.E.U. district committees, branches, and shop committees were urged in every *Monthly Report* to bring the matter before their local Labour Councils and by December 1932 the reduction in hours had come to be

---

[35] See e.g. *Standard Hours Case*, 1926, p. 1221.

regarded by the Commonwealth Council as representing 'the only immediate solution of the unemployed problem'[36] and the first item on the agenda of the 1932 A.C.T.U. Congress was an A.E.U. resolution in favour of a 30-hour five-day week and immediate wage increases. Following Congress' endorsement of this policy, the A.E.U. ceaselessly urged all unions to co-ordinate their efforts and press their claims on governments and arbitration tribunals. Other unions, however, were not quite so enthusiastic and concentrated most of their attention on the campaign for the restoration of the 10 per cent wage cuts.[37] In any case, few federal unions outside of the metal trades were as yet enjoying even a 44 hour week. During the 1933 New South Wales Enquiry into Standard Hours all other unions decided to withdraw their initial claims for 40 and 30 hours in favour of a simple defence of the 44 hour week currently operating in the state. The A.E.U. unsuccessfully persisted with its lone claim for 30 hours. In Queensland, however, the labour organisations approached the Full Bench of the state court for a 30 hour week but, despite the eloquence of their chief advocate, A.E.U. organiser R. J. Carroll, their arguments were rejected.

IV.

While A.E.U. leaders were participating in national political and industrial campaigns in an effort to halt the spread of unemployment, and investigating job possibilities in Russia[38] and China,[39] the members of the union were closely engaged in grim defensive actions at the shop-floor level, endeavouring both to soften the effects of the depression and to preserve long-established work conditions.

Unemployment statistics can provide only the barest outline of the impact of the depression. They do not indicate the physical and mental deterioration of men permanently out of work for periods of up to five years.[40] They do not convey the effect on either the youngest workers who were often immediately

---

[36] *M.R.*, December 1932, p. 5. It is in fact likely that during the worst of the economic stagnation any *increase* in hours would have resulted in an addition to the numbers out of work. The N.S.W. Railways Commissioners, for example, when applying for a reversion to 48 hours in 1933, stated that if their request were granted they would be able to dispense with 1,036 workers. *M.R.*, November 1933, p. 7.

[37] For typical A.E.U. complaints of other unions' lack of urgency on the hours issue, see *M.R.*, January 1933, p. 6.

[38] 'C.C.M.', 21/8/31. Russia had also been regarded as a possible source of work for A.E.U. unemployed during the postwar recession of 1921–2. Ibid., 24/5/21.

[39] *M.R.*, April 1932, p. 8.

[40] 'C.C.M.', 19/4/34.

dismissed upon completion of their apprenticeship,[41] or on the oldest who were sometimes sacked upon reaching an arbitrary age limit[42] and who were always handicapped in the search for work by their grey hairs. Some iron entered the soul of all who endured these dreadful years, and helps explain much subsequent industrial history.

Active union members were usually the first to be affected by retrenchment: half the members of the A.E.U. Melbourne District Committee, for example, were out of work in May 1930, and shop stewards were often the first to be sacked. In New South Wales the quasi-fascist New Guard asked the M.T.E.A. to give preference of employment to its members. The M.T.E.A. in turn passed on the information to employers that if they wished to ensure that any workers hired in future were non-communists they could apply for hands at the New Guard headquarters.[43]

The cuts in government expenditure had a particularly severe effect on the metal trades. One of the largest employers of engineering labour in Sydney was the Clyde Engineering Company which had always relied extensively on government contracts. Between 1929 and 1931 Clyde's workforce fell from 1,400 to a mere 70.[44] The number of metal workers employed by all members of the M.T.E.A. fell from 18,622 in October 1929 to 8,756 and 8,436 in the first quarters of 1931 and 1932 respectively. Further, betweeen May 1931 and May 1932 approximately 4,300 of these employees were 'rationed' to an average of 26 hours' work per week.[45] Such rationing schemes were supported by the union as a means of spreading available work as widely as possible. They were particularly common in the railways where men were generally rationed in a ratio of one week's unemployment in every five- or six-week period but in the worst cases, as in Queensland in 1931, single men obtained only three days' work per fortnight.[46]

Many engineers left the trade completely while others turned to assistants' work. The F.I.A. was naturally perturbed about this encroachment into its job territory, particularly in the railway workshops where many skilled men accepted regression to less skilled jobs in order to retain their positions. The problem became sufficiently important in Melbourne for the District Com-

---

[41] *M.R.*, June 1932, p. 4.
[42] Ibid.
[43] *Tariff and Industrial Information*, 31/3/32.
[44] *M.R.*, February 1931, p. 6.
[45] *Metal Trades Journal*, 24/2/33. These figures only cover workers governed by metal trades awards. Employees such as carters, storemen and clerks are excluded.
[46] *M.R.*, October 1931, p. 4.

mittee to agree to temporarily clear members to the F.I.A. during the period they were so engaged.[47] Friction of this nature was not confined to the iron-workers and from 1928 onwards long-standing demarcation problems assumed a new significance and bitterness as competition increased between the unions for the few jobs available. In 1932 alone the A.E.U. was involved in major disputes with shipwrights over aeroplane construction, with electricians over electrical work on motor vehicles, with ironworkers over fitters' work, with plumbers over pipe-work, and with coach-makers over work on electric railway cars.[48] Perhaps the fiercest struggles were waged with the coach-makers, for the depression intensified the natural divisions arising between craft and industrial unions as each side fought to retain job control. As early as 1928 the coach-makers sought to break the three-year-old agreement under which the A.E.U. had the right to provide all engineering labour at Holdens. In ensuing years the industrial union sought to gain a monopolistic position in the motor-trade labour market by bringing pressure to bear on individual A.E.U. members to join its ranks. Further clashes arose over the coach-makers' acceptance in 1933 of South Australian employers' proposals for the abolition of the system of indenturing apprentices.

Relief work assisted many unemployed members and they gladly accepted labouring jobs. The A.E.U. however, was anxious that the governments should provide relief work specifically for skilled men and their helpers because these categories of workers were often passed over in favour of the unskilled who were rostered for the work. When the authorities complied with this request, the union remained determined to retain skilled award rates for the members concerned. Here the union's attachment to the arbitration system proved to be an advantage since the Victorian and New South Wales governments were unable to use their strong bargaining position to lower skilled wages unilaterally. To accomplish this they had instead to apply to the Arbitration Court for a suspension of the federal award and the A.E.U. was able to persuade Beeby to reject their applications.[49] A.E.U. members who retained jobs in private employment were similarly protected by the arbitration system and the ability of their union to finance breach of award

---

[47] 'M.D.C.M.', 5/11/30. No figures are available to measure the exact extent of such regressions in the railways. However, in 1936, long after the worst of the depression, in answer to a claim by the N.S.W. Minister for Labour and Industry that there was a shortage of skilled engineers, the A.E.U. ascertained that there were still 75 engineering tradesmen working as labourers in the State railways. They consisted of 66 fitters, three machinists, two pattern-makers, two coppersmiths, one brass-finisher and one blacksmith. *M.J.R.*, October 1936, p. 29.

[48] *M.R.*, March 1932, p. 3, April 1932, pp. 6, 13, July 1932, p. 22.

[49] 31 *C.A.R.* p. 626. See also *M.R.*, September 1932, p. 4; October 1932, p. 6.

cases before the tribunals.[50] Some employers were tempted to pay less than the official rate but this left them open to prosecution by the union and consequent fines and reimbursement of back pay, and the M.T.E.A. warned its members on several occasions that the advantages were not commensurate with the risks.[51]

V

Although the depression imposed unparalleled hardship on engineers its impact on the internal politics and machinery of the A.E.U. was relatively slight. The activities of a vociferous 'Militant Minority' group within the union failed to produce any swing of rank-and-file support towards the policies urged by the communists. The fact that members were by and large satisfied with the administration and official policies of their union was illustrated in the election of full-time A.E.U. officers. Between 1928 and 1934 sitting members of the five-men Commonwealth Council stood for re-election thirteen times. Only once was one defeated (Pickard) and this occurred in March 1928 before the depression had assumed any alarming proportions. The eight organisers' positions were each balloted for three times in the same period but only two of them changed hand. L. J. Louis, however, argues that in Melbourne the A.E.U. was generally unsympathetic towards unemployed rank-and-file members.[52] As Louis himself points out, the A.E.U. was one of the few organisations which made provision for the retention of unemployed members within the union. Hence it might be expected that they would register their protests against the unsympathetic attitude of local officials in union ballots where their effect would have been considerable in view of the usual very low voting rate. In fact the three full-time A.E.U. officers in Victoria retained their positions quite comfortably in average polls throughout the depression. Further, upon the death in 1930 of Scoffin, the Victorian representative on the Commonwealth Council, he was replaced by J. A. Cranwell, the long-serving President of the Melbourne District Committee. Secondly, Louis does not mention in this context the financial aid extended to unemployed A.E.U. members. This aid, outlined below, was at its highest level in the period to which he refers, i.e. June—September 1930. Thirdly, the members of the district committee were, with the exception of the secretary, themselves working engineers who, as

---

[50] Members of the financially weak F.I.A. were not so fortunate. J. A. Merritt, 'The Federated Ironworkers' Association in the Depression', unpublished paper, Australian National University, January 1969.

[51] E.g. *Metal Trades Journal*, 31/5/34.

[52] Op. cit., pp. 158—9.

already indicated, were often the first to lose their jobs. Finally, the fact that supervision of unemployed members' activities was warranted is illustrated by the fact that in March 1931 a number of desperate out-of-work A.E.U. men decided to offer their services to the Victorian Premier, 'in return for food, clothing and shelter'. The district committee was able to prevent the implementation of this threat which was rightly regarded as 'the very antithesis of the principles of this Union'.[53]

One important factor underlying the A.E.U.'s internal stability was the extensive benefits system. Since no system of state-sponsored unemployment insurance existed outside Queensland during the depression, 'Donation' (out of work) benefits, benevolent grants and assistance from the branches' 'Local Purposes' levies were of crucial importance to A.E.U. members. So long as the payments were continued, the rank and file remained satisfied with the administration of their union's affairs. Criticism of the Commonwealth Council was only voiced when it was forced to ease the pressure on A.E.U. financial resources by a reduction in benefit and an increase in contributions.

The union entered the depression with what appeared to be ample funds. In May 1928 when Australian unemployment was still relatively low the Commonwealth Council sent £25,000 to assist the British Section which had experienced high unemployment throughout the 1920s. In September of the same year the Australian A.E.U. held over £98,000 in liquid assets alone. Over the ensuring months, however, payments to out-of-work members soared to unprecedented levels and, with the particular difficulty of older men obtaining jobs, so too did payment to the growing numbers claiming superannuation benefit. On the other side of the balance sheet, union income fell steadily because of declining total membership, the increase in the number of unemployed members exempt from the payment of fees, and generally growing *per capita* arrears. Financial economies were introduced in 1930 including the suspension of mortgage loans to members and cuts in grants to A.L.P. election funds. In November 1930 the Commonwealth Council was forced to request the British Executive Council for £20,000 which was remitted in four instalments of £5,000 — but the steady drain of funds continued. In April 1931 *net* expenditure was estimated to be over £1,200 per week[54] and the prospects of further assistance from London were slight because of the concurrent payment of benefits to over 50,000 unemployed British A.E.U. members. As a result, in May 1931 donation

[53] *M.R.*, April 1931, p. 11.
[54] *M.R.*, April 1931, p. 4.

benefit was reduced — for the first time in the history of the Austrialian A.E.U. — to a level which had been operating in Britain since April 1928. Officers' salaries were reduced and other administrative economies effected. Further, in accordance with Executive Council instructions, contributions were charged to members in receipt of donation, sick and superannuation benefits. Unsuccessful approaches were simultaneously made to the Scullin Government for a loan and to the New South Wales Lang Ministry for £100 per week from the unemployed relief funds.

The outflow of funds continued and in September 1931 the London office directed that the lowest scale of sickness and donation benefit be suspended and the weekly contributions of all membership sections be increased. Such drastic measures, particularly the rise in contributions, aroused protests within the union and the number of resignations rose alarmingly. By December the Commonwealth Council was sufficiently concerned to send urgent cables to A.E.U. headquarters requesting a retraction of the unpopular decision on contributions and London immediately acceded. Fortunately, during the second half of 1932, unemployment began to fall for the first time and the A.E.U. was able to see out the rest of the depression without having to tamper any further with benefits.

The A.E.U.'s maintenance — even at a greatly reduced level — of both statutory benefits to members of the benefit sections and benevolent grants and assistance from branch levies to all members was an achievement which was probably not equalled by any other union.[55] Between 1926 and 1932 the union handed out approximately £360,000 and, small though the individual payments were,[56] they represented an important lifeline for the unemployed

---

[55] Evidence of the benefit situation in other unions is scanty. Of the few that made provision for unemployment payments in their rules, the financial burden appears to have proved too great during the depression. As early as August 1930 only six Victorian unions (including the A.E.U.) were still paying unemployment benefits — Louis, op. cit., p. 156. In the wealthy printers' union only the N.S.W. branch was able to continue operating an unemployment fund throughout the 'thirties — Hagan, op. cit., p. 244.

[56] The scale of donation benefit varied between different benefit membership sections and according to length of membership. The maximum scale originally amounted to 10s. per week for 14 weeks and 6s. per week thereafter. In May 1931 it was reduced to 7s. for 14 weeks and then 4s. for 90 weeks. After the abolition of the lower scale of benefits in September 1931 members were entitled to 7s. for 14 weeks only. Benevolent grants amounting to 30 or 40s. were made at irregular intervals but after March 1931 a minimum period of twelve weeks had to elapse between grants to any one member. Unfortunately no estimate can be made of the scale and frequency of payments from individual branches' Local Purposes Funds since they did not enter into the general accounts of the union nor were they recorded in the surviving branch minute books of the period.

and promised some insurance for working A.E.U. members always fearful for their jobs.

Although A.E.U. members remained satisfied with their federal leaders, the Council's attitudes altered during the depression and an important new personality appeared on the scene. Scoffin's replacement, 'Joe' Cranwell, was to remain on the Council for 23 years and prove possibly the best, and certainly the most respected, leader the A.E.U. ever had. Cranwell, an Australian who had worked in Britain under the wartime munitions scheme, truly put the A.E.U. 'First, last and always', and the key to his character was that in pursuit of gains for A.E.U. members he was never inflexible. Although usually taking a stand to the left of centre he subscribed to no fixed creed. Each different situation was carefully weighed from the viewpoint of what would best serve the A.E.U. This pragmatic approach occasionally meant that after hearing all sides of the case Cranwell changed an earlier tentative judgment, thus angering colleagues of more inflexible nature. During his career he bruised many corns within the labour movement but his integrity was undisputed. From the first time he took his seat on the Council he took the leading role in the formulation of a more definite and aggressive federal policy.

Cranwell's lead was supported by Potter and by Pickard's successor, W. C. Long, a scholarly man who as a boy had distributed pamphlets for the infant Independent Labour Party in his home town of Bradford, England. Cranwell's vigour, and the disillusionment and bitterness engendered by the depression, had the effect of moving Evernden towards the acceptance of more radical ideas during his last years in office. When Evernden reached retiring age in 1934, Cranwell was elected Chairman by a two to one majority over his nearest opponent. The depression proved to most engineers' satisfaction that there was no substitute for ultimate reliance on industrial strength. With the A.E.U.'s bargaining power reduced to zero, members had witnessed the inability of Labor governments to aid workers during the emergency, while the arbitration tribunals had revealed their disregard for hitherto sacrosanct precedents. As the economy recovered the new leadership was to efficiently co-ordinate A.E.U. activities towards the betterment of members' conditions of employment. When the retention of the federal award became an obstacle to the attainment of this end the Council seemed prepared to abandon arbitration completely.

5

Counter-offensive

From 1934 the Australian economy recovered rapidly and by 1935–6 manufacturing employment had passed the previous peak level of 1926–7. The proportion of A.E.U. members out of work fell to 7 per cent in 1935, and 3 per cent in 1938. The fall in total membership of the union was halted in 1933, and by 1937 there were 28,000 on the roll. As it drove to take advantage of the economic upturn, only one factor marred the A.E.U.'s unity. This was an internal controversy, in 1936–7, in New South Wales, which initially arose over a political issue and which eventually demonstrated in the clearest fashion the checks to executive authority provided by the A.E.U.'s constitution.

During the years of economic recovery the labour movement sought to repair the damage to the A.L.P. caused by the party splits of the depression period. The Lang-Labor Party and federal A.L.P. were officially re-united in 1936, but within the New South Wales party the faction fighting continued until Lang's grip on the state machine was finally broken in 1939.[1] A.E.U. federal leaders urged the cause of party unity at every opportunity and heartily applauded the 1936 federal settlement.[2] This desire for amity within the A.L.P. led the Commonwealth Council into direct collision with those left wing members of the Sydney district who were determined at all costs to rid the state party of 'dictator' Lang.

In mid-1936 the anti-Lang N.S.W. Labour Council convened a conference of unions affiliated to the A.L.P. to initiate moves to reform the N.S.W.

---

[1] For details see L. F. Crisp, *Ben Chifley* (London, 1960), pp. 86–108; R. Cooksey, *Lang and Socialism* (Canberra, 1971); D. W. Rawson, 'The Organisation of the Australian Labor Party, 1916–1941'. Ph.D. Thesis, Melbourne University, 1954, pp. 277–315.

[2] *M.R.*, November 1934, p. 8. *M.J.R.*, February 1935, p. 4, November 1935, p. 7, March 1936, p. 6.

party. The state A.L.P. executive retaliated by banning the meeting and threatening unions concerned with disaffiliation if they were represented at it. In view of this, and desiring an end to faction fighting, the Commonwealth Council informed the Sydney District Committee that no A.E.U. delegates were to be sent to the conference. By six votes to five the Committee decided to disobey this instruction. The Council had been united thus far, but it divided when it actually came to implementing the threatened expulsion of H. Fountain, R. Miller and E. Bradshaw, the members who attended the conference. The majority of Cranwell, Long and G. W. Deverall, the Division 1 representative since Cranwell became Chairman, insisted that the Council's prestige and credibility were at stake. The minority of Potter and Wickham unsuccessfully argued in favour of compromise.[3] In response to many branch protests the Council majority made the error of setting out its views in a circular which attempted to paint those expelled as members of the C.P.A. This brought an immediate reaction from the three ex-members and, faced with the threat of legal action for defamation of character, the Council was forced to withdraw the allegations.[4]

Both sides in the dispute turned for support to London and in February 1937 the Executive Council decided in favour of the Commonwealth Council.[5] The three Sydney members then lodged an appeal to the Final Appeal Court, but by this time the controversy had become sufficiently embarrassing to the Commonwealth Council for it to settle for a compromise whereby the three were reinstated in June 1937, on condition that they withdrew their appeal and undertook to abide by Council's interpretation of rules. Ironically, in the succeeding two years the Council came fully to support the principles which had motivated the District Committee in its original act of defiance. In 1938 and 1939 the A.E.U. threw its weight on the side of the 'industrialist' movement which eventually overcame Lang with Chairman Cranwell becoming, as a result, President of the New South Wales A.L.P. and a member of the A.L.P. Federal Executive. But at the time when the rebel members rejoined the union the actual cause of their expulsion had been almost forgotten in the face of developments in the intervening period.

A 'Re-instatement Committee' had been formed at an early date to

---

[3] 'C.C.M.', 4/9/36. Only the Councilmen formally voted on the issue but Cranwell and Wickham later took the unusual step of recording their views in the minutes. ('C.C.M.', 2/10/36).
[4] 'C.C.M.', 20/10/36, 27/10/36.
[5] 'C.C.M.', 9/2/37.

campaign on behalf of the three expellees and, in 1937, it had contravened A.E.U. election rules by issuing a pamphlet vigorously attacking Long and urging support for candidates A. T. Douglas and G. Walker in the election in Division 2 (Sydney and Newcastle). In the ballot Douglas topped the poll with Long runner-up. The Council then fined the signatory of the pamphlet, disqualified both Douglas and Walker and unanimously declared Long re-elected.[6] A candidate in the Division 1 election was also disqualified because an illicit typewritten circular had been distributed on his behalf. Because he finished second in the ballot, this decision made no difference to the return to office of the winner, Deverall. The dissatisfaction of the branches centred on the voting in Division 2. While the Council was correct in invalidating Douglas' candidature it was generally held that his preferences — and those of Walker — should have been re-allotted.

Once again branches registered strong protests and appeals were forwarded to London. The communist newspaper, *Workers' Weekly*,[7] carried an article accusing the A.E.U. federal leaders of manipulating the election and the Council took legal action on the grounds of libel. The case was dismissed. Several branches then added to the Council's discomfiture by challenging its right to use the union's funds for its litigation, but the Final Appeal Court eventually dismissed their appeals. Objections to the non-distribution of preference votes met with more success and the Final Appeal Court ruled that a fresh election must be held in Division 2. In deference to the now re-instated Fountain, in whose cause the anti-Council campaign had been originally mounted, Douglas did not stand. In the new ballot in December 1939 Fountain secured three quarters of Walker's preferences and defeated Long by 972 votes to 862.[8]

When expelling the three rebellious members of the Sydney District Committee, the Council had at least acted in accordance to rule — albeit strictly. In the election controversy however, the council allowed its irritation with the dissidents to override its duty to ensure democratic and impartial administration of the rules. The union's balancing machinery, whereby members' grievances were heard as a last resort by rank and file representatives in the Final Appeal Court, ensured the eventual failure of the federal executive's misuse of its powers.

---

[6] 'C.C.M.', 14/4/37, 28/4/37. Naturally Long himself 'did not exercise voice or vote' in this decision.

[7] 11/5/37.

[8] *M.J.R.*, June 1938, pp. 16–9, February 1939, p. 26, September 1939, p. 8; 'C.C.M.', 6/10/38.

II

The industrial labour movement was in a generally bitter mood as it re-assembled its shattered forces and began the attempt to restore real wages and working conditions to pre-depression levels. Success in individual sectors depended on bargaining strength — and, just as in the 1920s, the unskilled, faced with much higher rates of unemployment, lagged far behind the van. A major aim of labour was to regain the Harvester equivalent for Basic Wage earners. The 1933 adjustment and the 'fresh start' of 1934 together restored about 60 per cent of the original cut. Eventually, in 1937, the Full Court made up the discrepancy by granting an increase averaging 5s. per week through-out the Commonwealth. The Bench did not, however, return to the old principle of wage fixation. While the 'needs' wage as fixed in 1934 remained adjustable in response to price movements, the 1937 addition represented a fixed 'prosperity loading' which it was visualised might be removed in any future economic recession.[9]

Union demands for a general reduction in working hours to forty per week or less remained insistent. They were spurred on when the federal govern-ment representative, Sir Frederick Stewart, voted in favour of a 40 hour week at the 1935 Geneva Convention of the International Labor Office. Stewart, on his return to federal Parliament, became an advocate of a shorter week but his party leader, Lyons, refused to ratify the convention. Instead the Prime Minister referred the unions to the Arbitration Court as the only medium through which their goal might be attained. The court proved willing to extend the 44 hour week to practically all industries under its jurisdiction but halted short of the further reduction.

The A.E.U. remained the prime agitator for the 40 hour week, and discus-sion of the issue was seldom absent from the pages of its journal. At times other unions differed with the A.E.U. on the order of priority of the hours and wages campaigns. In 1936 a special conference of federal unions decided, against A.E.U. protests, to concentrate on the full restoration of the 1931 wage cuts. Immediately after the 1937 Basic Wage re-adjustment, however, the shorter week was restored to pride of place. With evident satisfaction A.E.U. leaders described the special All-Australian Trades Union Congress at which this decision was made as '. . . one of the best that has taken place.'[10] Yet, despite the importance which the union attached to the campaign, and

---

[9] 37 *C.A.R.* 583.
[10] *M.J.R.*, August 1937, p. 7.

despite some successful local agreements on hours,[11] engineers were not to enjoy a general 40 hour week for another ten years.

The A.E.U.'s outlook on foreign affairs moved in step with the gradual shifts in official Labor policy.[12] In 1935 the Commonwealth Council denounced the use of economic sanctions against Mussolini's Abyssinian adventure on the grounds that they were likely to lead to war.[13] Two years later, however, the A.E.U. was party to resolutions of a Special All-Australian Trade Union Congress which, although opposing re-armament, supported the nebulous concept of 'collective security and mutual assistance' through the by now sadly discredited League of Nations.[14] By March 1939 the threat posed by the Axis powers was viewed rather more realistically. In that month the A.E.U. approved of Congress decisions which criticised policies of 'appeasement' and the failure of the Lyons government 'to request the British Government to stand firm against the demands of the aggressor nations.[15]

Although this Congress advocated rationalisation of the current defence programme, the labour movement remained opposed to compulsory national service. During 1939 the unions campaigned vigorously against the federal government's plans to create a National Register of Manpower which they feared could be used for the purpose of industrial or military conscription.[16] It was not until the very eve of war that Prime Minister R. G. Menzies, greatly aided by A.L.P. leader John Curtin, was able to assuage the unions' fears and secure the lifting of the current boycott of the Register.[17]

However, the A.E.U.'s main interest in the defence issue lay in its concern that increased arms production might bring in its train dilution of skill. World War I struggles over dilution were recalled, and the A.E.U. geared its organisation towards resistance of any proposals for a relaxation of qualifications for entry into the skilled labour market. In these circumstances the Arbitration Court's attitude to the apprenticeship system assumed additional importance. During the years between depression and war the problem of

[11] See e.g. *M.J.R.*, September 1936, p. 3, August 1937, p. 6.
[12] For details see E. Andrews, 'Australian Labour and Foreign Policy 1935–1939' in *Labour History*, 9, 1965, pp. 22–32.
[13] 'C.C.M.', 27/9/35.
[14] *M.J.R.*, August 1937, pp. 3–4.
[15] *M.J.R.*, May 1939, pp. 2–4.
[16] See e.g. *Statement by Executive of the A.C.T.U. re. National Registration Act, Supply and Development Act, and Amended Defence Act*. Pamphlet. A.C.T.U. 1939; *M.J.R.*, July 1939, pp. 2–3, 7, August 1939, pp. 2–3.
[17] G. Sawer, *Australian Federal Politics and Law 1929–1949* (Melbourne, 1963), p. 111; *M.J.R.*, September 1939, pp. 2–6.

junior and apprentice labour was one of the two major contentious issues in the metal industries. The other centred on the right of the A.E.U. to resort to direct action while operating within the federal arbitration system.

III

In his first Metal Trades judgment Beeby had given an indication that his views on the criteria upon which the level of skilled engineering rates should be based, differed from those which the court had followed under Powers' presidency. He had declared in 1930, 'If the industry since 1926 had displayed the buoyancy which characterized it during the preceding years, I would not have hesitated to increase margins in some directions in order to restore the ratio of allowance for skill of pre-war days.'[18] This apparent acceptance of the Higgins principle had drawn little attention because of the controversies over reclassification and concern with increasing unemployment. In the more prosperous conditions of 1935 Beeby revealed his opinion more clearly. He saw the central wages problem as being 'Whether under present circumstances there should be a *long delayed* increase in the margins of skilled tradesmen . . .'[19] [My italics]. The answer was to be based not on the overall condition of the economy but solely on the profitability of the metal industry. Although the members of the arbitration bench must take common action with regard to the Basic Wage, Beeby considered that,

In dealing with margins and general conditions of labour, awards cannot be standardized. The nature of the work done, the financial position of the industry, the extent to which the industry is protected from overseas competition and many other matters must be considered.[20]

Metal producers now enjoyed increasing demand for their products and foreign competition had been severely restricted by greater tariff protection. Yet while the demand for skilled labour was rapidly rising, the absolute number of tradesmen available for employment had decreased since 1930 because of the almost complete suspension of apprenticeship during the depression. Estimating that the industry's wage cost, insofar as it was controlled by the court, was 22 per cent lower than in 1929, Beeby considered that a 3s. increase in craftsmen's margins from 24s. to 27s. per week was fully justified since it would add only $1\frac{1}{2}$ per cent to the total wage-bill. However, he was not prepared to extend the pay rise to other than skilled occupations. Thus in the engineering section of the award, while tradesmen and

[18] 28 *C.A.R.* 923 at p. 967.
[19] 34 *C.A.R.* 449 at p. 454.
[20] loc. cit.

'Second Class' machinists received an extra 3s. and 2s. per week respectively, the rates of motor mechanics, 'Third Class' machinists, process workers, and other semi-skilled employees remained unaltered.

The marked fall in prices during the depression had meant that those tradesmen fortunate enough to retain their jobs had enjoyed an increase in the real value of their margins. In 1927, for example, the fitter's award rate was 28 per cent higher than an unskilled labourer. By 1932, with the Basic Wage following prices downwards, the differential had widened to 34 per cent. Beeby's 1935 decision meant an increase to 41 per cent which compared well with the Harvester ratio of 43 per cent.

The reversal of the precedents of the Powers era is even more significant when it is realised that this wage rise was granted before the bargaining power of the majority of metal tradesmen could secure any comparable increase by direct negotiations with their employers. Most engineers, for example, had not as yet begun to regain pre-depression over-award payments. By 1935 average A.E.U. unemployment through lack of work had fallen to 7 per cent of total membership, but it was still higher than in any year from 1905 to 1929 inclusive. In these circumstances the Commonwealth Council jubilantly described the wage increase as 'the greatest benefit secured from the Court by our Advocate in return for many well prepared and presented cases over a number of years'.[21]

The metal unions were able to secure an extension of the Beeby rates to members employed in the railways, automobile, and agricultural-implement industries. However, Judge Drake-Brockman, who now handled all railway cases, was less convinced than Beeby that the increases were warranted. The margins of tradesmen working in the New South Wales railways were traditionally higher than those applying to the general engineering industry. In 1935 a railway fitter received a 30s. margin, but it was only after urgent A.E.U. advocacy that Drake-Brockman was persuaded not to reduce the rate to the 27s. granted in the Beeby award. Even so his decisions concerning the classification of certain first class machinists, overtime rates, rest periods and travelling time aroused discontent among New South Wales railway workers.[22]

The 1935 Beeby award incorporated two other concessions to the unions. The first gave their officials the right under certain conditions to enter workshops at mealtimes. The second, and more important, gain was that the respondent employers in New South Wales, Victoria and Tasmania agreed

[21] *M.J.R.*, June 1935, p. 5.
[22] *M.J.R.*, July 1935, p. 3, August 1935, p. 3.

to be bound to the award in respect to all employees-including non-unionists. The employers did so because they preferred non-unionists to be covered by the federal award with its favourable classification provisions rather than by state awards which would otherwise apply as the common rule. In South Australia, however, there was no state award currently operating and metal employers there refused to be so joined to the Beeby award. The judge therefore referred the question to the High Court. In its decision in the *Metal Trades Employers' Case*,[23] the High Court went far towards establishing the principle of a federal common rule by affirming the power of the Commonwealth to make awards in respect to non-unionist employees.

Beeby's award was less favourable to the unions in its provisions for junior and apprentice labour. During the worst of the depression, the Full Court had permitted 'rationing' of apprentices as well as adults,[24] but the M.T.E.A.'s attempts to use 'unapprenticed learners' in New South Wales was nullified by A.E.U. litigation. The M.T.E.A. had originally been able to bypass the federal court on the learners' question[25] because most apprentices were not members of unions and hence did not come under the federal award. In March 1935, however, the A.E.U. secured a High Court decision which prohibited learners in any industry governed by a federal award.

The High Court judgment was issued while Beeby was still hearing arguments in the Metal Trades Case. After considering the employers' pleas he reversed the Full Court's 1932 decision not to allow learners[26] on the grounds that the depression had severely curtailed the training of new tradesmen and that the indenture system 'with its flavour of "master and servant" [was] inappropriate to modern youth'.[27] Hence he made provision for the simultaneous operation of the indenture and learner systems in New South Wales where the latter could be supervised by the state Apprenticeship Commission. He further indicated that the award would be similarly varied in other states as soon as they established the necessary regulatory bodies. In the meantime employers could, with the consent of the Industrial Registrar or state Apprenticeship Commissioner, employ a greater proportion of apprentices than set out in the award.

Beeby also rejected union arguments that employers were exploiting the 1930 award by replacing adult with junior labour. He therefore refused either to set fixed proportions between adults and juniors or to fix the wages of the

---

[23] 54 *C.L.R.* 387
[24] 32 *C.A.R.* 258.
[25] Above, p. 109.
[26] Above, p. 109.
[27] 34 *C.A.R.* 449 at p. 459.

latter according to age instead of experience. Beeby's only concession was to increase juniors' wage rates for their first two years of employment in order to reduce the high labour turnover due to dismissal of lads who were about to qualify for higher wages.[28] The judge felt that older youths should have every chance to enter the industry for it was, 'necessary to keep every possible avenue of employment open to these victims of the depression'.[29] Such sympathy for the school-leavers of 1930–4 was to become wide-spread among the Australian public during the remainder of the decade and employers were to find it a convenient lever.

In one important direction, Beeby indicated that his views were moving closer to those of the skilled unions. Referring to the difficulty in devising a wage schedule which would result in juniors retaining their jobs into adulthood he admitted,

In 1930 I thought that the adoption of piecework rates might have this result. But now it is evident that, where output is not regulated by the dexterity of the operative, but by the machine, piece-work may not be an appropriate system of payment.[30]

These doubts in the efficacy of payment by results contrast with the views set out in his earlier judgments and after this date the court refrained from attempting to force the skilled metal unions to accept payment by results.

Struggles over apprentice and junior labour continued. Faced with a disturbing rise in the numbers of junior workers and a mushrooming of 'Youth Occupation Committees' attempting to find work for unemployed youths, the A.E.U. decided in 1934 to organise the young process-workers.[31] In 1925 the union had considered enrolling juniors employed at a large-scale Sydney firm, but decided '. . . that no advantage would be gained by admitting them; in fact it would in all probability act detrimental [sic] to the interests of our members'.[32] Ten years later the situation had radically altered. The 1935 Interstate Conference, meeting to consider Beeby's award, decided a national organising campaign among junior workers was urgently needed '. . . not only in the interests of the process workers, but also for the

[28] For evidence of the high turnover of junior workers see 'Report of the Select Committee of the Legislative Assembly upon the Employment of Youth in Industry', *N.S.W.P.P. 1940–41*, Vol. I, pp. 347–9; *Our Jobs*, Pamphlet n.d. (1940?), Victorian Youth Parliament, Melbourne.

[29] 34 *C.A.R.* 449 at p. 461.

[30] Ibid., at p. 462.

[31] *M.R.*, March 1934, p. 17; 'C.C.M.', 5/6/34. No statistics are available to measure the influx of junior workers but some indication of their increasing numbers is provided by the fact that the proportion of metal workers aged less than 16 years rose from 2.3 per cent in 1931–2 to 4.2 per cent by June 1939. *Production Bulletin*, Nos. 26–33.

[32] Organiser E. C. Madden, *M.R.*, February 1925, p. 20.

protection of higher classifications'.[33] The F.I.A. had taken advantage of the initial lack of interest of the A.E.U. and other craft unions and had been attempting to organise juniors since 1929.[34] However, no jurisdictional disputes arose on the issue, and the A.E.U. seemed prepared to allow the unskilled union to continue enrolling juniors in those shops in which it had already established a foothold. Better organisation aided juniors to obtain improved working conditions but the threat to adults of displacement remained. John Danks & Sons, Melbourne, employed in 1929 approximately 100 journeymen and 25 juniors. By 1936 the proportions had roughly been reversed and it was claimed by the local A.E.U. organiser that the position in most other brass and nickelware firms had altered similarly.[35] Only the growing tightness in the skilled labour market prevented the accelerating influx of juniors from creating serious competition for work between them and engineering craftsmen.

Rising demand for skilled metal workers, in combination with the expansion of defence industries, prompted the federal government in 1938 to formulate a scheme to assist youths of all ages and in every state to obtain technical school training in a number of crafts. When they were classified as being 40 per cent efficient at their chosen trades, they would enter industry where their wages would be subsidised until they reached 100 per cent efficiency. The Victorian Government was tempted to take up the offer of a Commonwealth subsidy despite union opposition, but the scheme had barely got under way before the outbreak of war.

The New South Wales Government, on the other hand, had long been operating its own trainee scheme. Early in 1938 it applied for a 12 month variation of the federal Metal Trades Award to allow the appointment of apprentices between the ages of 19 and 25 who were to be given four years training.[36] The wage rates fixed under the scheme were lifted above apprentice award rates by government subsidy and employers' applications to take on these trainees were dealt with by the State Apprenticeship Council. On 2 March 1938 Beeby made the desired variation, largely on the grounds that the young men who would be able to take advantage of the scheme had missed their normal opportunity to be apprentices because of the depression.[37] In the following month the Full Court granted an application to

[33] *M.J.R.*, June 1935, p. 3.
[34] Merritt, 'A History of the F.I.A', Ch. 4.
[35] *M.J.R.*, March 1936, p. 9.
[36] *New South Wales Industrial Gazette*, 28 February 1938, p. 449.
[37] 39 C.A.R. 18.

extend the New South Wales Youth Employment Scheme to the timber, printing, coach-making, boot, and clothing trades.[38] Both the learner and trainee systems were abandoned by the court in 1941 in view of the current wartime dilution of skill by adults, but their joint impact is illustrated by the fact that in New South Wales, the state most affected, only 2,900 of a total of 11,100 new apprentices in all industries were engaged under indentures between 1934 and 1943.[39]

Almost simultaneously with his acceptance of the trainee project, Beeby suspended for one year the clause in the Metal Trade Award which fixed the proportion of journeymen to apprentices at 3 to 1.[40] Despite promptings from the M.T.E.A.,[41] employers had taken little advantage of the clause in the 1935 award which permitted firms to employ a greater proportion of apprentices if they could prove to Industrial Registrar or Apprenticeship Commissioner that they had exceptional facilities for training boys. Beeby considered that possibly they required a clearer direction. He therefore pronounced that, with the consent of Registrar or Commissioner, any employer could take on extra apprentices between March 1938 and March 1939 up to a proportion of one to every journeyman. After the expiry of this period apprentices so taken would not be counted in future calculations of proportions authorised by the award. Employers in all four southern states immediately made application to take advantage of this concession[42] but the threatening posture of the metal unions, together with the caution of the Registrars and Commissioners, restricted the inflow of apprentices during the twelve-month period. In April 1939, the M.T.E.A. applied for an extension of the privilege, arguing that at a time when defence industries were taking large numbers of craftsmen away from civilian production, only 159 extra apprentices had been taken on in New South Wales and 153 in Victoria. Beeby considered that his 1938 variation had accelerated the entry of youths into the industry ' . . . but not to the extent authorised by the amendment'.[43] He consequently ordered a six month extension in the trades of mechanical and electrical engineering, electrical fitting, and motor servicing and repair.

The outbreak of war was to throw an entirely different light on the problem of expanding the supply of skilled labour, but in the 1930s the court had

---

[38] 39 *C.A.R.* 220.
[39] *Metal Trades Journal*, 2/1/42.
[40] 39 *C.A.R.* 35.
[41] E.g. *Metal Trades Journal*, 30/10/36.
[42] *Metal Trades Journal*, 4/4/38; *M.J.R.*, May 1938, p. 4, June 1938, p. 4, July 1938, p. 22.
[43] 40 *C.A.R.* 161 at p. 162.

shown itself determined at least to loosen the unions' control on entry to the various trades. Beeby had attempted to imprint his ideas on the metal industry ever since his first award in 1927 but, even as he was putting the finishing touches to his 1938 and 1939 variations, he was involved in a struggle of wills with the A.E.U. which ended the dominant role recently played by the court in the metal trades.

IV

The head-on collision between judge and union came as the culmination of the A.E.U.'s post-depression campaign to restore over-award payments to its members. As soon as unemployment figures began to subside the various District Committees sought to commence negotiations with local employers for an improvement in wages. The degree of success varied from the 1/6d. per week secured from the Hobart City Council in September 1934,[44] to the 39/6d. obtained from the traditionally high-wage paying Melbourne news-paper proprietors in January 1935.[45] By June 1936 the Engineering Section of the Melbourne Chambers of Manufactures, faced with a demand for an all-round 15s. per week increase, expressed the opinion that 45 per cent of A.E.U. members in the district were in receipt of over-award payments.[46] Later in the same year the manager of Ford's automobile plant, Geelong, pointed out that the firm was paying 48 per cent of its employees from 4s. to 39s. per week in excess of the award minimum.[47] The Melbourne District Committee, how-ever, continued its agitation for the all round increase and, in November 1936, organiser N. Roberts was able to report that 22 firms had complied.[48] Members were constantly urged to take advantage of the increasing shortage of skilled labour and to negotiate their own wage increases directly with their employers.[49] For the remainder of the decade disputes and stoppages flared sporadically as A.E.U. members continued their wages counter-offensive.

The pace was originally slowest in New South Wales because unemployment there took longer to fall than elsewhere. The time lag in the state's recovery is illustrated in the following table.

[44] *M.J.R.*, October 1934, p. 16.
[45] *M.J.R.*, February 1935, p. 17.
[46] *M.J.R.*, June 1936, p. 3.
[47] *M.J.R.*, December 1936, p. 22.
[48] *M.J.R.*, November 1936, p. 16.
[49] See e.g. *M.J.R.*, June 1937, pp. 22–3.

Table 5.1: Percentage of A.E.U. Members Out of Work in June, 1933–9

Year	Victoria	New South Wales	Commonwealth
1933	13.5	24.1	20.2
1934	8.8	20.0	14.5
1935	3.5	11.1	7.0
1936	1.6	5.4	4.2
1937	1.8	2.9	2.6
1938	1.4	2.7	2.4
1939	2.0	4.4	3.3

Sources: *Monthly Report*, July 1933–4 inclusive. *Monthly Journal and Report*, July 1935–9 inclusive.

Note: Because of the inclusion by the A.E.U. of the last available return from branches failing to report in June these percentages over-estimate the true level of unemployment in this period of increasing prosperity. However, since the bias is likely to be roughly the same in both states, the table gives a fair indication of the differing rates of recovery.

As early as August 1933, when there were still over 1,300 A.E.U. members unemployed in the Sydney area, the District Committee asked the employers to meet the union in conference to discuss wage increases. The existing over-supply of labour made it easy for the employers to refuse. Faced with un-employment rates higher than the national average the Sydney district officials devoted their major efforts in 1935 to the curtailment of what they considered to be excessive overtime. Although the numbers out of work fell substantially during 1936, the District Committee in August placed an embargo on all overtime worked above four hours per week. Ship repairs and essential maintenance work were exempted from the ban. The immediate consequence was the convening of a compulsory conference by Chief Judge Dethridge who varied the award in the union's favour by ruling that no over-time was to be worked where shift work or additional employment was feasible.[50] By the end of 1936, this had had the desired effects, particularly in the direction of assisting the casual engineering workers commonly em-ployed on ship-repair work. With unemployment rates falling to levels closer to pre-depression years, the Sydney officials were now able to devote their energies to securing higher wages for working members.

The tactics of the District Committee were identical to those successfully pursued in the 1918–20 over-award campaign.[51] An overtime-embargo,

[50] 36 *C.A.R.* 477.
[51] Sheridan, 'A History of the A.E.U.', pp. 223–6.

although on this occasion originally applied for the purpose of work-spreading, came to fulfil the role of exerting pressure on employers enjoying a brisk demand for their products. Once again the union concentrated first on the waterfront firms whose ship-repair work was in a sense 'perishable' and thus most susceptible to threats of stoppages. After some months of fruitless negotiations the waterfront employers informed the union in January 1937 that the question of general wage rises was one which the Arbitration Court alone could settle. A stop-work meeting of members decided to accept Beeby's offer to deal with the matter. The judge's initial proposal proved unacceptable, but a stoppage of work was called off after one week in order that the A.E.U. could be represented at the hearing of the metal unions' arguments for a general variation of the 1935 award.

The main aim was to secure an extension of the 1935 margins increases to semi-skilled workers but the unions' log also called for an all-round increase of 13s. per week and a general improvement of working conditions. In his judgment Beeby made even clearer the degree to which he diverged from the principles of margins fixation adopted by Powers. He began by declaring 'I have never acceded to the contention that the 1921 award made by Mr Justice Higgins was an extravagant over-valuation of the relative value of the work of skilled and unskilled workmen.[52] In summing up the arguments presented by the two sides he indicated the criteria upon which, in his view, the level of margins should be based,

A great deal of evidence was tendered to prove that the general economic recovery of the Commonwealth during the past two years has been sufficient to justify reconsideration of wage rates and conditions of employment on their merits. Such evidence, however, is more appropriate to a basic wage inquiry and has not been considered in coming to a decision on the matters now before the Court. I confined my attention to the evidence as to this particular group of industries.[53]

Beeby justified this by explaining,

I have never agreed that margins for skill should be uniform in all occupations ... My decision in this group of industries is not therefore to be taken as an opinion that margins in all industries should be similarly assessed. I have always regarded skilled mechanics engaged in metal manufacture and in the generation and supply of electric light, heat and power as entitled to somewhat higher margins than those working in wood and other fabrics.[54]

Because of the rising demand for skill and the fact that many employers —

[52] 37 *C.A.R.* 176 at p. 179.
[53] Ibid., at p. 182.
[54] Ibid., at p. 183.

particularly in the moulding section — were paying over the award, the judge increased tradesmen's rates by a further 3s. per week and added the same amount to all other metal margins. This meant that the Harvester ratio between skilled and unskilled rates was completely restored.

The 1935 increase had soon been extended by the court to most other non-metal tradesmen who had followed precedent by citing the comparability of their skills to that of a fitter.[55] However, the important non-metal craft unions were slower to act after the 1937 adjustment. The powerful printing union, for example, did not apply until 1941 for a restoration of the pre-1937 relativities between the pay of its members and that of metal workers.[56] The intervention of war, its accompanying effects on the attitude of the court towards wage fixation, and the marked rise in the importance of metal skills in the war economy, meant that the earlier inter-industry relation between margins for various skills was not restored until 1947.

Beeby's award did not, however, satisfy Sydney A.E.U. members. On the contentious issue of ship-repair work the judge steered a middle course. He recognised that this section of the engineering industry enjoyed 'natural' protection from foreign competition and hence the waterfront firms could afford to compensate their employees for the more arduous nature of their work. The judge did not, however, believe that the difference between shipping and general engineering work merited the 8/6d. extra weekly payment which the unions were claiming. Instead he set the amount at 3s.

A.E.U. waterfront members were far from satisfied. Organiser J. Leary reported that, 'Immediately the members were advised of the terms of Judge Beeby's Award they were astounded at the inadequate increases granted.[57] A strike began immediately but after four days the engineers returned to work on condition that wages negotiations should at once be commenced. Conferences between the parties were held intermittently over the next three months. In the background the workers vented their discontent at mass meetings and demonstrations which included a march of 1,400 A.E.U. members on the Sydney Town Hall. Eventually, on 25 May, the waterfront employers agreed to pay 3s. per week over the award rate to all employees provided the A.E.U. lifted the current total embargo on overtime.[58]

The union immediately followed up its success and on 15 June the M.T.E.A. agreed to pay a general over-award payment of 3s. per week to all

[55] See e.g. the carpenters' (36 *C.A.R.* 324) and printers' (36 *C.A.R.* 738) cases.
[56] Hagan, op. cit., p. 271.
[57] *M.J.R.*, March 1937, p. 17.
[58] *M.J.R.*, April 1937, p. 19, June 1937, pp. 2, 21.

A.E.U. members in the Sydney district. The 1918–20 pattern had been reproduced in full and the Sydney precedent could now be used elsewhere. Negotiations began immediately in the Newcastle, Wollongong and Port Kembla districts and a mass meeting of South Coast members decided to prohibit all overtime. The numbers of New South Wales firms paying the extra 3s. rose during the remainder of the year but further disputes on the waterfront gave some general engineering employers the opportunity to withhold the increase[59].

On 20 August 1937 Beeby shocked the engineering unions by exempting the large ship-repair plants of Mort's Dock and Cockatoo Island from the payment of the extra *award* 3s. for work done on shore at these establishments.[60] The two firms had asked for this interpretation because the managements felt that the repair work performed on shore was no different from the work which engineers were expected to do in the general engineering branches of the industry and to which the extra shipping rate did not apply. The reaction of A.E.U. members was swift. As soon as it became obvious that the employers were determined to pay only the general engineering rate for shore work, 200 members ceased work, supported by members of the A.S.E. Within 10 days Beeby had suspended the extra allowance for *all* members of the two unions employed at Cockatoo and Mort's Dock.[61] In retaliation the unions decided to demand a general weekly increase of 5s. for all men involved in the dispute.

The Scullin government's 1930 amendments to the Arbitration Act had virtually abolished penalties against strikes and so, after three months of stalemate, the M.T.E.A. applied to the Court for the de-registration of the A.E.U. and A.S.E. In the preliminary hearings Beeby made it known that he would comply with the employers' requests if the union officials failed to ensure a resumption of work. He adjourned the case for a month in order to give the federal leaders time to take the necessary action.

Imagining that the fate of the union's registration hinged upon whether or not it could be demonstrated that the A.E.U. was financially supporting the strike, the Commonwealth Council formally ruled that benefits must cease and the strikers return to work.[62] In fact the Council was prepared to accept an actual return on tactical grounds, and it advised the District Committee and strike leaders of the serious results that would accrue if de-registration

[59] *M.J.R.*, July 1937, pp. 3, 21, December 1937, p. 22.
[60] 38 *C.A.R.* 328 at p. 333.
[61] 38 *C.A.R.* 247.
[62] 'C.C.M.', 29/12/37, 14/1/38, 27/1/38.

became an accomplished fact'.[63] When, however, the A.E.U. strikers decided to stay out, the Council readily accepted their view. A.S.E. rank and file similarly decided against their federal council's recommendation.

The outward attempt by the federal leaders to terminate the strike carried little weight with Beeby. When hearings resumed in January 1938, he remained convinced that the machinery of the union was being used in the collection of strike funds. He dismissed as irrelevant the A.E.U. Council's claims that the strikers were being supported by unauthorised voluntary subscriptions collected in engineering workshops. The men were receiving strike pay. Its exact source was immaterial — although the judge was correctly sceptical concerning Cranwell's supposed ignorance in the matter. Although 'frightfully upset'[64] about the whole matter, Beeby considered that he had no alternative but to make the de-registration order. As he saw it unions had freedom to choose between direct bargaining with employers and using the arbitration system. The A.E.U. and the A.S.E. had elected to operate through the court, 'but now in fact [they] contend that after securing awards they are free to aid strikes for claims refused by the Court after judicial inquiry. If the right is conceded the whole scheme of the Act falls to pieces'.[65] Bargaining with individual employers for over-award payments was permissible; strike action was not.

Beeby conceded that there was a possibility that his earlier ruling that the extra ship repair rate should not apply to the large waterfront shops had been mistaken. But until the whole issue was heard *de novo* the relevant clauses could not be altered. Finally, the judge was anxious that there be no mis-conceptions about his decision, 'An order for de-registration under the circumstances of this application is not a punishment. It is merely the assertion by the Court that registered unions cannot maintain a concurrent right to approach this Court and to resort to direct action'.[66] After allowing the order to 'lie in the Registry' for 17 days in the hope that the strikers would return to work, the two unions were officially de-registered on 17 February 1938.

Beeby's unprecedently rigid interpretation of the unions' responsibility undoubtedly took their leaders by surprise, but when presented with the *fait accompli* of de-registration, the A.E.U. Council showed little concern. No move was made to query Beeby's ruling in the High Court for it was felt that if operating through the arbitration system prevented the union from using

[63] 'C.C.M.', 25/1/38.
[64] *Argus*, 29/1/38.
[65] 39 *C.A.R.* 7 at p. 9.
[66] Ibid. at p. 10.

its strength to secure over-award payments then direct bargaining was eminently preferable. The Council's view was set out in the next issue of the A.E.U. journal. Wealthy companies, such as B.H.P. and the Colonial Sugar Refining Company, held that the rate prescribed by the court as a minimum was also the maximum. Union requests for extra pay were invariably countered by the stock argument that the court was the only place where wage rises were bestowed. If the unions took their case to the court that these profitable concerns could well afford the increases demanded, then they were informed that the financial position of individual firms could not be considered when the court was fixing wages for the industry as a whole. This vicious circle could only be broken by the unions making it apparent to wealthier firms that refusal to meet union demands would be countered by strike action.

If a union has to accept the Court's decision entirely and surrender the right to take any action that will result in securing better wages and conditions than the Court is prepared to give then it can be safely said that the price to be paid for registration is too high. . . .[67]

Yet within two months the Council completely reversed its opinion. In May 1938 the Council announced its decision to ballot members on the question of whether the union should re-register with the Court, and the manner in which the issue was presented to the rank and file left no doubt as to the leaders desire to revert to federal arbitration. In exhorting members to vote for re-registration the Council's primary argument rested on the fact that the 1935 Metal Trades Award as subsequently amended remained a virtual common rule in the industry insofar as the employers cited were concerned.

Hence . . . so long as there is a Commonwealth award in force in respect to engineers, employers who are respondents to that award could not legally be compelled to pay higher wages or observe conditions less advantageous to them than is therein prescribed.[68]

The existing award could continue to operate indefinitely and employers could apply for variations.

The Council listed several additional reasons why it was essential that the A.E.U. be re-registered. In the motor-body building, agricultural-implement, gas, and railway industries, the continued exclusion of the A.E.U. from the court would doubtless stimulate the aspirations of the relevant industrial unions to control all workers employed therein. Further, the coachmakers'

[67] *M.J.R.*, March 1938, p. 6.
[68] *M.J.R.*, May 1938, p. 16.

union was currently endeavouring to obtain a separate award for aircraft workers and, if this move were successful, then the A.E.U. could be completely shut out of this new and growing industry.

Lest A.E.U. members were tempted 'to take a parochial view' of the problem the Council reviewed the legal position of the various state arbitration tribunals. In all cases the local branches of the union would have difficulty in enforcing state awards which provided better rates and conditions than those granted by the federal court as long as employers remained parties to the Metal Trades Award. In Queensland and West Australia additional threats were posed to A.E.U. members. The M.T.E.A. had, in 1935, succeeded in extending the federal award to Queensland in respect to the 'manufacturing' section but strong union opposition had limited its application to only a handful of M.T.E.A. members.[69] The A.E.U.'s absence from the federal court would weaken the Queensland members in their fight to retain their more favourable state award. In West Australia the E.T.U. had long been refused registration by the state court because electricians were covered by the A.E.U.'s award. The E.T.U. was now applying for the extension of the federal award to this state and the A.E.U. would also be unable to oppose this move in court.

The Council also claimed the situation was urgent for if the A.S.E. re-registered first then the A.E.U.'s application might be rejected on the grounds that the Court already recognised an organisation to which A.E.U. members might conveniently belong. In conclusion the Council declared that it was always possible 'under favourable circumstances' for the union to use its strength to enforce the observance of wages and conditions in excess of those set out in Court awards. But the essential point was that the terms of existing awards constituted the basis of negotiations with individual employers. It was, therefore, in the best interest of the A.E.U. always to secure the best possible award for the metal industry.

In any case, until such times as we can exert some material influence in the direction of modifying, if not abolishing, the economic undulations that take place under our present system, it will be necessary for the Union to adopt a policy which will be most likely to protect and promote the interests of members during periods of depression as well as in prosperous times.[70]

---

[69] The M.T.E.A. absorbed the Queensland Iron Master's Association in January 1936. *Brochure to Commemorate The New Building* op. cit. Concurrently, the printing employers were successful in extending their federal award to Queensland. The result was a lowering in the wages of Queensland printers. Hagan, op. cit., pp. 255–7.

[70] *M.J.R.*, May 1938, p. 19.

A.E.U. members in the four southern states were convinced by their federal leaders' lengthy arguments and decided by 3,997 votes to 1,621 to apply for re-registration. On 8 September 1938 the union lodged a formal petition with the Registrar.

The real causes of the Commonwealth Council's sudden reversal of attitude were, however, largely unconnected with its public statements. All of the Council's arguments in favour of re-registration were, if valid, equally obvious and applicable immediately before and after Beeby's final order. The legal embarrassments of federal de-registration had long been apparent and had been often stressed by previous A.E.U. federal leaders in the arbitration controversies of the late 1920s. The threats posed by industrial unions and a possible downturn in the trade cycle had equally long been foreseen. Council could have been in no doubt concerning the effects of being struck off the register and Beeby had given the union ample time to end the waterfront dispute before registration was cancelled. It is true that the majority of the Council had already incurred the displeasure of many Sydney members by their handling of the Fountain—Douglas issues,[71] but this would not have deterred the federal executive from ensuring a return to work if it so desired. Tactical moves of this nature had taken place in earlier stages of the two year old waterfront agitation.

Nor had de-registration imposed any great practical disadvantages on the A.E.U. during the two months preceding the decision to hold the ballot. Beeby had varied the apprenticeship clauses of the Metal Trades Award in the A.E.U.'s absence but he was to extend the suspension of the proportion clauses in 1939 despite the union's strenuous participation in the opposition case. On the waterfront itself the A.E.U. made its point for, after empty threats to make a general call for labour, the employers settled their differences with the unions by conceding higher rates than had hiterto been offered. In future waterfront tradesmen were to receive 5s. per week above the wages set out in the award. The agreed rate was to be an inclusive flat rate for work defined as ship repairs in the award. Hence the strikers' main end was achieved and work was resumed on 31 March. In April the M.T.E.A. promised to recommend those of its members who were still only paying award rates to grant the extra 3s. agreed to in the previous year 'and it was further agreed that where merit money had been previously paid same was to continue'.[72]

Of the Council's remaining arguments in favour of re-registration that concerning the dangers inherent in the pending aircraft award disregarded

[71] Above, p. 120—1.
[72] *M.J.R.*, May 1938, p. 3.

the real relative strength of the coachmakers and the A.E.U. in this new industry. As we shall see the engineers were able, with almost contemptuous ease, to sweep aside the initially unfavourable conditions set out by the federal court. The possibility of the A.S.E. re-registering before the A.E.U. may have been more important. The rival engineering union did in fact register first, in May 1938, but it neither opposed the A.E.U.'s later application nor did the M.T.E.A.'s claim that there was no need for two bodies catering for men performing identical tasks carry much weight in arbitration circles. The A.E.U. was too large and powerful an organisation to be omitted from the court on these grounds and the Registrar, the Bench, and the M.T.E.A. itself knew too much of the facts of industrial life to believe otherwise. Employers' main objections to A.E.U. re-registration were to be based on somewhat more realistic arguments. It is, however, possible that the A.E.U. leaders feared that A.S.E. sole participation in future Metal Trades Awards might allow the smaller union to claim that it was responsible for any consequent improvement of engineers' working conditions. The A.E.U. would be out of the lime-light cast on federal court proceedings and hence might lose potential recruits. Thus fears of the union losing its traditionally dominant position among the metal unions may have possibly contributed to the A.E.U. Council's sudden change in attitude.

However, the major reason for the union leaders apparent inconsistency is provided by Mark Perlman in his study of the arbitration system,[73]

There is little doubt but that Chief Judge Dethridge ... had felt that Beeby had committed worse than an error when he had allowed himself to hear that the A.E.U. was paying strike benefits [during the waterfront dispute] for the Arbitration Court, like most quasi-legislative bodies, has to be able to close its eyes and ears to situations which it is not prepared to handle.

The A.E.U. leaders speedily learnt of Dethridge's attitude and realised that if the union were to re-register then it would be able in future to enjoy the best of both worlds; operating within the federal arbitration system and yet still able to obtain concessions from employers outside the court by direct action. That Beeby was made to realise that his exclusion of the A.E.U. was a bad mistake is borne out by his attitude during the hearing of M.T.E.A. appeals against the union's re-registration.

Thus when Industrial Registrar Stewart was initially considering the A.E.U.'s application to be replaced on the federal register in November 1938, he must have been influenced by the known views of the Chief Judge and

[73] *Judges in Industry*, (Melbourne, 1954), p. 108.

perhaps those of a chastened Beeby. But in addition to pressure from the Bench, Stewart was also faced with the insistent desire of the Prime Minister and the Minister of Defence that the A.E.U. be re-accepted into the arbitration fold. The interest of the federal government in the matter had been aroused by the manner in which the union had recently demonstrated its ability to disrupt the defence programme.

The Commonwealth Aircraft Corporation had been formed in 1936 and, when the first A.E.U. members were taken on at its Melbourne plant in January 1938, it was noted that the Commonwealth Government was displaying a very strong interest in this apparently private enterprise.[74] In June 1938 Beeby commenced hearing the counter-claims of the Corporation and nine unions for an award for the industry. The A.E.U. District Committee was not prepared to allow its members' wages and conditions to be determined by the court in the absence of official A.E.U. representation. It therefore requested the management to meet in conference with local A.E.U. leaders. The Corporation refused to acknowledge that the union's de-registration created special problems and declined to enter into negotiations outside of the federal court. C. A. Crofts of the A.C.T.U. attended the court and requested an adjournment of the proceedings because of the exclusion of the A.E.U. Beeby refused and in doing so he intimated that the Coachmakers' union could look after the engineers' rights.[75]

The court's eventual award,[76] although regarded by the judge as an experiment which could be reconsidered after six month's operation, was completely unacceptable to A.E.U. members. Unfavourable provisions included additional job classifications at low margins, unlimited numbers of apprentices and juniors, the introduction of 'trainees', ordinary rates for the first four hours overtime and ordinary rates for repair and maintenance work performed on Sundays. The aircraft award thus included many important departures from the conditions set out in the Metal Trades Award. A.E.U. leaders saw this preferential treatment for the Corporation as both a licence for the exploitation of their employees by the wealthy and powerful shareholders,[77] and as the first illustration of the federal government's intent to

---

[74] *M.J.R.*, February 1938, p. 22.
[75] *M.J.R.*, June 1938, p. 4, July 1938, p. 2.
[76] 39 *C.A.R.* 512.
[77] The Shareholders were Broken Hill Pty. Ltd., Broken Hill Associated Smelters Pty. Ltd., General Motors-Holdens Ltd., Electrolytic Zinc Company of Australasia Ltd., Imperial Chemical Industries of Australia and New Zealand Ltd. and the Orient Steam Navigation Co. Ltd. Helen Hughes, *The Australian Iron and Steel Industries 1848–1962* (Melbourne, 1962), p. 116.

break down traditional working conditions to expedite its current defence programme.

When no satisfaction was received from the Corporation following further demands for a conference, some 200 A.E.U. members, together with employees belonging to the S.M.W.I.U. struck work on 1 August. One week later the Trades Hall Disputes Committee ordered all unionists off the job. Simultaneously, A.E.U. members in Defence Department plants at Maribyrnong and Footscray (Melbourne), Garden Island (Sydney), and the Lithgow Small Arms Factory announced their determination to cease work in sympathy with the strikers if called upon.[78] The federal government at first refused to intervene but changed its mind as soon as the A.E.U. made it clear that it was prepared to authorise an extension of the strike. Acting in accordance with a personal pledge made in June that he would prevent any worsening of working conditions brought about by private employers under the pretext that such deterioration was necessary to place industry on a war footing, Prime Minister Lyons commenced negotiations with the striking unions.[79] Helped by the A.L.P. leader John Curtin and several other Labor parliamenterians, discussion between the parties proved fruitful and terms of settlement were agreed on 9 September. At this point doubts arose concerning the A.E.U.'s legal position in view of its de-registration. This problem was quickly cleared up by an unprecedented action on the part of the Prime Minister who issued a proclamation reducing from thirty to seven days the period allowed under the Arbitration Act during which objections could be lodged against an association's application for registration. The strikers returned to work on 12 September four days after the A.E.U. had filed its petition for re-admittance to the Arbitration Court.

The S.M.W.I.U. made the official application for the necessary variation of the aircraft award and Beeby incorporated the unions' demands in an amended judgment of 27 September 1938.[80] Thus the determined action of the de-registered A.E.U. had forced the employers, the federal government, and the court to accept its terms. It now seemed obvious, if the settlement of disputes by the arbitration process were ever to be effective in the metal trades, that the A.E.U. must be again included in the federal framework. The M.T.E.A. however, formally objected to the application for re-registration on three grounds; that A.E.U. members were currently engaged in strikes — notably at the Australian Gas Light Company's works and in association with

[78] *M.J.R.*, August 1938, pp. 7, 24, September 1938, p. 2; *Argus*, 2/8/38.
[79] *Argus*, 16/8/38.
[80] 39 *C.A.R.* 918.

the coalminers' union in New South Wales; that A.E.U. rules made provision for the settlement of disputes other than by conciliation and arbitration; and that the A.S.E. constituted a registered organisation to which A.E.U. members could conveniently belong.[81] The E.T.U. objected to A.E.U. rules covering electrical workers and argued that it already catered for such employees.

Before the A.E.U. entered its application the Registrar had insisted that the union rule prohibiting members from undertaking piece work be deleted. The Commonwealth Council, in view of the change in Beeby's attitude to incentive schemes and the relegation of the topic from the centre of the court's interest, agreed to make the alteration[82] although the A.E.U.'s opposition to payment by results was by no means altered by this step. This was the only concession which Registrar Stewart asked of the union. In his judgment[83] he tacitly admitted that Beeby's original order had been a mistake. Regarding the current gas and coal strikes, Stewart claimed that the Registrar was allowed to use his discretion and stated, 'I have come to the conclusion that there are factors present which render it inadvisable for me to dismiss the application upon the grounds so taken.'

As to the M.T.E.A.'s second objection, Stewart justified the A.E.U. rules on the grounds that they were necessary to enable the union officials to handle intrastate disputes which did not come within the jurisdiction of the federal Court. It was essential for the sake of industrial peace that the A.E.U. be re-registered for 'the absence from the arena of this large association cannot fail to be a clog on the satisfactory discharge by the court of the functions committed to it by Statute'. The employers' third objection and that of the E.T.U. were summarily dismissed as being at variance with the realities of inter-union relationships. The A.E.U. was officially re-registered on 8 November 1938.

The M.T.E.A. was still not satisfied and its appeal against Stewart's decision came before Beeby in the following month. The judge was placed in an invidious position. Although aware that his initial mistake must be rectified, he could hardly admit, as had Stewart, that the 'special circumstances' of the A.E.U.'s industrial power permitted the union to resort to direct action to enforce better working conditions for its members. Hence he

[81] *Metal Trades Journal*, 7/12/38.
[82] 'C.C.M.', 29/7/38.
[83] The following summary of Stewart's judgment is taken from *M.J.R.*, December 1938, pp. 3—4.

adjourned the hearings at the end of the first day in an attempt to persuade the Commonwealth Council to give some undertaking which would indicate '... a future policy of procuring observance of any awards of the Court to which it might become a party'.[84] The Council, while desiring to maintain the union's new registration, was not prepared to sacrifice the victories of the preceding twelve months and it decided 'That the matter of Judge Beeby's hostile attitude towards our Union be taken up with the Prime Minister per medium of Mr E. J. Holloway M.H.R.'.[85] It is not apparent whether this move produced any results but when the hearing re-opened five days later Beeby accepted the following empty guarantee,

The said Union undertakes that it will not support any of its members who go on strike without first giving the Executive an opportunity of bringing the subject-matter of the dispute before the Court and the Union will use all its influence to induce its members to observe the terms of the award.[86]

The employers' advocate justly argued that this declaration was devoid of real meaning and demanded that at least the word 'induce' be changed to 'compel'. In answer Beeby said,

You compel me to say something I did not wish to say. It may be that de-registration was the wrong remedy for the incidents that took place. It is obvious that this Union not being registered completely disorganises the Metal Trades Industry and the Metal Trades Award, which is one of the most important ever made by the Court. They should be back in the fold, and if after-events occur there are other remedies that the Court will not hesitate to apply.[87]

The reference to 'other remedies' was not developed further. The M.T.E.A. formally withdrew its objections and the A.E.U.'s registration was confirmed.

Beeby's retreat marks the end of a period in which the court was the dominant force in the metal industries, determining new conditions as it saw fit rather than adjudicating between employers and unions. Beeby resigned in 1941 and for the next decade the role of the bench was indeed largely that of an arbitrator between the forces of management and labour.

---

[84] 39 *C.A.R.* 1263.

[85] 'C.C.M.', 7/12/38.

[86] 39 *C.A.R.* 1263 at p. 1264. Perlman, op. cit., p. 109, n. 38, relates that it was commonly believed that Beeby composed this 'face-saver' himself. Cranwell and Mundy, the principal A.E.U. officials concerned in the negotiations, are both dead and surviving A.E.U. officials of the period were unable when interviewed to confirm or deny this version.

[87] *M.J.R.*, January 1939, p. 3.

6
World War II[1]

The shifts in Australian wartime economic policy coincided with the major changes in the military situation. The Menzies governments hesitantly sought to establish the necessary controls and re-allocate resources in order to achieve a 'maximum' war effort from the outbreak of war in Europe to the end of 1941 : but until the invasion of Russia large sections of the industrial labour movement remained highly suspicious of government motives and could not be counted on for full co-operation. The first Curtin Labour ministry took office in October 1941. Two months later the Japanese attacked Pearl Harbour. The war now became a true struggle for national survival. Backed by practically all sectors of the community the new government was able by use of stringent controls to place the economy on a total war footing. In mid-1943 the allies took the offensive in the Pacific and allied economic planning became more closely co-ordinated. The federal government slightly relaxed its concentration on the maximisation of the production of defence goods, easing off munitions output and redirecting manpower towards food production.

The major developments in manufacturing industry took place during the first four years of the war. Factory employment as a whole increased

---

[1] Much of the discussion of the war-time economy in this chapter is based on E. Ronald Walker, *The Australian Economy in War and Reconstruction*, (New York, 1947), and S. J. Butlin, *War Economy 1939–1942* in *Australia in the War of 1939–1945*. Series 4, Number III (Canberra, 1955).

Contemporary estimates of the allocation of national resources during the war are contained in *Facts and Figures of Australia at War* (*Australia in Facts and Figures* from September 1945) published quarterly from June 1943 by the Commonwealth Department of Information.

The social and political background of the early war years is best covered in Paul Hasluck, *The Government and the People 1939–1941* in *Australia in the War of 1939–1945* Series 4, Number I (Canberra, 1952).

An important source of information on the effects of government policy on industrial relations is Orwell de R. Foenander, *Wartime Labour Developments in Australia* (Melbourne, 1943).

from 565,000 in 1938–9 to a peak of 766,000 in 1943–4,[2] but the proportionate growth in 'essential' industries was even greater. The metal trades workforce practically doubled between 1938–9 and 1943–4 – from 177,000 to 341,000. This rapid expansion was accompanied by a revolution in engineering practice and the scale of operations.

New materials, tools and processes had begun to appear during the 1930s. One of the most important developments was the replacement of high-speed steel by tungsten carbide tipped tools in the more efficient workshops. This innovation could increase the output of turners, millers and other machinists six and sevenfold in some instances. Other innovations included non-shrink, alloy, and stainless steels, thermo plastics, roller bearings, Keller profile and die sinking machines, Theil punch shapers, metal saws, centreless grinders, thread grinders and gear hobbers and shapers. The pre-war period also witnessed the final defeat of steam and gas engines by electric power and an associated abandonment of belt-driven machinery in favour of individual motor drives.

The unprecedented acceleration of demand for metal products during the war had the effect of spreading these new techniques throughout the industry. Government armament contracts called for a much higher degree of precision than had been common for pre-war jobbing and repair work. Tool-rooms expanded rapidly in size. Firms which had demonstrated their ability to do accurate work changed almost exclusively to tool manufacture. Before the war six firms employed 700 workers to produce 2,000 machine tools per annum. By 1943 200 firms were manufacturing 14,000 machines per year with a workforce of 12,000.[3] Demand swung away from general-purpose towards specialised machine tools. Machines rare before 1939 became common. Much greater use was made of capstan, turrent and automatic lathes. Hydraulically operated millers and surface broaching machines appeared; gear cutting received a great impetus. Firms were encouraged to specialise in the production of one or two articles by the sub-contracting of component manufacture. Conveyor-belt flow systems became more common. A further very important stimulus to component standardisation and interchangeability was provided by the adoption of common threads in America and Britain. Lay-out was studied in order to make the most efficient use of available floor space. The value of good lighting was realised and its installation was made more feasible by the elimination of overhead belting.

The increase in specialisation and standardisation enabled many manu-

[2] *Production Bulletin*, Nos. 33–40.
[3] *Facts and Figures*, No. 10, p. 29.

facturers to take advantage of economies of scale. Government munitions factories usually operated on a large scale and contributed greatly to the wartime growth in the average unit of production in the metal industry. The proportion of metal workers employed in establishments with 100 hands or less on the payroll fell from 42 per cent in 1935−6 to 24 per cent in 1942−3. In this setting the numbers of semi-skilled metal workers rose markedly but there was no slackening in the demand for craftsmen, particularly toolmakers, turners and skilled machinists. Indeed the defence programme called for a rapid expansion of the supply of engineering tradesmen and the A.E.U.'s wartime history was one of efforts to safeguard its members' status and bargaining power in the face of drastic alterations in the composition of the skilled workforce.

II

Whereas the attitude of the rest of the labour movement altered markedly after the entry of Russia and Japan into the war, that of the A.E.U. remained consistent throughout. The union's leaders saw the war as an interruption − albeit a severe and lengthy one − to 'normal' economic activity and they judged that when hostilities ceased a reversion to something like pre-war conditions would be inevitable. Towards the end of the war it became apparent that the expansion of the metal trades would not be completely cancelled out with the advent of peace, but it was impossible for the union to foresee that in future there would be permanent full employment. Memories of the depression of the 1930s were too vivid for that. In the first issue of the A.E.U. journal published after the declaration of war the fears of the Commonwealth Council were plainly set out.

Whilst the Government is concentrating on its defence plans, it must be made to realise that very often the nation classed as having won a war is the one that is best prepared for peace. By that it is intended to emphasise the fact that whilst war is being waged plans on a large scale must be prepared to employ the nation in reproductive works immediately hostilities cease. Unless that organisation is commenced immediately we will be plunged into a depression the extent and suffering of which will cause the depression of a few years ago to fade into insignificance. Well might the question be re-iterated − *War! What then?*[4]

The question was re-iterated every time the union was presented with departures from customary working conditions. Each new problem was weighed in terms of the best way in which to safeguard members' interests

[4] *M.J.R.*, October 1939, p. 5. The A.E.U. order of priorities contrasted with that of the employers. The editorial of the first *Employers' Review* published after the outbreak of the war (30/9/39) was headed 'There Must Be No Strikes'.

in the post-war period. This pragmatic approach often put the A.E.U. out of step with the majority of other trade unions both before and after the important developments in the overall military and strategic situation in 1941.

A.E.U. policy is best illustrated by the line taken in the negotiations which began immediately after Pearl Harbour between the Curtin government, employers' organisations, trade unions, and the federal Arbitration Court concerning the best means of bringing about an 'all-in' war effort. At first the Cabinet considered that of the unions only the A.W.U., which was not affiliated to the A.C.T.U., should be separately represented and that the A.C.T.U. could speak for the rest. The Commonwealth Council immediately indicated that if the A.E.U. were not represented at the proposed conference then it would not consider itself bound by any decisions reached in its absence.[5] Because of this intransigence the A.C.T.U. asked the A.E.U. to send a representative. The Council agreed but informed the A.C.T.U. that its nominee, Cranwell, would represent only the A.E.U. and would express the union's policy even if it conflicted with that of the A.C.T.U. The government was separately advised that Cranwell would attend 'on the understanding that matters affecting this organisation can only be effectively dealt with by the Government and this Union'.[6]

The body which was set up following the conference of interested parties, the Industrial Relations Council, collapsed because the employers challenged the independence of the chairman.[7] However the Commonwealth Council's comments on the A.C.T.U.'s bases for discussion at the round-table conference are worth presenting in full for they set out clearly the A.E.U.'s unvarying approach to war-time problems. A summary of the A.C.T.U. proposals are given first, with Council views on each point in parentheses.[8]

(1) No stoppage of work to take place unless authorised by the union or unions covering the industry concerned (A.E.U. 'reserves the right to determine its action in these matters').

(2) Stoppages of work to be sanctioned only after complete exhaustion of conciliatory methods ('Opposed to this clause as it permits of too much delay').

(3) Improvement and speed up of the processes of arbitration ('Approved').

---

[5] 'C.C.M.', 16/12/41.
[6] 'C.C.M.', 19/12/41.
[7] Walker, op. cit., p. 63; *M.J.R.*, February 1942, pp. 5 and 7.
[8] The full A.C.T.U. proposals are set out in *M.J.R.*, February 1942, p. 3. Council comments are given in 'C.C.M.', 19/12/41.

(4) Production to be increased and made more efficient by means of elected workshop committees and through trade union representation on boards controlling production and distribution. Such representation to be selected through the A.C.T.U. or its branches ('Cannot agree').

(5) Living standards to be secured through readjustment of wage rates, elimination of wage anomalies and more rigid price control ('Agreed').

(6) Employment of women on work usually performed by men to be accompanied by safeguards in the form of equal pay and reinstatement of men when available ('Cannot agree').

(7) Consultation between trade unions and A.C.T.U., and A.C.T.U. and Government to take place when necessary ('Can only be dealt with by A.E.U. and Government').

(8) Absolute preference to Unionists in all industries ('Unnecessary eliminated').

These terse comments amply demonstrate the A.E.U.'s determination to act independently of the rest of the trade union movement if this were in the interests of its members. Its attitude towards the employment of females was to change, but the A.E.U.'s position on all other points was to be maintained for the remainder of the war. Above all it continued to insist on being directly represented in all discussions concerning possible industrial changes which might affect the conditions of working members. Because of the engineers' key position in the defence industries, they were almost completely successful in imposing this condition. The Council continued to view its members' right to strike as inalienable although at times even it was perturbed when engineers downed tools before even the District Committee or local organiser had been informed.[9] The A.E.U. objected to the proposal on workshop committees because it felt that the desire to assist the war effort by increased output should not degenerate into union co-operation in the worst aspects of 'speed-up'. The Council was particularly scathing in its comments on the communists and other left wingers outside A.E.U. ranks who had bitterly attacked its apparent co-operation with the government before the invasion of Russia but who, after July 1941, seemed prepared to sacrifice many of the workers' hard-earned rights.[10]

On the other hand, in June 1943 the A.E.U. helped to form the Metal

[9] See e.g. *M.J.R.*, August 1942, p. 7 and June 1944, p. 6.
[10] For an example of left wing attacks on the A.E.U. for its pre-1941 'co-operation' with the Menzies Government see *M.J.R.*, December 1940, p. 5. For the best statement of the Commonwealth Council's views on Production Committees and the reversal of left wing policy after the invasion of Russia see *M.J.R.*, November 1942, p. 6.

Trades Federation (M.T.F.) which aimed to co-ordinate the efforts of the metal unions in combating possible post-war problems. Only the E.T.U. failed to affiliate to the new body. Cranwell was elected Chairman and devoted much of his energy towards ensuring closer co-operation between the seven constituent members. The new organisation encouraged amalgamation discussions such as those between the A.E.U. and A.S.E.,[11] but the A.E.U. never allowed its membership of the M.T.F. to prevent it from pursuing its own independent policies.

The employers also moved towards closer federal organisation. In September 1943 the New South Wales and Queensland branches of the M.T.E.A. joined with the Iron and Steel Section of the Victorian Chambers of Manufactures and the Metal Industries Association of South Australia to form the Australian Metal Industries Association (A.M.I.A.). The retrospective reasons given for its establishment were the unique war-time conditions and the supposed fact that the metal unions were 'under the domination of the Communist Party and there were threats of a new social order and the abolition of the Arbitration system. These were times which called for clear sighted leadership and sound policy in this great and important war-time industry.'[12] In reality the new body was merely a loose federation which initially resulted in little more than the stimulation of friendly relations between the employers' state organisations.[13] As for the communist threat, we will later consider that question in detail. Suffice it here to say that employers at times found it a useful means of camouflage. For example they opposed Joint Production Committees largely because they feared greater union involvement in managemental affairs. They bolstered this basic point by claiming that the support for joint committees came from the 'militant' unions and that the leaders of 'the trade unions proper' were not enthusiastic about the idea at all.[14] The major unenthusiastic 'proper' union was, of course, the A.E.U. and one of the most fervent supporters of joint committees was the communist-led F.I.A. Yet it is hard to point to a more militant union than the A.E.U. during the war nor to less militant leadership than the F.I.A. after the invasion of Russia.[15] Throughout the war employers failed

[11] Above, pp. 49–50.
[12] *Brochure to Celebrate 20th Anniversary of Australian Metal Industries Association*, Sydney, 1962.
[13] *Metal Trades Journal*, 15/5/44.
[14] Ibid., 17/7/43.
[15] For official F.I.A. policy see Merritt, 'A History of the F.I.A', pp. 288–318. For an outline of the communists' 'Win the War' policy see L. L. Sharkey, *The Left. 'Dr' Lloyd Ross and Nationalisation* (pamphlet), Sydney, 1942.

to give credit to the communists for their devotion to the war effort and wrongly continued to blame them for all industrial friction.[16]

III

The process of formal wage settlement moved out of the Arbitration Court during the war. The maximum wage level was pegged by government regulations enacted under the 1939 National Security Act and although the court continued to settle industrial disputes it could not move independently of the framework set out in the regulations. In December 1940 regulations enlarged the powers of the federal court, including the right specifically to grant a common rule, to make awards not limited to the ambit of matters in dispute, to deal with intra-state disputes, to deal with industrial unrest before official disputes arose, and to speed up its working by cutting out inessential formalities. Provision was also made for the appointment of Conciliation Commissioners and, if necessary, temporary Conciliation Officers. At the same time however, the government itself was entering the field of wage settlement by means of other regulations and a confusing parallelism of action consequently arose.

In August 1940 the Full Court began hearing union arguments for an increase in the Basic Wage but rejected them largely on the grounds of the general uncertainty of war-time conditions.[17] The Bench's judgment was announced in February 1941 but shortly before it was known the federal government decided to introduce child endowment which hitherto existed only in N.S.W. The Basic Wage remained unaltered for the rest of the war. On the margins front a pre-war agreement between the Department of Supply and 13 unions for higher rates and favourable conditions at government munitions works was renewed for three years in December 1939. The government's aim was to attract skilled workers into the industry. As the munitions industry expanded, the payment of the extra margins (6s. for tradesmen) was extended by agreement to all government and private plants. When the Menzies government placed a ceiling on wages the extra munition rates were incorporated in the relevant regulations of July 1940. These regulations imposed severe restrictions on the movement of labour with the aim of channelling workers — particularly those with the requisite skills — into munitions work and to keep them there without employers competitively bidding up their wages. Employees who had been receiving payments before July 1940 in excess of the new maximum wage levels were not to suffer any

[16] See e.g. *Metal Trades Journal*, 17/8/43.
[17] 44 *C.A.R.* 41.

reduction in pay. After an important amendment to the regulations in December 1941 employers could also make excess payments due for long service or special ability, as bonuses based on output or the price of base metals, on incremental scales of wage increases, and to juniors occupying positions of responsibility.

In May 1941 the 6s. was extended to all areas covered by the Metal Trades Award — although the employers insisted that the extra amounts should be classified separately as a 'war loading' and should not become an integral part of the award rates. Their idea was that the loading could be eliminated after the war. The extra rates were later extended to all other awards under which engineering tradesmen were employed. In a series of judgments during 1941 Judge O'Mara also ended the trainee apprenticeship schemes, re-introduced weekly hiring and made provision for one week's annual paid leave for metal workers.[18]

After 1941 the only official adjustments to wage rates took place in response to upward movements in the cost of living. Government attempts to prevent price rises were largely successful. The Retail Price Index only rose by 23 per cent in Australia between the last quarter of 1939 and 1945 compared with increases of 27 per cent in the United States of America and 31 per cent in Great Britain. Yet this still meant that the increase in fitters' margins (30s. to 36s.) was more than balanced by the general wartime price rise. The discrepancy between nominal wage rates and the cost of living was more than made good, however, by increases in over-award payments and the great increase in overtime working at penalty rates.

Engineers were assisted in their initial efforts to gain higher over-award payments by the 'Cost Plus' method of pricing tenders for war work commonly used by metal producers. This usually meant that employers first estimated their total costs and then added a fixed percentage for profit. The actual level of wages paid to their employees did not affect their profit margins, and therefore firms competed for suitably skilled workers by offering rates substantially over the award.[19] Even after the successive tightening of the wage-pegging regulations employers continued to offer illegal financial inducements to skilled men. In part they did so by nominally transferring employees to higher paid classifications. But the majority of firms did not

---

[18] These decisions were consolidated into a new metal trades award on 5 December 1941. 45 *C.A.R.* 751.

[19] For examples of pre-Regulation over-award payments see *M.J.R.*, November 1939, p. 28, April 1940, p. 20, November 1940, p. 19. See also *Metal Trades Journal*, 1/9/41 for an example of the M.T.E.A.'s disapproval of earlier 'fancy wages' offered to engineers by N.S.W. metal producers.

attempt to disguise their evasion of the regulations. In July 1941, for example, the M.T.E.A. reported that the government was concerned over Sydney newspaper advertisements such as that offering employment to a toolmaker at £12 per week.[20] The current award rate was £6.11.0. Several employers were fined for these breaches,[21] but even in the last months of the war the M.T.E.A. was still remonstrating in vain against what it considered to be the short-sightedness of some of its members.[22]

Engineers' total real income was further added to by the great increase in daily and weekly hours of work. The commencement of hostilities saw the A.E.U. as determined as ever to secure a shorter working week. Attention was currently focussed on the coal industry where the Full Arbitration Court blocked Judge Drake-Brockman's attempt to grant a reduction in hours to surface as well as underground workers. The A.E.U. fully supported the unsuccessful ten week stoppage over the issue between February and May 1940 and its members employed at the State Coal Mine, Wonthaggi, Victoria, stayed out for some months after the general return to work.[23]

Yet even while wholeheartedly backing the coal strikers A.E.U. leaders were faced with a rapid acceleration in overtime working in all sectors of the metal trades. As we shall later see, the union was unable to oppose what in peacetime would be regarded as 'excessive' overtime because of its fears that any limitations would increase the impact and extent of dilution of engineering skill. The result was that, in response to an ever growing demand for metal tradesmen, efforts were made 'to supplement the 44-hour week with as much overtime as the human form can stand'.[24] The working of extremely long hours continued even after 'added tradesmen' began entering the industry in large numbers after the 1940 Dilution Agreements. Inevitably fatigue became a serious industrial problem and absenteeism and workshop friction increased in proportion.[25] Eventually the federal government was forced to intervene and in October 1942 special regulations were issued which limited working hours, excluding meal-breaks, to 48 for workers under 18 years of age, and to 56 for adults. A.E.U. members' reaction to this move seems to have been mixed. The Perth organiser, J. F. Newman, summed it by saying, 'The pegging of hours to 56 has concerned some of

[20] *Metal Trades Journal*, 17/7/41. See also ibid., 16/10/41.
[21] See e.g. ibid., 1/9/41, 2/3/42, 1/4/43.
[22] Ibid., 2/4/45.
[23] *M.J.R.*, October 1940, p. 21, January 1941, p. 26.
[24] Melbourne organiser, N. Roberts, *M.J.R.*, November 1940, p. 19.
[25] See e.g. *Metal Trades Journal*, 1/10/42.

the hungrier elements amongst us, and at the same time has not consoled some of the less energetic'.[26] Either way, with engineers working up to 12 hours overtime paid for at penalty rates, their real income remained at a level considerably higher than they had enjoyed in the pre-war years. Hence the wartime stabilisation of wages did not cause any great unrest among rank and file unionists who were largely content to wait until final allied military victory had been secured before pressing for further increases in nominal rates and a reduction in standard hours.

IV

Unemployment among Australian unionists was still high in 1939 and 1940.[27] The Menzies government therefore initially saw the main manpower problem as one of expanding the numbers of skilled workers in a relatively narrow range of metal, textile, and one or two other industries serving defence requirements. In February 1940 the Cabinet was informed that although less than 15,000 skilled workers had been employed in the Services and in munitions production at the end of 1939, an extra 10,000 were required in the next six months and over 20,000 more in the succeeding twelve months. Within the range of skills covered by the A.E.U. the position was similar. In January 1940 the R.A.A.F., for example, estimated that it required 5,000 fitters immediately and ultimately a further 13,000 mechanics. However, it was calculated that in October 1939 there were only 19,000 engineering tradesmen in Australia.[28]

The inducement of extra pay to munition workers was clearly insufficient to provide the skilled labour needed, and the government therefore introduced special training schemes to turn out new trademen in a short space of time. In the first instance the government restricted such schemes to the armed forces where suitable candidates were trained as part of their service. Courses began in December 1939 and by April 1940 there were 1,855 trainees of whom 498 had completed training.[29] The government felt, however, that it could not commence civilian training schemes until the craft unions had agreed to accept the dilution of their members' jealously guarded skills.

The A.E.U. had carefully considered the question of dilution in May 1939 at an Interstate Conference. It resolved that any proposals on the matter would not be entertained until all labour offered by the A.E.U. had been

[26] *M.J.R.*, January 1943, p. 13.
[27] *Labour Report* No. 33.
[28] S. J. Butlin, op. cit., p. 231.
[29] Ibid., p. 237.

accepted and employed. With the actual outbreak of war the problem became more urgent. Foreseeing the inevitability of an influx of new entrants into the skilled trades, and recalling the troubles arising in Britain during World War I because of the lack of adequate union control over dilution, the A.E.U. began to negotiate with the government within three months of the commencement of hostilities. The government for its part was anxious to avoid arousing the combined opposition of the trade union movement and saw that if the compliance of the A.E.U. could be secured then the other, smaller, metal craft unions might be expected to be drawn into a general network of dilution agreements. Throughout the protracted negotiations, therefore, the government was amenable to the acceptance of the various safeguards which the A.E.U. demanded should be incorporated in the agreement.

After some weeks of preliminary discussions the Commonwealth Council convened an Interstate Conference on 3 January 1940 to consider the government's proposals which at this early date still called for only 500 extra toolmakers to be drawn from the ranks of existing tradesmen, and some 2,800 other craftsmen. The Conference set out 14 points upon which the union would continue negotiations.[30] These were largely accepted by the government and on 11 March Cabinet approved the final formula. Actual training of civilians began on 18 March 1940 although the agreement was not formally signed until 8 May by which time the A.E.U. rank and file members had had a chance to discuss and approve it at branch and mass meetings.

The agreement was also signed by the M.T.E.A., the Victorian and South Australian Chambers of Manufactures and its terms were that: all propositions for dilution be consolidated under one government-controlled scheme; all available engineering tradesmen be first employed; no tradesmen to be debarred from employment on the grounds of age or minor disability provided he could perform the work required; no craftsman to be called into the armed forces unless his skill was fully utilised; any skilled servicemen not currently so engaged to be discharged; first preference in trainee schemes to be given to 'persons of engineering or appropriate classifications' and only when such sources had been exhausted could other classes of workers take advantage of the scheme; a Central Committee functioning under the administration of the Department of Supply and consisting of representatives of the Department, the employers, and the A.E.U. was to control and oversee the working of the scheme; Local Committees comprising of equal numbers

[30] For details see *M.J.R.*, April 1940, pp. 3—4.

of representatives of employers and the A.E.U. together with a Department chairman were to supervise the working of the scheme in each state; after a period of training determined by the Local Committee in a technical school or an approved industrial establishment during which he would be paid the Basic Wage, the trainee would be paid full tradesmen's award rates; a register to be kept containing the names of all trainees and copies to be supplied to A.E.U. and the employers' organisations; all trainees to sign an agreement to serve if and as required by the Local Committee for the period of the war; 'added' tradesmen not to be counted in determining the numbers of apprentices which employers could take on under the Metal Trades Award; 'recognised' tradesmen to have complete job preference over dilutees; the agreement was not to be used 'to deprive any employee of any rights under any existing award, agreement or determination' and nor was it to be cited before any federal or state wage tribunal.[31]

Within the A.E.U. the scheme was opposed only by a small paradoxical coalition of communists and the most conservative members, including many in the particularly craft conscious Newcastle district. The protests of the small minority of A.E.U. branches were, however, joined by those of the majority of other trade unions. Distrusting both the Menzies government and the 'Phoney' war, the left-wing sections of the industrial labour movement regarded the A.E.U.'s action as a betrayal of the unions' generally solid front. The A.C.T.U. and the smaller skilled metal unions, on the other hand, were chiefly aggrieved that they had not been advised of, or invited to take part in the negotiations. The A.C.T.U. Congress meeting in Sydney in April 1940 castigated the A.E.U. and carried a resolution opposing dilution in any industry and calling on the A.E.U. not to enter into any further discussions with the government. In return the A.E.U. ridiculed what it viewed as a dramatic pose rather than a practical policy.[32]

Not surprisingly the A.E.U. was in fact speedily imitated by the other unions. The A.S.E. moved first and signed an agreement with the employers and federal government in June 1940. The Boilermakers and the B.S.A. in November 1940, the Moulders in June 1941, and the E.T.U. and the S.M.W.I.U. in October 1941 all entered into similar agreements. In November 1941 the federal furniture trades award was varied by consent to allow for

---

[31] For full details of the original agreement see Foenander *Wartime Labour Developments*, pp. 33 and 145. The agreement was eventually brought down as an 'arrangement' under Clause 59A of the National Security (General) Regulations.

[32] *M.J.R.*, May 1940, pp. 7, 8, June 1940, p. 4.

a limited measure of dilution in that industry and, in June 1942, regulations were issued to allow for an engineering-type dilution agreement in the boot and shoe trades.[33]

The working of the dilution agreement largely fulfilled the A.E.U.'s aims in entering into it. A total of 37,472 male dilutees entered the trades covered by the A.E.U.[34] More detailed figures are unavailable but engineering added tradesmen represented 89 per cent of all metal trade dilutees by the end of May 1943.[35] Soon after this date, as the pressure on the defence industries began to ease, A.E.U. organisers began to report difficulties in placing dilutees. As a result the Central Dilution Committee suspended the trainee schemes and many dilutees began returning to their old jobs.[36]

In addition to the formal training scheme employers, if they could prove the need, were allowed to upgrade semi-skilled employees to higher job classifications. The A.E.U. usually opposed such 'elevation' both on the Local Committees and the shop floor but in New South Wales the A.S.E. supported the employers on this issue,[37] and the M.T.E.A. claimed that 40 per cent of added tradesmen were provided in this fashion to 1943.[38] Further, some firms by-passed the machinery set up by the agreement and elevated men to tradesmen's positions without reference to the Local Committees. In September 1940 regulations were issued to prevent this by tightening up on the registration of added tradesmen but the illicit practice continued until the rate of dilution slackened in the second half of 1943.[39] In retrospect the M.T.E.A. was prepared to admit that elevation had been responsible for inefficiency and higher costs.[40]

The A.E.U. had originally hoped that dilution could be restricted to rela-

---

[33] For details of dilution agreements in the non-engineering trades see Foenander, *Wartime Labour Development*, p. 41. Dilution of skill was not as extensive in the foundries as in the trades covered by the A.E.U. The moulders' union only accepted dilutees on plate and machine moulding and not on the more highly skilled jobbing work. See Hargreaves, op. cit., p. 84; *Metal Trades Journal*, 1/2/44.

    The Sydney branch of the Boilermakers' Society refused to acknowledge their federal executive's acceptance of dilution and opposed any dilution of their trade. However, the employers seemed able to secure the requisite numbers of dilutee boilermakers in all save waterfront shops. For details see Ibid., 1/3/41, 16/4/41, 2/1/42, 2/4/42.

[34] *M.J.R.*, September 1946, p. 8.

[35] *Metal Trades Journal*, 2/8/43.

[36] *M.J.R.*, October 1943, pp. 5, 11, December 1943, pp. 12, 13, April 1944, p. 15, May 1944, pp. 17, 21, September 1944, p. 13, November–December 1944, p. 3.

[37] *Metal Trades Journal*, 1/2/43.

[38] Ibid., 2/8/43.

[39] 'C.C.M.', 12/3/41; *M.J.R.*, July 1941, p. 10, December 1942, p. 11 and January 1943, p. 10.

[40] *Metal Trades Journal*, 1/4/53.

tively small areas of the metal trades. In the early months following the scheme's inception the union objected to the elevation of labourers employed in engineering shops and unskilled workers previously engaged in non-metal industries on the grounds that the ranks of lower grade machinists and other semi-skilled metal workers would be able to supply all the trainees required.[41] The A.E.U. also wanted to limit the employment of added tradesmen to lower class jobs leaving the recognised tradesmen free to undertake the higher grade (and generally more interesting) work.[42] This would have been satisfactory to the employers who noted that while many dilutees 'show certain promise . . . many do not measure up in ability to the third year apprentices'.[43]

A.E.U. efforts to limit dilution led to friction with other trade unions particularly those catering for unskilled workers who still had not been fully absorbed into the war economy. Skilled engineers worked very long hours of overtime and A.E.U. leaders did not feel able to call for any reduction in the working day or for the introduction of shift work because it was felt that such moves would strengthen the employers' case in demanding the induction of still more trainees. In early 1941 the F.I.A., wishing to widen its members' employment opportunities and also still opposed to the war-effort, sought to introduce a general overtime embargo in protest against the new tax provisions of the federal Budget. The Commonwealth Council refused to be associated with the campaign, explaining to the Sydney District Committee that because of the shortage of skilled labour the ban '. . . would widen the field for dilution and we desire to restrict dilution as far as possible'. Such hopes were swept aside by the rapidly accelerating demand for skilled labour, particularly after the entry of Japan into the war. Even while the Council was refusing to support an overtime ban A.E.U. organisers were commenting on the growing number of trainees who had had no previous experience in the engineering industry.[44] The proportion of such dilutees increased as the war economy expanded and A.E.U. leaders were forced to bow to the inevitable.

The very rapid expansion of the supply of skilled labour inevitably resulted in inter-union conflict as each organisation attempted to attract to itself the greatest possible numbers of new entrants into the industry. The A.E.U. and F.I.A. occasionally clashed because the latter seemed reluctant to give its newly trained members clearance to the craft union. At one time the New-

[41] The A.E.U. did not object to non-engineering craftsmen becoming dilutees as it was supposed that such men would return to their original trades after the war. *M.J.R.*, April 1940, p. 8.
[42] E.g. *M.J.R.*, August 1941, p. 11.
[43] *Metal Trades Journal*, 1/2/41.
[44] E.g. *M.J.R.*, January 1941, p. 26.

castle A.E.U. pressed the Commonwealth Council to apply to the Arbitration Court for the insertion of a clause in the F.I.A. rule book which would prevent it from retaining skilled members.[45] Eventually, the two organisations were able to settle their differences amicably by local agreements.[46]

The A.E.U.'s collision with its immediate rival, the A.S.E., was more direct and more serious. In its campaign to enrol dilutees the A.E.U. was initially at some disadvantage compared with the smaller union. With their minds always on post-war problems and believing that peace would mean a sharp cut-back in engineering production, the A.E.U. leaders envisaged the eventual exit of the great majority of added tradesmen. Hence dilutee members of the A.E.U. could not be assured of permanent retention of their war-time status. Even if the war lasted five years and thus enabled dilutees to serve the pre-war qualifying period at the trade they would still have to step down in preference to recognised tradesmen. In order to be able to ensure this the Commonwealth Council kept a detailed record of the movement of all added tradesmen through the Local Committees' registers.

The A.S.E. did not feel so restricted. Either because it realised earlier than the A.E.U. that engineering employment would not shrink greatly at the end of the war, or, more likely, because it simply hoped to expand its membership, the smaller union assured dilutees from the start that it would do its utmost to retain them in the industry after the war. As early as July 1940 A.E.U. organiser, C. Cowper, was complaining of A.S.E. action in sending to all trainees in the Sydney area a circular letter

... with the inference that it [A.S.E.] has been a party to the agreement [between the A.E.U., employers and government] since its inception. Some of their canvassers have also assured the trainees that they will be kept in the trade in spite of the conditions of the agreement.[47]

Cowper also claimed that the A.S.E. had lowered its fees to attract the newcomers and that A.S.E. members had held meetings protesting against their own officials' actions in the matter. Similar A.E.U. complaints of A.S.E. misrepresentation of the likely permanence of added tradesmen in the industry were regularly voiced by branches and organisers over the next two years.[48] A.S.E. growth was particularly noticeable in New South Wales where it made a maximum net gain of 12,288 new members as against the A.E.U.'s 10,928. However, with the slackening in engineering production and the exit of many dilutees after 1943 the A.S.E.'s membership fell much more rapidly.

[45] 'C.C.M.', 14/8/40, 29/10/40 and 4/11/40.
[46] See e.g. 'C.C.M.', 14/8/41; *M.J.R.*, September 1942, p. 12, January 1944, p. 12.
[47] *M.J.R.*, August 1940, p. 20.
[48] See e.g. *M.J.R.*, May 1941, p. 10, 'C.C.M.', 16/5/41, 30/6/41, 19/11/42.

By the end of the war the overall relative strengths of the two unions had roughly reverted to the pre-war situation.

The major initial concern of the A.E.U. leaders was that the A.S.E. might gain a foothold in shops which had hitherto been solely organised by the A.E.U. In particular the larger union sought to keep the A.S.E. out of the most skilled section of the industry — the toolroom. The extra dilutee tool-makers were selected from the ranks of recognised tradesmen but, in some cases at least, A.E.U. members did not apply in sufficient numbers for these key positions despite the exhortations of their local officials. Friction mounted between the two unions with the A.E.U. invariably the aggressor. The climax came in August 1941, when the A.S.E. applied to the Arbitration Court for an award to prevent the A.E.U. 'from inducing or endeavouring to induce by threat persons to resign from or to refrain from joining the claimant Society [A.S.E.] and join the respondent Union [A.E.U.]'.[49] Judge O'Mara declined to make an award as suggested by the A.S.E. but indicated that it had leave to apply again if the two organisations failed to settle their differences amicably. The unions' clashes over workshop control of added tradesmen seemed to die in the face of the new common danger arising from the entry of females into the skilled branches of the engineering industry.

V

The craft metal unions had long been uneasily aware of the potential threat posed to their members by female labour. Over the three decades preceding World War II, in the face of strong trade union opposition, small numbers of women had been introduced on such light repetitive metal work as core-making, nut and bolt making, and drilling, lapping and assembling. In the second half of the 1930s the primary union concern was to ensure the re-absorption of all out-of-work males. Believing that the incentive to the employers to introduce female workers was the disparity in wage rates, the A.E.U. and other metal unions became advocates of equal pay for equal work.[50]

The fear of an uncontrolled influx of women into the engineering labour

---

[49] 45 *C.A.R.* 310. For further details of the case and the back-ground to the toolroom disputes at the Small Arms Factory, Lithgow, and at Chas. Ruwolts Pty. Ltd., Melbourne, which gave rise to the A.S.E. application see 'C.C.M.', 19/7/40, 22/3/41, 25/3/41; *M.J.R.*, April 1941, p. 4, September 1941, p. 3, November 1941, p. 4.

According to O'Mara the A.E.U. members responsible for the Ruwolt's trouble were of English origin. O'Mara reported that A.E.U. Secretary Wickham claimed that the animosity towards the A.S.E. was 'based on a feeling which he expects to go out when the "old fellows go out"'. 45 *C.A.R.* 310 at p. 315.

[50] See e.g. *M.J.R.*, April 1937, p. 5; *Employers' Review*, 30/9/38.

market was one factor motivating the A.E.U.'s early acceptance of the dilution scheme. When the agreement came into operation the union's leaders realised that female dilution would be the next step if the training schemes did not provide sufficient tradesmen. Thus the A.E.U. opposed the F.I.A. proposals for an overtime ban at the beginning of 1941 not only because such an embargo would hasten the introduction of non-engineering workers into the trainee schemes but also because it would result in the entry of females into the industry.[51]

The first important pressure on the A.E.U. to accept females in the industry came towards the close of 1940. The organisers soon realised the necessity of this but when they passed on their views to the Commonwealth Council they were informed that under no circumstances would it agree to the entry of women into the skilled trades.[52] If employers or government forced the issue by unilateral action then the union reaction should be immediate, 'it is not a matter for a sectional dispute but it is a question that should be met by united opposition of all members in a district.[53] By April 1941, however, the Council had been persuaded to 'Communicate with E.C. [Executive Council] for permission to ... organise females in the industry if necessary, for our own protection'[54] — but the London office vetoed the proposal because it had been rejected by the 1940 Rules Revision Committee.[55]

Table 6.1:   Female Employment in the Metal Trades

	Total	Females	Females as a percentage of total
	(000)	(000)	%
1938–9	177.7	9.5	5.4
1939–40	184.5	10.6	5.8
1940–1	221.1	14.9	6.7
1941–2	276.1	23.5	8.5
1942–3	328.1	45.4	13.8
1943–4	341.0	55.2	16.2
1944–5	319.3	45.0	14.1
1945–6	292.5	30.4	10.4
1946–7	300.9	26.2	8.7

Source: *Production Bulletin* Nos. 33–41.

[51] 'C.C.M.', 28/1/41.
[52] 'C.C.M.', 29/10/40, 13/11/40, 15/11/40, 2/12/40.
[53] 'C.C.M.', 5/12/40.
[54] 'C.C.M.', 21/4/41.
[55] 'C.C.M.', 11/8/41.

This decision seriously handicapped the Australian section. As the rate of female entry to industry quickened it was able only to protest to the government. Male dilutees were eagerly enrolled but women performing identical tasks remained outside the A.E.U. The district officials were discontented at this state of affairs and they continually urged a change in union policy. Eventually in December 1941 the Coastal District Committee agreed to a consent award for females employed in general engineering in Perth. The Commonwealth Council formally reprimanded the Committee but the breach had been made. When the Council agreed to a conference on the matter in February 1942 district officials all reported the spread of females into A.E.U. trades in their areas. In the light of this the Council entered into extensive negotiations with the government in order to ensure that, if the A.E.U. ended its opposition to the employment of women, the position of male members would be suitably safeguarded.[56]

In December 1941 the Curtin government had approved of the principle of female workers being engaged in those sectors of the economy where the supply of males proved insufficient.[57] The Prime Minister also declared that he would give an undertaking that all women so employed would, if necessary, leave the industry after the war and that there would be no question 'of an invasion of men's work by cheap female labour'. A sub-committee of Cabinet was delegated to conduct negotiations with the unions and employers. The main problem to be solved was the rate of pay. Employers wanted the general adoption of the Arbitration Court's principle of setting the female Basic Wage at 55 per cent of the male rate. The unions insisted on equal pay for equal work. Eventually, in March 1942, the government decided to establish a special body to settle the issue. The Womens' Employment Board consisted of a chairman and two representatives each of employers and employees. One representative from each side was to be permanent and the other was drawn from the industry under consideration. Female wage rates fixed by the Board were to be not less than 60 per cent and not more than 100 per cent of the male rates. The actual wage level would depend on the Board's assessment of female productivity in each trade.

The employers refused to co-operate in the Board's operation[58] and their attempted obstruction was initially supported by the Opposition-controlled Senate. The government was able to circumvent these moves and the Board allayed the unions' main fears by deciding that, after a two week probationary

[56] 'C.C.M.', 23/12/41, 29/12/41, 6/1/42, 9/1/42, 9/2/42.
[57] Walker, op. cit., p. 302.
[58] *Employers' Review*, 31/3/42, 27/2/43; *Metal Trades Journal*, 16/3/42, 1/10/42, 1/3/43.

period at 60 per cent of the male rate, women employed on work in the munitions and metal industries usually performed by men were to receive 90 per cent of the male rate. Meanwhile the number of women performing work covered by the A.E.U. increased and the union continued to lose ground in the race to organise them because of the sloth of the British Section in altering the constitution. Eventually, in July 1942, the Executive Council wired instructions to take a postal ballot of Australian members on the advisability of recalling the Rules Revision Committee to amend the rules and allow females to join the A.E.U. In a high poll the Commonwealth members declared in favour by 13,726 votes to 8,257. Even so the General Rules were not altered until the end of the year and formal permission to enrol women was not received from London until January 1943.

As had been the case in the early days of male dilution, the A.E.U. hoped that the employment of women would be restricted to lower grades of engineering work. In this aim the union was initially supported by the federal government. In a letter setting out the Cabinet's original proposals in March 1942 the Minister of Munitions, and longtime A.E.U. member, N.J.O. Makin, wrote; 'I desire to add that it is intended that the foregoing [proposals] should apply only to semi-skilled and unskilled operations at present, and the objective will be to bring the female labour in on the lower grades of duties, thus releasing the men for higher and wider duties.'[59] Hence the A.E.U. fought hard to prevent the employment of women even on 2nd and 3rd class machinists' work whilst the toolroom was regarded as a strictly male pre-serve.[60] But it proved impossible to do more than slow down the rate of entry of women into the more highly skilled trades. A study of female entrants to the A.E.U. between 1943 and 1945 suggests that 35 per cent of the total of 4,300 were engaged in skilled occupations. Consequently, the union's emphasis swung round towards securing the introduction of specific legislation to ensure that absolute preference would be given to male engineers after the war.

In late 1942 and early 1943 the A.E.U., fully supported by the A.S.E., was involved in several important stoppages of work in sectors of the metal industry not covered by the Women's Employment Board's munition rates. Ostensibly the strikers were only fighting to secure at least 90 per cent of the male rate for female employees, if not equal pay. In fact, although the wages issue was of great importance the unions saw the stoppages as the best means of bringing pressure on the government to guarantee the post-war rights of male engineers.

[59] *M.J.R.*, April 1942, p. 4.
[60] 'C.C.M.', 14/9/42, 5/10/42, 10/4/43; *M.J.R.*, March 1943, p. 13.

For example, after the Women's Employment Board had approved of the employment of females on 1st class welding in the motor body building trade it reserved its decision on wages and conditions. In the interim the management at Ford's Motor Works, Homebush, New South Wales, had paid the female rates set out in the Metal Trades Award. Engineers employed at the plant immediately struck work and returned three weeks later only after the Board had announced that women should receive 90 per cent of male wages. Judge O'Mara regarded the A.E.U. stand as 'rather technical' and that

The dispute which is not really with the Company but with the Commonwealth Government is political rather than industrial and its purpose is to impress the Government of the day, not to persuade or coerce the employers. I understand that the Amalgamated Engineering Union has asked that legislation be passed making it a condition of the employment of females on men's work in the engineering trades and processes that they should be withdrawn from that work on the termination of the war or earlier if men can be found to take their places.[61]

In this the judge sympathised with the union which, in his opinion, had 'reasonable grounds for being apprehensive as to whether or not existing legislation is sufficient for that purpose'.

The pressure on the government produced results. After a similar dispute at A.C.I. Engineering Pty. Ltd., Sydney conferences were held between the union and the Attorney General. Sydney organiser, A. Shaw, reported that an understanding had been reached to the effect that 'a test case will be cited before the Women's Employment Board re 100 per cent wages for women and that the support of the Federal Arbitration Court will be given to Union claims. Judge O'Mara and the Attorney General, Dr Evatt, will also give their support'.[62]

However, after many further conferences with government representatives the A.E.U. accepted proposals contained in regulations gazetted in May 1943 which in effect provided for equal pay on tradesmen's or 2nd class machinist's work. In addition added male journeymen were to be given preference over their female equivalents and the Dilution Committees were to exercise full control over the selection and allocation of female dilutees.[63] After this date the A.E.U.'s immediate concern with the problem of female wages receded although it still supported the principle of equal pay in all trades and was associated with the unsuccessful attempt in 1945 to secure an increase in the wages of women not covered by the Women's Employment Board.[64]

[61] 48 *C.A.R.* 855 at p. 856. See also 49 *C.A.R.* 4 at p. 5.
[62] *M.J.R.*, February 1943, p. 10.
[63] *M.J.R.*, June 1943, p. 5, July 1943, p. 10.
[64] 54 *C.A.R.* 613.

7

The industrial front 1945—54: full employment and wages in inflation

I

The metal industries' plant and equipment had not been allowed to deteriorate to the same extent as in 'non-essential' industries during the war but the shortages of inputs, particularly of fuel and power, occasionally retarded progress in the immediate post-war years. Employment increased by 35 per cent to a total of nearly 400,000 workers between 1945—6 and 1953—4 but the 1943—4 peak wartime level was not surpassed until 1949—50.[1] The most noticeable growth occurred in the consumer-durable industries. General Motors—Holden produced the first all-Australian automobile in 1949 and the numbers employed in building and maintaining motor vehicles and accessories increased from 40,282 in 1945—6 to 90,449 in 1953—4. The workforce in the electrical goods industry rose by 47 per cent to a total of over 46,000 in the same period. On the other hand the proportion of metal workers engaged in railway workshops continued to decline, from 16 per cent in 1938—9 to 13 per cent in 1945—6 and 10 per cent in 1953—4.

With the federal government's withdrawal from arms manufacture and the proliferation of small enterprises, particularly garages, eager to take advantage of the peace-time seller's market, the proportion of workers employed in small-scale plants rose again. In 1953—4 38 per cent of the metal workforce were engaged in shops with less than 100 hands on the payroll. However, the larger producers had learned the advantages of specialisation and planned production and the increased product standardisation compared with pre-war years gave rise to renewed employer demands for the introduction of payment by results. Opposition to incentive schemes slackened within many trade unions during these years of continued full employment. In 1951 the A.C.T.U. Congress authorised an investigation into the question and in 1953 the Congress in effect lifted its 26 year old ban on payment by results.

[1] *Production Bulletin*, Nos. 40—8.

Within the metal trades, however, only the E.T.U. was prepared to co-operate to any important degree with management.

The decline in A.E.U. membership resulting from the exit of many war-time dilutees from the industry ended in 1947—8. Thereafter the numbers on the rolls increased steadily and the previous peak level was surpassed in 1951. Because of the acute shortage of skill in the post-war period the A.E.U. agreed to the continuation of a limited form of controlled dilution. When the war-time dilution regulations expired on 22 March 1946 they were replaced by new regulations, later incorporated into a *Tradesmen's Rights Regulations Act* (T.R.R. Act), which allowed for the entry to the metal trades of a limited number of ex-servicemen under strictly defined conditions. In all cases recognised tradesmen, i.e. those employed in the trade before 8 May 1940, were to have absolute preference over both war-time dilutees and returned servicemen. The Dilution Committees continued to control the training of the latter but independent elevation by management of unskilled employees to skilled work was now prohibited. This provision did not prevent some employers from attempting to continue the war-time practice but otherwise the new legislation worked well.

Of greater significance to the A.E.U. were the internal requests that all men who had worked at the trade for five years should be accepted as recognised tradesmen. The A.E.U.'s federal leaders, still fearing a post-war depression, at first insisted on preserving formal job preference for pre-1940 tradesmen. The Council moderated its attitude only when forced to by the impact of the post-war immigration schemes which saw a net inflow of 528,000 by mid-1952.[2] Whereas it was relatively easy to ascertain the true qualifications of British immigrants claiming to possess engineering skills, arrivals from war-torn and politically divided continental Europe posed much greater problems. Faced with a continued shortage of skilled labour and prevented by the T.R.R. Act from legally elevating unskilled workers, employers naturally tended to accept at face value migrants' claims to skill.

The Council's first reaction was that '... no Balts [are] to be employed on work covered by engineering awards'[3] but six months later the Council was instructing the Innisfail Branch to admit Europeans to membership 'where found on a job'.[4] Yet at this stage the Council still refused to accept any migrant, British or European, as a recognised tradesmen unless he could produce indisputable proof that he had worked at the trade for at least five

[2] *Report of the Committee of Economic Enquiry* (Canberra, 1965), Vol. I, p. 68.
[3] 'C.C.M.', 22/3/49.
[4] 'C.C.M.', 27/9/49.

years prior to May 1940. As the number of migrant engineers increased, how-ever, the Council bowed to the pressure for full recognition and job preference applied by dilutees who had entered the industry during the war. When the T.R.R. Act approached its expiry date of 3 September 1952 the A.E.U. pro-posed a suitable amendment to the legal definition of recognised tradesmen. Employers on the other hand were opposed to any extension of the Act because of the restrictions it placed on their freedom to elevate employees. After discussions between the two parties and the government a compromise agreement was reached. The 1952 amendments extended the operation of the Act to 2 September 1955. The definition of a recognised tradesman was widened to include all those who were currently employed on skilled work and who had been for at least seven years since 8 May 1940. This requirement effectively excluded from recognition any post-war dilutees. Migrants could obtain recognition only if they could produce proof of their qualifications in their country of origin. Men who had served in the armed forces in Korea and Malaya were now permitted to enter skilled trades under the same conditions as World War II servicemen. The major concession to the employers was contained in the clauses which allowed them to elevate unskilled employees, provided they had 'reasonable cause'. The unions did not hesitate to use the preference clauses during the 1952–3 recession.[5]

II

The immediate post-war period witnessed much industrial unrest culminat-ing in a six-month dispute in the Victorian metal trades in 1946–7 which brought the A.E.U. its greatest ever gain through direct action – but at a staggering financial cost and with side effects which were to help completely change the industrial and legal setting. Subsequent political and industrial events ranging from the Cold War to the A.L.P. Split have meant that, in retrospect, this stoppage, along with other immediate post-war industrial disputes, has been tagged in many quarters as simply part of a giant com-munist conspiracy to weaken the economy and subvert Australian society.[6] In fact it was nothing of the kind.[7] We have already noted the engineers'

[5] *Metal Trades Journal*, 2/2/53, 1/5/53.
[6] See, for example, B. A. Santamaria, '"The Movement". 1941–60 – An Outline', in H. Mayer (Ed.), *Catholics and the Free Society* (Melbourne, 1961), pp. 60–1; Probably the best evidence of the latter-day acceptance of this myth is its appearance in Robert Murray's authoritative book on the A.L.P. 'Split' which, he says, is based 'essentially on other people's recollections'. See *The Split* (Melbourne, 1970), p. 20.
[7] The author has endeavoured to demonstrate this in much greater detail elsewhere (T. Sheridan, '"Labour v Labor". The Victorian Metal Trades Dispute, 1946–47', in John Iremonger, John Merritt and Graeme Osborne (Eds.), *Strikes: Studies in Twentieth Century Australian Social History* (Canberra, 1973), pp. 176–224.

record of consistent industrial aggression since the Depression: for the A.E.U. the major difference between the 1946–7 dispute and previous shorter and narrower stoppages is the special ingredient inserted by the federal government. To this may be added the feeling of A.E.U. members that they had made considerable sacrifices during the war by accepting wage ceilings and co-operating with the general war effort, particularly through the dilution schemes. For less skilled and hitherto less fortunate workers there also existed an even more potent factor making for industrial aggression. These were not just the post-war years, they were also the post-Depression years. Few workers had been as fortunate as the skilled engineers in being able to commence an industrial counter-offensive in the late 1930s. The high demand for labour during the war was a new experience for most workers. So in addition to the natural desire to advance working conditions after a period of self-imposed restrain, all members of the workforce retained vivid, and usually bitter, memories of the Depression years. This meant that the attitude of organised labour was coloured by a desire for something akin to revenge, for a squaring of those industrial and social accounts left suspended with the outbreak of war. *This* time, it was felt, the bosses, the financiers, or however 'they' might be described, were not going to get away with it. This time the wage earning classes were going to make sure that their slice of the national cake was increased – and the time to do it was right now while business prospects were so good and labour in such high demand. Later on, perhaps, the situation might change in some unforeseen way so as to prevent industrial 'justice' being done – and despite all the new ideas of economic planning and financial management, despite all the election slogans, and despite all the White Papers in the world, there is plenty of evidence to indicate that, at heart, few Australians were completely convinced that the dole queue and all the other dreadful paraphernalia of the Depression had gone forever.[8] Such deepseated doubts added to the urgency of workers getting their cut *now* – lest the promised pie in the sky never actually eventuate.

As for the C.P.A.'s role, the truth of the matter is that it attracted support among an aggressive industrial workforce by its willingness to involve itself in, and if possible lead, what was a spontaneous grass roots drive in the post-war years for improved wages and conditions of work. The communist attitude

---

[8] The evidence for this is overwhelming. For examples of doubt at the highest levels see, E. Ronald Walker, op. cit., pp. 384, 386 and L. F. Crisp, op. cit., pp. 303, 305. And the fears lingered on for many years. In 1954 when 3,000 N.S.W. workers were asked to list 40 factors in order of priority an overwhelming 49 per cent placed job security first. Second came pay with 18 per cent. *Metal Trades Journal*, 15/1/55.

and performance contrasted favourably with the hesitancy of many A.L.P.
trade union leaders who found themselves in the invidious position of having
to defend industrial policies adopted by the Chifley government which were
completely out of step with the wishes of the great majority of rank and file
trade unionists. The communists certainly attempted to make hay while the
sun was shining, but without the particular contemporary industrial climate
all their efforts would have been in vain.

The fact that the post war industrial upheavals were not a communist
conspiracy is indicated by the fact that unrest began to surface long before
the end of the war – that is while C.P.A. members were still striving might
and main to avoid any industrial stoppages which might hinder the war
effort and consequently endanger Russia's struggle with Germany. As the
Australian correspondent of the conservative Empire quarterly, *Round Table*,
pointed out when discussing the 1944 coal dispute, unrest was not confined to
this traditionally turbulent industry,

New South Wales, during the 20 months ending August 31 (1944), had 1,432 industrial disputes involving 588,951 workers and resulting in a loss of 1,461,671 man-
days. At times in that period and since, industrial disputes wholly or partially
deprived the neutral citizen of meat, bread, laundry, newspapers, tyres, theatrical
entertainment, hospital attention, buses and trams, coke for stoves, potatoes, restau-
rants, hot baths, country and interstate travel and other amenities.[9]

An even longer list could be compiled for the immediate post-war period for
in the three years 1945–7, nearly $5\frac{1}{2}$ million working days were lost in 2,796
disputes. This contrasts with 2.4 million days lost in the last three peacetime
years 1937–9 but still falls short of the $8\frac{1}{4}$ million days lost in the post-World
War I triennium of 1919–21 during which the C.P.A., founded in 1920,
obviously had little industrial influence.

As for the A.E.U. itself, the controversial topic of C.P.A. influence within
the union will be considered at length in the next chapter. For our present
purpose of understanding the course and conduct of the 1946–7 dispute
we need only note certain central facts. Firstly the dispute represented probably the most popular issue ever in the history of the A.E.U. in Victoria.
Supported by public opinion the 21,000 Victorian A.E.U. members presented
a completely united front throughout and the only serious disagreements
occurred in Sydney on the Commonwealth Council. For the record we may
note that, of the 30 A.E.U. branch delegates who attended the 44 meetings

[9] March 1945. The *Round Table* correspondents were among those objective
contemporary observers who were quite clear as to the true origins of
industrial unrest and the communist role therein. See e.g. issues of December
1943, March 1946, March 1947.

of the Melbourne District Committee at which policy was hammered out during the strike, only five were C.P.A. members. Of the nine full-time Victorian officials, three were communists. The overwhelming majority of the strike leaders were A.L.P. men of impeccable credentials such as A.E. Fair, C. E. Mundy and H. J. Souter. A number of them, including J. E. Burke, W. H. White and F. P. Twomey, were among the union's leading anti-communists in the internal controversies just over the horizon. Understandably they, and officials such as G. W. Deverall and A. E. Horsburgh who both attracted electoral support from the A.L.P. Industrial Groups, were among those most disgruntled with retrospectively projected myths of C.P.A. master-minding the A.E.U.'s greatest victory — which at the time the union's best known communist correctly attributed to the 'splendid unshakeable unity of the workers of all shades of opinion. I have pointed to the complete unanimity of Communist, A.L.P., Catholic and even normally right wing delegates on the Melbourne District Committee, but this was in truth a reflection of the unity of the entire membership.'[10] The two Victorian federal officials who came to play the leading roles in negotiations were Cranwell — who by now was A.C.T.U. vice-president — and the current Councilman for Division 1, E. J. Rowe (C.P.A.). An ebullient personality and a gifted public speaker, Rowe was a perfect foil for his cooler, pragmatic colleague. The press painted Cranwell and Rowe in the reddest of hues but in reality one of their main tasks was to restrain the increasing aggression of the branch delegates. On several occasions only the two federal officials prevented the immediate extension of the A.E.U.'s biggest strike to other Victorian plants and to other states. In so doing they incurred considerable wrath from activists in Sydney as well as Melbourne.

The complex and rapid moving events occurring during both the dispute itself and during its lengthy prologue are particularly difficult to unravel and are interconnected with many other contemporary disputes of varying gravity and magnitude.[11] The key to understanding is to be found in the employers' oft-repeated claim that the A.E.U.'s real dispute was not with them but with the federal government. This is only a slight exaggeration for without the government's stand the dispute must have ended very much earlier. Indeed at times it seemed true to say that Prime Minister Chifley was the union's real opponent, for he was largely responsible for the firm anti-inflation line pursued by the government, including maintenance of wartime

---

[10] E. J. Rowe, *Communist Review*, June 1947.
[11] Full documentation of the following terse account is provided in Sheridan, 'Labour v Labor', op. cit.

wage ceilings. Chifley's view was that any relaxation of wage regulations in the contemporary labour market would only add more weight to the continued clamour from employers, opposition parties and the press for the relaxation of price controls, fuel rationing and other pieces of wartime machinery by which the government controlled the economy during its changeover to peacetime production. He maintained this position with all the doggedness and determination for which he was renowned, and in the face of considerable pressure within his cabinet, the A.L.P. caucus and from his otherwise natural allies in the union movement. When he yielded ground it was extremely reluctantly, at the last possible moment, and often with little grace.

Trade union frustration began when the government refused on constitutional grounds to introduce a national 40 hour week through legislation ratifying the 1935 I.L.O. Convention. The A.C.T.U. came in for considerable criticism when it settled for an offer in March 1946 to amend the relevant regulations to allow the Arbitration Court to deal with a general standard hours case. Hearings began in May but the A.C.T.U.'s hopes of a speedy decision proved sadly amiss as they dragged on and on for 16 months. The unions did not help by calling nearly as many witnesses as the stonewalling employers, but the government drew more criticism for its apparent refusal to ease the bottlenecks by appointing new judges to the understrength and overworked bench.

On the wages front the Basic Wage could only change in response to movements in the retail price index to which it was linked. Consequently the government made every effort through price control and subsidies to maintain constant the price of major goods in the regimen. These efforts were attended with almost complete success from 1943 onwards but workers still felt themselves the victims of a statistical confidence trick when told that their wages could not be raised because the index was stable. For, in addition to being subject to increased income tax rates they were painfully aware that some of the heavily weighted items in the index, such as a vacant house room, were virtually unobtainable. In addition items not included in the index had either risen considerably in price – such as fruit and vegetables, other than potatoes – or were in short supply, like beer and tobacco. Inevitably then, pressure mounted from all quarters for a change in the wage-pegging regulations. Eventually in March 1946 while making possible the 40-hours hearings Chifley also made the requisite amendments to allow the court to review the Basic Wage. The A.C.T.U., anxious to keep the two issues separate and anyway expecting a speedy hearing, decided to concentrate first on the 40-hours case. The employers, on the other hand continually tried to draw the Basic Wage issue into the hours' case in the confident belief that, faced with two sets of union demands, the court would grant only one. As the 40-hour hearings dragged on, union members felt doubly frustrated for neither their hours nor their Basic Wage expectations were being fulfilled.

In 1946 the A.E.U. began to concentrate its thoughts about margins. The ending of the war had several conflicting effects for engineers. On the one hand, as the Australian war effort tapered off, overtime earnings fell away temporarily for many workers, and employers began to tighten up on concessions such as unofficial tea breaks which had been accepted during the typically long working days during the war. In addition the disappearance of the cost plus method of pricing tenders for war work made employers more cost-conscious and chary of bidding-up skilled wages. On the other hand the lifting, towards the end of 1945, of regulations governing labour mobility stimulated other firms with an eye on peace-time prospects to offer illegal over-award payments to attract skilled men. In December 1945 Judge O'Mara varied the Metal Trades Award by making changes generally favourable to the unions including increasing annual leave to 14 days, but when it became clear that Chifley would not extend his March regulation amendments to margins, the A.E.U. districts began to implement the decision of an Interstate Conference by taking direct action to secure a margins increase of 20s. A progressive overtime ban was introduced first in Sydney and later in Melbourne, Newcastle, Wollongong and Adelaide. A major dispute seemed likely in Melbourne in October when the Railway Commissioner served dismissal notices on 100 A.E.U. men because of the impact of the ban, but this was masked and defused by the simultaneous eruption of a general transport strike in Victoria. This strike and many others occurred after a period of relative restraint during the federal election campaign and were the direct result of Chifley's rejection of A.C.T.U. post-election pleas to modify his wages policy. So explosive did the industrial atmosphere become, however, that Chifley was forced to arrange concessionary gestures. After secret discussions the Arbitration Court on 30 October declared its acceptance in principle of the 40 hour week and the Commonwealth government's counsel moved for a speedy hearing of a Basic Wage case. In fact the hours case dragged on for 11 more months and the A.C.T.U. soon discovered that the court did not intend to separate the wage and hours issues. By then, however, Victorian metal employers' anger with the A.E.U.'s overtime ban and with the separate wages campaign by the skilled moulders and their F.I.A. assistants had resulted in the commencement of the six month long metal trades dispute. On 1 November, 700 metal employer members of the

Chambers of Manufactures met and voted to lock out an estimated 100,000 employees if the ban was not lifted and the workers who had 'resigned' from 98 foundries did not return. Dismissal notices were in fact served to some 70,000 metal workers but a great many firms drew back from the brink as the deadline expired, and only some 20,000 were locked out on 14 November, including approximately 2,000 A.E.U. members.

With the advantage of hindsight it is obvious that the lock out was a mistake both tactically and psychologically. Labour market conditions were completely unsuited for such a move, while among unionists it recalled memories of 1918—22 and 1928—30, when it was believed the employers set out to 'smash' unionism. It provided the A.E.U. and its allies with lasting public sympathy and it crushed all hopes of compromise within the A.E.U. itself. From now on the officials' task of restraining outraged and belligerent members was made much harder. As it was, the locked out engineers determined not to return until the 20s. was granted and on 25 November they were joined by 1,500 A.E.U. maintenance engineers who had been retained by the firms involved.

The employers continued for some time to act as if pre-war conditions still obtained and that public relations were of no importance. In early December, for example, they refused to reopen the gates when, as a result of apparent concessions by Chifley, the foundry workers, with A.E.U. blessings, offered to return. In addition because of separate unrest over wages Adelaide employers locked out 1,100 foundry workers on 16 November. On 27 November, 62 Sydney waterfront shops followed suit, with the M.T.E.A. unsuccessfully attempting to persuade its other members to extend the lock out.

By Christmas the industrial realities of the strange new post-war world had finally impressed themselves on most employers. A steady stream of Victorian firms paid the 20s., and by mid-January both the Sydney and Melbourne firms had ended their ill considered lock out. The A.E.U., anxious as always to be in complete control of its own destiny and doubtful of the strength of purpose of the leaders of other unions affected, made no protest when they decided to return to work when the Melbourne shops reopened on 20 January. The F.I.A. however, was unable to secure suitable guarantees and its members remained out with the A.E.U.

In the meantime Arbitration Court and federal government had both flattered to deceive. The service of dismissal notices in Melbourne and Adelaide had been enough to persuade the Full Court that after all it should hear separate arguments for an interim Basic Wage increase as a matter of urgency, and the almost miraculously short 9 day hearings began on 25 November. Meanwhile further pressure was placed on Chifley by the threat of another transport strike over the court's declaration that the regulations did not allow it to accept the agreement on overtime rates which had been part of the October settlement terms. Chifley's stalling brought forth both a bitter public attack on him by A.C.T.U. Secretary, A. E. Monk, speaking for many 'moderate' unionists who had previously tried to defend Chifley, and rumours that the federal Minister for Labour and National Service, E. J. Holloway, was also privately critical. As stoppages in other industries mounted – including a national gas strike – the court's decision to award only a 7s. interim Basic Wage increase was greeted with anger and derision. On 14 December Chifley at last unveiled amendments to the regulations but then proceeded to ignore the outcry which followed when legal opinion, including one of the Arbitration Court judges, declared that the amendments did not allow for the marginal increases which Chifley claimed. Monk was one of the first to denounce the Prime Minister and further Cabinet dissension was rumoured. The metals stoppage continued.

In the New Year after an A.C.T.U. delegation had received no satisfaction from Chifley on its wages and hours claims, the A.C.T.U. Executive decided that the time had at last come for sterner measures. Its proposals for the first ever national stoppage on 1 May accompanied by the unilateral implementation of the 40 hour week were endorsed by a conference of federal unions on 5 and 6 February. Disappointment with the Chifley government was sharpened by the N.S.W. and Queensland A.L.P. governments' decisions to legislate the introduction of 40 hours for employees working under state awards.

Concurrently A.E.U. leaders were hard pressed to hold back their Melbourne and Sydney members who clamoured for an extension. The Commonwealth Council, however, was intent on first ensuring observance of the appropriate code of industrial conduct by kindred unions. Thus it waited until the M.T.F. and A.C.T.U. had formally endorsed an extension to all private firms in Melbourne not paying the 20s. When the A.C.T.U. established a Disputes Committee, however, the A.E.U. insisted that membership be limited to the A.C.T.U., the metal unions and the F.E.D.F.A., and made it clear that in the last resort it would make its own decisions. In an effort to cool the industrial atmosphere Acting Chief Judge Drake-Brockman made a public declaration of his belief that Chifley's December amendments did allow him to recommend unrestricted hearings into margins. Its extra 7,000 members still came out on 7 February but the A.E.U. was not uninterested when the employers referred the dispute to the court and Conciliation Commissioner Mooney decided to break precedent and conduct hearings while the strike was still on. On 25 February Mooney offered 9s. extra to all metal workers earning margins of 27s. and over, 7s. to those receiving margins between 20s. and 26s., and 5s. to all other classifications. During the hearings the employers had argued that the regulations only permitted a maximum increase of 4/6d. per week and had threatened to apply for an order of restraint if Mooney exceeded this figure. They soon shifted their ground when the A.E.U., F.I.A. and A.C.T.U. rejected Mooney's proposals as completely inadequate.

The next move open to the A.E.U. was to extend the strike to Victorian government plants. Had a non-Labor ministry been in power it seems certain that this would have been acceptable to the rest of the labour movement. In fact an A.L.P. government occupied the Treasury benches led by Premier John Cain who had made great efforts to settle the metals dispute – including trying to persuade Chifley to unbend. Thus the A.E.U. could not gain support for an extension on the Disputes Committee from other than the F.I.A. and F.E.D.F.A. The disagreement was well publicised and encouraged employers to reject union claims during negotiations at which the non-metal firms were clearly revealed as the most determined opponents of a margins increase. So fearful were they of an inevitable 'flow on' if the A.E.U. demands were met that members of the Chambers of Manufactures paid a voluntary levy of 2½ per cent of their February payroll to aid firms involved in the dispute. Mooney also was sufficiently encouraged by the union disagreement to forget his earlier declarations that he would not make an official variation of the award until the men returned. On 18 March he incorporated his '9–7–5' formula in an order varying the award. The metal union ranks then publicly split leaving the A.E.U. and its junior partner, the F.I.A., to seek support from individually sympathetic unions outside the M.T.F. The dispute now became irreparably entangled in the faction fighting of the Melbourne Trades Hall Council with the right wingers branding it a creature of the left. The A.C.T.U. decision to call off the May-Day stoppage because the court was at last to hear the hours and Basic Wage cases separately, added further fuel to the flames which raged over the A.E.U.'s decision to withdraw 3,000 members employed in the metropolitan power and transport industries on 22 March. Engineering tradesmen in the railwaymens', gasworkers', and tramway employees' unions also withdrew together with F.E.D.F.A. crane-drivers.

While creeping paralysis set into the Victorian transport system, the first divisions appeared in the A.E.U. in Sydney. Wickham's successor as secretary was J. H. Carney, a leader of the newly formed A.L.P. Industrial Group within the union. Councilman Fountain, the leading left winger of the late 1930s, had since then gradually moved away from his old allies. Removed from the heat of the Melbourne battleground, the rift with the A.C.T.U.

and the alarming drain on A.E.U. funds was enough to convince the two Sydney men that the five month old dispute had gone on long enough. They chose to make an issue of the on-the-spot 'endorsement' by Cranwell and Rowe of the Melbourne District Committee's unanimous decision to extend the stoppage to government establishments. It was quite common for such decisions to be made in expectancy of retrospective Council endorsement but Cranwell and Rowe had technically breached the rules. The third Councilman, W. J. Porter of Queensland, did not support the Sydney men and, in his absence on annual leave, Cranwell used his casting vote to officially endorse the extension. Not one branch recorded its support for Fountain and Carney.

On 31 March the Victorians' policy seemed to be vindicated by the interpretation of the wage pegging regulations offered by the Full Court when it presented its long-awaited decision on weekend penalty rates. This case, in which the A.E.U., A.R.U., F.E.D.F.A. and Gas Employees' Union represented the interests of all workers, was expected to implement the last gains from the settlements which had ended the October transport stoppage and the December–January gas strike. Instead, the court found that the regulations sufficiently limited its powers to prevent it granting increased weekend penalty rates to any other than shift workers. This decision meant that, if the A.E.U. had followed the advice of the Council minority and of the A.C.T.U., and returned to work to set the arbitration machinery rolling, the court, even if it were sympathetically inclined – which the Victorians doubted – did not have the legal power to award an increase. In other words Drake-Brockman's carefully stated opinion back in early February on the court's powers was incorrect.

The general union fury which greeted the Full Court's decision forced Chifley at long last to yield. On 4 April he announced amendments which appeared to allow, *inter alia,* for unrestricted margins alterations provided the Acting Chief Judge certified that an alteration was not opposed to the national interest. The question now was how the metals dispute could be brought into the court.

The last month of the stoppage became a simple test of whose nerves were the strongest. Deprived of Chifley's shield the employers, in rejecting continual A.E.U. demands for a conference relied on three factors; the refusal of Drake-Brockman to act while the strike continued; the increasing parliamentary pressure being brought to bear by the opposition parties on the Cain and Chifley ministries to somehow end the strike – even if it meant freezing A.E.U. funds and jailing Cranwell; and the soaring cost to the union of continuing the stoppage. While privately coming very near to surrender towards the end of April, Victorian A.E.U. officials maintained a bold public face, emphasising the £9 millions in the British General Fund and endorsing District Committee decisions to extend. The factor which won the day for the union was the determination, not to say by this stage the fanaticism, of the rank and file. The F.I.A. communist leadership appeared to have had enough by mid-April, but the engineers, not merely would brook no suggestion of turning back, but rather maintained continuous pressure for further extensions. On 11 April A.E.U. apprentices and lower grade staff withdrew from the Newport power house. On 29 April A.E.U. men in country railway depots came out. On 2 May during the final negotiations all remaining staff and apprentices withdrew from metropolitan power houses and railways. These moves were endorsed and paralleled by the A.R.U. and F.E.D.F.A.

Employers' hopes in the meantime were raised by increased A.L.P. pressure which led to Councilman Porter agreeing with Carney and Fountain that Cranwell and Rowe should be recalled to Sydney to re-assess the whole strike situation. In the event, Porter fully supported the Victorians against the Sydney men who again had no branch backing. On the following day summonses to show cause why they should not be deregistered were served on the A.E.U., F.I.A. and Chambers of Manufactures, but the engineers thought they could detect bias in the twin facts that the A.E.U. was dealt with first on 21 April and, after the court's decision to deregister the union in 14 days time, proceedings against the employers were adjourned. The A.E.U. extensions went ahead and the Executive Council was cabled for funds. As transport ground to a halt, power supplies diminished, and other industrial disputes continued to flare up, Opposition politicians forecast civil war and 'complete chaos and bloodshed' within a few days. The A.C.T.U. Executive threatened to disaffiliate the A.E.U. and eventually by 8 votes to 4, formally 'advised' it to return to work and put its 'unassailable' case in the hands of the court. For their part the A.E.U. rank and file urged interstate extensions.

Someone had to yield, and on 1 May the breakthrough came. Under pressure from Cain and almost certainly Chifley, Drake-Brockman gave in and convened a conference between the parties. Elaborate face-saving procedures were followed for the benefit of everyone except the A.E.U., but behind the outer facade employers and the A.E.U. got down to business. After often acrimonious negotiations, settlement terms were agreed to on 5 May and the A.E.U. allowed further face-saving for court and employers by not making public the fact that Mooney's '9—7—5' formula would be lifted by the court to '16—13—11' — thus giving the fitter a total gain of 23s. when the interim Basic Wage decision was included. Outwardly, the strikers were to return on the basis of the Mooney formula while the first Full Court ever to judge a margins case would immediately begin hearings with any decision to be made retrospective. This allowed the conservative press to talk in terms of an A.E.U. defeat and a triumph for the nation's unique arbitration system. The jubilant A.E.U. men who led the 7,000 strong May-Day weekend march— at which neither government, A.C.T.U. or T.H.C. were seen to be officially represented — knew otherwise. So did those who accepted the real terms at a mass meeting on 7 May and returned on 8 May after nearly deciding to leave private firms without their labour for a further week just to rub the victory in. The Sydney and Adelaide stoppages soon concluded on similar terms. The *Sun News-Pictorial* actually went so far as to indicate the true settlement terms and was lashed by the court for its temerity. Contempt charges were later dismissed.

Perhaps because of these revelations the Full Court's judgment, issued on 26 June, departed significantly from the terms on which work had been resumed. It decided that Mooney had radically distorted the correct relationships between the various classifications. In particular his award of 5s. had given 'disproportionate increases' to the lower paid metal workers. The court therefore made a new award on an entirely different basis. The fitter received 16s. extra and the process worker 5s. extra and all other margins were proportionately modified. The net result for tradesmen was that their nominal rates exceeded the Basic Wage by 49 per cent — a figure exceeding even the original 43 per cent Harvester ratio. On the other hand workers falling into classifications below that of process worker were subject to nominal reductions to the Mooney rates ranging from 6d. to 3s. per week. The court appears to have decided on reflection that the F.I.A. — which organised the vast majority of the tradesmen's assistants — did not deserve to gain its promised reward from a battle of wills essentially won by the skilled engineers.

Apart from its anger at the cut in wages experienced by tradesmen's assistants the F.I.A. had also expected that general labourers employed in the metal trades would receive a margin for the first time. In October 1947 the F.I.A., supported by the other metal unions, applied to Mooney for an increase in its members' wages on the grounds that the terms of the agreement ending the Victorian stoppage had not been fulfilled. Mooney's judgment, rebutted the Bench's attack on his previous findings,

I know of nothing more likely to prolong a dispute or create a further dispute, than for an industrial authority to fail to implement a settlement arrived at by the parties when the terms of the settlement are not opposed to the national interest, and are otherwise unobjectionable ...

To implement the agreement between the parties, I propose to further vary the

Metal Trades award to provide that the lower grades (that is the 7s. and 5s. grades in the 'Mooney award') receive an increase of 13s. and 11s. respectively on the margins existing before the variation by me and by the Full Court . . .[12]

He also granted a 3s. margin to general labourers employed in the industry.

In addition to providing a higher platform on which to build over-award payments the new metal trade rates flowed on speedily to other trades and ever afterwards the new relativities remained the ideal for the union movement. The end of the marathon 40 Hours Case in September 1947 saw the Bench postponing the inception of the shorter week until January 1948, but the A.E.U. still described 1947 as 'a year of outstanding industrial achievements', feeling that it had secured higher wages for all workers in the Commonwealth by its preparedness to conduct one of the most hard-fought and certainly the most costly strike for a single union in the nation's industrial history. Despite some two thirds of the 17,000 engineers involved obtaining other jobs and the fact that, until late January, the A.E.U. men who had been locked out were entitled to Commonwealth Unemployment Benefit, the cost of the dispute was enormous. The exact amount is impossible to calculate because of the A.E.U.'s practice of holding most of its cash in the form of branch balances. As some indication the Supplementary Fund went from a surplus of £101,845 to a deficit of £31,785 between June 1946 and June 1947, £120,000 of Commonwealth bonds were sold and spent, and in addition the Melbourne dispute fund raised £8,500 in voluntary donations. A conservative estimate of the direct cost of the 1946–7 disputes is £220,000 or approximately $1,800,000 in 1974 prices. As we shall see the erosion of the A.E.U.'s funds had important consequences in the 1950s. It also made it highly likely that the current A.E.U. leaders would want to avoid any similar large scale confrontations in the future. On the other hand direct action had been shown to wrest concessions from a government and arbitration system which had rejected the arguments and pleas of 'moderate' union leaders. Although willing to accept that their tactics might need altering, the events of 1946–7 could only strengthen the belief of A.E.U. officials and activists that constant on-the-job aggression was essential in order to make best use of the institutional wage-fixing framework. As we will see the Queensland members soon involved themselves in a costly stoppage but thereafter the legal environment changed too radically for any related tactical changes to be determined.

The employers learnt their lesson well. Now realising the futility of lock-outs in conditions of full employment they sought in future legal restraints on the withdrawal of their employees' labour. The Chifley government must

[12] 59 C.A.R. 1272 at pp. 1277–8.

have been influenced by the metal trades dispute — and other stoppages of the period — when it made provision for the use of 'penal powers' by the court in its 1947 amendments to the Arbitration Act. The court itself indicated the moral it drew from the strike by including a clause in the new 1947 metal trades award forbidding overtime bans under threat of fines.

III

A.E.U. officials barely had time to fully consider all the implications of the Victorian dispute before the Queensland members were involved in another major stoppage. The cause was the refusal of the Hanlon state A.L.P. government to permit a flow on of the 1947 federal award to metal union members employed under the state award in the railway workshops. After lengthy stalling the government's final offer of 6/10d. for a fitter was 9/2d. less than the 1947 federal increase and, more importantly, 5/6d. less than the recent state award increase for tradesmen in private firms. State legislation required a secret ballot be held before strike action could be taken but all workshop unions voted in favour, the A.E.U. members in a ten to one ratio. Work ended at midnight on 2 February 1948 and the men returned on 6 April after the government had agreed to support a retrospective pay increase formula before the state court ranging from 10/1d. for a labourer to 19/10d. for a toolmaker, with the fitter getting 12/4d. extra. This represented a definite victory for the A.E.U. and the other workshop unions, and when the Commissioner of railways later tried to back out of the agreement and substitute a formula ranging between 4/2d. and 12/4d. the threat of a new strike forced the government to stand by its agreement.

The Queensland stoppage stands out in the A.E.U.'s dispute-studded career for several reasons. It was the one about which most lies were told; the A.L.P. government over-reacted to a surprising degree; and an A.E.U. official was involved in a controversial episode which drew criticism from many A.E.U. activists in Queensland. The level of falsehoods surrounding the dispute is connected with the government reaction. On 9 February the state court judged that the government could legally stand down without payment 14,000 other workers affected by the workshop men's withdrawal. But rather than exerting pressure on the craftsmen to return, the long discontented transport workers extended the strike to all railway and tramway employees. In retaliation the Hanlon ministry introduced Emergency Regulations which gave the government 'the most drastic strike-breaking powers yet taken by Labour [sic] in Queensland or Australia'.[13] All strikers were ordered to

---

[13] *Courier Mail*, 28/2/48. The A.L.P. had been governing Queensland with only one short break since 1915.

return or lose all their accrued service rights. The press and radio were completely closed to the unions which henceforth had very great difficulty in putting over their viewpoint. The normally anti-union press became even more one-sided and even the final settlement was represented as some sort of union defeat. The A.E.U. bitterly noted the lack of critical comment on the Emergency Regulations by newspapers in other states which were normally ever ready to spring to arms when the 'Freedom of the Press' was threatened. The isolation of the unions from the Queensland media added to the conspiratorial instincts of communists and other left wingers and dramatised the situation even further in their minds. The feeling that perhaps a revolutionary atmosphere was developing in turn fed the government's excited suspicion of a vast communist plot. Thus when the waterside workers came out in sympathy on 1 March and the seamen placed a boycott on sea traffic to and from the state, the government reacted with a stringent Anti-Picketing Act which, *inter alia*, declared illegal all processions other than funerals. On 17 March a protest procession was broken up by a police baton charge and several strike leaders were injured and arrested. At this the A.C.T.U. and trade unionists all over Australia registered vehement protests which helped persuade Hanlon that he could not win.

While the repercussions of the original dispute seemed to threaten the very fabric of Queensland society, the local A.E.U. members continued to view the issue as essentially a question of workshop wages. The rhetoric of revolution largely passed them by. During the strike the main A.E.U. decision making body was the District Committee for Ipswich where the main railway shops were located. The A.E.U. worked particularly closely with the other metal unions but, although no rifts occurred as in Victoria, the T.L.C. Disputes Committee which was the natural focus of attention of the press was never able to dictate policy to the engineers. Just as in Victoria, the Commonwealth Council had to restrain the belligerent Ipswich district delegates, particularly early in the piece when for example, foremen members were withdrawn with the rest and had to be ordered back by the Council.[14] The A.E.U.'s major problem was the communications black-out. The Townsville District Committee, for example, wanted representation on the Ipswich Committee in order to be sure of what was going on. The Rockhampton Committee was so cut off that, two weeks before the end, it succumbed to the press canards that the strike was crumbling and approached the local Industrial Magistrate to hold a ballot on a return to work. The only other suggestion from within the A.E.U. that perhaps it should moderate its stand came from the Executive

[14] 'C.C.M.', 5/2/48.

Council when it forwarded £25,000 to aid the Australian Section's depleted finances. Yet while branches and districts in all states unreservedly supported the Queensland members' stand, they did divide on one issue connected with the stoppage. This was the behaviour of Councilman E. J. Rowe.

In addition to the Ipswich and Brisbane district delegates the main A.E.U. strike leaders were organiser C. Merrell and J. P. Devereux, a part-time official who was often placed on semi-permanent delegation to aid Merrell. Both were A.L.P. men, and in the political spectrum were generally regarded as being middle of the road — although in the industrial sense they were as aggressive in the pursuit of engineers' interests as any other A.E.U. officials. This distinction between affairs industrial and political was to escape many outsiders in the forties and fifties as we shall see: in 1948 it certainly fooled the Hanlon government which was surprised at the obduracy of these two 'moderate' A.L.P. men on the wages issue. Their determination and that of A.E.U. activists who could hardly be branded extremists in the political arena, once more belies contemporary and subsequent charges of communist 'control' of the dispute. Yet in the Queensland case it is easy to understand how outsiders — and several non-A.E.U. insiders — could be misled on this point. For the public spotlight was not focussed on Merrell, Devereux, or the Ipswich delegates. The centre of the stage was occupied instead by the dynamic and radical Councilman Rowe.

Probably the major criticism levelled at Rowe from within the A.E.U. was that since Queensland was not part of his electorate he had no business there. The outward justification for his presence was tenuous and the true explanation rests on the nature of the personalities involved. By this time Rowe was the senior Councilman and as such was Acting Secretary during the current illness of Carney. This fact provided the official explanation for his participation. In reality Porter, the Queensland Councilman, was well aware of his own limitations and did not relish the task of opposing an A.L.P. government. Although he paid several visits to his constituency he was only too pleased under cover of illness to let Rowe take over his duties. Rowe, on the other hand, seized the opportunity with positive zest. A man of action who liked best to be involved with rank and file affairs, Rowe had languished on the normal Council diet of paperwork and bureaucracy. The Victorian dispute had presented him with a great opportunity to act and organise and the Queensland stoppage seemed to present another. The difference in his reception rested on three factors. First, he was not personally known in Queensland. Second, the Hanlon government reacted very differently to the Cain ministry. Third, although playing a key role in the settlement Cranwell was prevented by Carney's and Porter's illnesses from visiting Queensland very often during the dispute. Thus no restraining influence was brought to bear on the ebullient Rowe.

At first most Queensland A.E.U. members were simply somewhat surprised by Rowe's fire, vigour and sense of the dramatic — the like of which they had never before encountered. They were certainly not antagonistic to his immediate and enthusiastic involvement in the T.L.C. Disputes Committee. The government and press naturally published his political affiliation and attempted to appeal to the strikers' parochial instincts by asking rhetorically whether Queenslanders would accept dictation from a '"Red" instructor' from the southern states.[15] What caused Rowe to lose some A.E.U. friends was a series of events beginning three weeks before the end of the dispute when 40 A.E.U. members employed at the Shell Oil Depot downed tools after the company succeeded in berthing a tanker despite the seamen and wharfies' embargo. One of the members concerned thereupon asked the state Industrial Court to hold a secret ballot on the issue, claiming that a majority of A.E.U. men at Shell would vote against striking. The court acceded to the request. Tne A.E.U. strongly objected, primarily because in October 1946 the court had judged that a similar 'sectional' ballot by A.E.U. members at another firm was illegal. The union further claimed that the ballot papers were numbered, potentially nullifying the supposed secrecy of the vote, and were also sent to apprentice and foremen members not affected by the dispute. Consequently at a meeting held on 22 March, 23 A.E.U. men in protest handed in their papers to be formally destroyed by Rowe.

For this action Rowe was fined £60, plus £31/10/- costs and committed to prison until such time as he 'purged his contempt'. The police were unable to execute the warrant for his arrest and Rowe remained at large for eight days. On 2 April he re-appeared to address a two-hour long meeting at the Brisbane Trades Hall despite a 50-strong police cordon around the building. At the conclusion of the meeting he voluntarily surrendered himself to the police. After spending four days in the Bogga Road prison Rowe offered his apologies to the court and was released on the same day as the general resumption of work took place.

To Rowe this episode represented a dramatic gesture of defiance to a repressive state, and one which also made figures of fun of the law enforce-

---

[15] See e.g. *Courier Mail*, 12/2/48, 13/2/48, 15/2/48. A recent student of the strike bears testimony to the impact of Rowe on the Disputes Committee. It must be stressed, however, that as far as the A.E.U. was concerned the main decision-making body during this successful dispute was the Ipswich District Committee, not the Disputes Committee. M. Cribb, '"State in Emergency": The Queensland Railway Strike 1948', in Iremonger, Merritt and Osborne, op. cit., pp. 225—48.

ment agencies. To many A.E.U. activists in Queensland, however, it represented behaviour ill-becoming a top official of their esteemed and ancient union. Rowe was therefore surprised to find that, rather than applauding his action, the majority A.E.U. opinion in the state was that he should have initially stayed to 'face the music'. The nickname 'Runaway Rowe' was quickly coined by anti-communists outside Queensland and used whenever possible. His own constituents returned him to the Council in 1949, but although his 1952 defeat was attributable to many other factors the tales of his Queensland escapade — which grew better with each narration — certainly did not help his image.

IV

Retail prices rose on average by 16 per cent between 1945 and 1948 but in September 1948 the Chifley government failed to secure electoral approval for a continuation of price control. This added new urgency to the longstanding union demands for an increase in the Basic Wage. Among the claims in a log served by the metal unions on the 17,500 employers in the metal, motor-body building, and agricultural implement industries was one for a £4 Basic Wage increase. The Full Bench decided to consider this demand in a national Basic Wage Case. On behalf of its affiliated organisations the A.C.T.U. adjusted its own separate claim upwards in order to correspond with the metal unions' figure.

Formal hearings began in February 1949 and dragged on for a further twenty months. Even while the parties were putting forward their lengthy arguments price inflation was lifting the Basic Wage by approximately 9 per cent per annum. The court twice refused to grant an interim increase but the A.E.U. was unable to obtain support for its suggestion of national stoppages in protest. Metal workers' discontent at the lengthy delays was exacerbated by their inability to obtain a new federal award until after the court had made its decision on the Basic Wage. A.E.U. District Committees undertook their own campaigns to ensure that members' real wages at least kept pace with rising prices. On 9 May 1950 all metal unions except the E.T.U. and Moulders were excluded from the Basic Wage hearings because of their action in imposing overtime bans at several Sydney firms which had refused to meet their wage demands.[16] Only the B.S.A. complied with an order to lift the bans and the Bench fined the five defiant unions £100 each.[17] The A.E.U. challenged the legality of this action but by the time the

---

[16] 67 *C.A.R.* 64; *M.J.R.*, May 1950, p. 4.
[17] 67 *C.A.R.* 351; *M.J.R.*, July 1950, pp. 3—4, August 1950, pp. 3—9.

High Court had decided in favour of the union[18] the Arbitration Court had at long last issued its final judgment in the Basic Wage Case.[19]

Chief Justice Kelly was opposed to any increase at all but the majority judgments of Foster and Dunphy J. J., granted a rise of £1 to adult males and set the female Basic Wage at 75 per cent of the male rate. After the first pay period in February 1951 the existing 1937 'prosperity loading' and the new increment of £1 would be incorporated into the 'needs' element and the whole wage would then be adjustable to changes in the cost of living. At the time the decisions were announced the A.E.U. Port Kembla District Committee was operating an overtime ban aimed at securing higher over-award payments. Two of the firms concerned, Lysaghts Pty. Ltd. and Australian Iron Steel Ltd., were respondents to the federal award as far as wages and overtime rates were concerned but other conditions of employment were governed by state awards. When appealed to, the N.S.W. Industrial Commission decided that overtime bans came within its jurisdiction and fined the A.E.U. £500 plus costs for the imposition of bans at each establishment.[20] This was the first time that the maximum permissible fines allowed by the state Arbitration Act had been imposed since the formation of the Commission in 1932. At first the A.E.U. refused to pay the fines, but was forced to submit when an order was served freezing the union's funds. At the same time A.E.U. members throughout the Commonwealth were rendered ineligible to receive the increases in the federal Basic Wage because the embargo on other Port Kembla firms contravened the overtime clauses of the 1947 metal trades award. Eventually the District Committee was forced to call off the ban and on 15 December 1950 the Full Court made a standard order granting the new Basic Wage to the engineers.[21]

These events coincided with the commencement of a new era in federal arbitration. The Commonwealth Court, encouraged by the Menzies Government, began to make greater use of penal powers originally provided in the 1947 Chifley amendments. The trend had begun with the fining of the five metal unions during the Basic Wage Case and when the High Court declared the action to be illegal in March 1951 the Act was promptly amended[22] and the new legislation increased the penalties for non-

[18] 82 *C.L.R.* 208. See also *M.J.R.*, March 1951, p. 3.
[19] 68 *C.A.R.* 698 at pp. 757–839. For a concise summary of the main provisions of the October 1950 judgment see Foenander, *Studies in Australian Labour Law* (Melbourne, 1952) Ch. VI.
[20] 49 *I.A.R.* 501, 509, 50 *I.A.R.* 100.
[21] 69 *C.A.R.* 829.
[22] For full details see J. Hutson, *Penal Colony to Penal Powers* (Sydney, 1966), pp. 174–5; R. O'Dea, *Industrial Relations in Australia* (Sydney, 1965), pp. 42–3.

compliance. Simultaneously, Conciliation Commissioner Galvin inserted the first ever 'bans clause' into the Metal Trades Award. The ostensible cause of his action was a dispute involving only five boilermakers and seven ironworkers at a single firm but Galvin took the opportunity to apply his Order to all parties to the federal award. The new clause took effect on 21 June 1951 and proclaimed that

(i) No organisation party to this award shall in any way, whether directly or indirectly, be a party to or concerned in any ban, limitation or restriction upon the performance of work in accordance with this award.

(ii) An organisation shall be deemed to commit a new and separate breach of the above sub-clause on each and every day in which it is directly a party to such ban, limitation or restriction.[23]

The A.E.U. protested vehemently at this decision which had been reached without notice to all parties concerned and with representatives of only two unions and the M.T.E.A. present at the hearings but, although originally inserted for a period of 12 months, the bans clause continued in operation for 20 years.

Concurrently the A.E.U. and other metal unions were engaged in presenting arguments to Galvin in the long delayed hearings of claims for a new metal trades award. Between November 1947 and November 1951 inflation and the court's 1950 decision had raised the Six Capital Cities Basic Wage by 86 per cent from £5.9.0 to £10. As a result the differential between it and a fitter's rate had fallen from 49 to 26 per cent. The extent to which employers paid in excess of nominal rates is illustrated by evidence submitted to Commissioner Galvin in March 1951 by A.E.U. organiser, C. M. Southwell, who demonstrated that Melbourne tradesmen currently received over-award payments averaging 22/6d. per week.[24] Yet even if this figure is taken as typical of the remainder of the Commonwealth, skilled-men's differentials were still below the level attained as a result of the 1946—7 dispute. The 1947 award rates had been by no means the maximum wages paid at the time of their inception. Some A.E.U. members continued to be paid over the rate and elsewhere the drive for extra wages was soon renewed. Southwell's evidence, on the other hand, indicates that in early 1951 tradesmen's average *earnings*, exclusive of overtime, were only 42 per cent more than the current Melbourne Basic Wage as compared with the 49 per cent minimum differential existing at the end of 1947.

The A.E.U. made an important gain in its wage campaign in June 1951

---

[23] 71 *C.A.R.* 507.
[24] *M.J.R.*, April 1951, p. 17. *Metal Trades Journal*, 15/3/51.

when paper and pulp manufacturers agreed that in future all margins in that industry should be automatically adjusted in accordance with changes in the C Series price index.[25] Employers' organisations in the main states, including the M.T.E.A., unsuccessfully appealed against the registration of the agreement but any fears they had that the 'escalator' clause might influence Galvin's findings in the metal trades case were soon dispelled.

Galvin, a former loco drivers' union official, indicated throughout the year-long hearings that he was fully aware of the potential ramifications of his decision. In his final judgment he admitted, 'As this case developed, the problem of inflation appeared to me to overshadow every other problem.'[26] Acting on his own initiative he called in an academic economist, D. W. Oxnam, to give evidence on the likely inflationary effects of an increase in national wage costs. Strongly influenced by Oxnam's 'cost-push' thesis, the Commissioner refused to grant any wage rises at all and he actually reduced the margins of one important classification, that of the welder, by 4/6d. per week. Thus the principles of Powers' 1924 judgment were once more re-established, this time quite explicitly. The wage rates of engineers and other metal workers were held constant not because they represented their current market value to employers but because it was considered by the arbitrator that any increase would have deleterious effects on the national economy.

Apart from the main wages decision the Galvin award set margins for females at 16s. when working in classifications for which men received 28s. or less, and at 75 per cent of the male rate in classifications receiving 28s. to 40s. The Commissioner left the settlement of rates for the few women who were employed in higher classifications to direct bargaining between unions and employers. Other provisions of the award included slight increases in apprentice rates and in special rates for hot, dirty and other unpleasant working conditions. Galvin also permitted employers to introduce payment by results provided employees could as a result earn at least 10 per cent more than the award minima. He further decided that in the case of trades employing 90 per cent of metal trades apprentices no firm need comply with the tradesmen: apprentice ratio set out in the award if the state apprenticeship authority approved its training facilities.

The reactions to the award when it was issued in January 1952 were predictable. After initially criticising Chifley's 1947 legislation employers

---

[25] *Industrial Information Bulletin*, Vol. 6, pp. 472–3; *Metal Trades Journal*, 15/9/51; *M.J.R.*, July 1951, p. 8.
[26] 73 *C.A.R.* 324 at p. 361.

had become increasingly reconciled to it — including the increase in ex-unionist Conciliation Commissioners once it was apparent that they were prepared to 'stand fast' against union demands. Galvin's decisions confirmed their opinion. The M.T.E.A. stated emphatically, ' . . . *the Metal Trades Case of 1951—52 must be regarded as one of the milestones in the history of Australian industrial arbitration*'[27] [italics in original].

For their part the unions were outraged. In Victoria the decision had the effect of helping finally heal the divisions lingering on from the 1946—7 dispute as the metal unions indignantly re-united to pursue a common offensive. The M.T.F. immediately organised a national 24 hour stoppage in protest and this was followed by spontaneous strikes in individual establishments. Further aggressive action was planned but a rift now occurred between the M.T.F. and the A.C.T.U. Executive which denounced the 'unauthorised sectional action' taken by the metal unions and sought to exert full control over the margins campaign.[28] The fact that M.T.F. members proved anxious to gain its support reflected the recent pronounced rise in the status and importance of the A.C.T.U.[29] Although A.E.U. members went ahead with strikes and overtime bans in all states[30] the A.C.T.U. attitude prevented any effective national campaign being mounted in support of them. In West Australia even the M.T.F. split, and the A.E.U. and the Boilermakers' Society were deregistered by the state tribunal for conducting a seven month strike concentrated in the railway workshops in a vain attempt to secure higher margins.[31]

The prospects of a successful outcome of the A.E.U.'s efforts were greatly lessened by the onset of the 1952—3 recession. The slackening of economic activity, although not greatly affecting engineering employment, resulted in a fall in overtime work and induced a general mood of pessimism among unionists. In October 1952, when the proportion of A.E.U. members currently reported out of work for all reasons amounted to less than one per cent, the Commonwealth Council gloomily considered that, 'The period of full employment enjoyed under the Curtin and Chifley Government is now a thing of the past.'[32] Attention was further distracted from the margins

[27] *M.T.E.A. Annual Report*, 1951/52.
[28] *M.J.R.*, March 1952, p. 4, April 1952, pp. 4—5.
[29] For details see R. H. Martin, 'The Rise of the Australian Council of Trade Unions', *Australian Quarterly*, 30, 1, 1958, pp. 30—42; O'Dea op. cit., pp. 109—10, 146.
[30] See e.g. *M.J.R.*, April 1952, pp. 14, 15, 17, June 1952, pp. 4, 19.
[31] *M.J.R.*, February 1952, p. 16, March 1952, pp. 20—1, April 1952, p. 18, June 1952, p. 3, September 1952, p. 4.
[32] *M.J.R.*, October 1952, p. 11.

issue by the action of employers' organisations in filing a federal log of claims which called for a reversion to a 44 hour week, a 46s. reduction in the Basic Wage, a cut in female rates, and the abolition of quarterly adjustments.

The hearings of these and the M.T.F.'s counter-claims lasted 12 months and on 12 September 1953 the Full Court unanimously rejected all save the employers' claim concerning quarterly adjustments which the Bench believed had 'undoubtedly been an accelerating factor in the rapid increase in prices which has afflicted Australia, notably in the years 1951 and 1952.'[33] Inevitably the unions regarded the decision as an attempt to make workers bear the burden of all future price rises. A.E.U. members were as disgruntled as other workers but their attention was partly diverted by the commencement of hearings on 14 September of the metal unions' claims for marginal increases. In their arguments for a variation of the Galvin award the unions were limited to the log they had submitted in the 1951–2 case. This log, compiled in 1949, had called for a fitter's margin of 80s. but subsequent inflation had outdated this figure and the unions considered that at least a doubling of the current 52s. margin was required.

The unions suffered their first setback when Galvin accepted the employers' arguments that the question of marginal increases was of such national importance that the matter should be dealt with by the Arbitration Court. Four judges began hearing the case on 13 October but on 25 February 1954 the court suspended hearings until November on the grounds that the state of the economy had not improved sufficiently since the Basic Wage judgment to allow for any increase in wage costs.[34] The court did betray a certain sympathy towards the deterioration of tradesmen's relative wage position and declared, 'If it were proper to set aside economic considerations there would appear to be a *prima facie* case for a complete review of the minimum margins appropriate to occupations covered by the present references.'[35] However, this did little to blunt the unions' resentment at the postponement. The A.C.T.U. placed most emphasis on lunch-hour mass meetings in factories. A.E.U. members, however, involved themselves in a number of important stoppages in order both to secure higher over-award payments and apply pressure to the court. The A.E.U. and other metal

---

[33] 77 *C.A.R.* 477 at p. 498. See also O. de R. Foenander, *Better Employment Relations* (Sydney, 1954), pp. 191–5. J. E. Isaac, 'The Basic Wage and Standard Hours Inquiry in Australia, 1952–53', *International Labour Review*, June 1954, pp. 570–93.

[34] 80 *C.A.R.* 3 at pp. 6–16.

[35] *ibid* at p. 15.

unions were fined under the penal clauses of the Arbitration Act. Although the rolling strike technique which the unions employed as a counter to court orders to return to work was seen by employers as an 'unnatural' and 'unchristian' tactic, which 'could have been conceived only in the minds of the Kremlin,'[36] the general increase in industrial unrest eventually produced results. Public sympathy for the unions' demands increased although attention was mainly focussed on the plight of the skilled workers. In June the government indicated that when court hearings recommenced it would intervene in support of the claims for increased margins for higher grades. Finally, in September the court agreed to re-open the case earlier than intended and its judgment was delivered on 5 November 1954.[37]

After an extensive review of the various indicators the judges considered that the requisite degree of economic stability had been reached which would allow a reassessment of the margins structure. They dismissed the unions' arguments that the adjustment should be aimed at restoring the real value of margin earners' nominal rates to the 1947 levels. The Bench further made it clear that in its view 'no case has been made out for any increase in the margins prescribed for ... unskilled or only slightly skilled employees'.[38]

Having thus cleared the ground the court looked for a 'sound basis' upon which to establish its new margins formula. Without offering any explanation it accepted the suggestion of the employers' advocate that the Beeby variation of 1937 was the 'proper datum point'. O'Mara's 1941 war loadings and the 1947 decisions were therefore 'distortions' of the correct scheme of margins assessed by Beeby because they had increased the margins of lesser skilled workers by relatively greater amounts than those of the 'really skilled' employees.

The court outlined the criteria upon which it would act in determining the exact adjustments to be made to skilled margins in the light of the great change in circumstances since 1937. The chosen principles were those set out by Powers in his 1924 engineering judgment as amplified in the 1947 Printing Trades Case by Judge Kelly who had declared,

that the following rules should guide me in the review of wage rates sought by the present application:—

1. That it must be put upon the applicant Union to satisfy the Court that material change in circumstances, occurring since the making of the award, has rendered the rates then prescribed as minima no longer just as such.

[36] *Metal Trades Journal*, 1/6/54.
[37] 80 C.A.R. 3 at pp. 21—55.
[38] Ibid., at pp. 31—2.

2. That the standard of justice must be the true value today of the work for which the rates are to be made payable as minima.

3. That the true value is not to be ascertained by reference to high wages being paid on account of accidental and temporary conditions connected with a shortage of labour.

4. That the true value is not to be ascertained by reference to variation in the purchasing power of money since the award was made.

5. That the assessment of the true value must have regard to comparisons of minimum rates payable for work in comparable industries or of comparable occupations.[39]

The Bench also accepted Kelly's rider to the fourth paragraph which stated, 'I have not forgotten that nominal values of all things, including the nominal value of work, must tend to increase with an increase in the nominal prices of essential commodities.'[40]

The fitter was taken as the representative skilled worker to whom the fivefold criteria should first be applied. After indicating its awareness that any increase in the fitter's rate would soon spread to skilled employees in other occupations, the court concluded that, 'viewed in the light of present monetary values and in the whole setting of marginal rates, the fitter's margin should now be assessed at 75s. That amount is two and a half times the fitter's 1937 margin.'[41] Other margins were similarly set at amounts 250 per cent above their 1937 levels but no change was made to the margins of process workers and lower classifications whose current rates would otherwise have to be reduced by application of this formula.

A striking feature of this judgment was that no explanation was offered of how the figure of 75s. for a fitter was arrived at. The court was careful to state that it had not been calculated by reference to any change in the value of money since 1937 but this disclaimer seems to have been made in order to prevent the unions from using the 1954 decision as a precedent for future claims that margins should be varied in proportion with rises in the cost of living. Immediately after making the statement the judges, in an apparent aside, pointed out 'for the benefit of those interested in such comparisons' that the C Series index had risen by two and two-thirds between 1937 and 1954. The court felt that the difference between

[39] 59 *C.A.R.* 278 at pp. 287–8.

[40] Ibid., at p. 304. In this 1947 award Kelly refused to grant the printing union's claim that the full increases recently granted to engineers by the Full Court should be extended to its members. However, in the following year Commissioner Portus ignored the principles expounded by Kelly and granted the union's claim in full. Hagan, op. cit., p. 281.

[41] 80 *C.A.R.* 3 at p. 32.

the purchasing power of the fitter's 30s. margin in 1937 and 75s. in 1954 'cannot be regarded as unjust' because of the intervening general improvements in conditions of employment including, 'the increase in the real value of the Basic Wage, the extension of paid annual leave, and the reduction of the standard ordinary working week from forty-four hours to forty.'[42]

The 1954 award, although increasing skilled margins, confirmed the principles espoused 30 years before in the Powers award. On both occasions the arbitrators were more influenced by the effect that their margins decisions might have on the national wage cost structure than the market value of engineering skill or the merits of the particular dispute before them. A.E.U. members were left to rely more than ever before on direct bargaining with individual employers to obtain what they considered to be a just return for their labour.

[42] Ibid., at p. 33.

8

The rise of the Groupers 1939—55

The rise of organised anti-communist forces in the trade union movement during the 1940s, and the subsequent course of events culminating in the disbandment of the A.L.P. Industrial Groups and the 1955 Split in the A.L.P. has by now been fairly well documented.[1] The major impetus behind the anti-communist crusade came from members of the Roman Catholic Church. The reason why they should prove the driving force rested both on a natural ideological antipathy towards 'atheistic communism' and on the fact that Australian Catholics, predominantly of Irish descent, had long gravitated towards the trade union-based A.L.P. as their natural avenue for political advancement. Consequently Catholic political activists and union officials were close witnesses to increasing communist influence in the industrial labour movement in the 1930s and 1940s.

It may well be, however, that the initial spark to the train of events which was to sear the labour movement for more than a generation was kindled by external, European events, notably the Spanish Civil War. Franco's insurrection was firmly supported by the Catholic hierarchy and press[2] and the heated debates in Trades Halls and at A.L.P. Conferences, particularly bitter in Victoria, served to illuminate for the first time in the minds of the young Catholic intelligentsia the exact degree of divergence between their social views and those of the left wing of the labour movement. For many more

---

[1] The most recent work on the Groups is that of Robert Murray, op. cit. Other standard references upon which the following outline of the organisation and career of the Groups and 'The Movement' draws heavily are, Tom Truman, *Catholic Action and Politics* (Revised and Enlarged Edition, Melbourne, 1960); Henry Mayer (Ed.), *Catholics and the Free Society*; Ian Campbell, 'A.L.P. Industrial Groups — a Reassessment', *Australian Journal of Politics and History*, Vol. 8, November 1962, pp. 182—99; D. W. Rawson, 'The A.L.P. Industrial Groups' in J. E. Isaac and G. W. Ford (Eds.), *Australian Labour Relations: Readings* (Melbourne, 1966), pp. 160—77; P. Ormonde, *The Movement* (Melbourne, 1972).

[2] E. Andrews, op. cit.

Catholics the Spanish War debates simply brought home the international nature of communism and consequently made the contemporary spread of communist influence among Australian trade unions seem more sinister.

Certainly as early as 1938 groups of Victorian Catholics were organising against communists in the Boilermakers' Society and the Australian Railways Union. The railway workshops with their relatively large concentrations of workers were the main spheres of this activity in both metropolitan and country areas. By 1939 a regular anti-communist newspaper was being issued at the Newport workshops in Melbourne. The meeting place for Catholic activists in the railways and elsewhere came to be the Melbourne office of the National Secretariat of Catholic Action. This body had been established in Melbourne in 1939 to formalise and channel the lay Catholic activity which had been growing for several years under the stimulus of the Distributist ideas disseminated by the Campion Society (founded 1931) and the associated *Catholic Worker* newspaper (founded 1936). The Secretariat consisted of two clergy and two laymen, with the latter providing the main inspiration and drive. F. K. Maher, founder of the Melbourne Campion Society, was Director until 1940 when he was succeeded by the young Assistant Director, B. A. Santamaria, who had been editor of the *Catholic Worker* between 1936 and 1940.

As the battle against the communists in the trade unions spread, Santamaria saw the need for better organisation. In 1941, encouraged by H. M. Cremean, the Deputy leader of the Victorian Parliamentary Labour Party, Santamaria secured the approval of Archbishop Mannix for his plans. During 1942 meetings of unionists and priests were held within the Melbourne Archdiocese which shaped the basic organisation of the famous Catholic Social Studies Movement, known to initiates simply as 'The Movement'. Since Santamaria had broken with the *Catholic Worker* in 1940, a weekly newspaper, *Freedom*, was launched in September 1943, the name changing to *News Weekly* in 1946.

For good or ill the founders of The Movement decided that its work should be confidential. Links with similar though less significant Catholic groups in Sydney and Broken Hill were soon established, but by 1945 Santamaria considered that a fully fledged national organisation to fight communism in the unions was called for. Consequently, he submitted a formal memorandum to a Sydney meeting of Catholic bishops requesting the establishment of a national Movement. The bishops acquiesced, entrusting formal control to Mannix, Archbishop Gilroy of Sydney, and Bishop O'Collins of Ballarat. In practice, however, the hierarchy kept to the background and Santamaria remained very much the leading figure.

The strength of The Movement varied greatly between states. It was always strongest in Victoria but was also firmly established in Sydney, Newcastle and the main N.S.W. country towns. In Queensland, Rockhampton and Townsville were the firmest bases. Movement strength in Brisbane was on a par with that in Adelaide and other South Australian industrial centres. Its influence in Tasmania and Western Australia was not great, despite the activities of full-time officials in those states. Only Catholics considered to be suitably dedicated were invited to join The Movement and its total membership was not very large, lying somewhere between 5,000 and 10,000, with perhaps half in Victoria and the majority of the remainder in New South Wales. Finances to support The Movement's activities came from individual Catholics, the bishops, and possibly from American funds available to anti-communist organisations.

The basic unit of organisation within The Movement was the parish group consisting of usually eight to ten parishioners, although sometimes more, who compiled lists of Catholic union members in their parish, indexed them by trade, and encouraged them to be active in their respective unions' affairs, particularly at election times. Other duties included fund raising, promoting sales of *News Weekly* and, of course, being active within political parties (overwhelmingly the A.L.P.). Overall, the cadre-style organisation, the low pay for full-time officials, the heavy calls on members' time, and the rather melodramatic air of secrecy and crusade surrounding The Movement were reminiscent of nothing so much as its combined *bête noire* and *raison d'être*, the C.P.A.

As elsewhere in the world, the invasion of Russia in 1941 and the subsequent whole-hearted communist support of the war effort brought increased acceptance of the C.P.A. in the Australian community. The success of communists in trade union elections which accompanied the C.P.A.'s popularity during the war perturbed not only youthful Catholic Actionists but also many trade union officials who opposed communists either on ideological grounds or because they saw the communist advances as threatening their positions and influence. In Victoria the Secretary of the Melbourne Trades Hall Council, J. V. Stout, and the President of the A.C.T.U., P. J. Clarey, worked closely with The Movement from 1942 onwards, informing it of areas where communist successes threatened. By the end of the war an anti-communist faction had openly emerged on the floor of the Trades Hall Council led by D. Lovegrove, the ex-communist secretary of the Fibrous Plasterers' Union.

It was, however, in New South Wales that what proved to be the most significant steps in the anti-communist crusade were taken. The right wing leadership of the Sydney Trades and Labour Council, faced with continuous gains by their opponents in union elections, decided towards the end of the war that the only possible way to stem the tide was to gain official A.L.P. blessing. Consequently, the 1945 Conference of the New South Wales branch of the A.L.P. was persuaded to form Labor Party organisations within industry. Ostensibly, these were to be mere educative or propagandist units but it soon became clear that they were being used to back the opponents of communists in union elections. Soon they were operating under the name of A.L.P. Industrial Groups.

Given the fact that the great majority of rank and file unionists gave their allegiance to the A.L.P., the New South Wales move in attaching that Party's imprimatur to anti-communist activities had obvious attractions for right wing unionists in other states. Consequently, after heated debate, majorities at A.L.P. Conferences in Victoria (1946), South Australia (1946) and Queensland (1947) voted in favour of establishing Industrial Groups. Attempts to gain A.L.P. backing for Groups in Tasmania and Western Australia proved unsuccessful although unofficial Groups operated in both these states. 'Groupers', as members of the Groups were known, were never strong enough to persuade the A.L.P. Federal Conference to approve a federal organisation for the Groups, although an unofficial Interstate Group Liaison Committee was formed in 1952.

With the formation of Industrial Groups in four states, The Movement directed its energies to assisting in every way possible the operation of the A.L.P.'s official anti-communist weapons. Movement members, of course, joined the Groups where possible and formed a disciplined minority within them. The Movement also recruited members for the Groups and, where necessary, tried to find suitable anti-communist candidates for union elections. In addition, Movement members distributed literature, addressed envelopes, provided finance, canvassers, cars, legal assistance, clerical help and useful advice for the Groups and Group candidates.

Groups could be formed within a single union or among members of several unions employed at a single work-site. Generally speaking, Group organisers concentrated first on the former type. In Victoria and South Australia only A.L.P. members were eligible for Group membership while in New South Wales and Queensland anyone could join although office bearers had to be members of the A.L.P. No A.L.P. member had the *right* to join a Group, and this provision prevented 'white-anting' by A.L.P. opponents of the Groups. Finance for the Groups' activities came from a variety of sources including membership subscriptions, raffles, lotteries, employers, The Movement, A.L.P. state Executives and, it was rumoured, U.S.A. government officials.

The strength and organisation of the Groups varied between states, with the major activity and controversy occurring in New South Wales and Victoria. The South Australian Groups led a brief and troubled existence until A.L.P. recognition was withdrawn in 1951. The Queensland Groups had no formal constitution until 1954 and appear to have operated largely at the direction and discretion of R. J. J. Bukowski, the A.W.U. leader, working in close partnership with The Movement's Queensland organiser, W. Thornton. Policy making by the New South Wales Groups was undertaken by an annual meeting of delegates elected from each Group. For the remainder of the year management was vested in a central executive consisting of five officers, 16 delegates elected at the annual conference and (after 1947) two nominees of the A.L.P. Executive. In the early years there was a considerable turnover among the Group executive's officers, many of whom, including the first secretary, H. Jensen, later came to oppose the Groups. One result of this turnover was that A.L.P. industrial organiser, W. R. Coulter, a permanent member of the Group executive and *ex officio* member of all N.S.W. Groups, provided much of the initiative before 1950. In that year J. T. Kane was appointed Group secretary and powers previously conferred on the industrial organiser were transferred to him. From this time on Kane, who in 1952 also became Assistant Secretary of the A.L.P., was the driving force behind the N.S.W. Groups. In Victoria the Groups were controlled by a committee appointed by the A.L.P. Central Executive and presided over by Lovegrove who in 1947 became Assistant Secretary of the A.L.P. In 1949 Lovegrove became A.L.P. Secretary and F. P. V. McManus succeeded him as Assistant Secretary and leader of the Groups.

The exact degree of success attending the Groups' efforts differed between states, between unions, and between branches of the same union in different states. In general Group successes were few in the early years but from 1950 onwards aided both by amendments to the Commonwealth Arbitration and Conciliation Act which provided for external control of trade union ballots, and by increasing public hostility to communism as the Cold War heightened, the Groups enjoyed a procession of electoral victories in important unions. In Victoria they gained control of the Clerks', Railways', Ironworkers' and Waterside Workers' unions and established the breakaway Amalgamated Society of Carpenters and Joiners as a rival to the Building Workers' Industrial Union. The Groups' major victories in New South Wales were in the Clerks' and Ironworkers' unions, while in Queensland success followed Group organisation in the Clerks', Ironworkers', Meat Workers', and Waterside Workers' unions. In all states and in diverse unions the Groups also gained lesser, partial victories as their candidates were elected to minor office or became members of union executives controlled by non-Groupers.

Then, in what seemed to many outsiders to be but a few short months, the fortunes of the Groups altered dramatically. From the crest of their victorious wave, they fell into utter disrepute within the labour movement. They were subject to increasingly vitriolic attack from all quarters, the influence of The Movement was reviled, they lost official A.L.P. endorsement, were disbanded in ignominy and the term 'Grouper' became an epithet to rival 'scab' in the orthodox labour movement's dictionary of opprobrium. Of course, the leaders of the Groups did not all mutely submit and perish in the onslaught. Many, notably in New South Wales, were able to ride out the storm and retain influence and office in unions and A.L.P. by tacking to the winds of change in a conciliatory fashion and by accepting the sacrifice of a few of their erstwhile colleagues such as Kane. Elsewhere, however, Group leaders went down with all guns blazing and the resultant splits in the A.L.P. between 1955 and 1957 and the eventual emergence of the break-away Democratic Labor Party (D.L.P.) proved disastrous for A.L.P. electoral fortunes, particularly in Victoria and Queensland.

The explanations for what appeared at first glance to have been a truly amazing reversal of fortune on the part of the Groups are several. In the first place the Groups' position at the height of their success was not quite as secure as it outwardly appeared. The tide which carried the Groups to their major successes was not solely the product of Group organisation and popularity. In particular, the C.P.A. itself contributed to the defeat of its own members in union elections through its poor tactics in the late 1940s. An often undifferentiating attack on all A.L.P. men meant that the communists lost many potential allies among those A.L.P. activists who had misgivings about the Groups and the direction in which they were taking the Labor Party. Such misgivings grew as communist strength diminished and the Groups became more powerful. At the personal level the typical Grouper was relatively youthful, imbued with crusading zeal and anxious for rapid change. As the successes mounted in the early 1950s, many of them found it difficult to conceal their impatience with older colleagues set in a more traditional mould, and often a youthful lack of tact overstepped the bounds into arrogance. By itself, of course, this was not fatal — the labour movement breeds pretty thick skins. On too many occasions, however, A.L.P. men opposing some facet of Groupers' policy were met either with scarcely veiled threats of organised opposition at re-election time or with abusive denunciation as 'Comms' or Red sympathisers.

While the introduction of standover and smear tactics were alienating increasing numbers of unionists, other erstwhile allies were perturbed to note that the Groups were not satisfied simply to storm the diminishing number of communist union strongholds. Instead they seemed to be probing in strange new areas including some staunchly right wing unions which did not conduct their affairs in a manner pleasing to the Groups. More generally, the Groups and their backers seemed determined to use the powerful position which they had acquired in the A.L.P. machine to mould Labor Party policy to their own ends. With the major industrial battles against the communists apparently won, Santamaria showed no signs of disbanding The Movement. On the contrary, it seemed that The Movement's influence in the Groups and the A.L.P. was to be used to push Movement policies — both domestic and foreign — within the A.L.P. In addition many unionists had been shocked by the implications of Movement social doctrine which they thought they could discern in the letter which the Catholic Chief Judge, Sir Raymond Kelly, circulated before the 1953 Basic Wage Case. Among other things Kelly suggested wage cuts and peasant immigration. The subsequent abolition of quarterly cost of living adjustments and the early 1954 margins freeze were seen in a number of quarters as fruits of the Movement seed. Simultaneously, dissent from Movement policies and actions was beginning to crystallise among several groups within the Catholic Church.

The exact weight to be attached to any one of these factors in the downfall of the Groups in 1954–5 is difficult to determine. It may well be, as D. W. Rawson argues, that the main contributing factor was simply that union leaders and A.L.P. machine politicians no longer *needed* the Groups by 1954. Communist strength had diminished and contemporaneous changes in C.P.A. policy towards A.L.P. unionists made those communists remaining in official union positions much easier to work with.

Whatever the reasons, the public facade of Group omnipotence within the labour movement crumbled with the dramatic suddenness already referred to. For our purpose of providing a background against which the internal controversies in the A.E.U. may be silhouetted, we need only to reiterate the differing course of events in the two major states and note certain changes in the status of The Movement. The 'Split' was greatest in Victoria — where the majority of the A.L.P. Executive were expelled and by far the greatest numbers of Groupers left the A.L.P. to form the largest branch of what eventually became the D.L.P. In New South Wales a more conciliatory approach was taken by the Groupers. As a result relatively few heads rolled and most N.S.W. Groupers decided 'to stay in and fight' within the A.L.P. The division of opinion within the Catholic Church about The Movement, begun before the Split, eventually came to focus upon the degree to which Movement policy should be determined by the hierarchy. The matter was finally settled at the end of 1957 by a commission of cardinals in Rome. The outcome was a voluntary disbandment of The Movement and its replacement by a completely lay body, the National Civic Council (N.C.C.). Led by Santamaria, the N.C.C. became closely linked with the D.L.P. and as an independent lay organisation it had the right, unlike The Movement in its latter days, to organise support for its policies in dioceses such as Sydney, Adelaide and Perth where the incumbent bishops had come to disagree with Santamaria's approach. Hence, although it was Victoria where Church approval was greatest and its union base firmest, the N.C.C. was able to play a significant role within the trade union movement in all other states in the post-Split era.

II

Several obstacles stand in the way of research into the activities of A.L.P. Industrial Groups within the A.E.U. The most obvious is that no records of Group meetings and decisions are available — if they ever existed. Because of contemporary controversies, references to A.E.U. Groups from sources outside the union must be handled with care and the bias identified and defused. As for internal A.E.U. records, the most promising source, the *Monthly Journal*, maintained a fairly strict neutrality on the subject of Groups for as long as they were officially recognised by the A.L.P., and virtually no reference was made to them until the New South Wales A.E.U. Group attempted to involve itself in the union's litigation in 1953.[3] Even then no details of the nature and operation of the Group were provided, for the debate outwardly concerned the merits of traditional A.E.U. election procedures compared with those of ballots supervised by the Commonwealth Arbitration Court. This leaves the researcher to pick his way through the stark minefield-maps set out in the bald minutes of the Commonwealth Council and in the equally sparse record of proceedings in the only extant District Committee and Political Committee Minute-books, those of the Melbourne District. Apart from the relatively greater gaps in our information about New South Wales and the other states, even the sign-posts which are uncovered in the minute-books may not always be interpreted literally. For, given the contentious nature of the issue, many A.E.U. officials and

[3] See below, p. 216 ff.

delegates who supported, or were supported by, the Groups preferred to gain the best of both worlds by not publicly endorsing the Groups and their activities. Indeed because of the overwhelming importance of tradition and of abiding by the Rule Book in the A.E.U., it would have been electoral suicide to support the Groups openly on issues such as 'court controlled' ballots.

While contemporary documentary sources require so much subtlety of interpretation, recollections of A.E.U. members after the A.L.P. Split provide no definite short cut to the actual course of events before 1955. This is partly because of a tendency on the part of those involved subsequently to exaggerate the strength of their opponents; but it is largely because of the stigma retrospectively attached to the Groups as a result of the bitterness and rancour surrounding both the Split itself and subsequent attempts by candidates supported by the N.C.C. to obtain a footing within the A.E.U. The complete, utter and undifferentiating denunciation of the Groups, and the tendency to identify all Groupers with what appeared to its opponents to be the more sinister aspects of The Movement is not confined to the A.E.U. It is common throughout large sections of the labour movement and hardly aids objective reassessment of events by the participants. Because of the acrimony surrounding the issue, to admit of association with the Groups — no matter how brief or sincere — now seems somehow tantamount to a confession of treachery to unionists who have remained loyal to the A.L.P. Indeed, such is the power of this retrospective alchemy that the outside observer sometimes finds it difficult to remember that the Groups were in fact officially endorsed organs of the A.L.P. rather than insidious cancers externally grafted onto the labour movement without its knowledge and consent.

From 1955 onwards events are relatively much easier to interpret. References to the A.E.U. in external sources still have to be treated with due allowance for bias, but since the union takes a more easily identifiable official line on the major contentious issues, the internal sources, including the *Monthly Journal*, are more specific and easier to handle. In the post-Split polarisation of issues participants stand up clearly to be counted on one side or the other and their affiliations are usually quite unambiguous. The middle ground has been swept clear and the contestants issue forth from boldly defined positions on the right and left of the field.

In general we can say that the experience of organised anti-communist forces within the A.E.U. was a paler reflection of the career of the Groups and their allies in the wider labour movement. Their efforts within the A.E.U. were never attended with as much success as in, say, the Clerks' union or the F.I.A., but the struggle was none the less fierce for that. There can be little doubt that both sides clearly recognised the central importance of the A.E.U. in the industrial movement and all districts of the A.E.U. witnessed the activities of anti-communists to some degree or another, with the major clashes occurring in the principal states of New South Wales and Victoria.

For tactical reasons largely based on A.E.U. activists' traditional independence and distrust of anything which smacked of 'interference' in their affairs, the Victorian A.E.U. Group did not publicise its existence to the same degree as in other unions.[4] For similar reasons it operated more independently of the controlling A.L.P. Group Committee. The core of the A.E.U. Group consisted of Catholic members who had been organising against communist candidates and influence through The Movement for some years before the A.L.P. Groups were established in 1946. The leaders in Melbourne during the 1940s and early 1950s appear to have been C. De Oliveira, F. Reilly, L. Fitzpatrick, A. J. Bailey, J. T. Hughes, F. Nolan, and father and son, T. P. and S. T. Corrigan. Group leaders in other centres included F. J. Singleton in Geelong and M. Calnin in Ballarat. The elder Corrigan was M.L.A. for Port Melbourne from 1942 to his death in 1952 when his son succeeded him in the seat. During the Groupers' rise to power Reilly in 1952 became a member of the Victorian Central Executive of the A.L.P. and in the same year Bailey became a Member of the Legislative Council after defeating the sitting candidate, P. J. Kennelly, in a notorious pre-selection battle. De Oliveira became manager of *News Weekly* and Bailey, the younger Corrigan, Hughes and Singleton all stood as parliamentary candidates for the breakaway party after the Split. On the A.E.U. District Committee, Fitzpatrick became the leader backed by a varying group of other delegates including Hughes, Nolan, F. A. Broderick, D. Henderson, and F. P. Twomey. At the branch level, where grass roots organisation was so important for electoral success, the Group came to be well served by a number of dedicated Branch secretaries such as Twomey, W. Hatters and L. Jenkins.

Associating themselves from time to time with this disciplined anti-communist core within the A.E.U. were a diverse group of other A.E.U. members. Prior to important A.E.U. ballots, the alliance was firm enough for this second set of members to be thought of as an 'Outer' Group whose

---

[4] For example, the A.E.U. was not numbered among the 16 unions in which official Industrial Groups had been formed by the time of the 1947 Victorian A.L.P. Conference. (For the list of 16 see Murray, op. cit., p. 18). Yet there is no doubt that an organised group sometimes calling itself 'the A.E.U. – A.L.P. Anti-communist Industrial Group' was already operating in the A.E.U. *M.D.C.M.*, 28/8/46.

composition varied considerably over time and the motives of whose members ranged from principled opposition to communism to a simple desire for Group and Movement aid in forthcoming election campaigns. Some members of this Outer Group held back from full participation in the 'Inner' Group because of a personal distaste for the predominance of Catholics therein, while, on the other hand, some of the latter felt that they could detect a Masonic influence among the anti-communists in the Outer Group. Be that as it may, A.E.U. officials in the Outer Group were always aware of the electoral dangers of being positively identified as a fully-fledged Grouper. A number began to shy away from contact with the Inner Group in the early fifties as they began to distrust the path Groupers were treading in the wider labour movement. The overall number of A.E.U. members who at least made electoral pacts with the Victorian Inner Group during these years was considerable, but the most important members of the changing Outer Group appear to have been three organisers, J. E. Burke, W. H. White and G. W. Deverall. Burke and White retained their Grouper links up to the Split, and when the former was elected to the Commonwealth Council in 1952 he proved the most energetic anti-communist ever to sit on the union's federal executive. On the other hand, Deverall, who had been a Councilman between 1935 and 1940, moved away from the Groupers in the late forties and once he became Commonwealth Secretary in 1949 he appears to have been equally at home with the Group's opponents.

In Sydney an official Industrial Group was formed in the A.E.U. almost immediately after the creation of the Groups at the 1945 A.L.P. Conference. Overall it appears that the membership of the Group was larger and the turnover greater in Sydney than in Melbourne. This fits the general pattern of N.S.W. Groups which allowed other than members of the A.L.P. to join and which saw many early Group promoters eventually turn against their creations. One of the founders of the A.E.U. Group was J. H. Carney, a Catholic who was Sydney District Secretary from 1940 to 1944 and Commonwealth Council Secretary from 1944 to his death in 1949. Other Sydney A.E.U. officials who appear to have actively supported the Group included organiser G. Herron, and H. Carr and E. Leaver who both worked full-time in the A.E.U. Sydney office 'on delegation' for several years after the war. Carr seems to have been the first secretary of the A.E.U. Group but later came to oppose Group policies as did another early supporter, J. A. Langton. On the Political Committee, support for Group policies was led by the secretary, J. Byrne, together with J. Brady and W. Molloy. By 1953 M. Malcolm had become secretary of the Sydney Group and his name was to the fore during the controversies surrounding the Group's efforts to obtain 'court-controlled' ballots in the important A.E.U. elections of that year. The A.E.U. Group seems to have been particularly strong in the Newcastle area, largely perhaps because of the backing given by organiser T. B. Ward who wielded great influence in the district by virtue of being its only full-time A.E.U. official for a quarter of a century. Upon Ward's retirement in 1949, his close friend and protegé, H. E. Low, was elected to succeed him. Another Newcastle man, J. J. Babbage, Commonwealth Councilman from 1954 to 1957, was also closely associated with the Group.

The four remaining states saw nothing like the same degree of anti-communist organisation in the A.E.U. as in Victoria and New South Wales in this early period. Most activity there came after the Split and the disbandment of the Groups. Before 1955 the minor states witnessed relatively isolated efforts to oppose 'communist' influences (however defined) and in most cases the stimulus was provided by The Movement acting through Catholic branch secretaries and district delegates. The relative lack of impact was partly due to the fact that, outside Queensland, there were few communists prominent in the A.E.U. in these states. In Queensland itself the A.W.U.-dominated Groups were generally unable to make much leeway among the metal unions although there were signs of informal organisation among A.E.U. Catholic members working in railway workshops.

Activity in the four minor industrial states was most effective during A.E.U. federal ballots and here the co-ordinating role of The Movement was of importance in getting out the anti-communist vote. Of particular value, in view of A.E.U. rules forbidding the circulation of printed election material, was The Movement's ability to handle the chore of compiling and distributing thousands of handwritten 'How to Vote' cards. The A.L.P. leaders of the Groups in different states also provided some measure of federal coordination during important A.E.U. ballots, particularly after the formation of the Groups' Interstate Liaison Committee in 1952. Within the A.E.U. itself those officials sympathetic towards the A.E.U. Group — particularly those holding federal positions like Carney, Babbage or Burke — were in a good position to relay information and advice between the various districts and states.

III

Having so briefly outlined the nature of the anti-communist forces within the A.E.U. we may now turn to some consideration of the actual course of the conflict. As was the case in many unions, communist influence first became of any significance in the A.E.U. during the bitter Depression years of the 1930s. However, while the mood of the union was certainly aggressive during the rebound from the Depression, the A.E.U. could provide many candidates other than communists to satisfy its taste for militancy in full time union positions during these years. Thus, while impressing their fellow engineers with their hard work and dedication, and slowly increasing their numbers and influence in workshops and on District Committees in the eastern states, the communists remained simply a part of the general spectrum of militant A.E.U. activists in the 1930s. Individual communists joined the ranks of the dozens of other candidates who were prepared to contest the numerous elections for full time office, but the A.E.U. rank and file remained largely satisfied with their traditionally militant officers like Cranwell and Carroll. In 26 elections in the years 1935 to 1939 inclusive only one sitting official was defeated — although natural retirements and the creation of two new organising divisions did result in the election of four other new faces to the ranks of the 17 elected full time officials which the A.E.U. employed at the outbreak of war.[5] The solitary A.E.U. official who was rejected by his constituents was Councilman Long who was replaced by Fountain in 1939.[6] As a result of general discontent with the Council's handling of the dispute over the 1937 ballot for this position Victorian G. W. Deverall was also replaced by a left winger, R. W. Hill, (A.L.P.), when he came up for re-election in the first year of the war. This defeat may help explain Deverall's flirtation with the Groups in the 1940s.

The opportunity for members of the C.P.A. to gain full-time A.E.U. positions was provided by World War II when a number of A.E.U. officials of long standing resigned to take positions in the rapidly growing Commonwealth Public Service endeavouring to control and co-ordinate the national war effort. It was not that communists directly replaced all six organisers concerned; it was rather that the effect of what was, for the A.E.U., a quite dramatic turnover of officials helped make A.E.U. activists more amenable to the idea of giving new faces, including communists, a turn in office.

The first communist to become a full-time A.E.U. official was J. F. Newman who was elected Perth organiser in September 1942. For several reasons, including the fact that Newman resigned from the C.P.A. in 1947, the election of the A.E.U.'s second full-time communist official proved more significant from the point of view of the internal struggles within the A.E.U. In June 1943 E. J. Rowe was elected as the representative on Commonwealth Council of South Australia, Victoria and Broken Hill. He replaced R. W. Hill

---

[5] One full time position, that of Arbitration Agent, was not elective. This position was held by C. E. Mundy an orthodox A.L.P. man, from 1922 until his retirement in 1947. The Assistant Arbitration Agent, H. J. Souter (A.L.P.), then took over the job until he moved on to the A.C.T.U. in 1954 when he was succeeded by E. G. Deverall (A.L.P.), the son of G. W. Deverall.

[6] Above, pp. 120–1.

whose defeat was largely due to his inability to assuage the suspicions of the Melbourne and Geelong districts that his term in Sydney had made him forgetful of his grass root origins in Victoria. For the next ten years 'Red Ted' Rowe was to be the stormy petrel of the A.E.U., personifying for his opponents what they saw as the sinister effects of communism on the A.E.U.

Rowe's election was symbolic of wider currents in several ways. He was a Ballarat railway worker and from early in the Spanish Civil War the Ballarat labour movement had witnessed a generally no-holds-barred contest for supremacy between Catholic-led forces and their radical opponents. Rowe, who broke Ballarat precedent with two successive years service as Trades Hall President, was the youthfully fervent ideologue who came to lead the left wing forces aided by A. C. Williams of the A.E.U. and J. Restarick of the Boilermakers' Society. The Catholic leader within the A.E.U. was M. Calnin who opposed Rowe in several A.E.U. ballots. The Holy Name Society seems to have provided some of the inspiration for the Catholic side which 'captured' the local A.R.U. branch early in the piece. However, the anti-Groupers always managed to maintain control of the Ballarat A.E.U. if only at times because of the explicitly sectarian overtones which the struggle took in this, as in some other, country towns.

Although Rowe's verve and oratory had made a considerable impact when opposing dilution at a 1940 Melbourne mass meeting, his supporters in 1943 felt he still might suffer from being a country resident. Consequently, in order to combat the advantage of Deverall, his main opponent in the contest to replace the now unpopular Hill, it was decided that he should campaign in person in districts outside Ballarat — particularly in the numerically all-important Melbourne branches. Hitherto only sitting officials had been able to indulge in relatively mild personal campaigning in their constituencies. From this time onwards all candidates faced with serious opposition formed unofficial committees to assist them in their campaigns, and endeavoured to address as many branches as possible. Further changes came in A.E.U. electioneering with the formation of the Groups. Previously candidates had emphasised only their A.E.U. qualifications — their experience and service in branches, District Committees and conferences. With the Groups' emphasis on unionists' political allegiances many A.E.U. candidates began also to refer to their A.L.P. credentials, while at least some A.E.U. members of the C.P.A. refrained from publicising their particular affiliation. Evidence exists that in one election Rowe sought aid from fellow communists in other unions in handwriting A.E.U. 'How to Vote' cards.[7] It is safe

---

[7] *Report of Royal Commission Inquiring into the Origins, Aims, Objects, and Funds of the Communist Party in Victoria and Other Related Matters*, 1950, p. 55.

to assume that such help was often given to counter at least partially the growing efficiency of the national anti-communist election machinery.

C. M. Southwell became the third communist full-time A.E.U. official when he was elected a Melbourne organiser in May 1944 ahead of six other candidates. This was three months after the same Melbourne members had selected G. W. Deverall to be their other organiser from another seven-man field. The two remaining war-time communist successes both came in New South Wales. In December 1943 A. E. Searle had run a rather distant second to J. H. Carney in a 16 man competition for a new Commonwealth Council Secretary, but in the June 1944 ballot to replace Carney as Sydney District Secretary, Searle finished ahead of four other candidates. Then, in March 1945, A. Wilson won a four man competition for the Sydney organising position just ahead of H. Carr who was soon to become first secretary of the A.E.U. Group in Sydney. The four communists stationed in the two principal states were exactly balanced by four anti-communists — Carney, Deverall and two N.S.W. organisers, Ward and Herron. The remaining ten officials were committed to neither camp.

In addition to the elected posts a number of members were placed 'on delegation' in the main industrial centres to assist in handling the war-time explosion of membership, and in Sydney and Melbourne they were retained long after the war. The District Committees appointed these 'temporary' assistant organisers and in each city they consisted of two anti-communists and two anti-Groupers. In Sydney Carr and Leaver balanced J. S. Dodd and H. Ewer, while in Melbourne Burke and White balanced J. J. Arter and L. Maxwell. When in 1948 a new permanent organising position was created in each city Dodd won election from Leaver in Sydney but White defeated Maxwell in Melbourne. In later years Ewer and Burke were also elected to organising jobs.

This even balance indicates two things about the A.E.U. at this time. First there was no question of either political extreme of the labour spectrum dominating the A.E.U. Secondly — and this remained true until at least 1955 — on *industrial* issues there was no noticeable divergence in the policies and tactics advocated and pursued by A.E.U. leaders who were diametrically opposed to each other politically. It is possible that A.E.U. Groupers and communists may have secretly desired to steer the A.E.U. in some preferred industrial direction. In fact there is no evidence that either side attempted to do so. It could be argued that the apparent unanimity within the A.E.U. on general industrial tactics and policy in the 'forties and early 'fifties is explicable in terms of one or both sides biding their time, waiting to build an impregnable power base before implementing industrial policies at variance to the standard A.E.U. approach. Again there is no evidence for this: but even if it were so and Grouper and/or communist officials took an A.E.U. approach simply to avoid providing their opponents with ammunition, their motives become irrelevant alongside the central observed fact that in the pre-Split period all A.E.U. officials, whatever their political affiliations, approached industrial issues from the standard A.E.U. viewpoint. In other words, whether or not they were obeying their own natural or ideological instincts, they were certainly implementing the wishes of their activist rank and file constituents.

As is the case with so many facets of the pre-1955 era, objective assessment of A.E.U. officials' industrial performance is bedevilled by stigmata retrospectively attached to those concerned after the Split. Because of the emergence of the D.L.P. and the N.C.C. opposing the A.L.P. with their own distinct and generally conservative industrial policies there has been a tendency to lump together all the ex-Groupers (and their allies) as always having been lacking in militancy and aggressive industrial policy. Whatever may have been the case in other unions, the record of A.E.U. anti-communists before the Split indicates that their opponents had no monopoly of militancy. In the period before the Split the active minority of A.E.U. rank and file members elected officials on their merits — and merits meant industrial militancy for the most part. One of the best proofs of the triumph of personality over political complexion in the A.E.U. electorate is provided by the fact that exactly the same Melbourne constituency which elected and re-elected communist organiser Southwell, also elected and re-elected anti-communist organisers, White and Burke. The form of A.E.U. elections, in which each position was separately voted for and multiple-candidate 'tickets' were virtually unknown, fortified the traditional A.E.U. emphasis on individual merits. Certainly intensive campaigning occurred before those ballots in which communists or their opponents fielded a candidate: but the issue was *never* alternative industrial policies. All candidates pledged themselves to the traditional A.E.U. approach, but, while the general failings of communism (or Catholicism) could be listed, it was difficult when opposing sitting A.E.U. officials to point to specific cases where the latter had diverged from A.E.U. policy as a result of their ideological allegiance. The most that could be argued in the great majority of cases was that at some unknown future date such officials *might* be swayed from following the A.E.U. line as a result of influences apparently emanating from Moscow or the Vatican. A.E.U. communists were not accused within the A.E.U. of being too militant before 1955 nor were A.E.U. Groupers charged with being 'bosses' men' in the same period. Often the two extremes recognised each others' industrial worth

and, when interviewed, ex-officials of the pre-Split period often spontaneously prefaced remarks about their opponents by saying they had
respected the latters' industrial policies and only opposed them 'politically'.
So A.E.U. industrial policies were unaffected in any direct sense by the activities of organised anti-communist forces — although already in this pre-
Split era the union's energies were being distracted by the need for many
officials to keep an eye on their opponents and to involve themselves in
campaigning for one side or the other during the innumerable A.E.U. ballots.

Where the Groupers' campaign within the A.E.U. did have an important
effect and did make for change was on the political front. For, as far as
election of delegates to the important Political Committees in the two main
centres was concerned, anti-communist arguments had a naturally greater
impact. It will be recalled that these Committees spoke for the A.E.U. on
political issues and, more to the point, controlled the large A.E.U. delegations to A.L.P. Conferences. Thus Grouper arguments that only A.L.P. members
should help determine A.L.P. policy came to seem reasonable to a majority of
A.E.U. activists and, as anti-communist organisation improved, the Melbourne
and Sydney Political Committees came to be dominated by Groupers and their
allies. This had rather paradoxical effects for official A.E.U. policy on Groups
in these two key districts. The District Committees, including their sizeable
quota of anti-communist delegates, continued to pursue the A.E.U.'s industrial aims with what to outsiders usually seemed to be an excess of militancy.
On the question of Groups the District Committees denounced them as representing outside interference in A.E.U. members' traditional rights to judge
a fellow member on his industrial record and nothing more. The two Political
Committees, on the other hand, were able to base their support of Groups in
general on the subtly different grounds that they were A.L.P. organs and, while
A.E.U. members might be a superior breed who would never become communist dupes or pawns, the Groups were necessary to save lesser organisations
subject to ballot frauds, standover tactics and all the other methods by which
communists were said to maintain their position.

In addition, of course, capture of the Political Committees enabled the
Groupers to align the A.E.U. delegations behind general Group tickets and
platforms at A.L.P. state Conferences. Despite the A.E.U. members' own
traditional ranking of the industrial side of things as far more important
than politics, this represented a very important success in the political sphere
for the A.L.P. Industrial Groups, for the A.E.U. was the largest union affiliated
to the A.L.P. in Victoria, and second largest (to the A.W.U.) in New South
Wales. Given the nature of A.E.U. records the course of Grouper ascendancy
may be traced with detailed accuracy only in Victoria, but if anything, it

seems that control of the Sydney Political Committee was acquired earlier and more completely, and was maintained for a longer period of time.

For nearly three years after the A.L.P. Groups' first establishment in Victoria the A.E.U. Political and District Committees remained united in their opposition. At the A.L.P. Conferences of 1947 and 1948 at which the continued existence of the Groups was in the balance, A.E.U. delegations voted against them. Significantly, however, in 1947 two Groupers, Bailey and Nolan, voted against the remaining A.E.U. delegates in the crucial division. They defended their action on technical grounds concerning the difference between an amendment and a motion, but were temporarily disbarred from representing the union at A.L.P. Conferences.[8]

In 1947 and 1948 the District and Political Committees vehemently opposed the attempts made by the Victorian A.L.P. Executive, notably in the case of T. Audley of the Shop Assistants' Union, to expel from the Party members of other unions who opposed Group nominees in union ballots. The A.E.U. attended joint meetings with like-minded unions to discuss possible tactics, including disaffiliation from the A.L.P., and although the A.E.U. delegation to the 1948 Conference was led by T. P. Corrigan M.L.A., and included at least three other Groupers in Fitzpatrick, Reilly and F. Dunn, the instructions given to the delegation were unambiguously to oppose the Groups and any 'Red-baiting'. A strong A.E.U. motion demanding the abandonment of the Groups did not get on to the A.L.P. Agenda Paper but Item 115 on the Conference's Agenda was a milder A.E.U. motion urging, in effect, that the solution to the industrial movement's current divisions over the Groups was to follow A.E.U. practice in separating affairs industrial and political by the creation in every union of an A.E.U.-style Political Committee to handle non-industrial matters. The Conference, however, was able to see little merit in what was, in the circumstances, a naive and rather patronising proposal. Indeed so far removed was the Conference from acceptance of the A.E.U.'s traditional unconcern for unionists' political affiliations that, out of 300 delegates, only W. Lewis of the Locomotive Enginemen's union joined the A.E.U. delegation in opposing a motion sponsored by the Central Executive which denounced the C.P.A. in the strongest possible terms.[9]

On the key issue of expulsion from the A.L.P. of opponents of Group nominees in union elections, the Groupers decided to pull in their horns a little in order not to antagonise beyond redemption the 'militant unions',

---

[8] 'Melbourne Political Committee Minutes'. (Hereafter 'M.P.C.M.'), 1/7/47.
[9] *Labor Call*, 2/4/48.

as the A.E.U.-led faction was popularly described.[10] Yet the Conference's agreement to reverse the expulsion decisions did little to soothe the A.E.U.'s irritation. Soon after the Conference the A.E.U. Political and District Committees held a joint meeting which among other things condemned the A.L.P. decision to continue the Groups and determined to reconvene meetings of unions opposed to the Groups.[11] Agitation against the Groups continued throughout 1948 and in January 1949 the Political Committee carried motions in favour of reducing the size of the A.E.U. affiliation to the A.L.P. and of withholding financial assistance to the A.L.P. during municipal, state and federal elections.[12] Yet all these efforts were to no avail. The A.E.U.'s campaign against the Groups aroused no major response in a labour movement which by 1949 was coming to accept the Groups as a fact of life. Within the A.E.U. itself the members had begun to exhibit what seemed to outsiders to be their schizophrenic distinction between affairs political and industrial by favouring Grouper candidates for the Political Committee while refusing to discriminate against anti-Groupers in other internal ballots. In fact the shifting balance on the Political Committee first manifested itself a mere fortnight after the decision to reduce affiliation to the A.L.P. At a lengthy, wrangling, and bitter meeting the original motion was rescinded by 12 votes to 10.[13] In April the motion withholding financial assistance to the A.L.P. was also rescinded by 11 votes to 8,[14] and a third key vote saw Fitzpatrick gain the secretaryship of the Political Committee by 11 votes to 10 against the leading anti-Grouper, K. Cameron.[15]

The 1949 A.L.P. Conference, beginning one week after Fitzpatrick's election, illustrated the changes which had occurred in the intervening year. Now firmly established and fully aware of the shifting balance on the A.E.U. Political Committee the Victorian Groupers saw no reason this time to make any conciliatory bows to the A.E.U.'s recent campaign against them. The particular object of their fury was the retiring Political Committee Secretary and leader of the A.E.U. delegation to the Conference, F. Simpson. By virtue of his handling of the correspondence announcing the cut in A.E.U. affiliation and his alleged delay in replying to A.L.P. queries Simpson, a prospective A.L.P. candidate for the senate, was refused admittance to the Conference. It also decided that in future automatic expulsion would be the lot of any A.L.P.

---

[10] *Argus*, 31/3/48.
[11] 'M.P.C.M.', 14/3/48.
[12] 'M.P.C.M.', 18/1/49.
[13] 'M.P.C.M.', 1/2/49.
[14] 'M.P.C.M.', 5/4/49.
[15] 'M.P.C.M.', 12/4/49.

member who opposed affiliation of his union with the A.L.P. In the process
the A.E.U. was scathingly attacked by Grouper delegates, some of whom were
taking the opportunity to relieve themselves of resentment against the
'Gentlemen Jims' accumulated over many years but notably during the
1946—7 Metal Trades Dispute. The general tenor of the assault and the reality
of A.E.U. consistency is conveyed by Lovegrove's description of the A.E.U.
as, 'nothing but a vehicle and appeal court for communists, fellow travellers,
parlour pinks, and spineless unionists, who did not have the courage to be on
one side or the other'.[16] The A.E.U. Political Committee formally supported
Simpson but no other action was taken. Later in the year the Committee
actually decided to increase the size of the A.E.U. affiliation to the A.L.P.[17]

A.E.U. agitation within the Victorian A.L.P. against the Groups ceased for
the next four and a half years as the Political Committee remained firmly
controlled by Fitzpatrick, Reilly, Bailey and their supporters, opposed only
by a relatively small core of anti-Groupers. During this period the Committee took the general Grouper line on all political issues approving, for
example, the 1949 imprisonment of C.P.A. Secretary, L. L. Sharkey, offering
only lukewarm opposition to the attempts by the Menzies' Government to
proscribe the C.P.A., fully supporting the U.N. intervention in Korea, refusing
to oppose conscription, rejecting calls for an investigation into allegations
of U.S.A. use of germ warfare, and opposing recognition of China. One direct
sign of the influence of The Movement came at the 1953 A.L.P. Conference
when Fitzpatrick moved a successful amendment bringing Conference endorsement of the primacy of agriculture and land settlement in the allocation of resources by A.L.P. governments.

On a number of issues, particularly the C.P.A. Dissolution Bill, the Committee's views differed from the line being pursued federally by the Commonwealth Council. Closer to home and of more significance was the increasingly
hostile surveillance of the Melbourne District Committee. The latter, on
which the Groupers remained in a minority, came painfully to realise that the
vaunted A.E.U. division of labour between Political and District Committees was feasible only if the complexion of the two bodies coincided. For a
start, of course, the Committees disagreed on the basic issue of the continued
existence of the A.L.P. Groups themselves and the District Committee's resentment was hardly lessened by public A.L.P. support in the press and on

---

[16] *Argus*, 18/4/49.
[17] From 8,100 to 10,100 members. 'M.P.C.M.', 7/6/49. In line with A.E.U.
practice, however, this was still well below the maximum figure possible for
A.E.U. Victorian membership then stood at approximately 21,000 of whom
some 18,000 paid the political levy ('M.P.C.M.', 22/3/49).

radio for Grouper candidates in A.E.U. elections. As a consequence the District Committee began to express views on matters which, strictly speaking, were not within its province. An anti-Grouper Commonwealth Council tended to overlook such incursions into 'political' affairs but the Executive Council, when appealed to, came down on the side of the Political Committee.[18] The upshot of this was not without its irony in view of the A.E.U.'s suggestion to the 1948 A.L.P. Conference:[19] the District Committee in early 1953 endeavoured to persuade Commonwealth Council to disband the Political Committee.[20] This move was unsuccessful and the opponents of the Political Committee had to wait until the Groupers lost favour with their electorates in the Branches. Significantly, this began to occur prior to the A.L.P. Split, but before discussing the swing away from the Groupers in the A.E.U. or the full implications for the A.E.U. of the Split itself it is necessary first to backtrack a little in time, and also to shift our attention to New South Wales. Here, in 1953, the Groupers set afoot moves which were to give rise to the biggest internal controversies in the A.E.U. since the ferment over the 1921 Biennial Conference. Their aim was simply to have the Commonwealth Arbitration Court supervise the conduct of the 1953 ballots to elect the Commonwealth Council Chairman and the New South Wales Councilman.

The decision to take this unprecedented step rested on the Groupers' disappointment at their failure, particularly in New South Wales, to make much impression in elections for full-time A.E.U. officers. It was indicated earlier that A.E.U. Groups were not very active in the four minor states. In the first seven post-war years, conventional A.E.U. candidates were returned without polemics or rancour to the five organising positions located in the lesser states. The position of Councilman representing West Australia and Queensland changed hands twice between 1939 and 1952, but on both occasions because of resignations due to ill-health. In 1952 the death of the incumbent saw a communist, C. G. Hennessy, elected to replace him. As had often been the case before, the election was a competition between the two vastly separated states' favourite sons, with the Queenslander having the slight advantage of numbers. The runner-up was the Perth organiser, H. J. Symons, who proved unsympathetic to the approaches of the A. L. P. Groups' Interstate Liaison Committee for an exchange of preferences with the Grouper candidate.[21]

The South Australian and Tasmanian members shared their Common-

[18] 'M.P.C.M.', 5/9/50.
[19] Above, p. 209.
[20] 'M.D.C.M.', 11/2/53.
[21] Campbell, op. cit., p. 197 and 198n.

wealth Councilman with the Victorians and the elections of 1946 and 1949 saw Rowe re-elected fairly comfortably ahead of his Grouper opponent, Calnin. In 1952, however, Rowe was defeated in a straight fight with Assistant Organiser Burke, behind whom all the anti-communist forces swung their full support. Over these same seven post-war years the long-serving A. E. Fair (A.L.P.) had comfortably retained the Melbourne District Secretaryship while the activists split the Melbourne organising positions between communist Southwell and anti-communists White and Burke. The joint Victorian country—Tasmania organising position was firmly held by A. E. Horsburgh, an unaligned A.L.P. member.

In New South Wales, although retaining control of the Sydney Political committee right until the eve of the key state A.L.P. Conferences of 1955, the Groupers often felt themselves to be slipping back in ballots for full-time officers. Sydney was the main area of Grouper weakness, for Newcastle continued to return organiser Low by large margins, and the South Coast and country branches favoured Herron until his resignation to become an In-spector of the Commonwealth Arbitration Court in 1949. The important Sydney area was largely responsible for a major Grouper setback which occurred in September 1947 when Fountain lost his Commonwealth Council seat to a communist opponent, Sydney organiser, A. Wilson. Two main factors contributed to Fountain's defeat. In 1946 unfavourable publicity arose from his unsuccessful attempt, made in company with Carney and two rank and file Groupers, to persuade Councilman Porter to support a round-Australia trip for Carney just prior to the ballot for Commonwealth Council Secretary.[22] The trip would, of course, have allowed Carney to do some campaigning. Early in 1947 the final nails were driven into Fountain's electoral coffin as a result of his role in the latter stages of the Victorian dispute when many activists were convinced that he 'ratted' on the strikers.[23] Wilson's election to the Council meant that two of the five members of Com-monwealth Council were now communists and the fact that they held two of the three voting positions was seen by some of their more naive opponents as an indicator that the C.P.A. had 'captured' the A.E.U. Certainly the fact made good propaganda for Groupers in all states of the Commonwealth and may have marginally aided Rowe's defeat in 1952 — although Hennessy's election at the end of that year appeared to restore the *status quo*. The one other change in the composition of the Council came in 1949 when Carney died after a long illness. The Grouper replacement candidate was Calnin

[22] 'C.C.M.', 10/7/46, 23/7/46, 13/9/46, 20/9/46, 1/10/46.
[23] Above, pp. 174—6.

from Ballarat, whose main opponents in a seven-man field were Searle and Deverall. As the lowest four candidates' votes were distributed, Calnin remained well ahead but the final count saw Deverall gain virtually all Searle's preferences and defeat Calnin by 522 votes out of 12,468 cast. Deverall's successful intervention in this election was resented in some Grouper quarters but his re-election was unopposed in 1952 and 1955.

In New South Wales the Wilson success was followed by further setbacks for the Groupers. Searle continued to be re-elected Sydney District Secretary and Grouper candidates were successively defeated in ballots to fill Wilson's old organising position, to fill the new permanent Assistant Organiser's post created in 1948, and to replace organiser Herron. By mid-1950 four of the five full-time state offices were held by communists — Searle, Buckley, Dodd and Ewer — and, along with Wilson, they were all re-elected when their terms in office ended. In these circumstances, with A.E.U. activists ignoring the Groupers' fulminations against the political affiliations of these officers, the Groupers decided that their only possibility of success was to draw into participation in the ballot the electorally apathetic majority of A.E.U. members. Hence the call for supervision by the Commonwealth Arbitration Court of the December 1953 Council ballots — for the court's practice was to conduct a pre-paid postal ballot through the auspices of the Commonwealth Electoral Office.

In order to justify to fellow members such 'interference' in the affairs of the independent and tradition-conscious A.E.U. the Groupers were sometimes to claim that court supervision, or 'court control' as it became popularly known,[24] was necessary in order to offset communist malpractices at the ballot boxes. While ballot-rigging seems to have definitely occurred in other unions, notably the F.I.A., no firm evidence was ever presented for such claims in the A.E.U. Only two charges are important enough to warrant further consideration. An ex-C.P.A. officer, C. Sharpley, claimed that he had witnessed ballot-rigging in the A.E.U. (and other unions) between 1946 and 1948. However, his blanket allegations were couched in vague terms and he gave only one specific example of supposed malpractice. This concerned the elections for the Melbourne District Committee in 1948 when non-members allegedly voted — although Sharpley says their attempt to rig the results proved a failure.[25] The second allegation came from leading Sydney

---

[24] Hereafter the contemporary phrases 'branch ballots' and 'court ballots' will normally be used to denote the alternative methods of electing A.E.U. officials.

[25] See Cecil Sharpley, *I was a Communist leader*, A Courier-Mail Publication 1949, pp. 16—17 and *The Great Delusion*, London 1952, p. 80; *Report of Royal Commission . . . into . . . the Communist Party in Victoria*, pp. 83—4.

Grouper, E. Leaver. After being narrowly defeated by Dodd for the new Assistant Organiser's position in December 1948, Leaver appealed to the Commonwealth Arbitration Court against the result claiming to know that he had received the majority of votes in the majority of voting branches.[26] His claims that irregularities were widespread were dismissed by the Arbitration Court and later by the N.S.W. Supreme Court.

Sharpley's allegations cannot be proved or disproved at this distance of time. Provided absent members' pence cards could be obtained, over-voting was a possibility although the A.E.U. rules made it very difficult by requiring voters to sign the teller's sheet which in turn was retained for 12 months as a safeguard. In an election contested by Groupers both they and their opponents would provide observers within the branches on Star Nights to check the ballotting procedures. Where possible, appeals would be made to the Commonwealth Council by one side or the other against branches wherein the appellants' opponents were expected to poll a majority of votes. Such appeals followed most A.E.U. elections and were mostly made on technical grounds such as the voting commencing too early or too late. No allegations of anything amounting to 'ballot rigging' were made through the A.E.U.'s internal appeal system although the Newcastle area was the subject of more controversy than most in this period. After the defeat of Fountain in 1947, for example, both sides claimed the other had misused pence cards in the district, although the A.E.U. London office found only the Groupers guilty.[27] A consideration of the intricate A.E.U. election procedure backed up as it was by the union's internal appeals system of many checks and balances confirms the opinion of British industrial relations authorities that A.E.U. elections were particularly democratic and corruption-proof.[28] Indirect evidence that communists were not elected to office by means of rigging A.E.U. ballots is provided by the defeat of Rowe in 1952, the simultaneous election of anti-communist and communist organisers in Melbourne, the election of Grouper majorities to the Melbourne and Sydney Political Committees, the election of large Grouper minorities to the same cities' District Committees, and the subsequent successes of communists in elections for A.E.U. office supervised by the Commonwealth Arbitration Court. When interviewed, Grouper leaders of the period freely admitted that their sole criticism of A.E.U. ballots was the fact that only the traditionally small percentage of activists participated.

[26] *Industrial Information Bulletin*, Volume 4, p. 408.
[27] 'C.C.M.', 13/2/48.
[28] See e.g. Roberts, op. cit., pp. 227–8.

In Sydney where, as we have seen, the Groupers had least success, the Leaver case greatly damaged their reputation in the Sydney district. His cardinal sin in the eyes of A.E.U. activists was, of course, that he did not attempt to use the union's appeal system in pursuit of his allegations. Even had the communists rigged the election result it would have been impossible for them to prevent an appeal being forwarded to the non-communist Executive Council and Final Appeal Court in Britain. He further weakened his case in the eyes of most members by arguing before the courts against Dodd's election on the technical grounds that A.E.U. rules did not provide for the office of an Assistant Organiser. This was despite the fact that he had been a candidate for the position and, like his opponent, canvassed for votes while filling the even more unofficial role of 'temporary' assistant to the Sydney organiser — a post which he had held 'on delegation' for five consecutive years. These facts were naturally well publicised by the anti-Groupers and made it very much harder for Group candidates in subsequent A.E.U. elections in Sydney.

In these circumstances the New South Wales Groups decided that their only chance of ousting Wilson from the Commonwealth Council was to secure a postal ballot through Arbitration Court intervention. Cranwell was to retire in February 1954 and the ballot to choose a successor was also to be held in December 1953. It was known that Rowe would attempt to succeed him so Groupers in all states backed the New South Wales proposal that this ballot should also be supervised by the court. Another ballot due in December was the annual election for Sydney District Committee President and this too was included in the application.

The Groupers did not use the mechanism provided by the Chifley government which allowed court intervention in cases of proven malpractices in union ballots. Instead, they used the 1951 Menzies amendments which simply required 1,000 members to petition the court to intervene. The petition sheets began circulating in May 1953, publicly backed by Grouper officers of the N.S.W. Branch of the A.L.P., and heatedly denounced by the A.E.U. Commonwealth Council, District Committees and many branches. Counter petitions were organised which quickly attracted over 38,000 signatures and the Council appealed to the 1,816 members who signed the original petition to retract formally if they felt they had been 'misled' by the Groupers.

Although appearing before the Industrial Registrar on 4 June with the legal representative of the petitioners to discuss the technical problem of whether the Sydney District President was an 'officer' within the meaning of the Act, the Commonwealth Council, including Burke, unanimously determined not to co-operate with the court in the event of the Registrar accepting the petitions. Meetings of District Committees, shop stewards, Branch Secretaries and Presidents were called to endorse the Council's stand and to consider proposals for a stopwork meeting. On 19 June the Registrar appointed the Commonwealth Electoral Officer for New South Wales to conduct the two Council ballots. The Electoral Officer then requested that the relevant information regarding A.E.U. membership be provided not later than 1 July. The Council response was to call for half-day stop-work meetings in the week beginning 6 July. The Executive Council was informed of developments.

It is certain that the majority of A.E.U. activists were opposed to court intervention. The pride which they took in their union, its history and independence is undoubted. The celebration of the centenaries of the English and Australian Sections in 1951 and 1952 amid much reminiscing and stirring speech-making may even have strengthened the pride in A.E.U. traditions — if that were possible. So effective a weapon was the call to repel outside interference that no matter how strongly they privately believed in the merits of court ballots — and indeed no matter how hard they may have been working for the success of the Groups — no full time official dared publicly say a good word for court ballots *per se*, nor for the petitioners. Even the Melbourne District Committee with its strong Grouper faction unanimously endorsed the Commonwealth Council's campaign. In these circumstances it required considerable dedication for A.E.U. Groupers to collect signatures in the workshops and stand up to the harassment of fellow members of all political hues — although actual attempts to use the union's rules to discipline the petition organisers could be prevented by Group supporters on the District Committees.[29]

The first break in the clouds for the Groupers came when the majority of Commonwealth Council decided that the risk of the court imposing fines outweighed the advantages of continued resistance. Burke was always a behind-the-scenes supporter of court ballots and Deverall tended to lean the same way. The key man, however, was the Chairman, Cranwell. There can be little doubt that Cranwell was strongly opposed to 'interference' in the conduct of the union's affairs. His record, containing such head-on clashes with authority as the 1938 deregistration issue and the 1946—7 Victorian dispute, in-

[29] E.g. 'M.D.C.M.', 1/7/53, 16/9/53. According to Burke a break-down of petition signatures revealed that 1,500 came from N.S.W. — 400 of them from Newcastle and presumably most of the rest from Sydney — 170 from 'Victoria', and 140 from Adelaide. 'Minutes of A.E.U. Melbourne StopWork Meeting', 8/7/53.

dicates that he was also unlikely to hold back from a confrontation with the government. In 1953, however, he appears to have greatly feared the effects on the union's currently weakened financial position[30] of any fines which the court might levy on the A.E.U. Another factor which must be borne in mind in weighing his last acts in office is that Rowe's main competitor for the succession was Cranwell's friend and protegé, A. E. Horsburgh, the organiser for the Victorian country and Tasmanian districts. At all events, 1 July, the deadline for providing the requisite membership details to the Electoral Office, saw history made in the Commonwealth Council. For the first time in the 36 years of its existence two of the voting members exerted their statutory power over the remaining Councilman and the non-voting Chairman and Secretary. Opposed by their three colleagues, Wilson and Hennessy passed a motion that the Council would not comply with the court's request. No heat or rancour surrounded the issue and the other three Council members were quite prepared to support the exploration by the 'majority' of all possible legal avenues of avoiding a court ballot. Naturally enough the split was played up by the Groupers,[31] but within the A.E.U. the stand taken by Cranwell and Deverall was generally seen to be based on financial fears. There can be little doubt that at this stage the two communists were taking the line backed by the great majority of the activist rank and file — outside Newcastle where at the July stopwork meeting 800 members decided in favour of accepting court ballots by a single vote margin.

On 13 July, the Council was summoned to the Commonwealth Arbitration Court where Malcolm and other leading Groupers were refused leave to intervene. On 15 July the A.E.U. application to the High Court for an Order Nisi was rejected, and when proceedings in the Arbitration Court were re-commenced an Order dated 24 July was issued against the A.E.U. to ensure compliance with the Electoral Officer's instructions. On the 29th the Council took the final legal step open to it by appealing to the Full High Court. In the background, the votes in what some expected to be the last ballots conducted by the A.E.U. were counted. In Sydney, Ewer was comfortably returned as Assistant Organiser. In Melbourne the electorate once again chose personalities at the opposite ends of the political spectrum with White being handsomely returned and communist A. Tennant narrowly defeating Fitzpatrick to succeed retiring District Secretary Fair. In the circumstances, a more useful result, from the Grouper's point of view, was in North Queensland where, in a result without A.E.U. precedent, the organiser for 25 years,

[30] See below p. 296.
[31] *Sydney Morning Herald*, 8/7/53, 9/7/53.

J. A. Willett, was overwhelmingly defeated by a communist challenger, F. B. Thompson.

At the beginning of August, the prospects for success of the Council's legal moves seemed remote. Consequently, Wilson and Hennessy sought again to commit the Commonwealth Council to continued resistance whatever the Full High Court's verdict. For the second time, they failed to secure agreement from the other three members of the Council. In the event the High Court reserved its judgment and the Council issued a compromise circular on 28 August. This referred to the divergence of opinion on the Council but played it down as largely one of tactics only and assured members that all confusion would be cleared up once the High Court decision was known. That this was wishful thinking was revealed by the fact that when the High Court made known its decision against the A.E.U. on 11 September the Council remained split in its outlook. On 14 September Wilson and Hennessy for the third time carried a 'minority motion', this time reaffirming A.E.U. opposition to court ballots and telling the District Committees to prepare for national stop-work meetings.

At this point then, the lines were clearly drawn and a crisis seemed imminent, with anti-Grouper isolation the more likely as a result of an A.C.T.U. decision advising the A.E.U. to comply with the court. The collision was averted as a result of discussions with 'responsible government departmental officers',[32] primarily it seems with Deputy Crown Solicitor, F. J. Mahoney.[33] Conducted by Cranwell, these discussions with Mahoney proved satisfactory. Cranwell later reported that the 'very strong impression' gained was that the authorities accepted A.E.U. arguments regarding the difficulties of postal ballots and hence would conduct the ballot in the branches after the normal A.E.U. fashion.[34] Consequently the Council decided to comply with the court — only hours before the arrival of an Executive Council telegram instructing it to do so.[35] On 30 September the rank and file were informed of the changes via a circular — which, however, contained an explicit threat regarding what would happen if 'the undertaking' was broken.

It seems certain that the Executive Council was greatly influenced by Cranwell in making its decision. His detailed views were made clear to the London office by means of private correspondence and the British executive could not help but be swayed by the opinions of this respected official whose years in federal office were double those of the other four Commonwealth

---

[32] *M.J.*, October 1953, p. 3.
[33] 'Letter of Appeal from A. Wilson to Executive Council', 6/11/53.
[34] *Ibid.*; 'C.C.M.', 18/9/53, 21/9/53; *M.J.*, October 1953, p. 4.
[35] 'C.C.M.', 22/9/53.

Council members combined. A further possibility is that, knowing the likely nature of Executive Council's imminent decision, Cranwell may have given rather too optimistic a slant to his negotiations with Mahoney when reporting back to Commonwealth Council. This would help explain the apparent total public disagreement between the parties as to what transpired[36] and also *News Weekly's* isolated claim that Cranwell privately admitted not receiving any 'undertaking' from Mahoney.[37]

In October events moved quickly. Armed with the Executive Council ruling Cranwell was able to rule out of order on 3 October a Wilson—Hennessy attempt to endorse a Sydney District Committee motion that all successful candidates in court ballots should resign. The importance of the Executive Council instructions appeared obvious when on the 7th the Electoral Officer issued instructions for a *postal* ballot and subsequently denied any knowledge of an 'understanding' being reached with the A.E.U. On the 9th, Cranwell was able to rule out of order Wilson—Hennessy motions for continued resistance, and the ensuing circular while denouncing the authorities' 'clear breach of the understanding' could only call for stop-work meetings to be held on 20 October 'in order that the membership can be informed on all aspects of the position, including instructions received from Executive Council'. On 13 October 'after much disagreement' *Circular S88* was finally drafted calling on Branch Secretaries to forward membership lists to A.E.U. headquarters in Sydney — but not to forward them to the Electoral Officer until advised by the Commonwealth Council.[38]

While these events were occurring at A.E.U. Head Office, in the background rank and file opinion was undergoing a change. From July onwards things had become a little easier for those A.E.U. officials who secretly supported the Groupers, for they were able to argue that it was fruitless (and expensive) to oppose the law — oppressive though it might be. In this, Grouper supporters at district and branch level were encouraged by the disagreement on the Council, knowledge of which spread speedily to the lower echelons of the union where Cranwell's opinions always carried particular weight. The argument in favour of accepting the inevitable and bowing to the law grew as the various legal avenues proved dead-ends for opponents of court ballots. Naturally the sentiment was cultivated by the

[36] For the Attorney General's Department's version of events see *C.P.D.*, Vol. H of R, 1, p. 1513. For the A.E.U.'s version see 'Letter of Appeal from A. Wilson'.

[37] *News Weekly*, 21/10/53.

[38] 'C.C.M.', 13/10/53. These lists included the names of 'unfinancial' members whom A.E.U. rules, rather unusually, allowed to vote in elections.

Grouper wing of the A.L.P. through argument, pamphlets and *News Weekly*, and by the daily press. However the real turning point came when the Executive Council intervened and instructed the Commonwealth Council to cease opposition. This meant that the so important weapon of appealing to the traditional pride and independence of A.E.U. members was largely nullified in the face of the ruling of a higher authority *within* the union. Appeals could be forwarded to the 1954 Final Appeal Court — with what success we shall later see — but until the deliberations of that body were known, the union's rules — the sanctity of which had been preached from the roof-tops by all court ballot opponents — quite clearly laid down that the Executive Council must be obeyed. Even if Cranwell had not ruled further opposition out of order, the jig was up. Not for the last time was one side in the internal A.E.U. struggles to be hoist with its own petard.

One immediate effect of the Executive Council ruling was to allow the press to confuse some rank and file members as to the purpose and the 'legality' (in A.E.U. terms) of the October stopwork meeting.[39] The dailies' false inferences that the Executive Council had forbidden the stoppage were a major factor in the relatively poor response to the meetings by those members who did stop work, and the failure of the Brisbane, Newcastle, Hobart and Geelong districts to hold stop-work meetings at all. Opposition to the October stoppages is also apparent in the correspondence to the Commonwealth Council from a number of District Committees, branches and workshops, but it is not clear how far this was from already committed pro-ballot supporters emerging to make public declarations now that the Executive Council ruling was known, and how much was induced by a misunderstanding of the Executive Council ruling.

In the districts where stop-work meetings were held, the mood varied. The smaller centres followed the Adelaide example where 700 members simply carried a unanimous resolution condemning the Grouper petitioners, the High Court's decision and the Electoral Officer's 'breach of faith'. At the key Melbourne and Sydney meetings, however, the rank and file debated motions in favour of continued resistance sponsored by their respective District Committees. The results differed. In Melbourne a stormy meeting rejected the proposal by 463 votes to 453 whereas in Sydney only 20 out of 2,000 members voted against the call to fight on.

The national feeling within the union was now such that Cranwell's subsequent decision to rule the Sydney vote 'out of order' did not arouse

---

[39] See in particular *Courier Mail*, 19/10/53, 21/10/53. See also, *Advertiser*, 18/10/53, 19/10/53; *Sydney Morning Herald*, 20/10/53; *News Weekly*, 7/10/53, 21/10/53.

much bitterness. From this point on Cranwell and other supporters of compliance had little real opposition — although since official A.E.U. acceptance of court ballots was still rationalised in terms of accepting an oppressive law, A.E.U. officers were still not free, even after the Executive Council ruling, to come out in favour of court ballots *per se*. In the week following the stopwork meetings Wilson and Hennessy passed another 'minority' motion condemning the Executive Council's 'unsolicited intervention' — but on the same day Cranwell ruled that, in accordance with Executive Council's instructions, branch secretaries must obey the Electoral Officer.[40] *Circular S90* consequently issued advising Branch Secretaries of this fact also contained reference to the Electoral Officer's 'breach of faith' and described the Executive Council instructions as unasked-for and constituting a 'devastating blow' to the Commonwealth Council and to the negotiations with the governmental officials. Hereafter, however, meaningful opposition ended, although Wilson, Hennessy and Cranwell did decide, against the objections of Burke and Deverall, that a ballot should be held in traditional A.E.U. fashion in the Branches on the December Star Night to 'check' the court supervised election.

Inevitably the election campaigns became inextricably linked with the furore over the court's intervention and therefore the general confusion over the nature of the Executive Council's instructions hurt the communist candidates, as did their attempts to resist the court in defiance of the A.E.U.'s London Office. Their image was particularly tarnished among the non-activist members who were persuaded to take part in the postage-paid court ballot. Such members were somewhat more receptive to the general anti-communist arguments of the press and radio — particularly when posed by A.L.P. officials such as Kane and McManus. In addition the A.E.U. Groupers ran a notably efficient and co-ordinated canvassing and pamphleteering campaign which completely outclassed their opponents' efforts. While the latters' election machinery was still geared to A.E.U. branch ballots the Groupers were able to call on all their recent experience of court ballots in other unions, backed by The Movement's national network and the Groups' Interstate Liaison Committee.[41] In this first A.E.U. court ballot the anti-Groupers were, for example, taken completely by surprise when their opponents exercised their right to obtain from the Electoral Officer copies of the lists of A.E.U. members sent in by Branch Secretaries. The Commonwealth Council was being flooded with complaints and allegations of the

[40] 'C.C.M.', 27/10/53.
[41] One item of expenditure in the 1952—4 Financial Statement of the Queensland A.L.P. Industrial Group was £50 for, 'John Maynes Expenses — A. Horsborough [*sic*] Ballot Queensland'. Campbell, op. cit., p. 199.

darkest conspiracies between public servants and Groupers while the latter were ensuring, quite legitimately, that their laboriously handwritten 'How to Vote' tickets were arriving almost simultaneously in the post with the ballot papers sent out by the Electoral Office. The Groupers' door-to-door canvassing teams, including many outsiders repaying similar help from A.E.U. Groupers in the past, were equally superior in efficiency to their opponents. The outcome of the election was never in doubt. In a record 51 per cent poll the voting for Chairman was; Horsburgh 18,961, Rowe 9,138, Symons 2,933, Willett 2,882, Shannon 2,136, Samuels 1,796, Informal 464. In N.S.W. a 53 per cent poll saw J. J. Babbage defeat Wilson by 8,199 votes to 4,034. The same winners emerged from the A.E.U.'s 'Check Ballot' although the distribution of the 21,446 votes cast therein for Chairman meant that Horsburgh only defeated Rowe on the final allocation of preferences — albeit quite comfortably by 11,546 to 9,136. The N.S.W. position was contested much more closely with Babbage only winning on A.E.U. returns by 3,055 votes to 2,921.

The election of Babbage, a Newcastle Grouper, and Horsburgh, an A.L.P. man regarded as 'safe' by the Groupers, was described as 'a very happy New Year's gift to Australian industry' by the federal Minister for Labour, H. E. Holt.[42] This naive sentiment was echoed in many other outside quarters and it is possible that even some of the younger A.E.U. Groupers were temporarily affected by the general euphoria. Experienced insiders were aware that gaining a majority of seats on Commonwealth Council would not mean any change in A.E.U. industrial policies. The election victories did not mean that the anti-communists had now 'captured' the A.E.U. any more than the previous communist voting majority had represented 'Red control' of the union. Yet in view of the genuine mistaken beliefs of many Groupers in other unions and among large sections of the general public, it will be useful to pause here briefly to review the implications and record of the A.E.U.'s communist officers in this period before the A.L.P. Split, the onset of which greatly complicates all such assessments.

In the first place, despite the post-Split oral tradition in the labour movement, it is not just Groupers and N.C.C. members who tend to magnify the effects of communists in trade unions.

In the words of D. W. Rawson, 'Nearly everyone, including the communists themselves, has a vested interest in demonstrating that a union under communist leadership is very different from a union under any other leadership'.[43]

---

[42] *Sydney Morning Herald*, 8/1/54.
[43] 'The Economic and Social Impact of Trade Unions in Australia' in Australian Institute of Political Science, *Trade Unions in Australia* (Sydney 1959), p. 137.

Thus, in general, communists are willing to take the 'credit' for all displays of militancy by rank and file members, particularly when direct action results in an improvement of working conditions, while their opponents 'blame' the communists for all stoppages and depict them as part of a master plan to disrupt the economy. Among A.E.U. activists, of course, no-one would have taken either claim seriously before 1955.

It may also be true as Rawson says that, 'communist officials have no inhibitions against strikes and it is in the interests of the Communist Party if the Australian economy is weakened as a result'.[44] But it is a very long leap from this to imply that virtually all industrial stoppages are attributable to the machinations of communist union officials or workshop cells. Even if it were accepted, for the sake of argument, that somehow communists were able to initiate strikes at will, such stoppages must speedily collapse without the support of the mass of non-communist rank and file union members. To believe otherwise is to ignore the realities of industrial conflict. The big post-war disputes in the engineering industry were the 1946–7 Victorian stoppage – which began as a lock out – and the 1948 Queensland railway strike. Both have been explained in terms of communist inspiration and control – but it is farcical to imply that the thousands of unionists involved could be kept on strike for so long simply by insidious communist influence. Communists excelled as strike leaders and propagandists by their conviction and hard work but their abilities in this direction would hardly have been sufficient to counterbalance the overwhelming opposition of government, Press and radio. If, in striking, the rank and file were acting as communist pawns there were plenty of vocal sources from which they could speedily learn of their mistake. The fact that they remained on strike for so long is evidence that they considered their cause to be just. To talk, for example, of the 1946–7 Victorian stoppage in terms of the A.E.U. being, 'in fact controlled by a communist, Rowe'[45] is not merely incorrect; it naively diverts the discussion of the post-war industrial relations scene away from its complex and varied reality into an artificial and sterile cul de sac.

Industrial friction in the metal industry measured in terms of working days lost subsided after the 1948 strike although the number of disputes

---

[44] Ibid., p. 138.
[45] Santamaria, op. cit., p. 59. Ex-communist C. Sharpley's equally unfounded allegation that the C.P.A. initiated and co-ordinated the Victorian dispute may just possibly point to the C.P.A.'s own delusions of grandeur in this direction. *Report of Royal Commission . . . into . . . the Communist Party in Victoria*, p. 93. See also, C.P.A., *Communist Leaders Speak*. (Pamphlet n.d.) p. 7.

increased after 1949. It might be argued, of course, by some non-A.E.U. members that a series of lightning strikes of short duration in the power, transport and other essential industries could have disrupted the economy in the approved communist fashion equally as well as longer stoppages in other sectors of the metal industry. There is, however, no evidence that the A.E.U. adopted any such plan of action in the remaining three years during which Rowe and Wilson 'controlled' the A.E.U. by virtue of sitting together on the Commonwealth Council. During this period as usual, strikes occurred randomly in single establishments where rank and file members considered direct action offered the best solution to their grievances. A temporary increase in working days lost in 1952 resulted from the Galvin award when the A.E.U. rank and file reaction was similar to that shown towards the Beeby awards of 1927 and 1937.

Nor is there any evidence that Rowe and Wilson sought to draw the A.E.U. into strikes involving other unions with communist officials. A.E.U. members employed in the coalfields, for example, were naturally affected by the bitter and controversial six-week stoppage in 1949 but the union's role was peripheral to the main struggle. The A.E.U. was not among the unions fined under the National Emergency (Coal Strike) Act of 1949 for attempting to support the miners financially.[46] Indeed, far from fomenting strikes the two communists, together with other Council members, refused to sanction A.E.U. coalfield's members' decision to stop work in protest against an unfavourable state award for colliery mechanics issued two months before the general stoppage. Dispute pay was withheld and although Wilson eventually came to support the strikers the remainder of the Council, including Rowe, enforced a return to work.[47]

One contentious issue in which anti-communists thought they detected C.P.A. influence was the Council's campaign against the Menzies' government's 1950 Communist Party Dissolution Bill. This measure would have rendered communists or any other 'declared person' ineligible for office in any industrial organisation. The A.E.U. was one of ten unions which con-

---

[46] Initially the A.E.U.'s funds were frozen along with those of the miners, the Waterside Workers' Union and the F.I.A. on the grounds that cash withdrawn immediately prior to the passing of the Emergency Act was intended to be used in support of the strike. The government apparently acted under the assumption that all unions with communist officials were united in their determination to continue the stoppage. However, the A.E.U. was able to demonstrate that the sum involved (£4,868) had been withdrawn in conformity with its usual banking pattern and the Crown withdrew its action. *M.J.* July 1949, p. 4; R. Gollan, *The Coal miners of New South Wales* Melbourne, 1963, p. 234.

[47] 'C.C.M.', 15/3/49, 18/3/49, 19/4/49.

ducted a successful case in the High Court to have the legislation declared unconstitutional. In this action the Commonwealth Council was supported by both the non-communist Executive Council which dismissed appeals by Grouper branches, and, eventually, by the majority of Australian electors who rejected in a referendum the government's attempt to make provision for the Bill by means of constitutional amendments.

A point of further significance when considering charges that A.E.U. policy was materially affected by the presence of two communists on the Commonwealth Council is that they did not always agree. Minor disputes on day to day tactics are naturally not recorded in the Council minutes but apart from their difference of opinion on the shortlived colliery mechanics' strike, one other matter led to a formal division. This was the question of whether members employed in the Newcastle steelworks would be better served by a federal award. These members had been covered by state awards since the 1930 Metal Trades Case but in 1952 Cranwell and Rowe outvoted Wilson in deciding that they should switch to federal arbitration.[48]

Thus it can be seen that the allegations made in certain quarters about the effects of Rowe and Wilson's terms in office were exaggerated. In some other unions the election of communist officials may have produced violent policy shifts but a study of the A.E.U. brings to light a basic consistency in the engineers' industrial policy. Whatever their political creed, the craftsmen members elected to the Commonwealth Council were first and foremost concerned to safeguard the status, working conditions, and job security of their fellow engineers, the majority of whom were also skilled tradesmen. Whether they consciously realised it or not, when considering questions like job preference for recognised tradesmen over wartime dilutees,[49] Councilmen such as Rowe and Wilson abandoned their radical views on Australian society and looked at the issue as craftsmen who had experienced unemployment and who sought guarantees for an uncertain future. Because of this consistency in official outlook no change occurred in A.E.U. industrial policy when Burke replaced Rowe in 1952, nor did it when Hennessy took his seat in 1953. When the two C.P.A. Councilmen then found themselves at variance with their colleagues on the court ballot issue — a non industrial matter be it noted — and used the Rule-book powers by which outsiders thought they 'controlled' the union to 'outvote' the Council majority, two results were inevitable. Firstly, their electoral stocks among activists fell,

[48] 'C.C.M.', 29/4/52. Cranwell here exercised his casting vote because the position of Councilman for Division No. 3 was vacant following the death of H. Jackson.
[49] Above, p. 165.

although the A.L.P. Split completely obscured this effect in Hennessy's case; secondly, use was made of the A.E.U.'s ultra-democratic structure and the impartial British links in the appeal chain.

Naturally enough when the fuss and applause died away after the election of Horsburgh and Babbage, the A.E.U. was seen to be continuing its consistent industrial programme in the same manner as before. It will be recalled that in 1954 the specific form of the union's perennial drive to improve engineers' standard of living was a federal campaign to increase margins.[50] When the Arbitration Court adjourned the Margins Case in February, A.E.U. members created stoppages and disputes in individual firms all over the Commonwealth. The court's resort to the use of fines was unable to halt the campaign. The dispute which most impressed itself on the public consciousness and which probably provided the greatest stimulus to the court's decision to reconsider the question of skilled margins in September was that concerning A.E.U. mechanics at Sydney bus depots. The rolling strike technique was employed so that as the court ordered a return to work at a particular depot the stoppage would jump to another depot. The strikers were supported by a £1 levy on mechanics still at work and the dispute continued from July to the end of September by which time the power industry had become involved. In the bus dispute the Sydney District Committee acted independently of the rest of the trade union movement and in the traditional A.E.U. manner upset the more peaceful forces therein by its disregard of their advice. Thus the A.E.U. came into direct confrontation with not merely the Arbitration Court but also the Labor Council Disputes Committee and the Cahill state Labor government. In the background the voices of the daily press, the Chambers of Manufactures and the Opposition were joined to the chorus of denunciation of what the T.L.C. Assistant Secretary described as the A.E.U.'s 'industrial lawlessness'.[51] A communist plot was a favourite explanation in many quarters but in fact A.E.U. members needed no prodding at all in this or any other of the 1954 margins' disputes. This the Leader of the Opposition in the N.S.W. Parliament admitted when demanding that the government declare the A.E.U. September 1954 Star Night ballot for District Committee delegates null and void. Mr Robson's declared aim was to keep out of office such militants as, 'Mr E. J. (Runaway) Rowe ... [whose] pose as a militant on the margin's issue had been attractive to the rank and file members and no doubt was responsible for his election, together with some of his cronies in the current Sydney

---

[50] Above, pp. 188—9.
[51] *Sydney Morning Herald*, 14/9/54.

District Committee ballot.'[52] Further evidence of the grass roots origin of the dispute is provided by the fact that despite the rising crescendo of disapproval and denunciation from all points of the political compass the rank and file of other unions gave their support to the A.E.U. men at different crucial times of the dispute. Sympathetic action was taken at one time or another by members of the Transport Workers', Railways', Salaried Officers', Vehicle Builders', Sheet Metal Workers', Electrical Trades', and Bus Employees' unions, often with complete disregard for the disapproval of their unions' leaders.

As a result of this typical display of A.E.U. members' militancy the Commonwealth Council found itself, as in 1938, in a position where in an attempt to avoid the penalties of the Arbitration Court, it formally had to renounce the strikers and order them back to work. Unfortunately, the 1954 court was as little swayed by the Council's disassociation as Judge Beeby had been, and the A.E.U. was fined a total of £1,000 on three separate occasions during the dispute. Unlike 1938, the Council this time was buffeted also from below — for the anti-Grouper majority on the Sydney District Committee gleefully took the opportunity to label the Council's directions for a return to work as a 'capitulation ... to the threats of the court to use the vicious Menzies — Fadden Government's amendments to the Arbitration Act'.[53] Yet while the bus dispute proved a useful stick with which to beat Horsburgh, Babbage and Burke — particularly Burke who answered for the Council in court — it is hard to believe that the Council's public stance would have been different if Rowe and Wilson had been elected. This doubt is strengthened, and the militant independence of the A.E.U. rank and file once more illustrated, by other events occurring in Sydney within a very short time of the bus dispute. In November, in order to preserve the imminent new margins award and to avoid still further fines, the communist district officers agreed with the Council that everything possible should be done to end a current strike at Ford's plant at Homebush over the dismissal of a shop steward.[54] However, neither the persuasive powers of organizer Buckley (C.P.A.) nor the Council's telegrams and registered letters instructing individual strikers to return to work produced any effect. The eventual exclusion of Ford's tradesmen from the new margins' award and fines of £1,000 levied on the A.E.U. also left the strikers unmoved. Only a threat initiated jointly by Grouper Babbage and communist Hennessy, to expel the strikers from the A.E.U. eventually

[52] *Sydney Morning Herald*, 23/9/54.
[53] *Sydney Morning Herald*, 18/9/54.
[54] For details of the Homebush Strike see 'C.C.M.', 8, 16, 17, 19, 30 November 1954, 14, 17, 21, 23, 24, 26 December 1954.

produced a compromise settlement — and even then delegates on the Sydney District Committee attacked their officials' joint stand. Six months later communist organisers and anti-communist Council members teamed together again to take similar drastic action agains stubborn A.E.U. strikers to avoid recurring fines as a result of a stoppage in Wollongong.[55]

While the opposing camps in the 1953 court ballot were thus closing ranks on the industrial front the main internal bickering between the new Commonwealth Council and the Sydney and Melbourne District Committees took two forms. Firstly, there were inconclusive arguments over the relative powers of the two bodies in appointing temporary organisers and holiday replacements for full time district officials — with each side endeavouring to ensure that, in future, nominees of its own persuasion would be appointed. Secondly, the parties differed in their reactions to the outcome of the many appeals forwarded to the Final Appeal Court against the Executive Council's 1953 ruling on court ballots. The first response from Britain came in June 1954 when the Executive Council took time out to rebuke the appellants by pointing to the much larger percentage vote in the 1953 court ballots compared with normal A.E.U. elections. The rank and file members who composed the October Final Appeal Court, however, were not impressed with the higher participation rate. Their finding was that Wilson and Hennessy had acted strictly according to the rules and consequently declared the Executive Council's decision to be incorrect. However, the ruling was not retrospective and it was suggested that the Australian Section should in fact alter its rules to fit in with federal legislation and thus allow for ballots supervised by the Arbitration Court. Suitable amendments could be discussed when General Secretary, B. Gardner, visited Australia in December. Given the unlikeliness of activist members voluntarily agreeing to such amendments to the rules it was not until 30 November that the Commonwealth Council decided to forward the decision to the appellants. Despite the unequivocal decision by the Appeal Court the Council issued circulars in January 1955 informing members that, as a result of petitioners' requests, the Electoral Officer would conduct the forthcoming ballot for Councilman No. 1. Inevitably, branch protests about this disregard for A.E.U. rules poured in to the Council and soon took the form of appeals to the Executive Council.

In March the Commonwealth Council shrugged off the admonitions of the London office for not commenting on the appeals, by claiming that it had no option but to obey the law. This argument must have been convincing for on 30 March, doubtlessly also influenced by Gardner who had now returned to Britain, the Executive Council rejected the appeals on the same grounds. While describing the Conciliation and Arbitration Act as, 'one of the most repressive and reactionary pieces of legislation ever enacted', it took time in its letter to chide the appellants by pointing to the illogicality of branches obeying the Electoral Officer but expecting the Commonwealth Council to do otherwise. Appeals immediately flowed from anti-Grouper branches to the 1955 Final Appeal Court, but even at the time the Executive Council had reached its controversial decision the traumatic A.L.P. Split was under way and the parameters of both A.E.U. elections and dissensions as a whole within the union had irrevocably altered. For some little time at least the issue of court ballots ceased to be the central battleground. The A.E.U. activist core redivided and redeployed themselves along bitter new lines dictated by the explosions occurring in the long, hot political summer of 1955.

9

The A.L.P. split and the defeat of the N.C.C.

The fortunes of the Groupers began to deteriorate perhaps as early as 1953 when dissension became apparent on the Victorian A.L.P. Executive. Certainly 1954 saw the anti-Grouper campaign achieve considerable momentum culminating in Dr Evatt's public attack. The Groupers' destruction within the A.E.U. roughly paralleled the trends within the wider labour movement and in Victoria, the scene of the bitterest struggle, the events in the A.E.U. may even have slightly preceded the larger drama.

The majorities enjoyed on the A.E.U. Melbourne Political Committee by Fitzpatrick, Bailey and their supporters began to narrow during 1953, reflecting increased suspicion of the Groupers felt both by uncommitted delegates to the Committee and also by its electorate of branch activists. The Fitzpatrick forces were defeated on a motion for the first time in October 1953 — albeit only on the casting vote of the Political Committee President.[1] Significantly, this officer was W. T. Butler who held the position by virtue of being District Committee President and who was now to lead the A.E.U. anti-Grouper forces within the A.L.P. Further reverses followed for Fitzpatrick and co. in 1954, including decisions by the Committee to protest against A.L.P. financial support for the Groups[2] and to reverse its policy towards the recognition of China.[3] Thus the Groupers had lost control of the A.E.U. body controlling the selection of A.L.P. delegates some months before the key resolution of no confidence in the Victorian A.L.P. was passed by the Melbourne Trades Hall Council in September. On an 'industrial' issue which helped lose the hard core Groupers their majority on the T.H.C. — that of the right of communist J. J. Brown of the A.R.U. to re-employment in the railways after electoral defeat by a Grouper candidate — Fitzpatrick could muster only one other supporter on the Political Committee.[4] When

[1] 'M.P.C.M.', 6/10/53.
[2] 'M.P.C.M.', 20/7/54.
[3] 'M.P.C.M.', 17/8/54.
[4] 'M.P.C.M.', 6/7/54.

the A.L.P. Split actually began, however, the first crucial motions in support of Evatt's attack on the Groups and against the 'old' Victorian A.L.P. Executive were carried by the narrowest of margins of 8 to 7 and 9 to 7 (with one abstention) respectively.[5] The closeness of the voting was a fair reflection of the initial reluctance of many A.E.U. activists to completely overturn the A.L.P. electoral boat while some hope of compromise remained. The Melbourne District Committee, with its by now large anti-Grouper majority, had also indicated its members' initial fears of irrevocably splitting the labour movement by rejecting proposals in July 1954 to ask the A.L.P. Federal Executive to intervene in Victoria because of the alleged 'capture' of the State Executive by The Movement. Instead the Committee merely requested the Federal Executive to bring about the dissolution of the Groups.[6] Several Grouper-controlled branches initially denounced Evatt for his attack on the Groups, but as the A.L.P. Split widened the great majority of A.E.U. activists in Victoria, as elsewhere, swung firmly behind the federal A.L.P. leader, and those who chose to defend the claims of the 'old' Executive were speedily isolated. At the centre of the storm the A.E.U.'s Reilly seconded the fateful resolution on the 'old' Executive which, by committing it to a boycott of the Special Conference called by the Federal Executive was, as Murray says, 'to lead directly to the ensuing split and formation of the Democratic Labor Party'.[7] However, Murray is incorrect to imply that the Groupers would have been able to control or influence the A.E.U. delegation to the Special Conference in the absence of a boycott[8] for, as we have seen, the anti-Groupers had already gained a majority on the A.E.U. Political Committee, and since 1948 A.E.U. delegations to A.L.P. Conferences had been rigidly controlled by the Committee. The consequent resignations from the old Executive included that of Deputy-Premier W. Galvin of the A.E.U. Of the other A.E.U. state parliamentarians Bailey and Corrigan stayed loyal to the old Executive while Minister of Education, A. E. Shepherd, followed Premier Cain — whom he was later to succeed as A.L.P. leader. The unanimously pro-Evatt A.E.U. delegation — which was one of the two largest at the February Special Conference — was led by Butler who, with Galvin, was elected to the new Executive. Accusations made by Groupers, including Corrigan, that the A.E.U. delegation had included some non-members of the A.L.P. were based on the fact that the Bendigo Branch, whose turn it was to nominate the A.E.U.'s country delegate, had selected a member who, not belonging to the A.L.P. (or any other party) refrained from attending the Conference at

[5] 'M.P.C.M.', 19/10/54, 14/12/54.
[6] 'M.D.C.M.', 21/7/54.
[7] *The Split*, p. 211.
[8] Ibid., pp. 212, 221.

Butler's request. Had there been any other irregularities of the order implied by the Groupers in the emotional atmosphere of the time there can be no doubt that Burke, Babbage and Horsburgh would have picked them up on the Commonwealth Council, while pro-Grouper activists would have called the A.E.U.'s internal appeals system into use. Following the February Special Conference Butler was the A.E.U. spokesman within both the A.L.P. machine and the ginger group of 25 'pro-Evatt' unions during the hectic events which saw the expulsion or resignation from the A.L.P. of all the main A.E.U. Grouper leaders.

The A.E.U. and its members played similarly important roles in New South Wales, particularly J. J. Cahill who, as A.L.P. Premier, helped ensure that the Split in his state never reached Victorian proportions. Inside the A.E.U. there is evidence that the Groupers' powerful grip on the A.L.P. machine had resulted in their A.E.U. opponents ceasing in the early 1950s to care greatly about Grouper control of the Sydney Political Committee. The group of young A.E.U.–A.L.P. members who were to break the Groupers' grip on the Committee during 1955 actually claim to have found difficulty in certain branches in ascertaining when and how the election of Political Committee delegates took place. The relative apathy concerning the complexion of the Committee was reinforced by the tendency in N.S.W. for the political limelight to focus on members of the Sydney-based Commonwealth Council. With the advent of the Split, however, interest in the Political Committee and the complexion of the A.E.U. delegation to A.L.P. Conferences was re-aroused. The Committee's minutes for 1955, which fortunately survive, reveal that in the early stages of the Split the Groupers continued to enjoy a bare majority over their opponents and this allowed them to select a Grouper-oriented delegation to the proposed A.L.P. 'unity conference' in April. By the time the A.L.P. Conference was actually held in August, however, the Sydney activists had returned a clear anti-Grouper majority to the Political Committee at the June elections. This in no way corresponds to Murray's assertion that, 'In April the communists had regained control of the [A.E.U.] political committee.'[9] The new majority, led by young A.L.P. members, J. D. Garland, M. O'Brien and R. A. Bruggy defeated Grouper attempts to have the delegation originally chosen in April represent the A.E.U. at the August Conference, and the union instead placed its considerable weight behind the pro-Evatt forces at the inconclusive August Conference. The union continued to oppose the Groupers in subsequent left–right battles within the A.L.P. which eventually resulted in the expulsion of Kane

[9] *The Split*, p. 287. For contemporary refutation of the charge that the new Political Committee was controlled by communists see R. A. Bruggy's letter, *Sydney Morning Herald*, 5/9/55.

and some other scapegoat Groupers and the establishment of a new, more 'balanced', though still essentially right wing, A.L.P. Executive in New South Wales. One member of the new Executive was P. D. Hills, M.L.A., future A.L.P. leader, A.E.U. member and Group supporter. In 1958 an increase in A.E.U. affiliation[10] and hence the size of its delegation was rewarded by the election of Garland to the Executive. From 1958 on A.E.U. delegates to the A.L.P. conference were elected directly by all members paying the political levy.

In Queensland, the third state to experience a violent division in A.L.P. ranks, no swing from right to left occurred in A.E.U. representation within the A.L.P. either before or during the Split. A.E.U. participants were typical of the Brisbane Trades Hall unionists, remaining anti-Grouper throughout. A.E.U. organiser J. P. Devereux, who was regarded politically as a right winger in many quarters, moved the motion on annual leave at the 1956 Queensland Labor in Politics Convention which, in its eventual version, proved to be the time bomb which destroyed the Gair government one year later.

At the federal level the majority of the A.E.U. Commonwealth Council who owed their election to Group organisation and support walked a tightrope during the Split. Despite many requests from anti- and pro-Grouper branches alike to declare its support for one side or the other, the Council refused to comment publicly on the Groups or other internal A.L.P. affairs. The communist Council member, Hennessy, made no attempt to force the issue for this neutral stance followed the Council's long established precedent which had been broken only during the A.L.P. Grouper's interference in the court ballot controversy. Privately, the Council members pursued their own political paths. Hennessy was naturally anti-Grouper while Deverall had by now drifted further away from the Victorian Groups and followed strictly the official A.L.P. line. Of the remaining three, Burke was most active in his support of the Groupers within the New South Wales A.L.P. although he personally was never as closely reliant on them as, say, Babbage. Horsburgh refused to commit himself one way or the other and, like Deverall, rigidly toed the official A.L.P. line during the Split.

The A.E.U. members' first reaction to the Split was clearly demonstrated in the internal election results of 1955 and 1956: anyone who could be identified as supporting the Groups suffered electorally. In 1955 Deverall was returned to office unopposed, but, with considerable irony, Burke, who had been elected in a branch ballot in 1952, was defeated in March 1955 by Melbourne District Committeeman, J. H. Stone (A.L.P.), in one of the court ballots

[10] Below, pp. 246–7.

which Burke had so vigorously supported in private. The result was something of a surprise for everyone but observers soon realised it to be one of the first industrial fruits of the Split for there can be little doubt that the publicly declared support given to Burke by the Victorian breakaway Grouper party was an electoral disadvantage. With the removal of the forceful Burke, the pro-Grouper drive on the Council died away, but in no way could Stone's victory be represented as a 'recapture' of the Council by the C.P.A., as the more fevered imaginations of the hard-pressed and bitter Groupers depicted it at the time.[11]

In May 1955 the A.E.U.'s convoluted internal system of checks and balances came into play to foil a move — which the pro-Grouper members of Council had initiated before the Split began — to abandon the traditional methods of electing A.E.U. officials in favour of postal ballots. The tactic adopted by Burke, Babbage and Horsburgh had been to make this proposal — which in the A.E.U. context obviously had revolutionary implications — to the 1955 Blackpool Rules Revision Meeting in the form of a late suggestion which did not appear on the original agenda. In this way little publicity was given to the radical proposal in Australia. Unfortunately for the supporters of universal postal voting, however, the Australian Section had to be represented at the Rules Revision Meeting not by Commonwealth Council nominees, but by two elected rank and file members: and the membership had chosen two New South Wales anti-Groupers in the persons of A. Shaw and ex-Councilman, A. Wilson. When the Council's proposal came up at Blackpool, Wilson and Shaw were able to impress the Meeting that the majority of Australian branches and District Committees would be opposed to the departure from A.E.U. tradition and the item consequently lapsed for want of mover and seconder.

In September 1955 three branch ballots resulted in anti-Grouper victories, with communists Hennessy and Arter being comfortably re-elected and D. T. Dean (A.L.P.) easily defeating Fitzpatrick for the vacant office of Melbourne District Secretary. Total votes cast in all three polls were down quite considerably on equivalent figures in recent years and this set a permanent trend in branch ballots — largely indicating disillusionment on the part of hitherto pro-Group activists. Two months later the second great irony of the internal A.E.U. controversies over court ballots was revealed when news

[11] E.g. S. M. Keon, *C.P.D.*, Vol. H of R 6 1955, p. 990. Since Murray surprisingly repeats this assertion without any qualification or explanation (op. cit., p. 255) it is worthwhile making it clear that, apart from the general dangers of talking of one faction or another 'controlling' the Council, after Stone's election the Council comprised of one C.P.A. member and four A.L.P. members of whom two had been elected with Grouper support and a third, Deverall, was unopposed by the Groupers in his re-election during the height of the Split.

reached Australia that the 1955 Final Appeal Court had *upheld* the anti-Groupers' appeals against the agreement of the Executive Council to Commonwealth Council's participation in the March 1955 court ballot. Consequently the Executive Council called for a new branch ballot for the Division 1 Councilman — the position now held by the anti-Grouper candidate, Stone. In this instance possession proved nine points of the law. The Grouper forces could hardly demand a new branch ballot after all their striving for court ballots — and in any case Babbage and Horsburgh believed their best chances of re-election lay in court ballots. So, letting sleeping dogs lie, both sides ignored the formal Executive Council instruction[12] — which in the circumstances the London office itself could hardly wholeheartedly support.

In 1956 the confusing political smoke began to clear and the old Grouper core began to re-assemble their battered forces within the A.E.U. The March ballots contained no surprises. The single ballot on the June Star Night was more significant in terms of the A.E.U.'s internal division and resulted in White barely fending off a challenge to his Melbourne organising position from leading anti-Grouper Butler.[13] The main electoral clash came in December during the emotional re-run of the ballots for the positions of N.S.W. Councilman and Council Chairman which in 1953 had caused so much drama and dissension. Both contests were essentially two-horse races — although opposing Babbage in addition to his old adversary, Wilson, was an outsider, L. J. Doherty. The candidate chosen to carry the left wing colours against Horsburgh was the young Sydney member, O'Brien. Campaigning and in-fighting for the two positions began early in the year and in April the rather strange waters in which the union found itself after ignoring the 1955 Final Appeal Court were clearly revealed. The occasion was an attempt by Stone and Hennessy to gain a tactical advantage for their side by separating the dates of nomination — and consequently of the election — for the two positions. This Horsburgh ruled out of order on the grounds that the motion in effect lacked a seconder because Stone's position was vacant under A.E.U. rules as a result of the Appeal Court decision on court ballots. This ruling was not seriously challenged by the left, and it did not prevent either Horsburgh from accepting other motions backed by Stone, or Hors-

[12] The Grouper-supporting Hawthorn Branch did enquire when the new election would be held ('C.C.M.', 6/4/56) and later on when memories had generally dulled, A.E.U. right wingers attempted to make useful propaganda out of the anti-Grouper Council's refusal to hold a fresh ballot, e.g. *Engineers' Voice*, November 1957.
[13] When preferences were distributed White's margin was 29 out of 1727 votes cast in a three-way contest.

burgh's supporters from ensuring by means of petitions that the December election was supervised by the Industrial Registrar. The Council, while vigorously protesting, did not attempt to fight the Electoral Officer's intervention in 1956, despite the unrelenting hostility of A.E.U. activists towards outside 'interference.'[14]

In the event, each side won one ballot. In polls 14 and 12 per cent down respectively on the 1953 figures, Horsburgh defeated O'Brien by 18,534 votes to 14,068, and after distribution of Doherty's preferences, Wilson defeated Babbage by 5,592 to 5,111. When the latter result is compared with Babbage's 1953 victory of 8,199 to 4,034 a considerable erosion of support for the Groupers is evident in New South Wales, which was also the only state to give O'Brien a majority over Horsburgh — although the fact that O'Brien was a native son was an important additional factor. Direct comparisons with 1953 are difficult in the ballot for Chairman because preferences were not distributed in the earlier six-man field. Any reasonable estimate of the likely direction of 1953 preference flow would, however, seem to indicate a swing to the left in 1956 despite Horsburgh's fairly comfortable victory. Horsburgh's return to office reflects the fact that he had endeavoured fairly successfully to remain above the worst of the mud-slinging and name-calling. Like so many other A.E.U. men, the Split had greatly shocked him and caused him to clutch gladly at the official A.L.P. banner. He had been drifting away from his original backers during 1955 and 1956, and from 1957 onwards he was to become evermore disenchanted with them, until eventually he played a key role in their final defeat within the A.E.U.

Several features of the 1956 campaign set a pattern for future A.E.U. elections contested by left and right and reveal some of the effects of the Split on the union. The first of these is the growing intolerance and public bitterness displayed by the two opposing sides. In many A.E.U. branches in Victoria and New South Wales following the Split high attendances were common, tempers were frayed, suspicion was mutual, issues were seen in stark blacks and whites, and 'Judas' was a word much abused by both sides. To take but one example of the lengths to which misplaced zeal could go, an angry, crowded and almost violent meeting at the Bondi Junction branch actually decided to 'expel' a leading petition organiser, K. J. Brock, from the union. Although his 'expulsion' had no official standing Brock successfully publicised the attempted injustice by taking to Court the Commonwealth Council and his branch secretary and president, G. J. Stead and J. D. Garland, both prominent anti-Groupers.

[14] See e.g. 'M.D.C.M.', 15/8/56.

Now that the A.L.P. was no longer officially supporting the A.E.U. petitioners the Council voting majority of Stone and Hennessy were able to denounce them in internal A.E.U. circulars in a manner even more unrestrained than that of Wilson and Hennessy in 1953. One such circular, headed 'A Warning to Members', urged members to 'take action' against petition organisers in workshops and branches and to report both the action taken and petitioners' names to the Council. The Council's opponents, while naturally appealing to London against this apparent incitement to violence, also informed the press of the circular's contents. In the ensuing controversy the A.E.U.'s legal advisers made it clear that the circular was intimidatory and a clear breach of the Arbitration Act, but the Council refused to withdraw or amend it until the Executive Council ordered it to do so in July 1957.

In this atmosphere then, in which the tone of the Groupers and their supporters was no less immoderate or vindictive, the activists within the A.E.U. polarised into two distinct and irreconcilable factions. At first this occurred only in New South Wales and Victoria, but as time went by the middle ground was eventually deserted in all six states. One of the best indicators of this is the gradual reduction in the numbers standing at important A.E.U. elections as all energy was concentrated on two main candidates. Also, within the A.E.U. at this period, to speak of the opposing forces as right and left wings of the union begins increasingly to make sense. It has been emphasised that before 1955 A.E.U. pro-Groupers were not 'right wing' in any sense that implies industrial passivism or lack of militancy. After the Split, with the formation of the D.L.P. and the evolution of its own distinct and generally conservative industrial policies its A.E.U. supporters – in some cases almost willy nilly perhaps – found themselves associated with and defending these views. This is particularly true in Victoria because of the course the Split had taken there – although, since the D.L.P. tag was seen to be a disadvantage, those A.E.U. men to whom it could properly be applied did not overly publicise the fact even in Victoria.

By far the greatest proportion of the A.E.U. activists who had always determined the complexion of the union's decision-making bodies, placed themselves in the 'left wing' camp. In the emotional, not to say hysterical, atmosphere of the mid-1950s it seemed to most concerned A.E.U. members, including many erstwhile supporters of the Groups, that all the old anti-Groupers' charges had been proven, and that a sinister plot to capture and control the A.L.P. and the trade union movement had been unveiled. The retrospective colouring of pre-Split events and motives set in among A.E.U. members just as it did in the labour movement at large. The effect was a

drastic cutback in Grouper-cum-right wing influence on any issues determined in branch ballots, including the composition of District and Political
Committees and all A.E.U. conference delegations. The reduction in influence
was most marked at first in Melbourne and Sydney, but over time the trend
could be seen in virtually all A.E.U. districts. There remained of course a
goodly number of branches wherein supporters of the D.L.P. and N.C.C.
remained a majority, and these continued to return dedicated men such as
Fitzpatrick and Bailey in Victoria as their representatives on A.E.U. district
bodies. But there was very little hope of gaining control of the union's
decision making machinery through usual A.E.U. channels in the near or
foreseeable future. This fact made the D.L.P.–N.C.C. supporters within the
union more anxious than ever to ensure that A.E.U. elections were conducted
under court supervision. The right's best, if not only hope of electoral success
was to persuade the electorally apathetic majority of A.E.U. members that
their union was threatened from within by a communist takeover. In this,
the generally conservative mass media might be expected to help – but in
order for there to be any chance of participation by sufficient communist-
fearing A.E.U. members a postal ballot was essential. A court supervised
ballot would also allow the right to bring into play the old, well-oiled,
Grouper-Movement electoral machinery for canvassing at members' homes.
The use of outsiders in door knocking, envelope addressing etc. would
help balance the left's numerical superiority both in the branches and,
increasingly over time, among the traditionally militant shop stewards
who were particularly effective campaigners in those workshops – still
a minority – which appointed stewards.

One feature associated both with the polarisation into camps and the
use of court ballots which emerged clearly during 1956 was the change
in A.E.U. candidates' campaign committees. These had originally been fairly
simple *ad hoc* affairs created to serve the needs of a particular election. From
1956 onwards, however, the committees supporting candidates of the right
and left, although still strictly unofficial, became virtually permanent
fixtures on the A.E.U. scene. They retained their respective machinery in
working order during the brief interludes between A.E.U. ballots and everyone was made well aware of their existence as they publicised their opposing
viewpoints. A suitable name was important and the N.S.W. left wingers
made an important coup by calling theirs the 'A.E.U. Rights Committee'.
When objections were made to the use of the union's initials, the secretary
(and converted ex-Grouper), J. A. Langton, replied with tongue in cheek
to a compliant Commonwealth Council that the full title was in fact the
'Australian Engineers United Rights Committee'. An 'A.E.U.' Rights Com-

mittee was also soon established in Victoria with Butler as secretary, and liaison between the two main states grew steadily more efficient over time. In Queensland and the other states where the contest was usually less vigorous the Rights Committee operated on an *ad hoc* basis as the occasion arose. The right-wing's body was known as The Rank and File Engineers' Defence Committee and its existence was made formally public in 1957 when it began to issue at regular intervals a handsome glossy news sheet called *Engineers' Voice*. Although it was to enjoy little local electoral success the Defence Committee was strongest in Victoria in the sense of dedication and funds. D. Henderson was President but the key figure was Fitzpatrick, the first secretary. Other prominent members included relatively newer faces such as G. Ind, L. W. Marantelli and I. G. Parkes. In New South Wales most of the A.E.U. Groupers stayed in the A.L.P., and those of them such as Malcolm who did not abandon their old cause during the Split were associated with the Defence Committee in that state. The main bastion of the N.S.W. Defence Committee was in the Newcastle district which provided its secretary, D. G. Fox. The Defence Committee does not seem to have established itself in firm physical reality in Queensland and the other states, and the right wing cause there had to rely as in the past on the Movement network. The connection between the Defence Committee and what became in 1957 the N.C.C. and the D.L.P. was not publicised but liaison was very close and the Movement/N.C.C. election apparatus was used as in the past. The 'A.E.U.' Rights Committee for its part, while seldom if ever needing non-A.E.U. canvassers, envelope addressers etc., accepted funds from sympathetic outside bodies such as the Victorian Trade Union Defence Committee which had sprung from the 25 'pro-Evatt unions' and which was to play so important a role in the Victorian A.L.P. for a further decade and a half. Another source of funds theoretically available to both sides was small donations made by branches from their 'Local Purposes' fund. However, despite Commonwealth Council sanction in 1958[15] many older branch officials frowned on the use of this fund for internal faction fighting. The left, by virtue of its majority support among activists, tended to gain most of the small flow from this source, as it did also from the more important unofficial collections organised on the job by shop stewards. Given the unofficial nature of the Rights and Defence Committees little is known about their budgets, particularly that of the latter. Evidence that expenditure was not inconsiderable is provided by the fact that during one election the Trade Union Defence Committee alone contributed £1,000 to the Rights Com-

[15] 'C.C.M.', 22/1/58.

mittee's campaign fund, while the ability of the Engineers' Defence Committee to finance both costly lawsuits and elaborate election campaigns was to draw comments from many neutral sources. Not the smallest irony of the A.L.P. Split then, was that it led to the establishment within the A.E.U. of two opposing bodies which, although more tightly organised, better disciplined and probably even more intolerant than their ill-fated predecessors, resembled nothing so much in all the world as the disbanded and disgraced Industrial Groups.

II

The right wingers' strategy in endeavouring to ensure that elections for full-time A.E.U. positions be conducted by the Electoral Office is understandable enough but, given the peculiar structure of the A.E.U., there were two weaknesses, one of them fatal. The first, and lesser, of these was the fact that the A.E.U.'s staggered electoral system whereby a ballot occurred on virtually every Star Night made the task of collecting petition signatures an unenviable and unending prospect, presenting continued occasion for scandal and indignation to the majority of A.E.U. activists in branches and workshops. Eventually in the early 1960s ways were temporarily found round this problem. The second, and deadly, weakness lay in the fact that court ballots could never detract from or overturn, the left wingers' advantage in the branches. Even if the right's campaign were to prove so much more efficient and persuasive than that of the left that A.E.U. members were persuaded to elect successively in postal ballots 24 right wingers to fill all the full time elective positions in the A.E.U.,[16] they would still face hostile District Committees and branches. In fact, of course, the right could only hope for partial victory in court ballots and its successful candidates were faced also with the opposition of their full-time colleagues — but the essential point remains that the only way to 'control' the A.E.U. was to have sympathetic majorities in the branches, i.e. have a majority of activists on your side. The D.L.P.–N.C.C. forces, like the Groups and Movement before them sought to persuade like-minded A.E.U. members, Catholics or otherwise, to attend branch meetings, but the fruits of such campaigns ripen over a long period, and even in the much more favourable period before the Split, the successes within the A.E.U. had been limited. The Split itself ensured a drastic cut in the right's support and thereafter there was, to say the least, little reason to expect the D.L.P.–N.C.C. share of A.E.U. activist support to increase more rapidly than that of their A.L.P.–C.P.A. opponents. There was

[16] 1960 figure.

no way round this problem of weakness in the branches. Court ballots could hardly help here for, even if candidates could be found in sufficient numbers — and we will return to the right's general problems in this direction later — it would be difficult to conceive the court being able to supervise each year elections for various offices in 236 A.E.U. branches[17] and the annual election of District Committee and Political Committee delegates and their substitutes.

A reading of the A.E.U. rule book indicated that virtually unlimited power resided with the Commonwealth Council. The older, more experienced, A.E.U. Group supporters had always been aware that it was only the tip of the A.E.U. iceberg, and many of the younger A.E.U. Groupers absorbed fully the lesson of 1954–5 — when, *inter alia* the Group-backed majority on the Commonwealth Council could not affect the disappearance of the Groupers' majority on the key Melbourne and Sydney Political Committees. After the Split, however, the 'politically' minded and legally trained decision makers in the D.L.P.–N.C.C. camp tended to forget, and to plump for dramatic dashes to control the top echelons rather than the wearying hard slog of proselytising at branch level. Ironically enough, while unlikely to prove fruitful at any time in the union's history, the tactic of attempting to 'capture' the A.E.U. by controlling its federal executive was particularly futile in the 1950s and the 1960s, for the very process of struggling to 'control' the Council acted to lessen the aura of respect surrounding the Council and to increase the importance and *de facto* autonomy of the districts. From 1953 onwards the image of lofty majesty which the Council had long projected throughout the Commonwealth was increasingly eroded as its members publicly hassled and fought in law courts and within the A.E.U.'s internal legal system. While respect for the Council was thus decreasing, the districts' autonomy and independence of action was simultaneously increasing for two reasons. First, the Council's involvement in the ongoing internal tussle meant that its attention and energy was continually diverted from its role of supervising all the union's multifarious activities. In addition, when the Council had a right wing voting majority, the districts — which were virtually all left wing after the Split — deliberately attempted wherever possible to avoid involving the Council in any issues likely to prove contentious. Left wing Council members encouraged them in this while, on the other hand, with the exception of Burke, the right wing Council members failed to wield their constitutional power either in a requisitely bold fashion or in the most effective manner. In the early 1960s the right wingers' clumsiness and uncertainty was due in large measure to the lack of both a firm base in the districts and the

[17] 1960 figure.

lengthy schooling in A.E.U. administration which most of their opponents and virtually all pre-Split Council members had undergone in the union's lower echelons. In all, the increased turnover of Council personnel which had begun during the war with the retirement of Potter and Wickham and which had accelerated after the departure of Cranwell, helped further the decline in the prestige and authority of the Council.

A third disadvantage under which the A.E.U. right wingers operated after the Split concerned their association with the N.C.C.–D.L.P. The point has already been made that the industrially aggressive A.E.U. members were hardly likely to view favourably the industrial policies which the D.L.P.–N.C.C. came to advocate. In addition on virtually every conceivable political issue the D.L.P. and N.C.C. were continually and publicly at loggerheads with the A.L.P., the party to which the majority of A.E.U. men owed their allegiance. The left wingers aggravated the general handicaps which association with the D.L.P. and N.C.C. imposed on their opponents by stressing the 'sinister' aspects of the N.C.C. which, the left argued, was a closed and secret organisation, outside the labour movement yet seeking to influence and control labour policy for its own dubious ends. The right's indignant counter-charges that the sinister outside organisation with ulterior motives was in reality the C.P.A. carried very little weight in A.E.U. activist circles after the revelations of the Split. In contrast to the mysterious N.C.C., A.E.U. activists felt that they knew all that was needed about the C.P.A., which had been in existence and subject to public scrutiny since 1920 and whose members had, with a few unfortunate exceptions during World War II, proved themselves to fit in well with the A.E.U. industrial tradition. In addition to such long-run empirical observations of C.P.A. members' industrial record, their stocks were naturally greatly enhanced within the A.E.U. – and in the labour movement in general – by the Split itself. As the original object of the Groupers' attack the C.P.A. could not help but gain increased sympathy among A.L.P. unionists, while C.P.A. members' charges about the true motivation of the anti-communist forces seemed to have been completely vindicated. Although the general political environment forced the A.L.P. Federal Executive to outlaw 'Unity Tickets', few left wing unionists could see any harm in them – particularly in the A.E.U. where a candidate's industrial record had always been the sole consideration and a united electoral front was now required against the common enemy. Thus A.L.P. strictures on Unity Tickets were, in principle, ignored by A.E.U. members – although the nature and frequency of A.E.U. elections meant that multi-candidate 'tickets' proper were unknown.

Many right wingers appear to have been genuinely baffled by the stance taken by the majority of A.E.U. activists. Tending themselves to view issues always in the starkest of blacks and whites they found it much easier to comprehend and stomach the position of A.E.U. communists than that of most A.E.U. members of the A.L.P. With the harsh fires of the Split annealing the right wingers' sense of crusade and embattlement, the main object of their resentment became not so much the C.P.A. men as the A.L.P. members who consistently rejected warnings about playing with the communist fire. For the dedicated A.E.U. Groupers who had fought communism for maybe ten or fifteen years before the Split, the A.E.U. – A.L.P. members who aided the destruction of the Industrial Groups, and thereafter permanently allied themselves with the communists, could fall into one of only two categories: they were either fools or rogues. As the A.L.P. rifts of 1955–7 set and hardened so too did A.E.U. right wingers' resentment of their A.L.P. confrères. Whereas an occasional hint of respect for a ruthless but worthy foe is evident in *News Weekly's* or *Voice's* treatment of C.P.A. members, nothing but scorn and vituperation is saved for members of the A.L.P. who are depicted as either spineless dupes or treacherous crypto-communists. No recognition is made of the existence of a genuinely radical strand of A.L.P. thinking independent of the C.P.A. The notion that A.L.P. unionists might initiate A.E.U. policy came to be treated with contemptuous disbelief by the right which increasingly viewed events in terms of an all too simple conspiracy theory. This misguided but genuine belief hardly aided the right wingers' credibility among informed A.E.U. members, nor did it bring nearer the possibility of any future reconciliation between right wingers and orthodox A.L.P. men within the A.E.U. The notion that a C.P.A. minority could manipulate the A.L.P. majority within the A.E.U. was regarded by the latter as the ultimate, far-fetched insult – made as it was about a union whose members prided themselves so fiercely on operating it successfully and independently for over a century, and coming as it did from what A.L.P. men saw as an authoritarian pressure group whose leaders had been publicly revealed as the would-be manipulators *par excellence* in Australian industrial history.

In the increasingly acrimonious atmosphere in which the right–left battle was fought, the A.E.U. right wingers did not, however, allow their personal feelings completely to overcome their tactical sense. Despite their public fulminations against so many leading A.E.U. members of the A.L.P. they were fully aware of the A.L.P.'s general popularity among the A.E.U. electorate, and the fact that, because of the Split, even in a court ballot the additional non-activist voters upon whom the right pinned its electoral hopes were increasingly unlikely to see any advantage in voting for an identifiable D.L.P.–N.C.C. supporter. Consequently, wherever possible the right attempted to put forward suitable members of the A.L.P. as its candidates in A.E.U. elections. This task was obviously easier in states other than Victoria, but it still proved difficult given the number and frequency of A.E.U. elections and the fact that the best known and most experienced A.L.P. members within the A.E.U. were usually hardly suitable from the right wing viewpoint. In most election campaigns the right wing freely applied the usefully euphemistic adjective 'Labor' to its candidates on election material and while canvassing. While the support given by the D.L.P.–N.C.C. forces to certain candidates in A.E.U. elections was clear enough to any regular reader of *News Weekly*, the right wing at first considered it politic not to publicise the connection among the uncommitted in the A.E.U. electorate. When such prudence was abandoned by N.C.C. leader Santamaria, the consequences were to be disastrous for the right wing cause.

Finally in the context of post-Split elections in the A.E.U. we should note that in several cases when right-supported candidates were actually elected they were to disappoint their backers. Partly this was the result of the false notions rife in non-A.E.U. circles about what 'control' of the A.E.U. involved – and associated overestimates of what election to full-time office in the union could produce in terms of changes in A.E.U. policy: partly it was because of the candidates' inexperience: partly it derived from the discovery that successful candidates are not necessarily as single-minded as their backers might think, and that election support did not automatically commit an A.E.U. official to carry out all the desires of his campaign managers, whether they be D.L.P., A.L.P. – or C.P.A.

Returning to the election scene itself, we pick up the story with the N.C.C.–D.L.P. campaign gathering increasing momentum and the scene is set for nine years of conflict more bitter than that experienced in any other union. Aggravating the fact that the A.E.U. formed the main industrial battleground for right and left forces in the post-Group period was the way in which A.E.U. elections were staggered. Whereas in other unions the sides might meet head-on only once every three years or so – and certainly not more frequently than once per annum – in the A.E.U. there was virtually no let-up in the tension and acrimony throughout this period. The union seemed to move without pause from one electoral crisis to another and from one law suit to the next. Only the main contests and controversies are listed below and it should be borne in mind that the A.E.U. story 1957–65 was far more tangled than even the following complex web would suggest.

The most important event in 1957 was the March ballot for a successor to the retiring Deverall. Surprisingly enough, given the furore over the petition lists circulated before this ballot, the petitioners failed to submit them 'in due time'. In the subsequent branch ballot the young Sydney left winger Garland polled 4,580 votes to win comfortably on the first count from Burke (2,198), who was now Sydney based, and Victorian, W. Sephton (943). The right pointed to the contrast between the 7,867 votes cast in the branches with the 32,602 participants in the court ballot for Chairman three months earlier, although the right wing's decision to marshal its resources and ease back its campaign once the Registrar rejected the petition obviously contributed to the low poll.

In November 1957, 15 rank and file delegates arrived in Sydney for an Australian Rules Revision Meeting followed by an Interstate Conference. No right winger had been elected as a delegate and the occasion presented the first chance for national liaison between activists who were virtually all prominent anti-Groupers in their respective districts. Among those already known in other districts because of electoral or legal clashes with the Groupers were O'Brien and Stead from Sydney, and Butler and Cameron from Melbourne. Also present were other lesser known members who were to become more prominent in the near future including H. J. Gillman from Brisbane and L. N. Carmichael from Melbourne. Another sign of the times and of the district activists' growing feeling of independence was the manner in which the delegates made it clear that they considered their decisions to be much closer to instructions to Commonwealth Council than mere suggestions. In this they were fully supported by the four left wing members of Council and the fifth, Horsburgh, after early resistance submitted to the otherwise unanimous will of the meeting. This demonstration that he was prepared to accept and move with the tide of activist opinion removed any lingering doubts about Horsburgh in left wing minds and in 1959 no opposition was offered to his re-election as Chairman.

The Conference, which was addressed by Evatt, passed resolutions on a great variety of topics. One which was a direct result of the Split and the left wing's determination to exert maximum influence in the A.L.P., declared that in the past the A.E.U. had not contributed as much to the A.L.P. as it might have. Therefore the Conference recommended that the union should in future affiliate to A.L.P. state branches on the basis of the union's fully effective membership and not, as was usual, on any lower nominal figure. Two months earlier the Commonwealth Council had taken away from the Political Committees the power to determine the size of the local affiliation. With the twin aim of increasing the proportion of the political levy available for affiliation fees, and being selective in its support of A.L.P. candidates, the Conference recommended that in future election donations be no longer automatic but should be individually determined by the Council. A.E.U. affiliation increased hereafter — but still remained below the maximum possible level.

Even while the Conference was sitting the Industrial Registrar was informing the union of his acceptance of a request from A.E.U. petitioners that he should supervise the March 1958 election for Stone's position. Yet for the second successive time the petitioners were to see their arduous and thankless efforts in collecting signatures largely wasted. In 1957 the fault had lain in their application, in 1958 it rested with an accidental miscalculation by their proposed candidate, Fitzpatrick, who, largely in order to keep his opponents guessing, held back his acceptance of nomination until the very last minute. To his dismay, however, his registered acceptance lay undelivered in a Sydney post office through the deadline because of the coincidence of a New South Wales public holiday. Upon urgent appeal to the Commonwealth Industrial Court[18] Mr Justice Dunphy decided that he had no power to make any order against R. C. Nance, the Commonwealth Electoral Officer for Victoria. He did, however, make it clear that in his opinion Fitzpatrick should have been admitted to the ballot. The A.E.U. claimed that Dunphy's opinion resulted in considerable pressure being applied to Nance to change his mind, but the only eventual consolation for the right wing lay in the evidence of the impartiality of administrators of court ballots which Nance's unyielding stand publicly provided. In the ballot itself Stone was comfortably re-elected.

The other Council position falling open in 1958 was Hennessy's, and some degree of confusion surrounded this also. Petitions ensured a court ballot but no eligible candidate was nominated other than Hennessy — leaving the left wingers claiming that not one A.E.U. member suitable to the N.C.C. could be found in West Australia or Queensland. In September 1958 a key branch ballot for Melbourne District Secretary was won by the left. Dean, the victor over Fitzpatrick in 1955, had not proved a success in the position and the Rights Committee gave its support this time to the dynamic Carmichael who, after distribution of Dean's preferences, defeated White, the Defence Committee's choice, by 939 votes to 774. Twelve months later White lost his organising position to Butler, thus sadly bringing to an end the remarkable A.E.U. Melbourne tradition of simultaneously choosing officials from opposite ends of the political spectrum. A.E.U. mem-

---

[18] In 1956 the arbitral and judicial functions of the federal arbitration tribunal had been separated and vested respectively in the Commonwealth Conciliation and Arbitration Commission and the Commonwealth Industrial Court. See below pp. 274 – 5.

bers in Victoria would never again elect a right wing candidate. The new tide of success which was about to carry the right wingers to a pinnacle of electoral achievement was not to flow in the main D.L.P.—N.C.C. stronghold of Victoria but in New South Wales and Queensland.

The first progress in the right wingers' recovery was made in New South Wales when the local Councilman election became due in 1959. The right's candidate to oppose the incumbent Wilson was C. Shearer, a relatively unknown branch official from the Newcastle district who had D.L.P. leanings but was a member of no political party. The campaign was among the most bitterly fought and vindictive of all A.E.U. ballots, with neutral observers noting N.C.C. involvement on Shearer's side and the expensiveness of his campaign.[19] Possibly because in 1956 the Rights Committee had matched them in the laborious chore of handwriting election material, Shearer's campaign directors decided on the bold, and at first puzzling, policy of ignoring the A.E.U. rule forbidding printed matter. Thus, after ensuring a court ballot through petition, and after conducting its usual door-knocking campaign, the right posted to all members an attractive brochure outlining Shearer's merits and warning of the communist 'menace'. The result was a win to Shearer by 5,775 votes to 4,765 in a poll slightly down on the 1956 figure. To nobody's surprise, the Commonwealth Council immediately disqualified Shearer for circulating printed material. The reason for the right's strange tactics now became apparent. While his supporters made use of the A.E.U.'s internal appeal system to counter-charge Wilson with various breaches of union rules, Shearer applied to the Industrial Court to disallow as contravening the Arbitration Act, the A.E.U. rule which restricted printed election matter to the official candidates' addresses which were available only to those members who attended the branch meetings. Proceedings commenced in February 1960 before Chief Justice Spicer and Justices Eggleston and Joske, but were interrupted while the Commonwealth Council asked for a High Court judgment on the validity of the Sections of the Act upon which Shearer's applications were based. In July the High Court gave a decision enabling the applications to continue and in September the Industrial Court handed down its reserved judgment in the matter. By two to one the bench dismissed Shearer's application in terms which the left wing activists were ever afterwards to quote in defence of their view that branch ballots were superior to court ballots. In part the majority judgment read,

[19] E.g. Alan Reid, *Sunday Telegraph*, 13/12/59.

Some people might think it would be better to have a wider distribution of election material, but it is at least a reasonable view that to obtain office bearers who will be devoted to the interests of the union is to limit the appeal of the candidates to those who would ordinarily vote, and not to allow candidates to exhort those who take no interest in union affairs to vote for reasons which have no relation to the affairs of the union. We are therefore not prepared to say that such a restriction as is involved in this case is oppressive, unreasonable or unjust as far as the candidate is concerned.[20]

Shearer decided to withdraw his second application, which argued that in any case it was not he who had actually transgressed the A.E.U. rule but the New South Wales members of the Defence Committee. This foiled the Rights Committee and Commonwealth Council hopes of publicising in court the N.C.C. connections with the Defence Committee. Internally, the impartiality of the A.E.U.'s appeals machinery was again being demonstrated. As well as disqualifying Shearer the Executive Council and Final Appeals Court upheld right wing appeals against both the Rights Committee for issuing 'How to Vote' cards favouring Wilson, and the Commonwealth Council for issuing a pamphlet condemning the right wingers along the lines of the contentious 1956 circular, 'A Warning to A.E.U. Members'.

In March 1960, during the Shearer litigation, the right had allowed the election for Council Secretary to be conducted in the branches and Garland retained his position fairly easily from Burke. However, the complications caused by the long vacancy of the Sydney—Newcastle seat were exacerbated by the lengthy illness of the Victorian, Stone, which left Hennessy as the only active Councilman. Rather than agree to a temporary filling of the post the Executive Council ordered Horsburgh to take over Stone's duties in March 1960. This decision severely hampered the depleted Council's effectiveness but London stood firm despite further appeals. Thus on several occasions Council business had to be conducted at Stone's hospital bedside. By the end of the year it was obvious that Stone's illness was fatal and when he died in February 1961 a bitter campaign developed for the vacancy between organiser Southwell and T. J. Taylor, the candidate backed by the right. Among other things, Taylor campaigned for the abandonment of the political levy, and useful ammunition was provided for the Defence Committee by the fact that, with Hennessy already in office and Wilson about to engage in the re-match with Shearer, three communist Councilmen were a distinct possibility. In the biggest poll ever recorded in the division, Southwell defeated Taylor in the final count by 8,750 votes to 8,313. In May the result of the Wilson—Shearer re-run went

[20] 1 *F.L.R.* 436 at p. 441.

the other way when, after the distribution of Burke's preferences, the right winger won by 6,187 votes to 5,487. In both elections the Defence Committee and *News Weekly* pointed to the close electoral alliance between A.L.P. and C.P.A. members in the A.E.U. and contrasted the reluctance of the A.L.P. to deal with the A.E.U. sponsors of 'Unity Tickets' with the relative speed with which certain A.L.P. members had been recently expelled from the Party for supporting D.L.P. candidates in elections in the Clerks' Union. Once the ballot had been declared Shearer, while careful not to mention his ties with the N.C.C. explicitly, went to some pains to publicly refute any notion that the A.L.P. had aided his victory — which he attributed to the support of 'those who have been loyal to the fight against communism from 1941 to the present day'.[21]

Greatly enthused by Shearer's victory and the relative closeness of the Southwell—Taylor battle the right wingers now turned with considerable optimism to the next batch of A.E.U. elections. Most important of these in their leaders' eyes was the ballot for Hennessy's Council position — for if the right wing candidate won this one then he and Shearer would 'control' the Council and consequently the union. The other elections scheduled for Star Nights in the second half of 1961 were also of considerable importance — as were those of 1962. Thus the intensive and virulent electoral campaigning in A.E.U. branches, workshops and members' homes continued non-stop — and indeed actually intensified as the right wing made successful moves to widen the coverage of court ballots. The importance of court ballots to the right wing's chances of success has been emphasised, and the right's election victories in the period 1961—3 were in no small part due to the fact that it was able to remove some of the main props on which the left's arguments against court ballots rested. Already the Menzies government, pressed on by the D.L.P. and its representatives in the senate, had amended the Arbitration Act to allow the government to pay the great bulk of the expenses associated with court supervision. That the amendments, which came into force in 1960, were introduced almost solely with the A.E.U. in mind was made clear by speakers in both Houses who alluded often to the A.E.U.'s key positions in both the trade union movement and the national economy.

To alleviate the problems associated with continual collection of petition signatures the right wingers began, early in 1961, circulating in Victoria, South Australia, Queensland and West Australia, petitions which asked simultaneously for court supervision of not one, but several A.E.U. ballots.

[21] *News Weekly*, 31/5/61.

Since the Defence Committee — N.C.C. machine was now running smoothly, the petitions for the first time asked the court to oversee ballots for A.E.U. district officials' positions. After due consideration, the Registrar accepted these multiple requests and the first court ballots for A.E.U. district officers were held in Melbourne and Perth in September 1961. The greatly increased polls induced by the postal ballot and the intensive and often scurrilous campaigns waged by the two sides resulted in all three left wing incumbents being returned. In Melbourne, District Secretary Carmichael defeated Fitzpatrick in a straight fight by 5,508 votes to 4,915 while organiser Hill defeated Hatters by 5,388 to 5,014 after distribution of preferences in a four man field. In Perth, after a campaign every bit as rough and tumble as the eastern states were now used to, organiser J. W. Coleman defeated W. Stewart by 1,213 votes to 990 in a three man field. Stewart appears to have relied particularly heavily on outside support and canvassers, and suffered from widespread left wing publicity of this fact. An incidental insight into the craft consciousness of both sides is provided by Defence Committee complaints that the Commonwealth Council had deliberately handicapped Stewart, a fitter, by describing him on official election documents as a mere machinist.[22]

At the end of the year organisers Devereux (Brisbane) and Arter (Melbourne) were allowed to return to office unopposed while the right wingers concentrated all their energies on the campaign to oust Hennessy from the Commonwealth Council in February 1962 and to ensure the return of suitable candidates in two ballots for New South Wales organisers. The re-election of Newcastle organiser, Low (2,180), ahead of left winger, J. G. Kidd (1,333), was hardly cause for surprise, but the other two results were. After 13 continuous years as an organiser Dodd lost by 5,321 votes to 4,815, to the Defence Committee candidate V. G. Clarke: and in the main bout J. McDowell's 6,182 votes swamped Hennessy's 2,957 and T. J. Elsey's 1,563. Four months later in June 1962 while unsuccessful in lesser challenges in four different states to left wingers Goss, Thompson, Butler and Ewer, the right wing's main effort was crowned by an extremely important victory. Malcolm (4,479) defeated Sydney District Secretary Searle (4,000) who had now been 18 years in office. Malcolm was far better known than McDowell and Clarke who were relatively obscure A.E.U. members, but all three owed their victories to the efficient Defence Committee–N.C.C. election machine which was now running in top gear and which managed their elaborate and

[22] *Engineers' Voice*, September 1961.

expensive campaigns in a manner which the left's machine could not match in New South Wales and Queensland at this stage.

McDowell was an A.L.P. member who had built up a considerable civic reputation in the Bundaberg area. Although not particularly well schooled in A.E.U. administration he had been President of the A.E.U. Bundaberg Branch for a number of years, and had been A.E.U. representative on several inter-union and negotiating committees in the region as well as acting as a country delegate to various A.E.U. conferences in Queensland. He was a fervent anti-communist and it was this fact plus his good local 'image' which apparently decided the N.C.C. to give him their full backing. As something of an electoral smokescreen T. J. Elsey, who had been closely associated with the right wing for a number of years in Brisbane, also stood against Hennessy, but there is no doubting behind whom the main weight of the N.C.C. drive was placed. An important figure advising McDowell throughout the campaign was the Bundaberg M.L.A., E. J. Walsh, who had been Treasurer under Gair and who still had considerable personal influence in Queensland labour circles. Walsh was closely associated with officers of the A.W.U., including state president G. Goding and fellow Bundaberg A.L.P. official, M. Tallon, who jointly provided McDowell's local organisation. Now that the dust of the Split was settling the A.W.U. leadership was quite prepared to oppose left wingers on principle, and A.W.U. officials' influence and legwork combined with N.C.C. support to see McDowell emerge an easy victor in what one industrial correspondent believed to be the most vicious in A.E.U. history.[23]

Strangely enough the reaction to the McDowell and Clarke ballots proved more important than the victories themselves. By this time the A.E.U. had been the centre of so much dissension and controversy that neutral observers were beginning at last to get the hang of the union's unique structure. Thus after supporting the right wing campaign and noting approvingly that the communists seemed to be on the way out, many press correspondents in 1962 made the point missed in 1953 that, by itself, a voting majority on Commonwealth Council hardly represented 'control' of the A.E.U.[24] However, a number of backers of the A.E.U. right wing forces overlooked the significance of this fact in the heady and euphoric atmosphere immediately following the McDowell and Clarke successes. *News Weekly's* first edition after the results were known spread its exultations all over the front page and more than half of the second. It saw the election as dealing the C.P.A. 'the most crippling blow it has suffered since its loss

[23] *Age*, 24/2/62.
[24] E.g. *Bulletin*, 17/2/62, *Age*, 24/2/62.

of the Ironworkers' Union [in 1952] ... The Metal Trades Federation is virtually lost to the Communist Party.'[25] The A.E.U. result was considered far more industrially significant than the gratifying election victory in mid-1961 of C. Fitzgibbon, (A.L.P.) over T. Nelson (C.P.A.) for the secretary-ship of the Waterside Workers' Federation — because while *News Weekly* had doubts about Fitzgibbon's value as an anti-communist, 'there are no doubts about the anti-communist records of Shearer and McDowell, or the effectiveness of their control over the union'. Of more immediate importance than the miscalculation which the latter comment revealed was another extensive article in the same issue which described the manner in which the daily press apportioned the credit for the defeat of Hennessy and Dodd as 'The Fraud of the Century'. For, strangely enough, it was over this question of who did what during the Shearer–McDowell–Clarke–Malcolm cam-paigns that N.C.C. spokesmen, led by Santamaria, did irreparable damage to the Defence Committee's standing within the A.E.U. and the broader industrial labour movement.

The curious revelatory outbursts were sparked off by the major dailies' and weeklies' references to McDowell's victory producing an 'A.L.P.' voting majority on Commonwealth Council. Santamaria immediately issued press statements which indignantly described as a 'hoax' any notion of the A.L.P. being connected with the struggle to break what he described as the C.P.A. 'grip' on the A.E.U. He outlined the determined efforts which the Defence Committee and N.C.C. had been making within the A.E.U. since 1959 at least. 'This campaign was backed to the hilt by the N.C.C. The A.L.P. had no part whatsoever in the campaign.'[26] Nor was this all, for when anonymous A.L.P. spokesmen replied that Santamaria exaggerated his organisation's role the N.C.C. leader again hastened into print to claim publicly that the cam-paign had been fought by the Defence Committee and 3,000 members of the N.C.C. and D.L.P. He further challenged the A.L.P. to state what action it had taken against A.E.U. communists. Shearer and McDowell supported Santa-maria reiterating that Shearer was not an A.L.P. member and that both of them were highly critical of the lack of support from the A.L.P.[27] At this stage the federal Leader of the Opposition, A. A. Calwell, stepped in to keep the pot boiling. He began by scoring some easy points in explaining that the reason why the A.L.P. did not officially support candidates for union office was because of the use to which the Industrial Groups had been put by Santamaria's Movement. Calwell then went on irrelevantly to talk about

[25] *News Weekly*, 28/2/62.
[26] *Sunday Telegraph*, 25/2/62.
[27] *Age*, 26/2/62.

the support he had given Fitzgibbon in the W.W.F. ballot and generally to sideswipe Santamaria, the D.L.P. and the N.C.C.[28] Amazingly enough Santamaria accepted the bait and on 4 March chose a Melbourne Catholic television programme to demolish as 'plain unvarnished bunkum' the press stories that the A.L.P. had won a victory in the A.E.U. He claimed that these stories had been 'carefully planted by Sydney industrial correspondents, who are strong A.L.P. supporters', and in attacking them he gave further details of the N.C.C.'s role in the Shearer and McDowell campaign. After describing the onerous task of collecting petition signatures, of canvassing, and the laborious consequences of A.E.U. rules forbidding printed material, Santamaria said,

> To sum up three aspects of this three-year-old campaign: Altogether 150,000 'how-to-vote' cards have been handwritten. This has involved 15,000 hours work done by 3,000 people.
>
> Altogether the posting of all these cards has cost £2,500. This money has to be raised by raffles and collections. Finally, over 1,000 people have been involved in the various canvasses.
>
> I know these facts personally since all of this work was done by the A.E.U. Defence Committee supported by unionist members of the National Civic Council.[29]

The Tasmanian state President of the N.C.C. publicly supported Santamaria's claims[30] while Queensland sources publicised the fact that, while Goding and Tallon were the only active A.L.P. supporters of McDowell in that state, no action was taken against A.L.P. members such as Gillman, the A.E.U. Brisbane District Secretary, who openly supported Hennessy.[31] A month later Santamaria's comments on the costliness and scale of the N.C.C. campaign within the A.E.U. were still being reported in the press. Among other things he revealed that, apart from the handwritten how-to-vote cards, some 20,000 letters were sent out in a single year.[32] Towards the end of May the issue flared up again as the Malcolm—Searle campaign reached its final stages. On this occasion the cause was press references to A.L.P. members backing Malcolm and handwriting his 17,500 how-to-vote cards, and descriptions of Clarke as an A.L.P. man.[33] This time, however, Santamaria did not personally enter the debate, leaving it to *News Weekly* to decry the reports and to Clarke to make a public declaration that he belonged to no political

[28] *Age*, 27/2/62.
[29] Quoted in *The Tribune*, 8/3/62.
[30] *Hobart Mercury*, 7/3/62.
[31] *Sunday Mail*, 4/3/62, *Courier-Mail*, 8/3/62, *News Weekly*, 21/3/62.
[32] *Australian Financial Review*, 19/4/62.
[33] *Age*, 23/5/62, 28/5/62, 29/5/62.

organisation and that his support came from the Defence Committee which, he said, was made up of men of all parties. Santamaria's silence, and Clarke's relative restraint when compared with Shearer's declarations three months earlier seem to reflect a growing awareness in right wing circles of the damage which the public association of the N.C.C. and Defence Committee had caused. The full effects of the damage would not be felt until later — and of course the revelations did not prevent Malcolm defeating Searle in June — but the left even at this stage could hardly believe its good fortune at this straightforward admission. Every press clipping was garnered, reproduced and quoted in workshop, branch, and on A.E.U. members' doorsteps. In future there need be no arguments about it — here it was straight from the horse's mouth, the N.C.C. was behind the Defence Committee; even the most attractive-looking of right wing candidates, such as A.L.P. man McDowell, was therefore either an N.C.C. dupe — or a rogue. The wheel had truly turned full circle, and in the abrasive propaganda war going on within the A.E.U. in the early 1960s the left wing had been handed the best possible weapon — for suspicions of the secretive N.C.C. could be fanned into a far brighter blaze within the A.E.U. electorate than any fear of communist control. The war was by no means over and, as we shall see, in the months that followed other weapons were to be placed in the left wingers' hands: but since they concerned the sacred rule-book their effectiveness would have been mainly limited to A.E.U. activists — most of whom were already converted to the left wing cause. After the Santamaria statements the way was clear for an increasingly efficient Rights Committee publicity machine to implant its message that the union was in danger of an N.C.C. takeover in the minds of a majority of non-activist A.E.U. members, and every move that Shearer and McDowell were to make was now capable of being interpreted in that alarming light. It was easy for left wingers to cast doubt on the N.C.C.'s true motives by pointing to unions like the coal-miners, sheet metal workers, plumbers and others which, although appearing to fit far more closely the N.C.C.'s definition of 'communist-controlled', were not subject to N.C.C. challenge. Many fringe A.E.U. activists, particularly in Queensland and in country branches in New South Wales and Victoria, who had done little more than shake their heads disapprovingly at the revelations of the Split, were now galvanised into active and indignant opposition by what they saw as an insidious and malevolent N.C.C. plot. As at least one political journalist prophesied would be the case, Santamaria, by his public revelations, in effect gave the 'kiss of death' to the right wing campaigns in the A.E.U.[34]

[34] Alan Reid, *Daily Telegraph*, 26/2/62.

It is difficult to understand why the N.C.C. leader made such a grave error. In the past the right wing within the A.E.U. had always played down any connections with the N.C.C. and had always euphemistically emphasised that their candidates were 'Labor' men. They had also derided the left's accusations of large numbers of non-A.E.U. men assisting the Defence Committee and had attempted to turn the charge by arguing that the Rights Committee was aided by C.P.A. members of other unions.[35] One possible explanation of Santamaria's reaction is simply that the comments of press-men and A.L.P. officials penetrated his guard, so that for a short while his usual public image of cool background calculation was replaced by one of an exasperated man witnessing the public acclamation for his own hard toil being given to his worst political enemies. Alternatively, Santamaria may genuinely have been naive enough not to have realised the effects his statements would have on A.E.U. members. In other words he may not have been aware of the N.C.C.'s connotations among rank and file unionists. In this case, whatever their motives, the newspaper reporters who so angered him were in fact proving themselves more effective anti-communist cam-paigners than Santamaria by helping persuade non-activist A.E.U. members that the A.L.P. was behind the Defence Committee candidates. Santamaria's television remarks of 4 March implied that he was not publicly unveiling the N.C.C. role because of any simple belief that the war was all over now that a simple voting majority on Commonwealth Council had been secured. Comments shortly afterwards by *News Weekly* about the hard slog ahead in the A.E.U. districts also indicate a belated awareness among right wing outsiders of how the A.E.U. operated.[36] Yet while not guilty of the excesses of exuberance that *News Weekly* at first displayed, there does seem to be some note of final triumph in Santamaria's comments, a certain sense that the end of a long hard road had been reached — or was definitely in sight. It is possible, therefore, that Santamaria felt that the moves soon to be made by Shearer and McDowell were certain to bring the right wingers' long campaign to a victorious conclusion. If this were the case he — and they — sorely miscalculated another aspect of the A.E.U. constitution — the appeals system. Overall, Santamaria's behaviour may reflect an unknown combina-tion of all three factors; exasperation with the press and A.L.P., naivety about the N.C.C.'s image, and over-confidence in N.C.C.-Defence Committee future strategy within the A.E.U.

[35] E.g. *News Weekly*, 17/5/61, 23/8/61, 11/10/61.
[36] *News Weekly*, 14/3/62.

III

It was not on the industrial front that Shearer and McDowell made their moves. They did little to steer the A.E.U. towards industrial policies commonly associated with the N.C.C. No effort was made, for example, to support the linking of wages and productivity which the Defence Committee occasionally advocated in *Engineers' Voice*. This rather disappointed their opponents who, while hammering away on the winning theme of how the N.C.C. openly backed the two Councilmen, had to be satisfied on the bread and butter side of things with reminding A.E.U. members of alleged Movement influence on the 1953—4 wage decisions. Virtually the only industrial 'betrayal' with which the eager District Committees could charge the right wingers occurred in November 1962 at a federal unions' conference in Melbourne. Here Shearer voted with the right wing unions against Horsburgh and representatives of other militant unions who supported a motion seeking to intensify the current campaign for increases in annual leave and margins. The Rights Committee made as much mileage as it could out of this fact, as it did out of an incident in February 1963 when Shearer and McDowell endeavoured physically to seize the Hurstville 2nd Branch's books after the Treasurer reported that £5 had been donated from the Local Purpose Fund to aid the Rights Committee's election campaign on behalf of organiser Buckley. For the rest, the two Councilmen did not pose any serious threat to the districts which increasingly went their own way.

For many A.E.U. members who became in any way involved in the union's affairs during the relevant period, Shearer and McDowell's joint two and a half years in office can be summarised in retrospect by the phrase 'court ballots'. Although much else was at stake during these months everything seemed to pivot around this issue. It was over court ballots that the major lawsuits were fought and it was as a result of court ballots that the Executive Council intervened so decisively. The climacteric battle between right and left in the A.E.U. began with Shearer and McDowell using their voting power to request the Registrar to supervise ballots for full-time A.E.U. officials. The move hardly came as a surprise to the left wingers for it would obviate all the problems associated with collecting petitions. Nevertheless, when in May the two Councilmen passed their first 'minority motion' over the protests of their three colleagues and requested the Registrar to conduct the elections for Council Chairman due at the end of 1962, hundreds of protests from individuals, workshops, branches and District Committees poured in and began to ascend the A.E.U. internal appeals ladder. The Registrar found the request 'duly made' by the union's official 'committee of management' and arrangements were made to hold the ballot in November. In July, Shearer and McDowell successfully made a request for simultaneous supervision of the ballot for the Sydney organising position held by Buckley. On 13 September, however, the Executive Council made it known that it upheld the left wing appeals. The British body sharply reproved Shearer and McDowell for so far departing from the rules as to initiate outside intervention in A.E.U. affairs. It made a clear distinction between their behaviour and the Commonwealth Council's enforced acceptance of intervention in the past after petitions had been lodged with the Registrar. While Shearer and McDowell accepted this finding without protest and immediately withdrew their request to the Registrar, the current secretary of the Victorian Defence Committee, I. G. Parkes, took action in the Industrial Court to prevent implementation of the Executive Council's instructions. At the same time the Hawthorn Branch secretary, A. J. MacDonald, was separately asking the court to disallow the A.E.U. rule which prevented members of the Industrial Section such as himself from standing for Council positions. On 5 November the court upheld Parkes' claim and indicated that in its view the Executive Council had no right to prevent the Australian Section from applying for court ballots. The Electoral Office had to delay the ballot for Chairman until the MacDonald case was decided but went ahead with the Sydney ballot in which Buckley ended the right wing run. Buckley thus became the first A.E.U. official in Australia to benefit from a rule change initiated by the British Section against Australian opposition which increased full-time terms in office from three to five years upon re-election.

The day after the Parkes decision, a key Council meeting took place. Argument hinged on whether the court's judgment relieved the Council in future of the necessity to observe the Executive Council's September ruling against direct requests for court supervision. Shearer and McDowell were adamant that it did, their Council colleagues were equally certain that it did not. In terms of A.E.U. 'law' and tradition there can be no doubt that the left wingers were correct and that unless and until the Executive Council gave a new ruling, the only recourse for the two right wing Councilmen was to do as Wilson and Hennessy had done in similar circumstances in 1953 and put their case before the Final Appeal Court. As it was, after long heated discussion, Shearer and McDowell moved and seconded a motion that the Registrar be requested to supervise the March elections for Council Secretary and for organisers for the Victorian country and Newcastle districts. Horsburgh sought to formally defer the matter on the grounds that the Executive Council needed time to consider the court's decision. He also argued that to defy the Executive Council's September ruling might invite the London office to use its powers in the rules unilaterally to commence action to sever the ties with Australia — which would be particularly unfortunate in view of the financial help which the Australian A.E.U. was currently seeking from Britain.[37] Considerable confusion was later to arise as to whether the motion had actually been deferred or not. Horsburgh and Garland were sure it had and Shearer and McDowell certain it had not.

While the Chairman and Secretary were addressing a long letter to the Executive Council setting out their alarm at the two Councilmen's line of thought, and suggesting a visit to London for verbal discussions,[38] the right wingers were independently placing a request for court supervision of the March ballots with the Registrar. In Britain the Horsburgh–Garland letter was received sympathetically and this for two main reasons. Firstly, Horsburgh was personally known as a result of several visits to London while a member of joint union delegations abroad, and the British officers considered him to be neither extremist nor alarmist. Secondly, the Executive Council — which was middle of the road in the British Labour spectrum and of course had no experience of divisions of the depth and feeling of those in post-Split Australia — was truly shocked by Shearer and McDowell's action and ideas. Hitherto British officials had not been too worried by nominal limitations imposed on Executive Council power by Australian industrial law because they were confident that Australian officials would, as in the case of West Australia,[39] remain faithful to the A.E.U. constitution in practice. The fact that members of the Australian executive would actually invite outside 'interference' in A.E.U. ballots was startling enough for British officials: from May 1962 onwards the Executive Council was predisposed to accept the Australian left wingers' charges about their opponents. The right wingers' subsequent decision to use the judgment in the key Parkes case to flout internal A.E.U. authority was the last straw. While formally acknowledging receipt of the Horsburgh–Garland letter in neutral terms,[40] General Secretary C. W. Hallett posed a stark alternative to Executive Council: either Commonwealth Council accepted the authority of its superior British Council, or the link between the two countries should be severed.[41] Thus, while seeking legal opinion on the Parkes case before giving an official

---

[37] Below, pp. 298–302.
[38] 'Letter to Executive Council', 9/11/62.
[39] Above, p. 28 n.8.
[40] Letter from Executive Council, 7/12/62.
[41] 'Submission to Executive Council', 20/11/62.

ruling, the Executive Council also asked its lawyers to give their interpretation of the A.E.U. rules governing severance.

Back in Australia the issue was raised again on 23 November when the Registrar asked the Commonwealth Council to clarify whether or not the Shearer–McDowell request for supervision of the March ballots was the result of a motion actually passed by the Council. In response the right wingers merely 'reaffirmed' the 'decision' of 6 November without really clarifying the ambiguous events of that earlier meeting. On 17 December the Registrar ruled that the ballot request had not been 'duly made'. This decision was indignantly criticised for its apparent sophistry by Defence Committee and N.C.C. supporters who were currently very dissatisfied with what they regarded as the apathy of the federal government and Industrial Court towards the right wing crusade in the unions.[42] Yet in this particular case it seems that the right wing Councilmen were strangely reluctant to put the matter beyond doubt by formally moving the requisite motion again, and that their backers' anger with the Registrar was consequently misdirected.

Shearer and McDowell's opportunity to rectify matters came in January 1963 as a result of the court's finding in the MacDonald case which was to the effect that the restriction of Council office to the minority of Benefit members was completely at variance with the Act. Such a decision was inevitable – and the Australians had unsuccessfully attempted to persuade the more Benefit-conscious British to alter the rule at the 1960 Blackpool Rules Revision Meeting. On 23 January the right wing Councilmen moved a motion calling for fresh nominations for Council Secretary and requesting the Registrar to supervise this ballot and also those for the Newcastle and Victorian organisers. This time no ambiguity was to arise – for Horsburgh ruled the motion out of order and informed the Councilmen that their only recourse against his decision was to use the A.E.U. appeal system. The A.E.U. right wingers thought otherwise and Fox, the Secretary of the N.S.W. Defence Committee, moved against Horsburgh in the Industrial Court. At the same time Marantelli, the editor of *Engineers' Voice*, was again challenging the A.E.U. rule prohibiting the distribution of printed election material. Marantelli's appeal was dismissed but Fox's action resulted in the court directing Horsburgh to accept the right wing motion on Council. When the Chairman – who with 16,236 votes had been returned to office for five years, well ahead of S. W. Seaton (5,500)[43] and MacDonald (5,279) – turned

---

[42] See e.g. *News Weekly*, 23/1/63.
[43] Seaton was the left wing's 'dummy runner' who used his official election address to attack the right wing and to support Horsburgh. *News Weekly*, 20/2/63.

to the Executive Council for advice he was informed that the British body was still considering the various legal aspects but that in the meantime he should obey the court.[44] Consequently, one day before the expiry of the court's deadline, Horsburgh finally accepted the Shearer–McDowell motion.[45] All three ballots covered by the motion had by now been conducted in the A.E.U. branches but, after MacDonald had successfully appealed to the court that fresh nominations should be called, the Registrar accepted the Council's request to supervise a new election for Council Secretary. The other two requests he declared to be 'out of time' and the results of the branch ballots indicated a sweeping success for organiser H. Walklate and a narrower victory for G. Firth, the right wing candidate, over J. G. Kidd in the competition for the retiring Low's Newcastle position. Appeals from both sides about irregularities in the latter ballot led, however, to the Council deciding to retain Low in the post until they had been decided. After due consideration the Council disqualified over 50 per cent of the votes cast and the net effect was to leave Kidd the winner. Shearer attempted to persuade the other Council members to hold a new ballot but McDowell stuck by the rule-book and voted with Southwell against him.[46] Firth then appealed to the court against the A.E.U. rule whereby *all* votes are disqualified in a branch where an irregularity occurs. The court decided in his favour and he took up the position for two short months until Kidd successfully appealed to the court against the age-old A.E.U. method of notifying members of elections. The eventual outcome, over eighteen months after the first ballot, was a fresh election, supervised by the court, which was comfortably won by Kidd, leaving right wingers with only the relatively sour comfort of pointing to the faults which the court had found with A.E.U. election rules.

The final result of the Newcastle ballot was in many ways symptomatic of the right wingers' experience in the key years 1963–5. Through Shearer and McDowell they had taken bold steps to short-cut their way to the capture of A.E.U. official positions. The A.E.U. members in Defence Committee– N.C.C. counsels must certainly have known that their strategy could only incur increasing resentment and fury among A.E.U. activists and that all chances of a firm base in the so important branches must disappear. Yet, when the gamble had been duly made, the expected short run gains failed to materialise. Despite the resulting economies of effort, the higher polls and

[44] Executive Council letter, 25/3/63.
[45] 'C.C.M.', 5/4/63, 9/4/63.
[46] 'C.C.M.', 13/9/63.

the skill and resources of the N.C.C. electoral machinery, right wing candidates were not rewarded with success. Indeed they met with such an electoral backlash that by the end of 1965 the main right wing forces had been almost completely routed and court ballots were a thing of the past. The central reason for this dramatic change in fortunes has already been indicated — the public identification of the N.C.C. with the Defence Committee. Other factors contributed, including the increasing efficiency of the Rights Committee in spreading its message of the imminence of an N.C.C. 'takeover' to A.E.U. members in workshops, branches and homes. In this field the Victorian Rights Committee led by Carmichael was particularly effective in getting its message across and eventually could boast of its ability in an 'emergency' to raise hundreds of dollars literally within hours by passing round the hat in the larger Melbourne shops. The dynamic Carmichael, who was, like Rowe, a considerable public speaker, now assumed in the eyes of the N.C.C. the role that 'Red Ted' had once played in the demonology of the Groupers and the Movement. During the early sixties Carmichael took every opportunity to 'expose' the N.C.C. and its designs, and in the still turbulent forum of the Melbourne Trades Hall Council he was aided by J. V. Stout, the T.H.C. secretary who had been so instrumental in the rise of the Groupers and who was now, in his last years, one of their bitterest opponents.

The major election stories in the period can be briefly stated. At the end of 1963 in the main and bruising bout Garland (16,914) gained an absolute majority on the second distribution of preferences in a six man field. Although Fitzpatrick (1,795) and Burke (2,217) also ran, the main N.C.C. backing went to I. C. Hodge (12,820) of Broken Hill.[47] In one of two concurrent ballots the candidate backed by the right wing managed to finish ahead of six unco-ordinated candidates all pledged to oppose the N.C.C. This was in West Australia where Stewart succeeded to the organising position vacated by Coleman, when he became Secretary of the Perth Trades and Labour Council. In the other ballot the leading Adelaide official, J. E. Shannon, whom the state A.L.P. executive had absolved of charges connected with Unity Tickets in 1962, easily retained his organising position. The election for Division 1 Councilman in January 1964 saw Southwell pip T. J. Taylor by 80 votes out of a total of 15,860 cast, after distribution of the third candidate's preferences. This was the closest to success the Defence Committee ever came in Victoria, the centre of N.C.C. power and support.

[47] In the original ballot held in the A.E.U. branches on the March 1963 Star Night, Garland headed a seven-man field with 5,448 votes out of 7,257 cast. Fitzpatrick was second with 610, Hodge came fourth with 196 votes. 'C.C.M.', 9/4/63.

Hereafter, the tide rapidly receded. Its ebb was aided by the three weeks visit to Australia in February–March 1964 by the A.E.U. General Secretary, C. W. Hallett. His trip was made in order to gauge at first hand the controversies surrounding the Commonwealth Council and generally to discuss and investigate the working of the Australian A.E.U. What he saw and heard confirmed the opinion Executive Council had formed via correspondence and in discussion with Horsburgh in London. In public statements and in private discussions Hallett made the Executive Council's stand quite clear: court ballots should be anathema to every A.E.U. member, but above all to elected officials. It was impossible to accuse Hallett of being either a communist, biased or misinformed. He expressed the considered opinion of Executive Council including its President Sir William (later Lord) Carron who was a Catholic and, in the British context, a noted right winger in the labour movement. Hallett also spoke for all the tradition-conscious and proudly independent A.E.U. activists of the old school,

It is fundamentally wrong for members and officers to go outside of the Rules to use this thing called Court Ballots, and to adopt the methods that are being adopted which take control of the Union away from the Union and put it in the hands of others outside of the Union.

Many years of working class thought had gone into the formulation of our rules, and it was a most disturbing thing to see that our Rules in Australia had become the playground for lawyers. It is incomprehensible to the leaders of the Union in England that there should be such a level of interference in Union affairs by Government direction which relate to registration, arbitration of disputes, the so-called 'court-ballots' etc. . .

Executive Council have discussed the whole situation of Australia, and are deeply disturbed at the whole trend of events. It is my own opinion that if the membership wants to protect their rights, then they could not hesitate to remove those that break the rules.[48]

So, while left wingers made more than usually fervent toasts and speeches to the 113 year old tradition of the A.E.U., and District Committees and Branches competed for the honour of entertaining their British secretary, many right wing A.E.U. members began to concede final defeat. By their essential defensiveness and fatalism in all discussions with the General Secretary, Shearer and McDowell gave clear indication that they realised the war had been lost even before the Executive Council formally decided in April against their actions in requesting court ballots. Shearer in particular had given up the struggle as it became obvious that his standing had slumped disastrously in New South Wales. His backers were among the first to realise this and when he came up for re-election they swung their support behind

[48] Address to Melbourne District Committee, 19/2/64.

Burke who was here contesting an A.E.U. full-time position for the last time. Even so the N.C.C.'s campaign in 1964 was half-hearted compared with its efforts in 1959 and 1961, and Bruggy (4,530), the Rights Committee's current Secretary, easily defeated Burke (2,547) on the first count in a five-man field. Shearer collected only 765 votes.

The Defence Committee continued to ensure court ballots in 1964 and 1965 by the old method of lodging petitions but the end was obviously in sight. One month after the Shearer defeat Melbourne organiser Hill (6,062) easily defeated the old Grouper, F. A. Broderick (3,817). Even more symbolically, in a contest between the two men who, similar in age, dedication and ability, personified the opposing factions in the Victorian A.E.U., Carmichael (6,062) out-polled Fitzpatrick (3,703). This was Fitzpatrick's last attempt to gain full-time A.E.U. office. In the sixties, as the tide of activist opinion flowed even further away from the right wing and his supporters dwindled away, Fitzpatrick earned the grudging respect of even his bitterest opponents as he continued his lone and hopeless fight on the Melbourne District Committee. Eventually in 1965 he too gave up the struggle and he left the union in which he had led the Victorian Grouper–Defence Committee forces for over 20 tumultuous years.

In New South Wales Malcolm, the man who played a roughly similar role to Fitzpatrick on the Sydney District Committee, made it clear to his hostile Committee after defeating Searle that he would conscientiously carry out their instructions – provided always they remained within the A.E.U. rules. The Sydney left wingers were naturally quite pleased with Malcolm's attitude and they found him to be a particularly efficient and dedicated Secretary. No-one sought to oppose his return when his first term of office ended in 1966 and his second in 1971.

The remaining successful right wing candidates of the crest years 1961–3 were all rejected when time came for re-election. In March 1965 McDowell went down to Brisbane District Secretary Gillman, Clarke lost to J. C. Doyle, and in the following year Stewart lost to A. J. Marks. In between, in two isolated and surprise results, right wing-backed candidates were elected Adelaide District Secretary and Tasmanian organiser. Both proved particularly independent-minded and both survived only a single term before being defeated by left wing candidates.

Outside the union, right wing enthusiasm for the crusade within the A.E.U. also faded from 1963 onwards, ebbing most quickly perhaps in New South Wales and slowest in Tasmania and Queensland. *News Weekly* sadly chronicled the changes and whereas originally it had been the anti-Groupers and left wingers who had cast aspersions on the neutrality and integrity of the officials of the Commonwealth Industrial Court and Commonwealth Electoral Office alike, it was now the N.C.C. supporters who declared that, 'confidence in the clean ballot legislation has materially suffered over the last twelve or eighteen months, in particular, as a result of what many regard as certain "political" judgments, as well as administrative actions'.[49] In its annual New Year review of the union scene in 1965 the *News Weekly* correspondent tacitly admitted that the battle had been lost. He came as near as he could to revealing that the key factor was the public identification of the N.C.C. with the Defence Committee when he complained of the 'utterly filthy and vicious propaganda' directed at the N.C.C. and D.L.P. and the resultant fact that, 'sufficient normally decent A.E.U. members allowed themselves to be stampeded into restoring communist and United Front control to the A.E.U., and through the A.E.U. back into the metal industry'.[50] By 1966 the right wing had ceased to tender petitions and so for the last six years of its existence the A.E.U. returned, as in its first 100 years, to conducting its own elections undisturbed by any outside 'interference'.

[49] *News Weekly*, 28/8/63.
[50] *News Weekly*, 14/1/65.

10

The industrial front 1954—72: towards national bargaining and amalgamation

In the period between the commencement of the A.L.P. Split and the final defeat of the right wing forces within the A.E.U. the economy continued to enjoy a strong growth trend interrupted only by the 1960—1 recession and a milder check to most growth series spread over the longer period 1956—8. The rate of increase of consumer prices rose above 5 per cent for about 12 months in 1955—6 but for the remainder of the decade the annual rate of inflation was generally less than 2 per cent. In the sixties consumer prices continued to rise on average at less than 3 per cent until the pace quickened towards the end of the decade. At the core of the steady rise in manufacturing output, employment and productivity observed in this period was the performance of the metals sector. While total factory employment grew between 1953—4 and 1967—8 by 34 per cent to 1,339,605, two-thirds of the total increase occurred in the metal sector which grew by 58 per cent to 628,953, and expanded its share of the total factory workforce from 40 to 47 per cent. The production of consumer durables was a particularly important stimulus to growth within both the metal sector itself and in the economy at large. Between 1953—4 and 1967—8 employment in metal firms directly associated with the motor car increased by 80 per cent to 163,136 and in the electrical goods sector by 90 per cent to 90,006. Together, these two industries accounted for 40 per cent of the total metal workforce in 1967—8.[1]

As the fifties progressed and consumption standards grew, the fears which so many people had harboured of a return to the bad old days of high unemployment and sharp cyclical swings began to disappear. Consequently expectations altered and the 1961—2 recession, although of no greater

---

[1] Figures given in this paragraph are taken from A.M.C. Waterman, 'Fluctuations in the Rate of Growth: Australia 1948—49 to 1963—64', Ph.D. thesis, Australian National University, 1967, Chs. x and xi, and Commonwealth Bureau of Census and Statistics, *Secondary Industry Bulletins*, Nos. 47—58 and *Manufacturing Industry*, Nos. 1—5.

magnitude than the 1952–3 episode, evoked a degree of public discontent and criticism which cannot be wholly explained by either its comparatively longer duration, the misleading statistics to hand, or the wide impact of the federal government's initial credit squeeze.[2]

The relative facility with which the economy was steered during the fifties past various shoals including the 1958 world recession had helped persuade even A.E.U. leaders that an economic catastrophe was unlikely. The 1961 recession brought briefly at its peak general unemployment rates as high as 4.5 per cent to the metal trades but although some communist officials tended at first to look for underlying weaknesses in the capitalist system throughout the world[3] the general picture in 1961 is of A.E.U. leaders attacking the Menzies government's economic mismanagement and calmly, albeit forcibly, urging the stimulation of national expenditure by lowering hours of work, lifting wages, increasing spending and controlling imports. These were, of course, the very policies which the A.E.U. and the rest of the union movement had demanded so unfashionably during the 1930s. Given the intervening intellectual conversion of economists and businessmen both the tone in which the A.E.U.'s urgings were made the atmosphere in which they were received was very different.

The incidence of unemployment in the metal trades in 1961–2 was slightly lower than that in manufacturing in general.[4] For most skilled A.E.U. members the slackening in industrial growth rates in 1956–8 and 1961–2 at worst involved a cut in overtime but seldom outright unemployment. Over-award payments were almost universally retained by engineering craftsmen as employers hoarded their skilled workers during the recessions. Many factories used the slack time for long-delayed overhauls of plant, often transferring skilled personnel from manufacturing departments to their service divisions.[5] Thus as in years gone by the incidence of unemployment was highest among less skilled metal workers.

II

Despite the conflicts over Adult Training Schemes outlined below there can be no doubt that over the last 20 years employers' organisations have wholeheartedly agreed with the craft unions that the apprenticeship

---

[2] For a detailed comparison of the two downswings and the public reaction to them see Waterman, op. cit., pp. 477–97.

[3] E.g. *M.J.*, March 1961, pp. 1, 26.

[4] The 1961 Census revealed 4.5 per cent of the metals work force 'not at work' on 30 June 1961 as against 5.3 per cent of the total manufacturing work force. Waterman, op. cit., p. 480.

[5] For evidence of the continued shortage of skill during the 1961–2 recession see, e.g. *Metal Trades Journal*, 1/2/62, 1/3/62, 6/6/62.

system provided easily the best means of supplying the economy's rapidly expanding need for skilled tradesmen.[6] On every possible occasion employers' leaders and representatives urged firms to apprentice more lads, yet the major single cause of the continuing shortage of skill and its inevitable consequences on the level of skilled wages was the refusal of individual employers to take on apprentices. Although a formal apprentice-tradesman ratio remained in the Metal Trades Award and other major awards covering metal craftsmen, Galvin's decision in 1952[7] meant that interested employers could in fact train as many apprentices as they liked.[8] Generally speaking it was the larger employers like B.H.P. Co. Ltd., Australian Iron and Steel Ltd., Qantas, and the various Electricity Commissions which made the effort to train extra lads. It appears that the formal ratio may have acted as a psychological barrier to certain employers who felt that they had done their 'fair share' if they employed apprentices up to or close to the nominal proportion,[9] but all too many firms —particularly the smaller ones — simply refused to 'waste' money training apprentices who might move on when qualified. Instead such firms preferred to find their tradesmen by offering over-award payments to men already fully trained. In 1955 an M.T.E.A. survey of its membership revealed that only 52 per cent of over 800 firms which replied to its questionnaire employed apprentices.[10] In 1962 it was generally accepted as a rough national estimate that whereas perhaps half of all employers were taking the nominally permissible proportion of apprentices, one quarter were taking none at all.[11] An M.T.E.A. survey of its larger members in 1965 revealed that the average apprentice: tradesman ratio among the 64 respondents was 1:4 while 41 metal establishments inspected by the federal arbitration tribunal in 1967–8 had an average ratio of 1:3.4.[12] In this context the A.E.U. and the other unions had few worries about the general acceptance of the Galvin 'capacity to train' criteria after 1952 and, unlike the printers, the metal unions seldom seriously opposed employers' applications to train extra lads. In 1962 they had few qualms in agreeing to a variation of the Metal Trades Award to allow for short term apprenticeships for boys with higher educational qualifications, and two years later they agreed to the removal of the original age limit.

[6] Virtually any issue of the *Metal Trades Journal* will endorse this view but see, e.g. the issues of 15/1/53 and 16/1/61.
[7] Above, p. 186.
[8] For a detailed exposition of this point see the *Beattie Report*, pp. 176–88.
[9] Ibid., p. 187.
[10] *Metal Trades Journal*, 15/4/55.
[11] *Metal Trades Journal*, 15/5/62.
[12] *Beattie Report*, p. 52, Appendix 47.

Employers involved in training apprentices had mixed views about the short term scheme with a minority opinion emerging that while the shorter terms might suit the specialist, five years was necessary to train an 'all round' tradesman.[13] The Victorian Apprenticeship Commission refused to accept the scheme set out in the Metal Trades Award, preferring its own state system whereby all applicants for apprenticeship were automatically granted time credits for educational qualifications.[14] Even so, it seems that the Victorian system was not attracting any more apprentices in 1968 than in New South Wales where the effect of the short term scheme was 'insignificant' during the first three years of its operation, accounting for only 281 of the 6,408 lads commencing apprenticeships as fitters and turners.[15] Another variation to the Metal Trades Award in 1962 which allowed for a lad to be apprenticed to more than one employer attracted even less interest among firms despite promotion by the M.T.E.A.[16]

With no fears of an over-supply of apprentices the A.E.U. rather aimed throughout this period to improve the apprenticeship system lest its failure to attract lads strengthened arguments for adult training.[17] Among other things the A.E.U. aimed to improve the quality of instruction and to persuade employers to take on more lads both by formal representations and by individual deputations from the shop floor. With the object of ensuring that lads received an all-round training the union came to support the idea that they should be apprenticed to the state apprenticeship authority which would allocate them to approved employers. Another important strand in the A.E.U.'s efforts on behalf of apprentices was its campaign to ensure that all training in technical schools took place during working hours and not in the lads' spare time. Complete daylight training had been recommended by many concerned with apprenticeship matters, including the majority of members of the 1953–4 Joint Commonwealth–State Inquiry into apprenticeship,[18] but to the A.E.U. its nationwide establishment seemed painfully slow. South Australia had to wait until the demise of the Playford Government before an Act based on 1959 A.E.U. submissions to the Trades and Labor Council was passed by the new A.L.P. ministry in October 1966.[19]

[13] Ibid., pp. 274–6.
[14] Ibid., pp. 279–80.
[15] Ibid., p. 286.
[16] Ibid., pp. 247–52.
[17] For typical A.E.U. views on apprenticeship see *Minutes/Reports of National Conference of Officials* 1960, 1964, *Interstate Conference* 1961, 1965.
[18] *Commonwealth–State Apprenticeship Inquiry Report of Committee 1954*, p. 32.
[19] As in some other states the deficiency in South Australian technical school accommodation delayed the full implementation of daylight training for several years after the legislation came into force.

On the wages side the main aim of the craft unions was both to raise apprentices' pay and to make it a fixed proportion of the tradesman's rate rather than a proportion of the Basic Wage. While employers were generally prepared to give bonuses to proficient apprentices and in some cases made straight-out over-award payments to senior apprentices, for a long while they firmly opposed any link with the tradesman's rate. Consequently although the Arbitration Commission accepted the union arguments in the case of the ship joiners' apprentices in 1956 the principle was not incorporated in the Metal Trades Award until 1966 when the employers decided that the need to make apprentices' pay less undesirable in comparison with youths' wages in other occupations outweighed the costs involved. In the 1960s the A.E.U. also began a campaign to establish apprentices' rights to participate fully in industrial action with adult workers.

The second source of metal craftsmen was from overseas. The available data on immigrants' skills contain all the usual problems connected with 'self-described' occupation statistics and are complicated by changes in the Commonwealth Statistician's classifications in 1959 and 1961.[20] The best we can do is simply to note with Mr Justice Beattie that it would appear that in the years 1946—60 inclusive, Australia made a net gain of some 56,000 self-described metal-tradesmen immigrants, with the biggest inflow occurring in the three years 1949—51. In the five and a half years after June 1961 the net gain was approximately 31,000. Beattie estimated that in 1966 the addition to the N.S.W. skilled workforce was probably equal to about 70 per cent of the contribution represented by tradesmen who had just finished their apprenticeship. The mechanism set up under the T.R.R. Act was the means by which migrants were sifted and, as might be expected, A.E.U. representatives remained among the sterner judges on the Engineering Trades Committees. In 1956—7 in particular the A.E.U. incurred public odium by its inflexible stand in the aftermath of the Hungarian uprising. The union's steadfast refusal to endorse the Central (Engineering Trades) Committee's proposal to make it easier for Hungarian refugees to obtain Recognised Trade Certificates was seen in many quarters as a simple by-product of the alleged communist 'control' of the A.E.U. This reaction was the more understandable in view of the fact that, hardened both by the local anti-communist mud slinging during the A.L.P. Split and the wider contemporary Cold War environment, A.E.U. officials, like so many other left wingers in the West, refused to condemn Russian actions in Hungary. Misunderstanding of the A.E.U.'s stand on Hungarian tradesmen was fortified both by A.E.U. communists' outright

[20] For details see *Beattie Report*, pp. 28—30 and Appendices 15—24.

defence of Russia[21] and by the initial acceptance of the Central Trades Committee's sympathetic approach by the A.E.U. representative, Horsburgh. The latter soon withdrew his unauthorised stand when challenged by his Commonwealth Council colleagues and by angered rank and file activists, but by then the public relations damage had been done and the post-war consistency of the A.E.U. position on immigrant tradesmen whether fleeing from fascist or communist oppression had been obscured.[22] It was not until the overall immigrant flow began to decline in the second half of the sixties that the stern A.E.U. watch on Europeans' qualifications began somewhat to relax.

The third source of skilled tradesmen lay in the 'elevation' to craftsman status of adults already working in industry at less skilled jobs. As we have seen the 1952 amendments to the T.R.R. Act made legal provision for elevation. At first the A.E.U.'s firm policy was to discourage employers from elevating men on the shop floor wherever possible. As time went by the union took a milder view of elevation and this for several reasons: the economy showed no sign of a return to the bad old pre-war days, the shortage of skilled men persisted and, not least, the A.E.U.'s rivals showed no disinclination to accept elevatees as members. The exact A.E.U. attitude to elevatees varied, with full time officials being more amenable to change than the more traditional-minded branch secretaries, and the metropolitan centres proving more liberal than the country areas and Newcastle.[23]

The diminution of A.E.U. fears of a sudden downturn in demand and a consequent oversupply of tradesmen were reflected in the union's acceptance of the progressive liberalisation of the conditions governing the issue of tradesmen's certificates to men who had acquired their skill through substantial trade experience. In 1958 with A.E.U. agreement the issuance of the old Recognised Tradesman's Certificates ceased, although all existing Certificates and the job preference they implied remained valid until 30 June 1960. From September 1958 a 'Tradesman's Certificate' was issued which carried no rights, preference or privilege but simply provided evidence that the holder was qualified in his trade. The next amendments to the Act came into force four months after a 1960 A.E.U. Conference of officials had decided to

---

[21] *M.J.*, February 1957, p. 21. For an opposing A.E.U. view see *M.J.*, July 1957, p. 24.

[22] 'C.C.M.', 15/2/57; *Commonwealth Council Circular* S217, 19/2/57; 'Minutes of Melbourne Shop Stewards' Quarterly Meeting', 5/4/57; M.D.C.M. 17/4/57; *Sydney Morning Herald*, 1/4/57; *Metal Trades Journal*, 1/5/57.

[23] See e.g. the report of Newcastle organiser, H. Low in *A.E.U. Minutes of National Conference of Officials 1960*, p. 15. The conservatism in the Newcastle area was not confined to the A.E.U. For evidence of E.T.U. craft resistance to upgrading in Newcastle, see *Beattie Report*, p. 31.

make every effort to ensure that the more conservative of A.E.U. branch officials accepted as a fully fledged tradesman any member who had been employed as such for seven years. From March 1961 the Trades Committees could issue a Tradesman's Certificate to any applicant who had been employed as a craftsman for seven of the ten years prior to March 1961. This in effect represented a final acceptance of successful elevations in the 1950s, for previously Certificates were issued only to those employed for seven years and within one month prior to 3 September 1952. Hereafter the date on which the seven years experience was based was brought forward whenever it was considered necessary. By the mid-sixties the number of certificates issued by Trades Committees was averaging 1,000 per annum.[24] In addition, as the workforce came to accept full employment as the norm, fewer upgraded workers felt the need to gain formal recognition of their status from a Trades Committee, although A.E.U. officials found that whenever the demand for labour slackened there was a noticeable upturn in the application for certificates. In 1964 a Department of Labour and National Service investigation revealed that 19.5 per cent of the 16,746 workers engaged in metal tradesmen's tasks in the 262 large private firms surveyed had neither served an apprenticeship nor been issued with a certificate. The trades in which such workers were most common were welding and first class machining with percentages of 41.2 and 38.0 respectively. In fitting and turning, easily the largest single trade category, the proportion was only 10.7 per cent.[25]

An indication that upgrading did not produce sufficient suitable all round qualified tradesmen is provided by the employers' continued interest in the introduction by the Commonwealth Government of fully fledged Adult Training schemes including intensive full time technical school training. On this issue the A.E.U. and most other metal craft unions stood firmly in opposition, for they saw quite clearly that, if the rate of remuneration offered to the trainees was high enough, sufficient would be eventually forthcoming to end the sellers' market for skilled labour. The unions' fundamental objection is clearly revealed by the 1972 decision of the new Amalgamated Metal Workers Union to work for the removal of all barriers of age and sex from apprenticeships in the metal trades — with the single proviso that all apprentices must be paid the same rate.

The two major confrontations over adult training came in 1955 and in the period 1962–5. On the first occasion after lengthy negotiations the federal government threatened to let the T.R.R. Act lapse unless the unions agreed

[24] Ibid., p. 32.
[25] Loc. cit.

to a scheme under which it was proposed to introduce annually 2,000 extra tradesmen into the workforce after six months full time training in technical schools and two years workshop experience all on full pay. The A.E.U. was naturally one of the fiercest critics of the proposal. Grouper and communist members of the Commonwealth Council united whole-heartedly in warning the government of inevitable industrial unrest, in attacking A.C.T.U. President Monk for his relative lack of firmness, and in hoping that the E.T.U. would not break the common front.[26] In fact the unions stood firm, but so too did the government and the Act duly lapsed on 2 September. The A.E.U., envisaging a long hard haul in order to restore the favourable features of the Act, was gratified − and the M.T.E.A. duly annoyed[27] − when, to everyone's complete surprise, the government in October 1955 simply renewed the legislation in an unchanged form.

In 1962 a series of national conferences were convened by the Department of Labour and National Service. At these discussions all parties lamented the decline in the proportion of boys taking apprenticeships since 1956.[28] The unions' acceptance of the desirability of short-term and group apprenticeships resulted in the consent variations of the Metal Trades and other major awards referred to earlier. On the issue of adult training, however, the unions refused to budge. When the employers applied to the Arbitration Commission for the incorporation of an adult training scheme in the Metal Trades Award they were met with unified resistance, stop-work meetings and demonstrations. The A.E.U. again was in the van of what its leaders considered to be one of the most effective campaigns ever organised by the joint unions,[29] with Councilmen Shearer and McDowell as determined in their opposition as any of their colleagues.[30] In view of the obvious union hostility the Commission, while encouraging further conferences between the parties, did not attempt to implement the claims of employers who thus had to be satisfied with the

---

[26] For details see 'C.C.M.', 24/5/55, 17/6/55, 29/7/55, 16/8/55; C.C. Circulars S139, 24/6/55 and S146, 3/8/55; M.J., May 1955 p. 23, August 1955, pp. 3, 5.

[27] *Metal Trades Journal*, 1/10/55.

[28] Absolute numbers of annual new indentures in all trades remained constant between 1956 and 1960. They rose in the metal trades by 727 or 10.8% but this contrasts with a 28.4% increase in the 15-year-old male population in the same period. See Dept. of Labour and National Service, *Training for Skilled Occupations*, (Melbourne, 1962), Tables 1−5.

[29] *A.E.U. Addresses, Reports and Decisions of National Conference of Full-Time Officials 1964*, p. 8.

[30] For details of A.E.U. reaction and that of other metal craftsmen see *Metal Trades Journal*, 16/4/62; M.J., March 1962, pp. 1, 7, April 1962, pp. 1, 10, May 1962, pp. 8−9, September 1962, p. 17, October 1962, p. 5, November 1962, pp. 11−14.

new short term and group apprenticeships. The government and its advisers, however, still supported the notion of adult training[31] and in April 1964 it unveiled detailed proposals for its implementation which were similar in most respects to the abortive 1955 formula.[32] Once again the metal unions backed by the A.C.T.U. rejected the proposals point blank, in effect challenging the government and employers to prove that a shortage of tradesmen existed for any reason other than the failure of employers to engage sufficient apprentices. A series of conferences resulted in modifications in the government's proposals but brought no yielding on the part of the metal craftsmen apart from the minor concession of agreeing to the removal of the 17-year age limit on short term apprenticeships. Consequently the impetus behind the scheme died away in 1966 and 1967.

III

An important institutional change occurred in the wage fixing arena in 1956 when amending legislation separated the arbitral and judicial functions within the Commonwealth arbitration system. This followed the High Court's decision in the *Boilermakers' Case* which saw the metal unions again successfully challenge the Arbitration Court's ability to both make and enforce awards.[33] When appeals to the Privy Council against the High Court decision failed, the Menzies government took the opportunity to reorganise the system in such a manner as to ensure more uniformity of wages and conditions throughout the Commonwealth.[34] The judicial function of interpretation and enforcement of awards was given to the Commonwealth Industrial Court manned by judges appointed for life. This Court and the Industrial Registry remained within the province of the Attorney General's Department. The powers of conciliation and arbitration were vested in the Commonwealth Conciliation and Arbitration Commission which was placed under the auspices of the Minister of Labour. Although the personnel later increased, the Commission originally consisted of a President and four Deputy Presidents all of whom were judges retiring at 70 years of age, and nine lay Commissioners retiring at 65. All industries covered by federal

[31] For Department of Labour and National Service views see, *Training for Skilled Occupations*, op. cit.
[32] *Industrial Information Bulletin*, Vol. 19, pp. 468–9.
[33] 94 *C.L.R.*, 254. The first challenge was made in 1951 by the A.E.U. (above pp. 183–4).
[34] For further details of the 1956 amendments see O. de R. Foenander, *Industrial Conciliation and Arbitration in Australia*, (Sydney, 1959), especially Chs. III and IV.

awards were divided among the various Commissioners, jurisdiction was extended to include a number of commonwealth instrumentalities formerly under the sole jurisdiction of the Public Service Arbitrator, and those industries operating under special federal tribunals were more closely integrated with the Commission. Appeals from a decision of a single member of the Commission could be heard normally by a mixed Bench of two Presidential members and a Commissioner, while appeals from decisions of single Presidential members were to be heard by a full Bench of three Presidential members which also heard appeals from decisions of the Public Service Arbitrator. Major matters including the basic wage, standard hours and long service leave could only be dealt with by a full Presidential bench. Other matters considered to be of sufficient public interest such as general margins cases could be handled by a bench consisting of at least three members, one of whom, where practicable, being the Commissioner responsible for the industry concerned. Provision was also made for the appointment of Conciliators who were employees of the Commission lacking arbitral power to whom the parties to a dispute could be referred by the Commissioner.

As the reality of continuous full employment finally sank in among the Australian community, public debate began to concern itself increasingly with some of its apparent implications. By the end of the 1960s, in addition to wider studies of inflation, a whole body of literature had been written describing and analysing the phenomena of earnings and wage drift and their components, and suggesting feasible national wage policies.[35] Despite union complaints that wages represented the price of but one commodity and that control of wage rates was not an incomes policy, the existence of centralised arbitration machinery proved an irresistible temptation for academics, public servants and politicians to join employers in arguing that the Commonwealth Arbitration Commission could be an important instrument for moderating inflation.[36] For its part, the Commission was seen to zig-zag this way and that

---

[35] For a representative selection and review of this literature see, J. E. Isaac and G. W. Ford (Eds.) *Australian Labour Economics Readings* (Melbourne, 1967), Chs. 1–15; J. E. Isaac, *Wages and Productivity* (Melbourne, 1967); N. F. Dufty, *Industrial Relations in the Australian Metal Industries* (Sydney, 1972) Ch. 5.

[36] At times of course influential outside advice suggested other priorities — one example being Sir Douglas Copland's 1961 arguments in favour of a return to wage adjustments in response to cost of living movements.

During the gap between completion of the manuscript and publication of this book the wheel appears to have taken a further and somewhat ironic turn. In 1974 a growing number of economists are urging a restoration of cost of living adjustments — which they prefer to call 'wage indexation' — on the grounds that it will prove a key weapon in reducing the current accelerated rates of inflation.

as it attempted to reconcile its own changing notions of the national interest, with on the one hand, union pressure and the realities of the industrial market place, and on the other, the strictures of the federal government to keep increases in wage-rates as low as possible. The changing principles and apparent inconsistencies in the Commission's major judgments have been catalogued and analysed by a variety of interested observers[37] as well as by the main parties to the hearings who attempted to use their interpretations of the tribunal's current thinking to their own best advantage in subsequent cases. Whatever the reasoning, the outcome was that the gap between award rates of pay and earnings steadily widened, although in the mid-sixties empirical studies seemed to show that over award payments were not perhaps so important a component of the drift as had been previously imagined.[38]

With the abolition of cost of living adjustments in 1953 the periodic margins cases came in effect to represent a second bite at the same arbitration cherry, and the cases came to be argued on increasingly similar grounds. In margins cases the unions continued aiming to get some yardage out of both the general concern for the shortage of skilled workers and the sympathy felt by community and tribunals for the notion of wage justice for skilled men. They also continued to hold up the Higgins and 1947 awards as the desirable relativities, but the need to base the desired margin on a hypothetically higher basic wage recalculated for cost of living movements since 1953, naturally obscured the original simplicity of the formula. Throughout the period the Metal Trades Award was the vehicle for the presentation of most major arbitration cases including Basic Wage and margins, with the A.C.T.U. formally presenting the latter from 1954 onwards. Table 10.1 sets out the main decisions of the Commonwealth Arbitration Commission to 1965.

The principles on which the decisons were apparently based changed considerably. The degree to which the A.E.U. and other unions may have influenced the Commission's thinking will be considered in a moment but in the annual Basic Wage reviews of 1956–8 the Commission was largely concerned with the economy's capacity to pay and only restrained award in-

[37] In addition to the standard works already referred to, the *Journal of Industrial Relations*, established in 1959 is a useful source of contemporary analysis of both the Commission's decisions and general developments in industrial relations. See also, J. Hutson, *Penal Colony*, and *Six Wage Concepts* (Sydney, 1971); J. H. Portus, *Australian Compulsory Arbitration, 1900–1970* (Sydney, 1971).

[38] See J. E. Isaac, 'Wage Drift in the Australian Metal Industries' *Economic Record*, 41, June 1965, pp. 145–72 and *Wages and Productivity*, op. cit., p. 120; K. J. Hancock, 'Earnings Drift in Australia', *Journal of Industrial Relations*, 8, July 1966, pp. 128–57.

Table 10.1:   Commonwealth Conciliation and Arbitration
Commission Basic Wage, Margins and Annual Leave
Decisions 1956—65

Basic wage		Fitter's margin	Annual leave
1956	+ 10s.	—	—
1957	+ 10s.	—	—
1958	+ 5s.	—	—
1959	+ 15s.	+ 21s.	—
1960	No change	—	No change
1961	+ 12s.	—	No change
1962	No change	—	—
1963	No change	+ 10s.	+ 1 week
1964	+ 20s.	—	—
1965	No change	+ 6s.	—

creases were given. In 1959 the Commission decided the economy's capacity
to pay could stand larger increases representing a 6 per cent rise in the Basic
Wage and a 28 per cent rise in margins — this latter proportion although
not restoring margins to their 1947 value was greater than the rise in prices
since the 1954 judgment. In 1960, however, despite what the unions regarded as the best case they ever presented on capacity to pay grounds, the
Commission swung away from this criterion and refused to increase the Basic
Wage. It also rejected union claims for an extra weeks annual leave. In 1961
the Commission, although again rejecting the annual leave claims, lifted the
Basic Wage by 12s and swung back towards the old pre-1953 notion that price
changes should be considered when setting rates, along with productivity
movements. It therefore indicated its desire for a triennial review of productivity and annual consideration of price movements. In the succeeding two
years the Consumer Price Index did not move sufficiently to allow any cost of
living adjustment to the Basic Wage but in 1963 the Commission lifted
margins by 10 per cent on the grounds of increased productivity and price
changes since the last margins judgment in 1959. It also increased paid
annual leave to three weeks. In 1964, after rejecting employers' arguments
for the merging of Basic Wage and Margins into a Total Wage, and after
considering national productivity movements in the last triennium, the four
man Bench split strongly on the amount by which the Basic Wage should be
lifted. The President's casting vote determined that the figure was 20s. but
the other two judges voiced strong fears of inflationary consequences and
argued for only 10s.

In 1965 a differently composed bench split strongly again, three to two, but in granting a graduated rise in margins, moved in a fresh direction. The employers' Total Wage was again formally rejected, but so too were the guiding principles of 1961–4. In future, Basic Wage and Margins claims would be heard annually together in a National Wage case, and the major criterion would be the likely economic effects of wage changes. In 1966 the first National Wage Case saw yet another bench move towards the 1965 minority judgment and unanimously lift the Basic Wage by $A2.[39] It also introduced a new criterion when it declared that general margins should not be altered until a 'work value' investigation had been conducted into the metal trades classifications – but in the interim offered relief to the lowest margins earners by creating a Minimum Wage $A3.75 above the Basic Wage. In effect this decision heralded the end of the Basic Wage and prepared the ground for the Total Wage. Later in 1966, in response to a union application for an interim increase for higher margins during the inevitable delay before a metal trades work value decision, the bench granted a rise amounting to $A1.10 for tradesmen. The 1967 National Wage Case saw the formal abolition of the Basic Wage and a $A1 rise in both Total Wage and Minimum Wage. In future there were to be only two types of wage case; the National Wage Case, the result of which would hinge on a general review of the economy, and Work Value cases which would decide whether specific occupations deserved wage changes.

Despite considerable exhortation only Victoria among the states followed the Commission's example and abandoned the historic Basic Wage. The 1968 and 1969 National Wage Cases resulted in respective Total Wage rises of $A1.35 and 3 per cent, while the Minimum Wage – which came to be adopted by all states save New South Wales – was increased by $A1.35 and $A3.50. Meanwhile in December 1967 the Commission ended the metal trades first Work Value Case with a complete surprise by awarding tradesmen $A7.40 – the full amount of their claim. The unions' pleasure was marred both by the fact that the Commission firmly broke hitherto accepted relativities by awarding much lower increases to most less skilled classifications, and by the Commission's explicit encouragement to employers to absorb the rises in existing over-award payments. The stage was then set for the 'absorption' battle of January and February 1968 which saw 400 stoppages of work and 180,000 metal employees taking part in the first total 24 hour stoppage in the industry since 1952. Eventually the issue was referred back to the Commission which in a majority decision on 21 February 1968, decided that the 60 per cent of

[39] When decimal currency was introduced in February 1966 £1 became $2 and one shilling became 10 cents.

metal workers awarded a $A1.60 increase or less should keep the original amount without absorption, while the others should receive only 70 per cent of the original increases. The remainder was deferred until the National Wage Case was held in August when the Total Wage rise gave the fitter an extra $A1.35.

In the 1969 National Wage Case which resulted in a 3 per cent increase, or $A1.65 for tradesmen, the Commission, in response to employers' requests, set out a detailed statement of the relationship between the National Wage Cases and Work Value reviews. In brief, the Commission indicated that National Wage decisions reached after consideration of economic factors would be the main avenue of wage rate change. It appeared that the National decisions would tend to preserve the existing wage relativities by being made on a uniform percentage basis while changes in the wage structure through Work Value reviews would not be too frequent or radical. The Commission in the early seventies faced considerable problems in implementing its 1969 principles, while for their part the metal employers at last moved collectively towards settling wage claims by direct bargaining with unions. In 1971 lengthy negotiations preceded Commissioner Hood's decision of 16 July providing an approximate 10 per cent rise in metal wage rates, and the employers indicated their desire for an annual review of the award by means of direct negotiations. As a result, in 1972 the first ever consent award was made in the industry. A completely new vista of wage settlement appeared to be opening in the metal trades.

The A.E.U.'s wages policy during these two decades of full employment and inflation can be readily imagined. As far as its own members were concerned its officials in the various districts sought to assist and to co-ordinate the continual efforts of the rank and file to use their bargaining power to extract higher wages and better conditions from individual employers. While it is impossible to quantify the effect, it seems reasonable to assume that the internal A.E.U. controversies of the period must have diverted officials' energies to a certain degree. Employers may be pardoned for doubting this, given the overall success of A.E.U. members' non-stop offensive in these years: in fact it seems likely that two factors helped compensate for the faction fighting. First there was the increasing *de facto* autonomy gained by the District Committees which had traditionally always been more aggressive than the Commonwealth Council. Secondly the A.E.U. tradition of independent rank and file action continued in this period, fortified by the contemporary spread of Shop Committees. Needless to say, A.E.U. members and officials were among the most enthusiastic supporters of this latter trend and invariably A.E.U. men formed a ginger group on Shop Committees pressing aggressive policies. With its British connections, the A.E.U. was particularly aware of just how far the relative role and influence of Shop Committees lagged behind their equivalents in some larger industrial economies.[40] To many employers and to the more pacific minded leaders of other unions the Committees seemed to promote the influence of the A.E.U. and other militants within workshops. The employers pointed to the 'communist' threat in Shop Committees and the way in which they bypassed 'responsible unions'.[41] Unsuccessful moves were made in the early sixties by both the M.T.E.A. and Victorian Chambers of Manufactures to persuade their members not to recognise the Committees. Industrial stoppages often occured in individual plants over the basic principle of Shop Committees but this underlying factor was often obscured to outsiders by the immediate issue sparking off the dispute. Among notable stoppages in this category were a 14 week strike at Metters, Sydney, in 1957[42] and also, despite the public focus on wages, the big 1964 General Motors dispute.[43] Within the union movement the 1961 A.C.T.U. Congress had endorsed a fairly conservative charter for Shop Committees, but in 1963–4 the A.C.T.U. Executive and its state councils denounced the alleged usurpation of the powers of both the A.C.T.U. itself and of individual union executives. Nevertheless, Shop Committees slowly continued to grow in number and importance.[44]

While defending Shop Committees from attack, and commonly defined as a militant, 'communist controlled' union, A.E.U. officials — A.L.P. and C.P.A. alike — still regularly had to face the old A.E.U. phenomenon of rank and file engineers with the bit between their teeth determined to engage in direct industrial conflict with employers in circumstances which their leaders considered inappropriate. As always in such cases A.E.U. officials had to risk the immediate unpopularity involved in attempting to cool-off the members

---

[40] For percipient comments by an A.E.U. rank and file member on the contrasts between British and Australian Shop Committees see the report of N. Gow, Australian representative at the 1960 Blackpool Rules Revision Committee Meeting in *M.J.*, December 1960, p. 15. Gow indicates the growing rift in Britain between union executives and the shop floor which was later to occupy the attention of the Donovan Royal Commission. See also J. D. Garland's article in *M.J.*, March 1966, p. 9.

[41] *Metal Trades Journal*, 2/4/62. See also National Employers Policy Committee, 'Enforcement of Awards: Conciliation and Arbitration Act Sections 109 and 111', in Isaac and Ford, *Australian Labour Relations*, pp. 400–408.

[42] *M.J.*, June 1957, p. 22, September 1957, p. 22.

[43] *Addresses, Reports and Decisions of National Conference of Full-Time Officials* 1964, p. 28.

[44] For some discussion of the spread of the Shop Committee movement see Orwell de R. Foenander, *Shop Stewards and Shop Committees*, (Melbourne, 1965); Hutson, *Penal Colony* pp. 216–20.

concerned. Usually the members listened, but when they did not they occasionally laid the union open to heavy fines and costs as a result of the application of the penal provisions of the federal or state arbitration acts.[45] Needless to say not every dispute resulted in fines. Partly this was because of the unions' flexible tactics which adjusted to the harsher legal setting of the 1950s and 1960s. Just as important, however, was the need for employers not to overplay their hand. The threat of heavy fines was a useful deterrent often capable of persuading even the most militant unions such as the A.E.U. to request their members to make a tactical withdrawal — but indiscriminate use of the legal sanctions was likely to create such a groundswell of resentment that reform in the direction desired by the unions would become inevitable. In the sixties, the size and number of fines increased but it was not until the end of the decade that such an atmosphere was in fact finally created. The fundamental cause was the lavish use of the penal provisions by the metal employers in the 1968 absorption battle. Thus the A.E.U., which in the previous 18 years 1950—67 had incurred total fines under Commonwealth law of $A33,050,[46] now incurred fines totalling $A23,192 by the end of July 1968 — the overwhelming proportion in the first two months of the year. Overall, the Commonwealth Industrial Court levied $A100,000 in union fines in 1968, which represented ten times the 1967 total. In this atmosphere of widespread rank and file involvement and resentment, demands grew for A.C.T.U. action but the issue was largely decided in the unions' favour as a result of the jailing on 15 May of C. O'Shea, the Secretary of the Victorian Branch of the Tramways Union, for refusing to pay outstanding fines. On the morning of his arrest 5,000 shop stewards demonstrated in Melbourne and over the next few days an estimated one million employees were involved in stopwork meetings of protest. O'Shea himself was released after six days when an anonymous benefactor paid the fines but as a result of the industrial turmoil the federal government entered into negotiations on the penal provisions with the unions and employers. In 1970 the Act was amended to allow the Industrial Court to at least make some inquiry into the merits of the situation giving rise to a particular strike, instead of,

---

45 For an interesting discussion of such cases involving what he calls 'super militants' by a communist A.E.U. official see Hutson, *Penal Colony*, pp. 220—6.
46 Calculated from J. E. Isaac, 'Penal Provisions under Commonwealth Arbitration', *Journal of Industrial Relations*, 5, 1963, pp. 110—19, Table 2; and Dufty, *Industrial Relations* . . . , Table 2.3. The figure does not include legal costs which until October 1964 at least were actually greater than the total fines incurred under Commonwealth law. The relative figures to then were, fines $A22,100, costs $A24,000. 'Addresses etc. National Conference 1964', pp. 16—17.

as in the past, simply being required to determine whether a union was breaching an award and, if so, to apply the penal clauses. Nevertheless the Gorton and McMahon ministries refused to accede to union demands for a complete withdrawal of the sanctions. In March and December 1971 confrontations on the issue were avoided by other anonymous benefactors paying outstanding fines before the expiry of government deadlines. Thereafter, apart from the payment of outstanding fines by two metal unions in order to ensure amalgamation with the A.E.U., no union paid a fine until the election of the sympathetic Whitlam A.L.P. government in December 1972.

The increased resort to penal provisions in the sixties reflects to some small degree the increasing union acceptance of the theme, emphasised almost *ad nauseam* by the A.E.U., that on-the-job agitation was essential in order to persuade employers and arbitrators of the desirability of granting general improvements in wages and conditions of work. The experience of union campaigns was always interpreted in the same unvarying light by A.E.U. officials: when other unions and the A.C.T.U. united with the A.E.U. important gains were made and confirmed by the tribunals; when the A.E.U. and its militant allies were unsupported, or union campaigns were 'short circuited' by less militant union leaders through premature resort to arbitration, then no gains were forthcoming. In preaching the gospel of direct action there was a tendency sometimes to overlook valuable gains derived from A.L.P. state governments, particularly in N.S.W., in such spheres as long service leave, apprentice training and annual leave. In the strict wages sphere it is difficult to fault the A.E.U. analysis on the evidence — although how lasting the gains were in view of employers' ability to absorb labour cost increases by price rises is another matter altogether.

The 1954 margins increase was not enough to alter the general trend towards collective bargaining which had begun among metal unions in the Korean War inflation and been accentuated by the Galvin decision. The months immediately after the 'two and a half times' award saw both its flow on to the rest of the workforce despite the disapproval of the Arbitration Court, and successful opposition by the A.E.U. to metal employers' attempts to absorb the increases in pre-existing over-award payments. With the 'absorption' battle won by mid-1955 the A.E.U. went over to the attack to establish higher over-award payments. As a reference point, the districts aimed for a standard 30s, for tradesmen on top of the 75s. award rate. This target conformed with the standing A.C.T.U. policy of 'double the [1952] margins'. In general the campaign was reported a success particularly in the two major industrial centres of Melbourne and Sydney, with many employers paying much more, and a number agreeing to cost of living adjustments.

The biggest single dispute in 1955 was that at the Naval Dockyards in Sydney and Melbourne which involved 24 unions and some 4,000 workers between July and September. The campaign continued into 1956 with rank and file militancy feeding on the wage anomalies appearing in those states where cost of living adjustments were still being made on the state Basic Wage. Only South Australia had imitated the federal court's abolition in 1954 — and in N.S.W., where the state Basic Wage had been tied to that of the Common-wealth since 1937, the A.L.P. government in 1955 reintroduced adjustments which were maintained until 1964. This move annoyed the federal govern-ment which made every effort to persuade all states to abandon adjustments. Victoria and Tasmania did so in 1956 but the A.E.U. was still able to per-suade a number of firms of the need for adjustment to price changes[47] and metal employers generally made very little effort to absorb the 10s. federal Basic Wage increase.

The major disputes in 1956 occurred in Queensland and Sydney. In Queensland a state-wide campaign involving lengthy overtime bans and stoppages brought increased overaward payments, and an upward varia-tion of the state awards by 27/6d. with no absorption. In Sydney an 18 week stoppage at Bradford Kendall Ltd. ended in a compromise whereby part of the A.E.U.'s wage claim was granted while the engineers agreed at least to consider the firm's proposals for a bonus plan. Such offers of higher wages linked to schemes to increase productivity was a common reaction among employers in the fifties. Available estimates suggest that there was little change in the proportion of metal workers participating in incentive schemes between 1949 and 1969, and the A.E.U. remained the spearhead of the anti-incentives movement.[48] It remained as difficult as ever to apply payments by results directly to craftsmen's work and most of the employers' offers to the A.E.U. were aimed at stimulating skilled engineers' interest in overall plant output through bonus schemes and/or accepting work study evalua-tions which would improve productivity. The employers were helped by the fact that some other skilled unions, notably the E.T.U., were more flexible in their approach after the 1953 A.C.T.U. decision, and their acceptance of incentive schemes increased the pressure on A.E.U. members employed in the relevant shops. One notable example concerned five Australian Paper Manu-facturers Ltd plants where E.T.U. craftsmen and their assistants earned res-pectively £4 and 10s. more than the A.E.U. fitters in 1955. After three years

---

[47] E.g. *M.J.*, April 1956, p. 29.
[48] N. F. Dufty, 'Unions in Action; aims and methods', in Matthews and Ford, op. cit., p. 47; and *Industrial Relations . . .*, p. 154.

of friction and negotiation in which the rank and file at the Botany Bay plant took a harder line than A.E.U. officials, all plants accepted an 'efficiency payment'.[49] There were a number of other instances of A.E.U. members eventually accepting some kind of work study or incentive scheme but in the vast majority of cases the spontaneous and successful reaction was the traditional craftsman's opposition.[50] Some of the strongest opposition came from the particularly craft conscious Newcastle district,[51] and in New South Wales generally the memory of the notorious Taylor card system which had sparked off the 1917 General Strike was commonly invoked.[52] The A.E.U.'s biggest and longest contest in this field was with the Department of Supply when it attempted to introduce time and motion study into its various establishments. This battle of wills began in 1958, probably reached a peak of intensity with stoppages in Melbourne and Lithgow in 1963 and 1964 respectively, and dragged on for virtually the remainder of the decade. The A.C.T.U. backed the A.E.U.'s stand but the A.S.E. and F.I.A. broke ranks. The disadvantages of applying conspiracy theories to industrial relations were demonstrated by N.C.C. leader Santamaria who viewed the disputes at the munitions factories not as lineal descendants of the 1852 lock out, the 1917 New South Wales general strike, or hundreds of other disputes over payment by results and methods engineering, but as part of a C.P.A. scheme aimed at sabotaging Australia's contribution to developments in Indonesia and Vietnam.[53]

On the regular wages front 1957 saw the Newcastle and South Coast A.E.U. members pushing their somewhat unwilling leaders – and through them the Metal Trades Federation – into arranging for the reversion to the state award of workers in the steel companies and their main associates. The object was to gain the extra 21s. which was the current difference between state and Commonwealth Basic Wages.[54] Within a very few years, however, the A.E.U. steelmen had cause to reflect on the wisdom of their decisions. By 1959 the four successive federal Basic Wage increases totalling 40s. actually placed workers 2s. better off than in 1953 in real terms, while the A.E.U. steelmen found their minority position in the state arena made it difficult to extract margins increases.[55] In the federal field A.E.U. leaders looked on the first

[49] 'M.D.C.M.', 13/7/55, 17/8/55; *M.J.*, July 1955, p. 26, November 1955, p. 17, August 1956, p. 30, February 1957, p. 28, February 1958, p. 27.
[50] E.g. *M.J.*, January 1956, p. 28, December 1957, p. 25, February 1958, p. 26, June 1958, p. 25.
[51] E.g. *M.J.*, December 1954, p. 5; *Industrial Information*, volume 9, no. 12, p. 924.
[52] E.g. *M.J.*, April 1960, p. 16.
[53] B. A. Santamaria, *Point of View* (Melbourne, 1969), pp. 187, 191–3.
[54] *M.J.*, January 1957, pp. 5, 16–18, 27.
[55] *M.J.*, July 1959, p. 1, September 1959, pp. 6, 11.

three Basic Wage increases as particularly derisory — but all that could be expected in the absence of widespread agitation on the job by all unionists. This was of course the constant theme of A.E.U. spokesmen in joint union conferences and, although often impatient with the failure of other bodies to accept their representations, A.E.U. leaders were not completely dissatisfied with the overall trend of the union movement's thinking. The 1957 A.C.T.U. Congress was described as 'the greatest ever'.[56] The granting of representation on the A.C.T.U. Executive to six 'industry and services' groupings in addition to the generally conservative state Labor Councils was viewed as a particularly important breakthrough for the industrially aggressive unions. Another major step from the A.E.U.'s viewpoint was the direction by the 1957 Congress to the Executive to pursue wage claims through direct negotiations with employers if necessary. Almost immediately afterwards the Executive accepted an A.E.U. proposal, endorsed by the M.T.F., that the fitter's margin should be set at 126s., or 51s. more than the 1954 award rate.

The A.E.U. and a few of its aggressive allies were first off their marks — for the A.C.T.U. decision simply meant that their ongoing wages drive had now been formally endorsed, an official target had been set, and other unions were expected to join in the campaign. In fact A.E.U. officials were soon complaining about the lack of effort on the part of the non-metal unions. By June the M.T.F. had successfully negotiated an advantageous agreement with the oil companies which proved so useful a bargaining reference that, as well as calling on its members not to bow to the metal unions' wage demands, the M.T.E.A. unsuccessfully attempted to block its acceptance as a consent award by the Commission. Non-metal unions made little move until July when, after A.C.T.U. invitations to negotiate nationally on margins were rejected by employers' organisations, a conference of 54 federal unions decided that a campaign should be initiated under the supervision of the state Labor Councils. Even so the A.E.U. continued to complain of lack of active co-operation and of constant attempts to 'short circuit' the campaign by premature submission to the Commission. When the A.C.T.U. Executive called on the state Councils to put out educational propaganda on the margins' issue, A.E.U. organiser Southwell sardonically argued that it should be aimed at union officials rather than the rank and file.[57] At the end of 1958 A.E.U. reviews of the campaign revealed but patchy success, with state-government undertakings proving particularly obstinate. In the new year, as the A.E.U. kept grinding away, the Labor Councils finally began to put their

---

[56] *M.J.*, October 1957, p. 2.
[57] *M.J.*, November 1958, p. 27.

full weight behind the margins drive. In Melbourne a leading A.E.U. activist, N. Hill, was appointed full-time organiser of the T.H.C. campaign. By March respondents to a District Committee questionnaire in 60 shops in Melbourne revealed an average over-award payment of 45s. The 15s. Basic Wage rise in June was seen as a by-product of the national wage drive by A.E.U. leaders who insisted that industrial pressure be maintained even after the margins case itself began in August. In the background large-scale stoppages and overtime bans greeted the N.S.W. Industrial Commission's new award for the steel industry.

In the federal margins hearings the employers quoted extensively from the A.E.U. journal, particularly Southwell's reports, in an effort to show how the A.E.U. had led the way with direct industrial action to wrest wage concessions from metal employers 'under duress'. In turn the A.E.U. submitted its final Melbourne survey figures which revealed that the 120 shops covered paid an unweighted average of 47s. over the award rate and that three-quarters of them averaged between 55s. and 60s.[58] Outside the Commission the engineers continued to prise concessions from individual employers right up to the announcement of the bench's decision in November 1959 to lift margins by 28 per cent, or 21s. for fitters. In its judgment the four-member bench, while steering a middle course between the main arguments put forward by the two sides, took the 1954 principles as its criteria and arrived at this arbitrary percentage after consideration of economic capacity to pay and intervening price changes. No details were given as to how 28 per cent became the formula[59] but the A.E.U. had no doubt that the national campaign had helped make up the Commission's mind and was particularly cynical about the bench's view that union members' welfare would have been better served by simply bringing their claims to the Commission rather than first establishing higher wages on the job.[60]

Since the new fitter's rate was still 38s. less than the desired relativity to

[58] This compares with the Australian Metal Industries Association survey average figure for the same year of approximately 47s. for all males and 44s. for fitters in New South Wales. The A.M.I.A. figures for all states combined except Tasmania were 38s. and 36s. respectively. Isaac, 'Wage Drift in the Australian Metal Industries', p. 171.

[59] Hutson (*Six Wage Concepts*, pp. 97—8) points to an interesting picture which emerges when one puts to one side the standard comparison made by all contemporaries between the fitter and the Basic Wage earner. If instead the process worker's rate is lined up against that of the fitter it appears that the successive margins increases from 1947 onwards all restore relativities eroded in the process workers' favour by intervening flat rate increases in the Basic Wage. The relativity restored in these five cases is in the strikingly narrow band between 81 and 83 per cent.

[60] 92 *C.A.R.* 793 at 807.

the increased Basic Wage, the Commonwealth Council publicly expressed its dissatisfaction and immediately issued instructions to all organisers to be on their guard against any attempts by employers at absorption. These were not slow in commencing and Southwell, for example, considered the 1959 Christmas period as the busiest in his 16 years in office with, 'too many disputes to record'.[61] Yet, as in the past, the buoyant market for skill meant that the A.E.U. line held in all states. Similarly the new rates flowed on to other industries and this fact, together with criticisms levelled by the cost-push inflation school of thought at the Commission's 1959 decision helped persuade the bench to make no change in the Basic Wage at the end of the 1960 hearings. The A.E.U. saw this decision as a natural outcome of not preparing the ground with effective nationwide agitation, and one which clearly revealed the Commission as an agent of the Commonwealth government's fiscal policies.[62] The remainder of 1960, a boom year, saw the A.E.U. still disappointed with the overall approach of the rest of the labour movement. After a federal union conference to plan strategy after the Basic Wage decision the Commonwealth Council complained that recommendations ultimately acceptable to the A.C.T.U. Executive fell short of the militant tone of the debate.[63] The A.E.U.'s next main objective – apart from the everlasting striving for higher wages – was an extra weeks annual leave. This aim was stimulated by the friction arising in New South Wales where workers under state awards had gained three weeks in 1958. The A.E.U.'s recommendation for concerted action on the issue was unanimously accepted by the federal unions but in its leaders' view the campaign was short-circuited by the A.C.T.U. approaching the Commission before anything like sufficient groundwork had been laid through coordinated national agitation.[64] The Commission in its December judgment was sympathetic to the notion of extra leave but dismissed the application because of the current over-tight labour market. In the same year the coalminers' application for a 35 hour week which, if successful, the union movement hoped to use as a lever in other industries, was rejected by Mr Justice Gallagher – although he did grant them an extra week's annual leave.

In the eyes of the A.E.U. rank and file higher wages remained a dominant theme – so much so that officials often found themselves unable to tackle the backlog of organisational matters which had built up during the 1958–9

---

[61] *M.J.*, February 1960, p. 28.
[62] *Minutes of National Conference of Officials 1960*, p. 23; *A.E.U. Interstate Conference 1961*, p. 12; *M.J.*, April 1960, p. 6, May 1960, p. 2.
[63] *M.J.*, May 1960, p. 2.
[64] *A.E.U. Interstate Conference 1961*, p. 12.

campaign. The biggest single dispute occurred in Brisbane between July and September where a joint union campaign to maintain the advantageous pre-1959 relativities between state and federal awards resulted in a two months strike by employees at the Commonwealth Engineering Co. Ltd. works. The application of penal provisions brought increased solidarity and a stop-work meeting of 6,000 metal workers. The state government then declared a state of emergency in order to break the strike. This forced the Commonwealth Engineering workers to return to work but an estimated 150,000 Queensland workers stopped for 24 hours in protest, and record attendances were reported at meetings in all major centres. Overtime bans followed, but as trade slackened in 1961 the employers collectively stood firm, leaving the Queensland unions — whose members were still on rates higher than the federal award — to attempt to pick them off individually.

The year 1961 began with a 23 day stoppage at the Newcastle B.H.P. steelworks by 1,400 tradesmen over the alleged victimisation of an A.E.U. shop-steward. The state Commission levied £5,275 fines on the ten unions involved and the A.L.P. government withstood constant union pressure and the instructions of the 1961 A.L.P. Conference for their remission. The rest of the year saw most union campaigns pause as trade slackened. Skilled unemployment remained minimal but some of those A.E.U. craftsmen who were laid off found that over-award payments offering in their next job were below recent accepted levels. In South Australia employers made a determined but unsuccessful effort to absorb the 12s. Basic Wage increase and A.E.U. organisers in all centres reported a generally tougher employer approach in plant bargaining. An attempt to inaugurate a four day working week met firm metal union resistance.

In 1962 the campaign for three weeks annual leave began to gain some momentum but the Commission's acceptance of the principle in 1960 made many union leaders confident that the decision was a foregone conclusion. A.E.U. suggestions for a 24 hour stoppage on the combined issues of leave and the federal government's adult training proposals were rejected by the M.T.F. In the event the Commission now declared that the slackness in the economy prevented the inception of extra leave. Proceedings were adjourned until early in 1963. This delaying tactic proved to be the spur for the all-out campaign long urged by the A.E.U. and now co-ordinated by the state Labor Councils. In August Sydney organiser Buckley described the campaign as, 'the biggest effort that has been made since the end of world war No. 2' (*sic*).[65] In succeeding months it was linked to a drive to ensure an increase

---

[65] *M.J.*, August 1962, p. 23.

in marginal rates. Mass meetings, demonstrations and stoppages marked the progress of the campaign while, despite the pleas for solidarity from the employers' organisations, the A.E.U. and other metal unions continued to gain favourable concessions when establishing or renewing agreements with various employers. Only Shearer's vote against more aggression at the federal unions conference in November[66] marred the general picture of unity and progress.

When hearings before the Commission began in February the T.H.C. paralleled a meeting held in Sydney the previous September by organising a mass meeting of 3,000 delegates from works all over Melbourne. The A.E.U. regarded official sponsorship of such a demonstration while hearings were proceeding as a major step forward in union tactics.[67] Joint union agreements made at this time with the oil companies, I.C.I.A.N.Z. Ltd. and Cadbury–Fry–Pascall Pty. Ltd. all included suitable leave arrangements. A.E.U. leaders' calls for continued pressure in other plants met with a ready response and, in addition, shop stewards, financed by shop floor collections, attended the hearings. In the final stages of the hearings 3,000 metal unionists marched through the city to demonstrate outside the Commission.

In its April judgment the Commission granted the extra week, beginning in November 1963. Because of the leave concession the bench was not so greatly influenced on the margins issue by the considerable evidence presented by the unions on over-award payments — evidence which incidentally suggested that the Boilermakers' Society's shopfloor drive since 1959 had been even more successful than that of the A.E.U.[68] After lamenting that no work value evidence had been presented the bench decided that price movements since 1959, changes in productivity and the state of the economy warranted a 10 per cent rise in margins.

The remainder of 1963 went by in a fairly predictable fashion. After publicly condemning the inadequacy of the margins rise and the delay in implementation of the extra leave, the A.E.U. helped secure their flow on to other awards, successfully opposed before the Commission an M.T.E.A. attempt to give employers the right to split the annual leave period, and ensured no absorption of the new rates. At the A.C.T.U. Congress the A.E.U. delegation supported aggressive industrial policies and in the main debate on

---

[66] Above p. 257.

[67] *M.J.*, February 1963, p. 1.

[68] The A.E.U. average figures of 56/8 in Sydney, 53/10 in Victoria and 42/4 in Adelaide; compared with the Boilermakers' average of 70/10, 60s and 47/1 for the same three areas and the A.S.E.'s 53/5 in New South Wales and 43/3 in Victoria. 102 *C.A.R.* 138 at p. 145.

the penal provisions of the Arbitration Act helped amend the official recommendation along more aggressive lines. In industry itself the key dispute occurred in the rubber industry, climaxing in a three week strike of engineers, boilermakers and electricians in Melbourne. The penal provisions were invoked and £3,350 fines imposed before fruitful negotiations were initiated. The final settlement established in effect a 72s. over-award payment for tradesmen.[69] This was seen as the major breakthrough but increased payments were extracted from other employers before, during and after the rubber dispute.

The next year, 1964, followed an increasingly familiar pattern. The target was an increased Basic Wage and again the A.E.U. was pleased to see that a national campaign was to be co-ordinated by the state councils. In the two main centres the degree of determination differed with Melbourne, where Hill was again appointed full time T.H.C. campaign organiser, fulfilling A.E.U. expectations better than Sydney where the A.E.U. activists complained of the moderation of the Labor Council's stance.[70] One of the biggest disputes during the campaign was at C.I.G. Ltd., Melbourne involving nine unions and heavy fines under the penal provisions. By May the average Victorian engineer's over-award payment approximated 80s. The eventual decision of the Commission to lift the Basic Wage by 20s. and, more particularly, its apparent rejection of the employers' arguments for a Total Wage, were seen by the A.E.U. as a considerable victory.[71] Absorption attempts once more were defeated. Employers did, however, enjoy success in one important area. Employees had first gained long service leave rights in the previous decade and hitherto they had been regulated by varying state legislation. Considerable improvements to the N.S.W. system introduced by the A.L.P. government in 1963 added weight to insistent employer pressure for uniformity among federal award workers and the Commission issued its first long service leave awards during 1964.

September and October 1964 saw considerable industrial drama particularly in Melbourne, and probably marked the identification in the minds of a section of the general public of District Secretary Carmichael as the 'red' agitator behind all industrial unrest in the metals industry. In September a series of stoppages, demonstrations and marches through the city occurred in protest against price rises, the state budget, and the long delays in adjusting upwards the wages of workers in state instrumentalities. Although sub-

---

[69] For details see *M.J.*s August 1963–January 1964.
[70] *M.J.*, March 1964, pp. 23–4.
[71] E.g. *M.J.*, July 1964, p. 26.

stantial wage concessions were secured for government workers the campaign was marred by disagreement on tactics between the industrially aggressive unions led by the A.E.U. and the more pacific-minded state A.L.P. parliamentary leaders and the newly right wing T.H.C. Executive.[72] In October a similar tactical split occurred during a stoppage of some 18,000 workers including 1,700 A.E.U. men at General Motors-Holden (G.M.H.) plants. The roots of this dispute dated back to 1963 but the immediate cause was the company's rejection of a £3 wage claim put forward by the Vehicle Builders' Union and backed by A.E.U., A.S.E. and E.T.U. There is no doubt that all G.M.H. workers supported both the claim and the subsequent strike which spread to Adelaide, but the timing could hardly have been better from the viewpoint of G.M.H. which took an uncompromising stand throughout.[73] Heavy fines, other unions' lack of funds, the involvement of the A.C.T.U., the open opposition of the federal government and a very poor press all made it harder for the A.E.U. to gain support for an extension of the dispute. After four weeks a contentious secret ballot of the strikers brought a return to work on the understanding that negotiations on the wages issue would then take place. A.E.U. members denounced the A.C.T.U.'s role.[74] During the negotiations G.M.H. proved a hard bargainer and although some concessions were forthcoming the unions were forced to take their basic £3 claim to the Arbitration Commission. The research teams of the A.C.T.U. and the main unions concerned undertook detailed examinations of G.M.H.'s profitability and of productivity change in the industry. When the case began in 1966, an official of the United Auto Workers' Union was brought out from the U.S.A. to give evidence about the parent company. Despite this elaborate preparation the Commission rejected the union arguments, basically on the grounds that it would set a dangerous precedent if award rates distinguished between employers.[75] By this time, however, union attention was also being diverted by the general radical changes occurring in the arbitration sphere.

The 1965 joint hearings of the Basic Wage and margins cases, while giving 6s. more to the fitter, were described sincerely by A.E.U. leaders as 'one of the worst decisions the Commission has ever brought down'.[76] The rejection of the 1961—4 criteria was particularly resented, but after the amazing scenes of the unions trying to avoid being paid the margins increase and the employers

[72] For details of the relevant contemporary shifts in Victorian union politics see, R. M. Martin, 'Australian Trade Unionism, 1964', *The Journal of Industrial Relations*, 7, 1, pp. 77—87.

[73] Ibid., p. 83.

[74] *M.J.*, December 1964, p. 5.

[75] 115 *C.A.R.* 931.

[76] *M.J.*, July 1965, p. 1.

insisting that workers accept it,[77] the A.E.U. and its allies failed to persuade the other unions that direct action was called for. The 1965 A.C.T.U. Congress decided to argue the 1966 case along the prices—productivity lines which had held in 1961—4, only to find the Commission accepting the employers' proposals for a Total Wage concept and deciding to initiate a work value study on margins. Since the 1961 Professional Engineers' Case, in which the bench had awarded large increases on work value criteria this last notion was not seen as a particularly retrograde step by many in the union movement. Work value supporters included the E.T.U., the A.C.T.U. advocate, R.J. Hawke, and A.E.U. right winger C. Shearer[78] but the majority of metal unions were against the idea because of the work involved and fears for less skilled workers. Metal employers too had considerable reservations largely because of the upward movement of skilled margins recently occurring outside the Metal Trades Award. The trend began in Queensland in 1965 where the state Commission accepted union arguments based on existing over-award payments to lift the fitter's rate to $A15.50 or $A4.30 more than the federal rate. Thereafter, decisions, based *inter alia* on work value considerations, lifted the tradesman's rate by $A4.30 in the West Australian state engineering award, the federal shipwrights' award, the federal aircraft industry award, and the Tasmanian shipbuilders' wage board determinations. The Commission's decision at the end of the Metal Trades Work Value study led to the 1968 absorption struggle already referred to — which in turn helped bring confrontation on the penal provisions in the Commonwealth Act. In the background the new criteria for wage fixation were reaffirmed in successive National Wage Cases.

The A.E.U. and its allies viewed the swing away from the traditional dual wage structure of Basic Wage and margins with suspicion.[79] In essence, and despite some of the setbacks for employers which emerged from the work value study, the A.E.U. saw the changes in the sixties as evidence of employers taking the initiative away from a union movement too often divided on peripheral political issues to concentrate fully on industrial and arbitration policies. The employers' strategic superiority in the period was felt to derive from the increased pooling of their intelligence and research resources. The various employers' organisations had long attempted to co-ordinate national policies through *ad hoc* committees and when the Arbitration Court indicated in 1953 that evidence from individual employers would no longer be required the M.T.E.A. in

[77] For an A.E.U. description of this 'Mad Hatters' Tea Party' see Hutson, *Six Wage Concepts*, pp. 66—73.
[78] 'Election Address' 1964.
[79] For details see Hutson, *Six Wage Concepts*, p. 231.

particular aimed to integrate its research with other associations.[80] The important breakthrough came in 1959 with the formulation of the National Employers' Policy and Consultative Committee (N.E.P.C.C.) which formalised the *ad hoc* arrangements and consisted of Presidents or nominees of the A.M.I.A.' the Associated Chambers of Manufactures of Australia, the Australian Council of Employers' Federations and the Australian Woolgrowers and Graziers Council.[81] The Working Party for the N.E.P.C.C. was made up of the senior staff industrial officers of each of the member organisations. In 1961 the N.E.P.C.C. became the National Employers' Policy Committee (N.E.P.C.) and the Working Party became the National Employers' Industrial Committee (N.E.I.C.). The N.E.I.C. is the executive of the N.E.P.C. and, through its experienced industrial officer members, it acted as the employers 'think tank' initiating national policy during the sixties. The metal employers organisations were particularly pleased with the development, and the comments of the A.M.I.A. President in 1960 on the significance of N.E.P.C.C. and the need for metal firms both to take the lead and to ensure a growth in national unity among employers are reminiscent of nothing so much as an A.E.U. leader talking of his union's role in the wider union movement.[82] Just as with the metal unions, unity among metal employers' organisations was not always perfect. The ever dynamic and forceful M.T.E.A. moved into Victoria in 1965 inducing the state Chambers of Manufactures to change the name of its Engineering and Allied Trades Division to that of the Metal Industries Association of Victoria (M.I.A.V.). But although relations between M.T.E.A. and M.I.A.V. were not very cordial at first, in February 1970 they merged into the Metal Trades Industry Association of Australia.

A major response of the A.E.U. to the growing co-ordination of employers' industrial policies was to seek closer links with other metal unions than the M.T.F. provided. This time the momentum towards amalgamation proved irreversible.

IV

The major advantage to the A.E.U. of the ties with Britain in the post-war years was the existence of an appeals system to which both sides in the internal controversies had equal recourse and in whose impartiality both sides reposed equal confidence. Thus the Executive Council and the Final Appeal Court played a key role in the internal Australian contro-

---

[80] *Metal Trades Journal*, 15/1/54.
[81] *Metal Trades Journal*, 16/2/59; see also Isaac and Ford, *Australian Labour Relations*, pp. 256–7; Dufty, *Industrial Relations*, pp. 59–68.
[82] *Metal Trades Journal*, 15/8/60.

versies. One result of this was to focus British attention on the desirability and feasibility of maintaining the link with Australia: and even as the right wingers were losing their last electoral skirmishes in Australia, moves were being set afoot in both countries which were to bring about the complete separation of the two Sections on 30 June 1968. Yet although the actions of Shearer and McDowell and the decisions of the Industrial Court — notably in the Parkes case — brought the issue of separation to a head on the British side, the severance of the link between the two countries was in fact the culmination of older post-war trends within the union. On the British side the original stimuli were the endemic general difficulties of long distance supervision and specific financial problems which arose in Australia in the 1950s. On the Australian side there was an increasing post-war awareness of the need to gain complete autonomy — although for some time this was tempered by an anxiety first to place the union's finances on a sounder footing.

The rapid expansion of Australian membership in the 1940s threw into even bolder relief the drawbacks of operating with an administrative structure essentially designed for British conditions. The low officer: rank-and-file ratio became a more significant disadvantage in the post-war years. On the one hand A.E.U. officials were increasingly distracted from their normal duties by internal dissensions — which were exacerbated by the A.E.U. constitution, particularly its election procedures. On the other, rival unions free from faction fighting found that the advent of full employment and associated healthy union finances enabled them to expand their organising staff as the situation demanded. Thus A.E.U. officials, prompted by the complaints of the activist rank and file, became increasingly aware that the union was being surpassed in organisational efficiency by its competitors — particularly by its arch rival the A.S.E. Until the appointment of a full-time District Secretary in 1956 for example, the Adelaide A.E.U. organiser using public transport competed single-handed with three A.S.E. full-time officials each with a union car. In Sydney in 1964 seven A.S.E. full-time officials were matched with three A.E.U. equivalents assisted by a fourth who was also supposed to organise the whole South Coast industrial complex. The situation in other capitals was no better while country members were particularly vocal about their neglect by overworked organisers. Their reaction ranged from the threats of the Werris Creek and Tasmanian country branches to resign *en masse* and join the A.S.E., to Geelong members' repeated pleas for the restoration of the A.E.U.'s 'prestige' in their area.[83]

[83] 'C.C.M.', 16/11/56, 24/3/59, 28/4/59, 24/7/63.

Although each side in the internal A.E.U. conflict tended publicly to blame the other whenever remotely possible for the union's organisational problems, both left and right wingers in their saner moments attributed it to the restrictions placed by the union's constitution on the ability of the A.E.U. to compete with the A.S.E.[84] It seems likely that, outside Newcastle, right wingers were often more radical in their thinking in this direction than their opponents who tended to have a greater respect for the time-honoured way of doing things in the A.E.U. That this was not always the most efficient way, and that the A.E.U.'s organisational problems were not wholly due to the British link, is indicated by General Secretary Gardner's finding during his 1955 visit to Australia that federal officials wasted far too much time performing office-girls' jobs — including writing long-hand minutes of proceedings and sorting mail.

In addition to being under-staffed the Australian Section was also prevented from establishing suitable permanent offices in outlying metropolitan areas such as Paramatta, or in newer industrial centres such as Wollongong or Geelong. Even in the capital cities accommodation was a perennial problem and the Executive Council long acted as a brake to expansion of office space although eventually it aided modified extensions in Sydney and Melbourne in the late 1950s. Transport was another bone of contention — for the geographically compact British Section refused to agree to the provision of organisers' cars from the General Fund. This left the Australian leaders with the task of persuading the rank-and-file to agree to an extra voluntary levy. In 1955 a postal ballot on the issue drew 25,520 votes and with the activists heavily outnumbered the suggestion was rejected by a two to one majority — leaving Australia's largest manufacturing union in a unique and ludicrous position. The problem was not solved until 1959 when the activists decided overwhelmingly in favour of a levy in a branch ballot one fifth of the size of the 1955 vote.

The desire for amalgamation again grew among metal unionists in the 1950s. There were a variety of reasons for this, including technological change, the further integration of metal union activity before arbitration tribunals and growing feelings of solidarity induced both by the tribunals' use of 'penal powers' and the rising importance of shop committees. Among left wingers in particular the events surrounding the A.L.P. Split seemed to point to the need for unity against a dangerous outside foe. This feeling

---

[84] See e.g. C. Shearer's comments in 'Report of Proceedings at Meetings of Commonwealth Council with the General Secretary, Bro. C. W. Hallett, commencing 24/2/64'; and W. Buckley's and V. Clarke's reports, *1964 National Conference of A.E.U. Full-Time Officials.*

became particularly prevalent in the A.E.U. where, in addition, the old and lofty feelings of exclusivity had been further eroded by the growing awareness that the union was no longer in a markedly more secure financial position than its fellows.

The essence of the problem was benefit payments — and superannuation benefit in particular. In the eight financial years between 1950 and 1958 £418,000 was paid out to superannuated members with the annual sum growing from £38,000 to £70,000. By the end of this period the fewer than 2 per cent of A.E.U. members entitled to this benefit were draining off nearly 24 per cent of the union's income. As a result in 1958 — a year when dispute benefit was as low as £8,000 — General Fund expenditure exceeded General Fund income by over £23,000. The British Section, whose membership topped one million in 1960, suffered from a similar actuarial imbalance and its expenditure exceeded contributions for eight years 1951–7 inclusive. Yet British A.E.U. funds continued to rise steadily as a result of interest derived from the union's investments. In 1954, for example, when combined funds stood at £11 millions the increment was £290,000 (sterling). By contrast in Australia the 1946–7 Victorian stoppage had absorbed the A.E.U.'s hitherto ample resources and thereafter the General Fund was only kept afloat by nominal borrowing from the Supplementary and Superannuation Reserve Funds. Industrial fines and costs of litigation arising out of the internal controversies did not improve matters.

In 1951 Executive Council instructed the Australians to follow British practice of charging an 'all-in' contribution instead of continuing to separate the basic contribution and the extra Supplementary levy.[85] The Commonwealth Council took this opportunity as an excuse to cease maintaining separate balance sheets for the three main funds. It was not long, however, before the Executive Council picked up this move and the capable and indefatigable Gardner thereupon commenced an investigation on Australian finances. He combined this with a detailed examination of the Australian Rule-book to ascertain the degree of divergence from the General Rules. This second task was prompted by the many 'illegal' suggestions forwarded to London by the 1949 Australian Rules Revision Meeting. Given the many other demands on his time and the usual difficulties arising from long-distance communication, it took Gardner over three years to complete his investigation. In all he found that some 540 alterations were required in the Australian rules to bring them into conformity with the General Rule Book. The main cause of the vast majority of these minor discrepancies was

[85] Above, p. 31.

the failure of the Australian Section over the years to adopt all the changes made by the British Rules Revision Meetings. Commonwealth Council's excuse for this was threefold: the fact that Australia had not been represented at Rules Revision Meetings in Britain between 1919 and 1945; the irrelevance to Australia of many of the rule changes; the existence of overriding labour legislation in Australia which prevented implementation of certain British rules. The third factor was to prove the main source of disagreement over rules in the next few years, for it involved differing definition of the key word 'conditions' in the rule allowing the Australian section to amend the General Rules in order to bring them '... into conformity with Labour legislation and conditions prevailing in the Commonwealth'.

With the aim of viewing the operation of the Australian Section at first hand, Gardner visited Australia at the beginning of 1955. During his stay he made many suggestions towards improving administrative efficiency, including central auditing and purchasing systems. He also became aware of some of the problems unique to Australia. His death in 1956 removed a sympathetic voice from Executive Council just prior to a serious rift between it and the 1957 Australian Rules Revision Meeting. The British saw the latter's main task as the incorporation of Gardner's 540 alterations in the Australian Rule Book, together with the further changes since made by the 1955 Rules Revision Meeting. The Australian delegates had other ideas. In part they were spurred on by conferences on possible amalgamation convened by the M.T.F. earlier in the year which had resulted in the Commonwealth Council tentatively approaching London about holding a ballot in Australia on autonomy. But they were also resentful of Executive Council's decision, when twice recalling the 1955 Rules Revision Meeting, not to include the two Australian delegates on the grounds that the expense was not justified since no specifically Australian matter was involved. The 1958 Final Appeal Court was to accept the Australian complaints, and the 1960 Blackpool Rules Revision Meeting was to reject an Executive Council suggesting that the rules should be altered to allow it to use its discretion in such cases. But in 1957 these rank and file judgments still lay in the future and the Australian Rules Revision Meeting passed a resolution expressing its resentment in terms which Executive Council was later to describe as 'almost impertinent.'[86] The London office was taken aback by other decisions of the Meeting when, after considerable delay, they finally obtained galley proofs of the proposed new Australian Rule Book. To their alarm they found that many of

---

[86] 'Report of Meeting Between Executive Council and Bro. A. Horsburgh, Commonwealth Council, held in General Office on 8th September, 1958'.

Gardner's suggestions had not been implemented while other changes had been introduced which the London office considered to be 'illegal'.

While the disagreement over both the Australian and Gardner amendments basically hinged on the definition of local 'conditions' in the rules, two other factors influenced the Executive Council's attitude to the Australian Branches in 1957. The most important of these was the state of the Australian finances. After Gardner's visit the Executive Council ordered a separation of the three main funds and a reconstitution of the Supplementary Fund balance at a notional figure for the year ending September 1955. Even so the Commonwealth Council was unable to implement the instruction, for the low nominal sum recommended still exceeded the Australian Section's total liquid assets. Instead it asked for London's help to counter the problem of Superannuation Benefit which was aggravated by immigrant Benefit members who had already paid part of their contributions to the British General Fund. The Executive Council did help with funds for the purchase of office space in Victoria Parade, Melbourne, but the failure to reconstitute the separate funds according to what London saw as a reasonable timetable, plus the 'impertinent' behaviour of the Australian Rules Revision Meeting made the British executive sceptical of Australia's goodwill.

A second factor influencing British thinking was the recent negotiations leading to the separation in 1957 of the South African branches from the parent union. The cause of the break was the South African government's insistence that its apartheid policy be confirmed in A.E.U. rules in that country but, distasteful though this issue may have been, the actual discussions over financial settlement between the two Sections had proved most amicable. Given their completely different industrial experience the South African engineers had marshalled their financial resources far better than the Australians in the post-war years, and separation occurred without any transfer of funds in either direction. Thereafter A.E.U. President W. J. Carron never tired of pointing to the *ex post* fact that the South African separation took place on the basis of, 'What we have we hold.'

Given their basic financial problems the members of Commonwealth Council were not too keen to push for autonomy until London had provided aid. Thus they swallowed their pride, accepted the British strictures, agreed to go along with the London interpretation of local 'conditions' in the rules — and consequently, with the reluctant agreement of the activists, deleted all the 'illegal' 1957 amendments and implemented the Gardner suggestions in a new Rule Book printed in February 1959. Commonwealth Council also promised to buckle down to a thorough reorganisation of the union's finances. Efforts in this latter direction were aided by the energy of Garland, the new Council Secretary, and the appointment as Finance Officer of G. J. Stead whose meticulous endeavours were to earn the praise even of the Executive Council. From 1959 onwards the creaking A.E.U. administrative structure in Australia was progressively transformed along modern office-management lines. In return the London office set out a new and more realistic formula for the reconstitution of the three main funds and repayment of the General Fund's 'debt' to the two other funds. It also transferred £82,751 (sterling) from the British to the Australian Superannuation Reserve Fund. While still keeping a strict watch on Australian expenditure, even to the extent of admonishing Commonwealth Council for not using airmail paper when sending bulky correspondence to London, the Executive Council's worst fears and suspicions were gradually assuaged. In the new harmonious atmosphere only the occasional irritation broke the surface. Of these the Executive Council's refusal to permit a temporary replacement during Councilman Stone's lengthy illness was perhaps the most annoying. Yet both sides drew morals from their experience in the second half of the fifties and at the 1960 Rules Revision Meeting each tried to have the Rules amended to its advantage. The Australians endeavoured to gain *de facto* autonomy by deleting the clause giving the Executive Council control over the Commonwealth Council, while the Executive Council tried to delete all reference to the Australian branches' power to alter the rules in accord with local industrial legislation. In their wisdom the rank and file delegates rejected both moves alike.

The years 1960—3 saw the British executive coming slowly to realise that the Australian branches had not been merely awkward or rebellious in the past when they had argued that many British rule amendments would not be acceptable to the Commonwealth Industrial Registrar. The occasion of this painful lesson was the attempt, made at Executive Council insistence, to register the 1959 Australian Rule Book. A long, complicated three way correspondence ensued, with Commonwealth Council playing a mainly passive liaison role between Registrar and Executive Council. After much haggling and lengthy argument before the Industrial Court, the 1959 Rule Book was perforce amended by an Australian Rules Revision Meeting and finally registered with the Court in July 1962. No sooner had the London office heaved a sigh of relief than the Registrar refused to accept some of the changes necessitated by decisions of the 1963 Recalled Rules Revision Meeting. This time the Executive Council did not even bother to argue with the Registrar for by now, in addition to long-distance battle-weariness, the MacDonald case had necessitated further rule alterations and, most significant of all, the court's decision in the Parkes case challenged the whole idea of British jurisdiction in Australia. Thus by the time of Hallett's visit the Executive Council had been fully primed to accept severance as inevitable.

On the Australian side the desire for autonomy had grown again as the worst of the financial problems began to recede – but calls by a conference of officials in 1960 and by a rank and file Interstate Conference in 1961 for a ballot on the issue were temporarily set aside during the climacteric left – right struggle of 1962–4. When the battle ended attention inevitably reverted to organisational problems. The prospects of amalgamation had once more brightened when in 1964 the A.C.T.U. Executive decided to call the Metal Group unions together to discuss the matter. A 1964 A.E.U. conference of officials, after thoroughly debating organisational problems and the need for amalgamation, again called for a ballot on autonomy so that members' feelings could be known before the 1965 Blackpool Rules Revision Meeting. Although this suggestion was not implemented, it was at the Blackpool meeting that the crucial steps were taken which led to severance of the link between the two Sections three years later.

On the Blackpool agenda there were no fewer than 190 suggestions for alteration to the Australian rules – virtually all of them stemming from the Parkes case and other recent Industrial Court decisions. The considered intent of the British leaders was made clear on the opening day when, to the surprise of the two Australian delegates, two suggestions from Queensland branches were listed for immediate attention. One of these in effect called for a ballot to establish Australian members' views on autonomy and, if they were in favour, for Commonwealth Council then to commence negotiations with Executive Council. The other suggestion simply called for Commonwealth Council to complete autonomy negotiations in 1965. Sir William Carron, in introducing these suggestions, argued that the second was preferable. The Australian delegates, veteran ex-official A. Wilson and fellow N.S.W. activist N. Clapton, were taken aback by the determination of the British executive to settle the separation issue so quickly, and sought to stall for time by arguing that the call for a ballot was more democratic and should be considered first. The Meeting decided against them by 40 votes to 12 (2 abstentions) and went on to endorse the commencement of negotiations. Other important decisions included agreement to close the Australian Benefit Section to new entrants and to double the Supplementary Levy from 3d. to 6d. Among the rule amendments enforced by the Parkes and other cases were the creation in Australia of a biennial equivalent of the National Committee to be known for its short life as the Commonwealth Delegate

Meeting, the restriction of the right to vote in A.E.U. elections to 'financial' members, and the extension to all members of eligibility for any elective office. Yet despite the obvious imminence of separation, the meeting rejected the Australian delegates' arguments for three more organisers to be paid from the General Fund.

There were two bouts of roundtable negotiations on separation: the first in January 1966 when Horsburgh and Garland visited London, the second in February–March 1967 when three Executive Councilmen assisted by the new General Secretary, J. Conway, visited Australia. The key issue was the terms of the final financial settlement. The British tacitly accepted that some transfer of funds to Australia was inevitable but, as bargaining ploys, they pointed to the 'What we have we hold' outcome of the South African separation, emphasised the past 'mismanagement' of the Australian finances, and implied that a reduction of arrears to average British levels would considerably improve the current Australian balance sheets. For their part the Australians stressed the unity of the international union, recalled transfers of funds from Sydney to London in 1897, 1922 and 1928, pointed to the fact that the past financial problems would not have arisen if the Australian branches had not loyally accepted British-made rules governing the scale of Benefit contributions and payments, and reminded the Executive Council that Australian funds had never benefited from the huge British investments from the Superannuation Reserve Fund. While prepared to settle for a lot less the Australians outwardly claimed that their share of A.E.U. funds should be increased by a transfer of £519,000 sterling from London.

The Sydney bargaining sessions eventually ended in agreement that £209,216 sterling would be transferred to Sydney to bring the Australian Section's assets up to a round £500,000 — but at this point the Executive Council in London informed its delegation and Commonwealth Council that it had separately reached a final and unalterable decision. The Australians were to be offered £146,749, take it or leave it. The British delegation then left for home accompanied by Australian anger at both the arbitrary nature and peremptory tone of this communication. Further haggling continued long distance and a final agreement was clinched in August 1967 on the basis of a transfer to Australia of £155,008/11s/2d. The final steps in the negotiations were taken at the Recalled Rules Revision Meeting held in Brighton in March 1968. The Meeting's two main tasks were to delete all reference to Australia from the General Rule Book and to incorporate therein the necessary changes following from the British Section's recent amalgamation with the Foundry Workers' Union. The latter included a change in name to the Amalgamated Union of Engineering Workers. Of more interest to Australian members than these formalities, however, was the reception given by the Executive Council to Wilson and Clapton's arguments that in order to offset the recent devaluation of sterling the financial settlement should be increased by $A60,000. H. P. Scanlon, who had been on the 1967 delegation to Australia and who had since succeeded Carron as President, proved sympathetic to this view and after the Meeting ended Executive Council formally agreed to the Australian proposals. On 30 June 1968 the 116-year-old ties were finally severed in a completely amicable fraternal atmosphere confirmed by the subsequent visit to Australia of Scanlon in January 1969 and negotiation of an interest-free loan from the British union of £100,000 for the purchase of land and the building in Sydney of a new Head Office.

While the financial details of separation were being hammered out over these three years, the Australian Section's internal efficiency and domestic financial resources had been further improved both by administrative action and by decisions of Commonwealth Delegate and Rules Revision Meetings in 1967 and 1968. One of the most important changes was the decision to transfer the Supplementary Fund surplus to the General Fund to assist in Benefit payments. However, the fact that nine-tenths of the surplus was channelled in this direction indicated the drain on Australian funds that the closed Benefit Sections still represented. In 1967 it was estimated that of $A200,000 paid out in Benefits only $A76,000 was covered by the extra 20 cents per week paid by Benefit members. Consequently in April 1968 the resumed Australian Rules Revision Meeting decided to terminate these sections completely at the end of 1975. A compensatory scheme of increased funeral benefit or contribution exemption was provided for those Benefit members who elected to transfer before then to the Industrial Section (under its new name of Adult Male Section). Superannuation payments would cease completely after 31 December 1985. The Meeting also determined to increase contributions and create 10 new elective positions upon gaining autonomy.

The delegates at the 1967 and 1968 Meetings also fashioned the constitution of the post-autonomy A.E.U. and their natural desire to create a structure more suitable to Australian conditions than the nineteenth century 'New Model' was strengthened by the implications of amalgamation discussions currently being held with other metal unions. The old A.E.U. atomistic branch structure was replaced by 68 larger branches meeting monthly, and the administrative work of the old branch secretary was largely taken over by the respective state offices. Branches were grouped into zones for the election of delegates to State Councils which met quarterly and included all full-time state officials. Annual State Conferences became the main policy making bodies on state matters. At the federal level the old Commonwealth Councilmen became National Organisers and the Council was extended to include elected state representatives. Council meetings were to be held when necessary and at least every six months. The supreme policy, rule-making and final appeals authority of the union was a biennial Commonwealth Conference consisting of the Commonwealth Council, 45 elected rank and file delegates and 8 state officials.

The new rules were successfully registered in September 1968 and the words 'Australian Section' were officially dropped from the A.E.U.'s title in February 1969. Increased officer strength, a rise in contribution rates, further administrative streamlining including computerisation of the union's membership accounts, and the opening of offices on the South Coast and at Paramatta all had their effects on the union's finances and its membership levels. The numbers on the A.E.U. rolls had picked up slowly in the early sixties as a result of the first administrative shake-outs but with the post-autonomy changes membership climbed by nearly 11,000 to 93,583 between January 1969 and March 1971. A growing atmosphere of enthusiasm and zest for change and growth became apparent in this period and it was augmented by the long awaited amalgamation.

The first post-war metal union amalgamation occurred in 1966 when the Boilermakers' and Blacksmiths' Societies combined into a single union (B.B.S.). This move was applauded by the A.E.U. and agreement was speedily reached for a working integration between it and the B.B.S. This involved the establishment early in 1967 of a Combined Research Department and the reciprocal movement in Sydney of the B.B.S. federal office to Chalmers Street and the A.E.U. district office to the B.B.S. premises in George Street. Joint occupancies were initiated almost simultaneously in Tasmania and West Australia. In January 1968 a committee of federal officers from the two unions began discussing amalgamation details and it speedily decided that, given certain difficulties posed by the Arbitration Acts, the best method of carrying out the actual process was that used in the B.B.S. merger i.e. for one of the unions to change its rules and broaden its structure to accommodate the members of the other union. As soon as this became effective the registration of the other union would cease. Since the A.E.U. was the larger of the two and since its new rules were actually being drawn up at this time in preparation for autonomy it was agreed that they should form the basis for the amalgamated union. Approaches were made to the other metal unions.

Not surprisingly in view of the differing industrial and political outlooks of the two unions' leaders, the A.S.E. failed to show any great enthusiasm for amalgamation with the A.E.U. even after the removal of the British control which had nominally stood between the two bodies for three quarters of a century. Similarly the right wing F.I.A. leadership declined A.E.U.–B.B.S. advances. The Moulders showed more interest but eventually they too decided against abandoning their separate existence. Approaches to the Sheet Metal Workers' Union met a positive response and representatives of this third large union joined in the discussions in 1970. A detailed timetable of amalgamation was soon compiled and, in March 1971, the rank and file of all three unions endorsed the proposals. In April 1971 the federal conferences of the three unions were held simultaneously to iron out various problems. Metal employers supported the merger and, despite some last minute litigation by right wing members of the B.B.S. and some unsuccessful pressure applied by the D.L.P. to the McMahon government, the giant new Amalgamated Metal Workers union of 160,000 members was officially born on 2 April 1973. While many members doubtless experienced a twinge of regret for the final passing of the old order, A.E.U. activists now felt much better equipped to cope with the new era of industrial relations ushered in by contemporary radical changes in the arbitration and bargaining arenas, and the appearance in Canberra of the first Labor government in 23 years.

Selected Bibliography

I: Manuscripts, Theses and Other Unpublished Material

(a) Transcripts of Cases heard before the Commonwealth Court of Conciliation and Arbitration. Lodged in the Archives of the Registrar of the Commonwealth Court, Melbourne

Application of H. V. McKay for an Order under the Excise Tariff Act October/ November 1907.

Amalgamated Society of Engineers and The Commonwealth of Australia, (1918).

Amalgamated Society of Engineers and The Adelaide Steamship Company and Others (1920/1).

Federated Moulders' (Metals) Union of Australia and The Adelaide Steamship Company and Others (1924).

The Amalgamated Engineering Union and J. Alderdice & Company Pty Ltd and Others (1926).

Australian Coach Motor Car Tram Car Waggon Builders' Wheelwrights' Stock Makers' Employees' Federation and Holdens Ltd and Others (1929).

Amalgamated Engineering Union and Others and The Metal Trades Employers' Association and Others (1928–30).

(b) Transcripts of Cases heard before the New South Wales Arbitration Court. Lodged in the State Archives, Mitchell Library, Sydney

Amalgamated Ironworkers' Assistants' Union of New South Wales v Chapman and Co. Ltd (1907).

The Stove and Piano-Frame Moulders' and Stovemakers' Employees' Union of New South Wales v Fred Metters & Co. (1907).

Amalgamated Society of Engineers (N.S.W.) and The Iron Trade Employers Association (1908).

(c) Records of the Amalgamated Engineering Union

Australasian Council Minutes.

Commonwealth Council Minutes.

Investment Committee Minutes.

Commonwealth Council Bulletins.

Commonwealth Council Circulars.

Melbourne District Committee Minutes.

Melbourne Political Committee Minutes.

Sydney Political Committee Minutes.

Lithgow District Committee Minutes.

Minutes of Interstate Conferences.

Minutes of National Conferences.

Minutes of Rules Revision Meetings.

Minutes of Commonwealth Delegates Meetings.

Minutes of Melbourne District Shop Stewards Quarterly Meetings.

Adelaide No. 2 Branch Minutes.

N.S.W. Railway and Tramway Sub-Committee Minutes.

Addresses of Candidates for Commonwealth Council Positions.

Files of Correspondence between Commonwealth and Executive Councils.

(d) Other trade union records

Australasian Society of Engineers, Federal Council: Official Quarterly Membership Returns to the Commonwealth Statistician, 1941–53.

Australasian Society of Engineers, South Australian Branch: Secretary's Half-Yearly Report, 1936–54. Half-Yearly Statements of Income and Expenditure, 1920–54. Minutes of Executive Meetings, 1924–54. Minutes of Branch Meetings, 1924–54.

Federated Moulders' (Metal) Union of Australia, Victorian District: Minutes of the Executive Committee, 7 December 1906–9 January 1934. Minutes of General Meetings, 18 January 1912–16 December 1920.

Stove and Piano Frame Moulders' and Stovemakers' Employees' Union: Minutes of Meetings, 4 April 1906–22 September 1924.

(e) Theses

Dixson, Miriam: Reformists and Revolutionaries: An Interpretation of the Relations Between the Socialists and the Mass Labour Organizations in New South Wales 1919–1927 with Special Reference to Sydney. Ph.D. Thesis, Australian National University, 1965.

Isaac, J. E.: Economic Analysis of Wage Regulation in Australia 1920–1947. Ph.D. Thesis, University of London, 1949.

Keating, Michael: The Growth and Composition of the Australian Workforce 1910–11 to 1960–61. Ph.D. Thesis, Australian National University, 1967.

Macarthy, P. G.: The Harvester Judgment — An Historical Assessment. Ph.D. Thesis, Australian National University, 1967.

Merritt, J. A.: A History of the Federated Ironworkers' Association of Australia,

1909–1952. Ph.D. Thesis, Australian National University, 1967.

Rawson, D. W.: The Organisation of the Australian Labor Party, 1916–1941. Ph.D. Thesis, Melbourne University, 1954.

Sheridan, T.: A History of the Amalgamated Engineering Union (Australian Section), 1920–1954. Ph.D. Thesis, Australian National University 1967.

Turner, I. A. H.: Industrial Labor and Politics 1900–1921. Ph.D. Thesis, Australian National University, 1962.

Waterman, A. M. C. W.: Fluctuations in the Rate of Growth: Australia, 1948–49 to 1963–64. Ph.D. Thesis, Australian National University, July 1967.

(f) Unpublished or Privately Circulated Papers, and Drafts or Manuscripts

Blake, J. D.: Communist Party of Australia, 1945–66 (mimeographed draft).

Davenport, R. F.: Report of the All-Australian Trade Union Congress, February– March 1930.

Goodwin, K.: History of the A.S.E. (typed draft).

Howard and Associates Pty Ltd.: Research Service: Report on the Pattern of Industrial Disputes in Australia, The United States and Great Britain.

Merritt, J. A.: The Federated Ironworkers' Association in the Depression, unpublished paper, Australian National University, January 1969.

Paterson, J.: A.C.S.P.A. Census Report (mimeographed) Australian Council of Salaried and Professional Associations, 1965.

Stevens, S. P.: A preliminary report on the effect of the 40-Hour week in Australian industry, Economic Monograph 116, Economic Society of Australia and New Zealand, N.S.W. Branch, September 1949.

II Published Material

(a) Royal Commissions

COMMONWEALTH

Royal Commission on the Tariff, *Parliamentary Papers*, 1906, Vols. 4 and 5.

Royal Commission on the Basic Wage, *Parliamentary Papers*, 1920–1, Vol. 4.

Commonwealth-State Apprenticeship Inquiry, *Report of Committee*, 1954.

NEW SOUTH WALES

Royal Commission into the Cause of Decline in Apprenticeship, *Parliamentary Papers*, 1911–12, Vol. 2.

Interim Report of the Royal Commission into the Alleged Shortage of Labour in New South Wales, *Parliamentary Papers*, 1911–12, Vol. 2.

Interim Report and Minutes of Evidence of Royal Commission on Industrial Arbitration in the State of New South Wales, *Parliamentary Papers*, 1911–12, Vol. 2.

Report and Minutes of Evidence of Royal Commission on the Job and Time Cards

System in the Tramway and Railway Workshops of the Railway Commissioners of New South Wales, *Parliamentary Papers*, 1918, Vol. 6.

Report of the Royal Commission on Standard Hours, *Parliamentary Papers*, 1920, Vol. 2.

Report and Minutes of Evidence of Royal Commission into the Administration, Control and Economy of the Railway and Tramway Services of New South Wales, *Parliamentary Papers*, 1922, Vol. 3.

Report of the Select Committee of the Legislative Assembly upon the Employment of Youth in Industry, *Parliamentary Papers*, 1940–1, Vol. 1.

SOUTH AUSTRALIA

First Progress Report and Minutes of Evidence of Royal Commission on Manufacturing and Secondary Industries in South Australia, *Parliamentary Papers*, 1926, Vol. 2.

VICTORIA

Royal Commission Inquiring Into The Origins, Aims, Objects And Funds Of The Communist Party In Victoria And Other Related Matters, *Report*, 1950.

GREAT BRITAIN

Royal Commission on Trade Unions and Employers' Associations 1965–8, *Report*, 1968.

(b) Other Official Publications

COMMONWEALTH

Census of the Commonwealth of Australia, 1911, 1921, 1933, 1947, 1954, 1961, 1967.

Civilian Register 1943.

Commonwealth Arbitration Reports.

Commonwealth Law Reports.

Commonwealth Year Books.

Commonwealth Bureau of Census and Statistics, *Labour Reports; Manufacturing Industry; Overseas Trade Bulletins; Production Bulletins; Secondary Industry Bulletins.*

Commonwealth Department of Information, *Facts and Figures of Australia at War; Australia in Facts and Figures.*

Commonwealth Department of Labour and National Service, *Industrial Information Bulletin; Training for Skilled Occupations*, Melbourne, 1962.

Commonwealth Department of National Development, *The Structure and Capacity of Australian Manufacturing Industry*, Melbourne, 1952.

Development and Migration Commission, Report on Unemployment and Business Stability in Australia, *Parliamentary Papers*, 1926–8, Vol. 5.

Federal Law Reports.

Inter-State Commission, Tariff Investigation 1914–16, Report, *Parliamentary Papers*, 1914–17, Vol. 7.

Occupation Survey, 1945.

Report of the Committee of Economic Enquiry, Canberra, 1965.

Tariff Board, *Reports*.

NEW SOUTH WALES

Industrial Arbitration Reports.

Industrial Commission of N.S.W., *The Apprenticeship System in N.S.W. A Report by the Commission to the Minister for Labour and Industry — July 1968*, (Sydney, 1969).

Industrial Gazette.

The New South Wales Strike Crisis 1917. Report by the Industrial Commissioner of the State (J. B. Holme). *Parliamentary Papers*, 1917–18, Vol. 2.

QUEENSLAND

Legislative Record of the Labour Government of Queensland, 1926.

Report of Economic Commission on the Queensland Basic Wage, 1925.

VICTORIA

Reports of the Chief Inspector of Factories and Workshops to the Victorian Parliament. *Parliamentary Papers*.

Government Gazette.

OTHER

Conference of British Commonwealth Statisticians, Canberra, November 1951, *Summary of Proceedings*.

(c) Newspapers and other Journals

Advertiser, Adelaide,
A.E.U. Monthly Journal, Sydney.
A.E.U. Monthly Journal and Report, Sydney
A.E.U. Monthly Report, Sydney.
A.E.U. Monthly Trade Report, Sydney.
A.E.U. Quarterly Report, Sydney.
Age, Melbourne.
Argus, Melbourne.
Australasian Engineer, Sydney.
Australasian Manufacturer, Sydney.
Australian Financial Review, Sydney.
Australian Labour, Melbourne.
Bulletin, Sydney.
Catholic Worker, Melbourne.
Century, Sydney.
Communist Review, Sydney.
Courier-Mail, Brisbane.
Daily Standard, Brisbane.
Daily Telegraph, Sydney.

Engineers' Voice, Melbourne
Hobart Mercury, Hobart.
Industrial Information, Sydney.
Industry and Trade, Melbourne.
Labor Call, Melbourne.
Labor College Review, Melbourne.
Labour News, Sydney.
Metal Trades Journal, Sydney.
News Weekly, Melbourne.
Round Table, London.
Sunday Mail, Adelaide.
Sunday Mail, Brisbane.
Sunday Telegraph, Sydney.
Sun News-Pictorial, Melbourne.
Sydney Morning Herald, Sydney.
Tariff & Industrial Information, Sydney.
The Australian Worker, Sydney.
The Employers' Review, Sydney.
The Ironworker, Sydney.
The Tribune, Melbourne.
Tribune, Sydney.
Voice, Sydney.
Whyalla News, Whyalla.
Worker, Sydney.
Workers' Weekly, Sydney.

(d) Reports of Employers' Associations and Trade Union Congresses

Central Council of Employers of Australia, *Report of Proceedings at Annual Interstate Conference of Employers' Federations.*

Metal Trades Employers' Association, *Annual Reports.*

Metal Trades Employers' Association, *Directory of Products and Services of Members.*

Minutes of the All-Australian Trade Union Congress.

Official Report of the New South Wales Congress of Trade Unions.

Official Reports of the All-Australian Trade Union Congress.

Report of Annual Meeting of the Employers' Federation of New South Wales.

Report of Proceedings of the Interstate Congress of Trades and Labor Councils, Adelaide, 1913.

South Australian Chambers of Manufactures, *Annual Reports.*

Victorian Chambers of Manufactures, *Annual Reports,*

(e) Books

Anderson, George. *Fixation of Wages in Australia*, Melbourne, 1929.
    Problems of Industrial Administration in Australia, Melbourne, 1938.

Amalgamated Engineering Union. *Souvenir. 25th Anniversary*, Sydney, 1945.
Amalgamated Society of Engineers, *Jubilee 1901*, London 1901.
Arius. *Social Unrest (Universal and Local) And Its Causes*, Sydney, 1919.
Atkinson, M. (Ed.) *Trade Unionism in Australia*, Sydney, 1915.
Australian Institute of Political Science. *What Should We Do with the Australian Wage System?* Proceedings of Winter Forum, Sydney, 1952.
   Productivity and Progress, Sydney, 1957.
   Trade Unions in Australia, Sydney, 1959.
Barou, N. *British Trade Unions*, London, 1947.
Brennan, Niall. *The Politics of Catholics*, Melbourne, 1972.
Brigden, J. B. and others. *The Australian Tariff — an Economic Enquiry*, Melbourne, 1929.
Buckley, K. D. *The Amalgamated Engineers in Australia, 1852–1920*, Canberra, 1970.
Butlin, S. J. *War Economy 1939–1942* in *Australia in the War of 1939–1945*, Series 4, Number III, Canberra, 1955.
Campbell, E. W. *History of the Australian Labor Movement. A Marxist Interpretation*, Sydney, 1945.
Child, J. *Unionism and The Labor Movement*, Melbourne, 1971.
Childe, V. G. *How Labour Governs*, London, 1923.
Clegg, H. A. Killick, A. J. and Adams, Rex. *Trade Union Officers*, Oxford, 1961.
Crisp, L. F. *The Parliamentary Government of the Commonwealth of Australia*, London, 1949.
   The Australian Federal Labor Party 1901–1951, London, 1955.
   Ben Chifley, London, 1960.
Cooksey, R. *Lang and Socialism*, Canberra, 1971.
Cooksey, R. (Ed.) *The Great Depression*, Canberra, 1970.
Davidson, A. *The Communist Party of Australia*, Stanford, 1969.
Dufty, N. F. *Industrial Relations in the Australian Metal Industries*, Sydney, 1972.
Dunlop, John T. *Wage Determination under Trade Unionism*, Oxford, 1950.
Dunlop, John T. (Ed.) *The Theory of Wage Determination: Proceedings of a Conference held by the International Economic Association*, London, 1957.
Ebbels, R. N. *The Australian Labor Movement, 1850–1907*, Sydney, 1960.
Ellis, M. H. *The Garden Path*, Sydney, 1949.
Fitzhardinge, L. F. *W. M. Hughes, A Political Biography: vol. I, The Fiery Particle, 1862–1914*, Sydney, 1964.
Fitzpatrick, B. *The British Empire in Australia*, Melbourne, 1941.
   A Short History of the Australian Labor Movement, Melbourne, 1944.
   The Australian People, Melbourne, 1946.
Foenander, Orwell de R. *Towards Industrial Peace in Australia*, Melbourne, 1937.
   Solving Labour Problems in Australia, Melbourne, 1941.
   Wartime Labour Developments in Australia, Melbourne, 1943.
   Industrial Regulation in Australia, Melbourne, 1947.
   Studies in Australian Labour Law and Regulations, Melbourne, 1952.
   Better Employment Relations, Sydney, 1954.
   Industrial Conciliation and Arbitration in Australia, Sydney, 1959.
   Trade Unionism in Australia, Sydney, 1962.

Shop Stewards and Shop Committees, Melbourne, 1965.

Recent Developments in Australian Industrial Regulations, Sydney, 1970.

Forster, Colin *Industrial Development in Australia 1920–1930*, Canberra, 1964.

Galenson, W. (Ed.) *Comparative Labour Movements*, New York, 1952.

Giblin, L. F. *Growth of a Central Bank*, Melbourne, 1951.

Gifford, J. K. *Wages, Inflation and Productivity*, Sydney, 1961.

Goldstein, Joseph. *The Government of British Trade Unions*, London, 1952.

Gollan, Robin. *The Coalminers of New South Wales, Melbourne, 1963.*

Goodman, J. E. B. and Whittingham, T. G. *Shop Stewards in British Industry*, London, 1969.

Hagan, J. *Printers and Politics*, Canberra, 1966.

Hargreaves, W. J. *History of the Federated Moulders' (Metals) Union of Australia 1858–1958*, Sydney, n.d.

Hasluck, Paul. *The Government and the People 1939–1941*, in *Australia in the War of 1939–1945*, Series 4, Number I, Canberra, 1952.

  The Government and the People 1942–1945 in *Australia in the War of 1939–1945*, Series 4, Number II, Canberra, 1970.

Healey, George. *A.L.P. The Story of the Labor Party*, Brisbane, 1955.

Higgenbottam, S. *Our Society's History*, Manchester, 1939.

Higgins, H. B. *A New Province of Law and Order*, London, 1922.

Hobsbawm, E. J. *Industry and Empire*, London, 1969.

Hogan, E. J. *What's Wrong with Australia?* Melbourne, 1953

Hughes, Helen. *The Australian Iron and Steel Industry 1848–1962*, Melbourne, 1964.

Hunter, Alex (Ed.) *The Economics of Australian Industry*, Melbourne, 1963.

Hutson, J. *Penal Colony to Penal Powers*, Sydney, 1966.

  Six Wage Concepts, Sydney, 1971.

Iremonger, J., Merritt, J. and Osborne, G. *Strikes: Studies in Twentieth Century Australian Social History*, Sydney, 1973.

Isaac, J. E. *Wages and Productivity*, Melbourne, 1967.

Isaac, J. E. and Ford, G. W. (Eds.) *Australian Labour Relations: Readings*, Melbourne, 1966.

  Australian Labour Economics: Readings, Melbourne, 1967.

Jefferys, James B. *The Story of the Engineers 1800–1945*, London, 1945.

Jupp, James. *Australian Party Politics*, Melbourne, 1968.

Kewley, T. H. *Social Security in Australia*, Sydney, 1965.

Lang, J. T. *The Great Bust: The Depression of the Thirties*, Sydney, 1962.

Louis L. J. *Trade Unions and the Depression: A Study of Victoria 1930–1932*, Canberra, 1968.

Maclaurin, W. R. *Economic Planning in Australia 1929–1936*, London, 1937.

Mann, T. *Tom Mann's Memoirs*, London, 1923.

Matthews, P. W. D. and Ford, G. W. *Australian Trade Unions*, Melbourne, 1968.

Mayer, Henry (Ed.) *Catholics and the Free Society*, Melbourne, 1961.

  Australian Politics, A Reader, Melbourne, 1966.

Murray, Robert. *The Split*, Melbourne, 1970.

O'Dea, Raymond. *Industrial Relations in Australia*, Sydney, 1965.

Ormonde, P. *The Movement*, Melbourne, 1972.

Oxnam, D. W. (Ed.) *Payment By Results, Addresses to the Third Labour—Management Conference of the University of Western Australia*, Perth, 1958.

Palmer, Nettie. *Henry Bournes Higgins, A Memoir*, London, 1931.

Perlman, Mark. *Judges in Industry*, Melbourne, 1954.

Perlman, Richard (Ed.) *Wage Determination. Market or Power Forces?* Boston, 1964.

Phelps Brown, E. H. *The Growth of British Industrial Relations*, London, 1954.

Piddington, A. B. *Report on the Productivity of Queensland and the Remuneration of Labour*, Brisbane, 1925.

Political and Economic Planning. *British Trade Unionism*, New Revised Edition, London, 1955.

Portus, J. H. *The Development of Australian Trade Union Law*, Melbourne, 1958.

Australian Compulsory Arbitration 1900—1970, Sydney, 1971.

Pratt, A. *Australian Tariff Handbook 1919*, Melbourne, 1919.

Rankin, M. T. *Arbitration and Conciliation in Australia*, London, 1916.

Rawson, D. W. *Labor In Vain?*, Melbourne, 1966.

Rawson, D. W. and Wrightson, S. *A Handbook of Australian Trade Unions and Employees' Associations*, Department of Political Science, Research School of Social Sciences, Australian National University, Occasional Paper No. 5, Canberra, 1970.

Roberts, B. C. *Trade Union Government and Administration in Great Britain*, London, 1956.

Trade Unions in a Free Society, London, 1962.

Ross, E. *A History of the Miners' Federation of Australia*, Sydney, 1970.

Santamaria, B. A. *Point of View*, Melbourne, 1969.

Sawer, Geoffery. *Australian Federal Politics and Law 1901—1929*, Melbourne, 1956.

Australian Federal Politics and Law 1929—1949, Melbourne, 1963.

Schedvin, C. B. *Australia and the Great Depression*, Sydney, 1970.

Scott, E. *Australia During the War, Official History of Australia in the War of 1914—1918*, Vol. XI, Sydney, 1937.

Shann, E. and Copland, D. B. *Crisis in Australian Finance*, Sydney, 1931.

Sharkey, L. L. *The Trade Unions, Communist Theory and Practice of Trade Unionism*, Supplemented and Revised Edition, Sydney, 1959.

Sharpley, Cecil H. *The Great Delusion*, London, 1952.

Shaw, A. G. L. *The Economic Development of Australia*, New Impression, Melbourne, 1962.

Singer, C., Holmyard, E. J., Hall, A. R., and William, T. I. *A History of Technology*, Vol. 4 (The Industrial Revolution), Vol. 5 (The Late Nineteenth Century), Oxford, 1958.

Spence, W. G. *Australia's Awakening*, Sydney, 1909.

History of the A.W.U., Sydney, 1911.

Sutcliffe, J. T. *A History of Trade Unionism in Australia*, W.E.A. Series, No. 3, Melbourne, 1921.

Timbs, J. N. *Towards Wage Justice by Industrial Regulation. An Appreciation of Australia's Experience under Compulsory Arbitration*, Louvain, 1963.

Truman, T. *Catholic Action and Politics*, Melbourne, 1960.

Turner, H. A. *Trade Union Growth, Structure and Policy. A Comparative Study of the Cotton Unions*, London, 1962.

    Wage Trends, Wage Policies, and Collective Bargaining: the Problems for Under-developed Countries, University of Cambridge, Department of Applied Economics, Occasional Papers 6, Cambridge, 1965.

Turner, I. A. H. *Industrial Labour and Politics; The Dynamics of the Labour Movement in Eastern Australia 1900–1921*, Canberra, 1965.

    Sydney's Burning, Melbourne, 1967.

Walker, E. Ronald. *Australia in the World Depression*, London, 1933.

    The Australian Economy in War and Reconstruction, New York, 1947.

Walker, K. F. *Industrial Relations in Australia*, Cambridge, Mass., 1956.

Walker, K. F. (Ed.) *Automation*, Perth, 1957.

Webb, Leicester. *Communism and Democracy in Australia, A Survey of the 1951 Referendum*, Melbourne, 1954.

Webb, Sydney and Beatrice. *Industrial Democracy*, London, 1913.

    The History of Trade Unionism 1666–1920, London, 1920.

Wildavsky, Aaron, and Carboch, Dagmar. *Studies in Australian Politics*, Melbourne, 1958.

Windett, Nancy. *Australia as Producer and Trader 1920–1932*, London, 1933.

Yates, M. L. *Wages and Labour Conditions in British Engineering*, London, 1937.

(f) Articles

Andrews, E. Australian Labour and Foreign Policy 1935–1939, *Labour History*, No. 9, 1965, pp. 29–32.

Beeby, G. S. The Artificial Regulation of Wages in Australia, *Economic Journal*, Vol. 25, No. 99, 1915, pp. 321–8.

Bentley, P. R. Trade Union Leadership and Strike Incidence, With Specific Reference to the Waterside Workers' Federation, 1950–66, *The Journal of Industrial Relations*, Vol. 12, March 1970, pp. 88–97.

Bland, F. A. Unemployment in Australia, *International Labour Review*, Vol. 30, July, 1934, pp. 23–57.

Buckley, K. The Role of Labour; the Amalgamated Society of Engineers, *Labour History*, No. 4, May 1963, pp. 3–10.

    A New Index of Engineering Unemployment 1852–1894, *Economic Record*, Vol. 43, March 1967, pp. 108–18.

    The Membership of the Amalgamated Society of Engineers in Australia 1856–1889, *Australian Economic History Review*, Vol. 7, September 1967, pp. 142–9.

Butlin, N. G. An index of Engineering Unemployment 1852–1943, *Economic Record*, Vol. 22, December 1946, pp. 241–60.

Campbell, Ian. A.L.P. Industrial Groups — A Reassessment, *Australian Journal of ·Politics and History*, Vol. 8, November 1962, pp. 182–99.

Churchward, L. G. Ten Years of Research into the Australian Labour Movement, *Australian Political Studies Association, News*, Vol. 2, 1957, pp. 1–3.

    The American Influence on the Australian Labour Movement, *Historical Studies of Australia and New Zealand*, Vol. 5, November 1952, pp. 258–77.

Trade Unionism in the United States and Australia: A Study of Contrasts, *Science and Society*, Vol. 17, Spring 1953, pp. 119—35.

Clarey, P. J. The Trade Union Attitude to Incentive Payment Schemes, *Economic Papers*, No. 9, Economic Society of Australia and New Zealand (N.S.W. Branch), Sydney, 1950, pp. 22—9.

Cruise, H. F. Some Restrictive Practices in Australia, in Australian Institute of Political Science, *Productivity and Progress*, pp. 236—306.

Dixson, Miriam. The Timber Strike of 1929, *Historical Studies of Australia and New Zealand*, Vol. 10, May 1963, pp. 479—92.

Dufty, N. F. The Skilled Worker and his Union, *Journal of Industrial Relations*, Vol. 2, October 1960, pp. 99—109.

Forster, Colin. Australian Manufacturing and the War of 1914—18, *Economic Record*, Vol. 29, November 1953, pp. 211—30.

Australian Unemployment, 1900—1940, *Economic Record*, Vol. 41, September 1965, pp. 426—50.

Hancock, K. J. Earnings Drift in Australia, *Journal of Industrial Relations*, Vol. 8, July 1966, pp. 128—57.

Isaac, J. E. The Basic Wage and Standard Hours Inquiry in Australia, 1952—53, *International Labour Review*, Vol. 69, June 1954, pp. 570—93.

The Prospects for Collective Bargaining in Australia, *Economic Record*, Vol. 34, December 1958, pp. 347—61.

Penal Provisions Under Commonwealth Arbitration, *The Journal of Industrial Relations*, Vol. 5, October 1963, pp. 110—19.

Wage Drift in the Australian Metal Industries, *Economic Record*, Vol. 41, No. 94, June 1965, pp. 145—72.

Knowles, K. G. J. C. and Robertson, D. J. Differences between the Wages of Skilled and Unskilled Workers, 1880—1950, *Oxford Institute of Statistics Bulletin*, Vol. 13, April 1951, pp. 109—27.

Earnings in Engineering, 1926—1948, *Oxford Institute of Statistics Bulletin*, Vol. 13, June 1951, pp. 179—200.

Laffer Kingsley. The Economic Aspects of Incentive Payment Schemes, *Economic Papers*, No. 9, The Economic Society of Australia and New Zealand (N.S.W. Branch), Sydney 1950, pp. 30—44.

Problems of Compulsory Arbitration in Australia, *International Labour Review*, Vol. 67, May 1958, pp. 417—33.

Maclaurin, W. R. Recent Experiences with Compulsory Arbitration in Australia, *American Economic Review*, Vol. 28, March 1938, pp. 65—81.

Martin, R. M. Australian Trade Unionism, 1964, *The Journal of Industrial Relations*, Vol. 7, March 1965, pp. 77—88.

Oxnam, D. W. The Relation of Unskilled to Skilled Wage Rates in Australia, *Economic Record*, Vol. 26, June 1950, pp. 112—18.

Strikes in Australia, *Economic Record*, Vol. 29, May 1953, pp. 73—89.

Some Economic Aspects of the Scientific Study of Industrial Relations, *Australian Quarterly*, Vol. 27, June 1955, pp. 30—41.

Industrial Arbitration in Australia: Its Effects on Wages and Unions, *Industrial Labour Relations Review*, Vol. 9, July 1956, pp. 610—628.

Arbitration in Perspective — A Further Comment, *Economic Record*, Vol. 34, April 1958, pp. 96—103.

Issues in Industrial Conflict: Australian Experience 1913—1963, *Journal of Industrial Relations*, Vol. 9, March 1967, pp. 13—25.

Portus, G. V. Development of Wage Fixation in Australia, *American Economic Review*, Vol. 19, March 1929, pp. 59—75.

Rawson, D. W. Politics in Trade Unions — Does it Matter? *Australasian Political Studies Association, 8th Annual Conference, Canberra 22—26 August 1966.*

Rosenberg, Nathan. Technological Change in the Machine Tool Industry, 1840—1910, *Journal of Economic History*, Vol. 23, December 1963, pp. 414—43.

Ross, Lloyd. Problems of Participation of Members in the Administration and Activities of Trade Unions (With Special Reference to the Australian Railways Union, New South Wales State Branch) in Australian Political Studies Association, *Proceedings of Fourth Conference, Canberra, 8—10 August 1962.*

Russell, F. A. A. Industrial Arbitration in New South Wales, *Economic Journal*, Vol. 15, September 1915, pp. 329—46.

Sawkins, D. T. The Effect of the Living Wage Policy on Wages for Skill, *Economic Record*, Vol. 6, November 1930, pp. 159—69.

Sheridan, T. Partial Anatomy of a Union: A Sample of A.E.U. Recruiting 1914—1952, *The Journal of Industrial Relations*, September 1972, pp. 238—63.

Scott, W. D. Incentive Payment Schemes Operating in Australia, *Economic Papers*, No. 9, Economic Society of Australia and New Zealand (N.S.W. Branch), Sydney 1950, pp. 6—21.

Taft, R. The Social Grading of Occupations in Australia, *British Journal of Sociology*, Vol. 4, 1953, pp. 181—7.

Weiner, H. E. Communists in Australian Trade Unions, *Political Science Quarterly*, Vol. 69, September 1954, pp. 390—400.

(g) Pamphlets

Aaron, E. *The Steel Octopus, The Story of B.H.P.*, Sydney, 1961.

Anderson, N. C. *O.B.U. for Australia*, Melbourne, 1917.

Australasian Council of Trade Unions. *A Survey of the Lukin Award*, Melbourne, 1929.

Statement by Executive of the A.C.T.U. Re National Registration Act, Supply and Development Act, and Amended Defence Act, Melbourne, 1939.

The Trade Unions and the War, Melbourne, 1941.

Australian Metal Industries Association. *Brochure to Celebrate 20th Anniversary*, Sydney, 1962.

Baker, W. A. *The Commonwealth Basic Wage, 1907—1953*, Sydney, 1953.

Black, George. *Arbitration a Failure — Why? Arbitration's Chequered Career from 1901 to 1927*, Sydney, 1927.

Blackburn, Maurice. *Trade Unionism — Its Operation Under Australian Law*, Melbourne, 1940.

Clarke, Duncan. *No Arms for Japan*, Melbourne, 1951.

Communist Party of Australia. *Ballot Riggers at Work! Defend the Unions*, Melbourne, n.d.

Catholic Action at Work, Melbourne, n.d.

Communist Leaders Speak, n.d.

Demand a Better Deal in Workers Compensation, Melbourne, 1944.

Dixon, R. *Towards Militant Trade Unionism*, Sydney, 1935.

Fabian Society of N.S.W. *Secret Ballots in Trade Unions*, Sydney, 1949.

Federated Ironworkers' Association. *B.H.P.*, Sydney, 1941.

Forty Hour Week Committee of the Labour Council of N.S.W. *The Case for the 40 Hour Week*, Sydney, 1936.

Hade, M. *The Case for the Forty-Four Hours Working Week*, Sydney, 1926.

Heagney, Muriel A. *Arbitration at The Cross Roads*, Melbourne, 1954.

Hughes, J. R. *Keep the Unions Free*, Sydney, 1949.

Illawarra Trades and Labour Council and Newcastle Trades Hall Council. *The Story of the Steel Strike of 1945*, n.d.

Lindsay, Jack. *Factory Front*, Sydney, n.d.

McPhillips, Jack. *The Work of Our Union*, Sydney, 1944.

B.H.P. Loses £15,000, Sydney, n.d.

Arbitration?, Sydney, 1952.

Act Now to Defend Living Conditions, Sydney, n.d.

Penal Powers. Menzies' Weapons Against Unions and Wages, Sydney, 1958.

Todays Wage Fight. The Way Forward, Sydney, 1961.

Metal Trades Employers' Association. *The Late John Heine, An Appreciation*, Sydney, 1947.

Brochure to Commemorate New Building, Sydney, 1958.

Metal Trades Federation. *Incentive Schemes Based on Output*, Sydney, 1951.

Olive, D. *The Queensland Railway Strike*, Brisbane, n.d.

Returned Servicemen's League. *Subversion, The R.S.L. Case Against Communism in Australia*, Canberra, 1962.

Rowe, Ted and Wright, Tom. *United Action Wins*, Sydney, n.d.

Sharkey, L. L. *The Left. 'Dr' Lloyd Ross and Nationalisation*, Sydney, 1942.

The W.E.A. Exposed!, Sydney, 1944.

Sharpley, Cecil. *I Was a Communist Leader*, Brisbane, 1949.

Schreiber, O. *Case for the Forty Hour Week*, Sydney, 1937.

Thornton, E. *Trade Unions and the War*, Sydney, 1942.

Stronger Trades Unions, Sydney, 1943.

Trautmann, W. E. *One Great Union*, Melbourne, 1915.

Turner, H. A. *Arbitration, A Study of Industrial Experience*, Fabian Research Series, No. 153.

Wage Policy Abroad: and Conclusion for Britain, Fabian Research Series, No. 189.

The Trend of Strikes, Leeds, 1963.

Victorian Youth Parliament. *Our Jobs*, Melbourne, n.d.

Workers International Industrial Union. *Job Control*, Adelaide, 1928.

Worker Newspaper. *Unions' Case for a 30 Hour Week*, Brisbane, 1933.

Wright, Tom. *Lenin and the Trade Unions*, Sydney n.d.

World Trade Union Federation, Sydney, n.d.

Index

work study, *see* incentive schemes
Work Value, 278–9, 289, 292
workers' compensation, 16
Workers' Weekly, 121
World War I
  British dilution of skill, 123, 154
  effects on A.E.U., 40–1
  government shipbuilding scheme, 65, 89
  see also industrial disputes, wages
World War II, 144–63

A.E.U. policy, 146–8
effects on A.E.U. ballots, 35; on amalgamation discussions, 49; on Commonwealth Council, 33; on metal trades, 19, 21, 144–6, 164; on office holders, 204
see also defence
Women's Employment Board, 161, 162, 163

Yallourn, 102, 108

5oc
HD
6894
> M512
A437